THE PITY

OF IT ALL

THE PITY
OF IT ALL

A Portrait of the German-Jewish Epoch,
1743–1933

AMOS ELON

PICADOR
A METROPOLITAN BOOK
HENRY HOLT AND COMPANY
NEW YORK

www.picadorusa.com

Picador® is a U.S. registered trademark and is used by Henry Holt and Company under license from Pan Books Limited.

For information on Picador Reading Group Guides, as well as ordering, please contact the Trade Marketing department at St. Martin's Press.
Phone: 1-800-221-7945 extension 763
Fax: 212-677-7456
E-mail: trademarketing@stmartins.com

Designed by Fritz Metsch
Maps by James Sinclair

Library of Congress Cataloging-in-Publication Data

Elon, Amos.
    The pity of it all : a portrait of the German-Jewish epoch, 1743–1933 / Amos Elon.
        p. cm
    Includes bibliographical references and index.
    ISBN 0-312-42281-4
    1. Jews—Germany—History—18th century. 2. Jews—Germany—History—1800–1933. 3. Jews—Germany—Intellectual life. 4. Germany—Civilization—Jewish influences. 5. Jews—Cultural assimilation—Germany. 6. Germany—Ethnic relations. I. Title: Portrait of the German-Jewish Epoch, 1743–1933. II. Title.

DS135.G33 E57 2002
943'.004924—dc21   2002067833

First published in the United States by Metropolitan Books, an imprint of Henry Holt and Company, LLC

D 30 29 28 27 26 25

It is not what they built. It is what they knocked down.
It is not the houses. It is the spaces between the houses.
It is not the streets that exist. It is the streets that no longer exist.
It is not the memories which haunt you.
It is not what you have written down.
It is what you have forgotten, what you must forget.
What you must go on forgetting all your life.
And with any luck oblivion should discover ritual.
You will find out that you are not alone in the enterprise.
Yesterday the very furniture seemed to reproach you.
Today you take your place at the Widow's Shuttle.

JAMES FENTON, "A German Requiem"

CONTENTS

CONTENTS

THE PITY
OF IT ALL

Introduction

IN the fall of 1743, a fourteen-year-old boy entered Berlin at the Rosenthaler Tor, the only gate in the city wall through which Jews (and cattle) were allowed to pass. The boy had arrived from his hometown of Dessau, some one hundred miles away in the small independent principality of Dessau-Anhalt. For five or six days he had walked through the hilly countryside to reach the Prussian capital.

We do not know whether he was wearing shoes; it is more likely that he was barefoot. The boy, later famous throughout Europe as the philosopher Moses Mendelssohn, was frail and sickly, small for his age. Early years of poverty had left him with thin arms and legs, an awkward stutter, and a badly humped back. The hump may have been the result of a genetic disorder (the most severe type, according to modern medical textbooks, is thought to affect mostly Jews of Central European origin and is often accompanied by a stutter), or it may have been caused by rickets, a common childhood disease at the time. The boy's overall appearance "would have moved the cruelest heart to pity," claimed one contemporary, and yet his face was remarkably attractive.[1] Under the finely arched forehead, his eyes were deep and sparkling, his nose, cheeks, lips, and chin delicate and well-formed.

The boy was all but penniless and traveled alone, carrying his few possessions in a satchel on his hunched back. In 1743, the movements of Jews—many of whom were wandering peddlers—were tightly regulated and controlled. Only a limited number of rich Jews (and, occasionally, a scholar) were allowed to settle in Berlin, but peddlers were barred. Jews requesting admission to Berlin, even for only a few days, were sternly interrogated as to their background and purpose. If temporarily admitted, they were *verzollt,* that is, subject to a "commodity tax," as though they were merchandise, at the same rate as imported Polish oxen. The gatekeeper's task, according to one report, was "to stop and register all incoming Jews, keep an eye on them during their stay, and expel the foreign ones" as soon as possible.[2]

Prussia, under the enlightened despot Frederick II (later known as "the Great"), was, relatively speaking, more tolerant than most other German states; the official disposition was to regard most Jews (and all serfs) as less than human. The gatekeeper's surviving log for 1743, the year Mendelssohn trudged through the Rosenthal Gate, includes this notation: "Today there passed six oxen, seven swine, and a Jew."[3] Several versions of what transpired during Mendelssohn's interrogation have been passed down. According to one, the gatekeeper teased the young hunchback, suspecting him of being another peddler. "Jew, what are you selling? I may want to buy something from you." Mendelssohn is said to have responded, "You'll never want to buy anything from me." "Out with it! Tell me what you deal in," the gatekeeper insisted. "In r . . . r . . . reason!" the boy stuttered. According to another account, Mendelssohn was asked what he wanted in Berlin. His answer: "To learn."

BOTH versions are apocryphal, yet they sum up, as such stories often do, the main facts of the case. At fourteen, Mendelssohn was a promising young Talmudic scholar. His former teacher was now a rabbi in Berlin and had given his consent for Mendelssohn to attend his religious seminary. The boy's passage from Dessau to Berlin was as through a time machine, a journey across centuries, from the hermetic insularity of the medieval ghetto into which he was born to the relative enlightenment of eighteenth-century Berlin. Here, Frederick II, upon his coronation as king of Prussia only three years earlier, had proclaimed the reign of reason and invited Voltaire to stay with him as chamberlain. In Frederick's eyes all religions were equally false and equally useful politically. "All religions must be tolerated," Frederick declared (the first European ruler to do so formally). "Every man may seek spiritual salvation in his own manner." With regard to the role of authority, he decreed that "the exchequer must only see to it that none would injure the others."[4] There was, of course, no freedom of speech in Prussia, not even on the subject of religion, but disrespect toward religious practice was punished only mildly. In France, more than twenty years later, the nineteen-year-old Chevalier de la Barre would still be tortured by inquisitors and executed for failing to doff his hat at a passing religious procession.

At the time of his arrival, Mendelssohn knew only Hebrew and *Judendeutsch,* a raw medieval German dialect mixed with Hebrew. German suffixes attached to Hebrew verbs produced the infinitives; the limited, rudimentary vocabulary of *Judendeutsch* permitted only the simplest exchanges. On the rare occasions when it was written, *Judendeutsch* was spelled in Hebrew letters read from right to left. Non-Jews derided it as a mongrel and barbaric dialect, a form of *mauscheln,* whining, the "accents of an unpleasant tongue" (Goethe). Mendelssohn's education had been exclusively religious. He was still unable to speak German or read a German book. Less than two decades later, almost entirely self-taught, he had become a renowned German philosopher, philologist, stylist, literary critic, and man of letters, one of the first to bridge the social and cultural barrier between Jews and other Germans.

His life suggests a saga not only intellectual but human and dramatic. No fabulist would have cast this stuttering ghetto hunchback as the central character in a unique drama of language and *Kultur.* Mendelssohn's great ambition was to end the age-old social and intellectual isolation of Judaism, some of which had become self-imposed. In some ways he fully succeeded. His impact on his time was considerable. A recent guidebook to the city of Berlin goes so far as to claim that, apart from the modest attempts of a few forgotten writers and the founding of the Prussian Academy of Sciences by Leibniz in 1695, "the history of literature in Berlin begins on an autumn day in 1743 when a fourteen-year-old Talmudic student named Mendelssohn entered the city through the gate reserved for Jews and cattle."[5]

As a religious thinker he preached a doctrine of "reason" that, as first expounded by the great Maimonides in the twelfth century, had long been suppressed by German rabbis as heretical. In Mendelssohn's view, God was not a hypothesis, a logical postulation, as later Jewish theologians would claim; rather, reason itself was a gift from God. Mendelssohn became the father, albeit inadvertently, of modern Reform Judaism—he himself remained traditionally devout and observant throughout his life. He was as passionate about language (becoming fluent also in French, English, Hebrew, Greek, and Latin) as about German literature, and for a man of his time and place, passionate about social justice as well: he wished he could turn "Jewish boys into craftsmen and . . . serfs into free peasants."[6]

One of the first practicing Jews to be fully assimilated into high German culture, Mendelssohn became the first German Jew to achieve European prominence as a philosopher and a man of letters, admired by Kant and Herder and by *beaux esprits* everywhere, a close friend and collaborator of the leading German playwright Gotthold Ephraim Lessing (one of the foremost liberals of his age) and other prominent figures of the German Enlightenment. His contemporaries hailed him extravagantly. The poet Christian Martin Wieland saluted Mendelssohn "in the sacred name of friendship." For his achievements as a philosopher and religious reformer, he was acclaimed as the "German Socrates" and the "Jewish Luther." For his advocacy of an enlightened secular state, the French philosophe Mirabeau placed him on the same pedestal as the authors of the United States Constitution.

Throughout the nineteenth century, German Jews celebrated, idealized, and drew hope from Mendelssohn's famous interreligious friendships. Their pride in these friendships was indicative of, and perhaps eased, their own difficulties in winning a similar degree of acceptance. Mendelssohn became their patron saint, a model for all who sought to preserve their ethnic or religious identity but share in the general culture. He was the first of a long line of assimilated German Jews who worshiped German culture and civilization and whose enterprise, two centuries later, would come to such a horrendous and abrupt end. Some were more gifted than others, some not gifted at all; most were unswerving in their attachment to the country of their birth.

Their story, from the days of Mendelssohn until the rise of Nazism—a story of such promise but also so vexed, so tangled, and ultimately so terrible—is the subject of this book. To tell that story, it uses Sartre's definition: Jews are those considered by others as Jews, irrespective of their religious or ethnic allegiance. It is a history, not a work of sociology; the historian, unlike the sociologist, can live with the unique. It traces the fates and ideas of a number of interesting, mostly secular, and often very appealing people; though perhaps not representative, they were emblematic. Many were fully assimilated or acculturated, but neither term reflects the complexity of a predicament that eventually became a kind of identity. The history of assimilation has long been a subversive subject for which Zionists have offered only self-interested interpretations and assimilationists have avoided because they did not want to draw attention to themselves. No one foresaw the end. The duality of German and Jew—two souls within a single body—would preoccupy and torment German Jews throughout the nineteenth century and the first decades of the twentieth. Nowhere in Western Europe was this duality as deeply felt and finally as tragic.

THERE are no reliable early population statistics. In the eighteenth century, there can hardly have been more than sixty thousand Jews in the German states, less than half of 1 percent of the total German population. This exceedingly small, widely dispersed community was soon considerably augmented by the Jews of Silesia, Poznan, and other largely Slavic territories in the East conquered by Prussia in three successive wars. When, in 1870, more than thirty independent German states consolidated to establish a united Reich, Jews were still an insignificant minority of slightly more than 1 percent. Sixty years later, on the eve of the Nazi takeover, when the total German population had risen to sixty-five million, the relative number of Jews had dropped to 0.8 percent. One wonders how so small a presence could have triggered, even indirectly, such vast enmity. Other ethnic groups were far more numerously represented in the German-speaking territories. Yet in economic and cultural terms there has rarely been an ethnic or religious minority so visible—and, for better or worse, so magnified and often overrated in the public mind. In a relatively brief period, this small community produced a staggering array of entrepreneurs, artists, writers, wits, scholars, and radical political activists. The high visibility of Jewish success elicited intense feelings of envy, resentment, and a sick, almost pornographic, curiosity. In the distorted mirrors of popular imagination, Jews loomed ominously larger than their number, a presumed threat to national integrity, identity, culture, "health," and the general well-being.

The brief legal emancipation of Jews during the Napoleonic wars released unparalleled economic, professional, and cultural energies. It was as though a high dam had suddenly been breached. In Jewish history, something similar had happened once before, in Moslem Spain, albeit on a smaller scale. Shortly before the onset of the Inquisition, a Spanish Jew boasted that the kings and lords of Castile had the advantage over their many adversaries in that their Jewish subjects "were amongst the most learned, the most distinguished in lineage, in wealth, in virtues, and in science."[7] During the Weimar Republic—the high point of their integration and assimilation into German life—German Jews might have claimed the same.

There has rarely been a confluence of two cultural, ethnic, or religious traditions that proved so richly creative at its peak. Frederic Grunfeld writes that had the end not been so awful we would now hail the decades before the Nazi rise to power as "a golden age second only to the Italian Renaissance."[8] In literature alone, German Jews accounted for such luminaries as Heine, Börne, Kafka, Werfel, Zweig, Wolfskehl, Broch, and Kraus; in the sciences, Willstätter, Haber, Ehrlich, Einstein, and Freud; in music, Mahler, Weill, Schoenberg, and Mendelssohn's grandson Felix Mendelssohn-Bartholdy. Given the Jews' late entry into European civilization, the wealth and variety of their contribution to the arts and sciences was startling.

In politics, they were the midwives or founders of most of Germany's parties. As political activists, they were prominent mainly on the liberal and radical left. As voters, they mirrored the most enlightened sections of the rising German bourgeoisie, tending to support the liberal center and the moderate left. Herder anticipated their liberalizing influence early on. Long before Jews were emancipated and given the vote he predicted they would have fewer or none of the prejudices that other Germans cast off only with great difficulty. As social and political critics, a few were sometimes impertinent, unmindful that stepchildren must always be on their best behavior. In general, they were, of course, as conformist as most other Germans and, occasionally, even more so. Yet their constantly precarious situation induced many to cultivate a skepticism and a sense of irony that became, almost, their hallmark. Many retained an outsider's sharpened sensibility and wakefulness. The ironist Heine's memorable lines come to mind:

> *I think of Germany at night*
> *The thought keeps me awake till light.*

and

> *I had, long since,*
> *a lovely fatherland.*
> *The oaks would gleam*
> *And touch the skies;*
> *the violets would nod.*
> *It was a dream.*

These qualities of skepticism, irony, and wakefulness produced some great polemicists, satirists, literary critics, and pioneers and connoisseurs of avant-garde art. Thomas Mann, who in many ways was ambivalent about Jews (though he was married to one), hailed them as Germany's finest judges of literature and the arts. Among all things "German" in the arts, he claimed, only those that also passed the acid test of approval by Jewish critics were truly valuable.

As involuntary outsiders, they occupied extraordinary vantage points from which to observe and, if need be, castigate the majority. They remained at the very heart of the German culture and their own, scathing in their criticism of German authoritarianism but also of the foibles and failings and dogmatism of their own ethnic and religious community. The major revolutions in European and American Jewish life during the nineteenth century, from religious reform to political Zionism, originated in Germany or Austria among Jews passionately devoted to German culture. As their own tribal idols crumbled, they did not simply borrow those of the Christian majority but invented new ones—communism, psychoanalysis, and other systems based on the utopian conviction that the world could be rationally reordered and vastly improved on a "scientific" basis. The best among them tended to be indifferent to all religion and to view both their Jewish and their German heritage with detached irony. Heine does just that in his parody of Schiller's celebrated "Ode to Joy," a hymn to . . . cholent, the traditional Jewish Sabbath meal:

> *Holy cholent, dish celestial,*
> *Daughter of Elysium:*
> *If he'd only tasted cholent,*
> *Schiller would have changed his hymn.*

> *God devised and God delivered*
> *Unto Moses from on high,*
> *And commanded us to savor*
> *Cholent for eternity.*

Heine, after his reluctant conversion, remained loyal to his Jewish heritage only, as he put it, out of a deep antipathy to Christianity. (The Jewish heritage, he insisted, was love of freedom and of good cooking.)

For all their irony and skepticism, the Jews of Germany never ceased in their effort to merge German and Jewish identity. The heartstrings of their affection were tied early; their overriding desire was to be complete Germans. Many succeeded. If their success appears in retrospect an illusion, it was often a highly creative one and with a grandeur of its own. Accepted or rejected, German Jews continued to potter with their identity, inventing, suppressing, rediscovering, or professing it. The vast majority never hid the fact that they were Jews. There were long intervals when this forthright approach was no impediment, especially in smaller communities. A great many intermarried. Tens of thousands converted and disappeared within the majority. Those who converted often seemed no less remarkable or creative than those who, spurred by the force of a divided allegiance, found themselves in the vanguard of modern art and inquiry.

Their true home, we now know, was not "Germany" but German culture and language. Their true religion was the bourgeois, Goethean ideal of *Bildung* (high culture). With few exceptions, the main thrust of their intellectual and political efforts—and of their reckless magnanimity—was a desperate but vain attempt to civilize German patriotism: to base citizenship not on blood but on law, to separate church and state, and to establish what would today be called an open, multicultural society. Ironically, the only time German Jewish intellectuals abandoned this effort and joined in the jingoism of most other Europeans was during the First World War—"the seminal catastrophe of the twentieth century," as George Kennan calls it—without which the Nazis might never have risen to power.

The prominence of German Jews and the contributions they made became fully apparent only after they were gone. In 1933, in a last-minute attempt to counter the Nazi threat, the traumatized leaders of the Centralverein (Central Union of German Citizens of the Jewish Faith), the most representative organization of assimilated German Jews, commissioned the compilation of a list of Jewish "achievers" and "achievements" in all fields. The project, pathetic only in retrospect, included Jewish luminaries in literature and the arts, in Jewish as well as Christian theology, in politics, warfare, industry, and the natural sciences. The result, entitled *Jews in the Realm of German Culture,* was a vast, meticulously detailed encyclopedia of Jewish contributions to German life and culture during the past two centuries. The task was executed with overwhelming thoroughness by a committee of experts headed by Siegmund Kaznelson, well known during the Weimar period as an editor and publisher. The oversized book ran to 1,060 pages and comprised thousands of entries and names. Richard Willstätter, a Nobel Prize winner in chemistry, wrote the introduction. To avoid possible misunderstandings, the book even included an appendix on "non-Jews widely regarded as Jews," from Lou Andreas-Salomé and Johann Strauss to Charlie Chaplin, Igor Stravinsky, and Albert Schweitzer. The Gestapo outlawed the book and ordered the entire edition destroyed. The manuscript survived, however, and was reprinted after the war. An enormous body of literature on the subject has since grown up, mostly in Germany. It continues to bemoan the incalculable loss Germans inflicted, as it were, on themselves after 1933.

BEFORE Hitler rose to power, other Europeans often feared, admired, envied, and ridiculed the Germans; only Jews seemed actually to have *loved* them. The links—and the tensions—between Jews and Germans were sometimes described as stemming from an alleged family resemblance. Heine was one of the first to emphasize the similarities. He hailed Jews and Germans as Europe's two "ethical peoples"; together they would yet give birth to a new messianic age. Heine went so far as to claim that the ancient Hebrews had been "the Germans of the Orient"! Goethe expressed a wish that Germans be dispersed throughout the world as the Jews had been and strive like them for the improvement of mankind. The poet Stefan George hailed Jews and Germans for living "in God's image, blond or black, sprung from the same bosom: estranged brothers."[9] Ludwig Bamberger, the Jewish patriotic hero of the 1848 uprisings, boasted that Jews were "Germanized" not only within the confines of German lands but far beyond: in Eastern Europe, Jews more than any other people were rooted in the German language, he claimed, and "language means *Geist* [spirit]."[10] Walter Benjamin said in 1917: "The German and the Jew are like two related extremes that confront each other."[11] Kafka maintained that Jews and Germans "have a lot in common. They are ambitious, able, diligent, and thoroughly hated by others. Both are pariahs."[12]

More recently, Gordon A. Craig, the prominent American historian of Germany, has alleged a "striking resemblance" between nineteenth-century Germans and Jews, evidenced by their industry, thrift, and common proclivity for abstract speculation. A shared respect for the written word, he writes, "has made Jews the People of the Book and Germans *das Volk der Dichter und Denker* (the people of poets and thinkers)."[13] Less positively, Jews and Germans stand accused of a similar combination of arrogance and self-loathing, tactlessness and hyper-sensitivity. Even when such generalizations contain a grain of truth, they do not explain the one-sided love or the one-sided hatred or what happened in the end.

At various times there has also been speculation—much of it rather tedious—as to whether there ever was a real "dialogue" between the two peoples or even, as some put it, a "symbiosis." But dialogue is possible only between individuals; peoples normally only scream or shoot at one another. The term *symbiosis*—borrowed from, of all things, biology—is even more dubious. In a symbiosis, one life-form is unable to *exist* without the other! Not surprisingly, symbiosis between humans was first preached by the Romantics as part of their organic notions of friendship, "race," biohistory, and civilization. Before the Holocaust, it was mostly Jews who spoke, hopefully, of symbiosis. Martin Buber rhapsodized about a German-Jewish symbiosis as late as 1939: it had been abruptly interrupted by the Nazis, he claimed, but it might be resumed again in the future. After the Holocaust, only penitent Germans evoked it, guilt-stricken and rueful over "their" loss. Altogether, the idea of symbiosis was always suspect. Why does nobody ever speak of an American-Jewish, French-Jewish, or Dutch-Jewish symbiosis?

SOME claim to have discerned an inexorable pattern in German history preordained from Luther's days to culminate in the Nazi Holocaust. According to this theory, German Jews were doomed from the outset, their fate as immutable as a law of nature. Such absolute certainties have eluded me. I have found only a series of ups and downs and a succession of unforeseeable contingencies, none of which seem to have been inevitable. Alongside the Germany of anti-Semitism there was a Germany of enlightened liberalism, humane concern, civilized rule of law, good government, social security, and thriving social democracy. Even Hitler's rise to power in January 1933 was not the result of electoral success (the Nazis' share of the vote had seriously declined in the fall of 1932). Rather, Hitler's triumph was the product of backstage machinations by conservative politicians and industrialists who overcame the hesitations of a senile president by convincing him (and themselves) that they were "hiring" Hitler to restore order and curb the trade unions. Installing Hitler as chancellor was not the only alternative at the time.

Hindsight is not necessarily the best guide to understanding what really happened. The past is often as distorted by hindsight as it is clarified by it. Jean-François Lyotard, a wise Frenchman, has said that the Holocaust was an earthquake that destroyed not only the topography but the seismographs as well, leaving us to wander dumbfounded in the ruins.[14] Circular, self-fulfilling arguments are of little help in recovering the topography. Such arguments tend to deflect backward from the Holocaust to the Middle Ages or to the eighteenth century, when Jews were beginning to trade their "nationhood" for the pottage of an illusory emancipation. From here they plunge ahead to a seemingly preordained end. Accusations of "self-hatred," so frequently flung at assimilated German Jews, usually with scarce justification, are also of little use. In most cases, it was eminently possible to assimilate without hating oneself or despising one's roots. The history of Jewish assimilation, not only in Germany, has long been a subversive subject, which the assimilated have suppressed so as not to draw attention to themselves, and the Zionists, for equally self-interested reasons, have distorted. Fritz Stern, perhaps the foremost expert on this subject, has argued that the history of the assimilated Jews of Germany was much more than the history of a tragedy; it was also, for a long time, the story of an extraordinary success: "We must understand the triumphs in order to understand the tragedy."[15] We must see the German Jews in the context of their time and, at the very least, appreciate their authenticity, the way they saw themselves and others, often with reason. For long periods, they had cause to believe in their ultimate integration, as did most Jews elsewhere in Western Europe, in the United States, and even in czarist Russia. It was touch and go almost to the end.

As we contemplate the story of the German Jews we are seized with a sense of the transience and precariousness of human achievement. We are moved by the losers, by their struggle and pain. A line by Cato the Elder that Hannah Arendt, a quintessential assimilated German Jew, often cited approvingly, comes to mind: "The victorious cause pleases the gods but the defeated one pleases Cato."

Ancient Renown

BERLIN, as the young Mendelssohn first saw it in 1743, was little more than a garrison town. The capital of Prussia, a kingdom named after an extinct pagan tribe, Berlin was the seat of the Hohenzollern dynasty. Prussia was inhabited by nearly as many Slavs as Germans—as late as 1815, at the Congress of Vienna, it registered as a "Slav kingdom."[1] Berlin was a walled city, neat and orderly, surrounded by lakes and forests. The streets were laid out in straight military lines, paved even in the suburbs. Madame de Staël in *On Germany* complained that as a city Berlin was altogether too new, as new as the excessive military power of Prussia. There was "too little past" in Berlin, she complained, nothing Gothic! "One sees no evidence of former times."

The recently built royal palace was a severe block of dark stone, relatively modest, built along the river Spree. By enabling barges to reach the Baltic and North Sea ports, the river facilitated the growth of commerce and industry. Berlin's population totaled about 100,000, including 25,000 Prussian soldiers and some 2,000 Jews. Tolerated in the city only for their economic usefulness, the Jews were granted right of residence that was revocable at any time. To renew it they were obliged to pay the king an annual poll tax, in addition to a long list of other discriminatory dues. But unlike most other German cities, Berlin did not confine them to a ghetto. They lived anywhere they pleased.

Their presence in the city was fairly recent. Until 1669, Jews had been banned from settling in Berlin or anywhere in the adjacent region. When, in that year, the Austrian emperor Leopold I, under the influence of a fanatic cleric, ordered all Jews expelled from the city of Vienna and from all of Lower Austria, they pleaded with the Prussian *Kurfürst* Frederick I (his descendants would call themselves kings) to show mercy. Would he allow some of them to move to his lands? "The earth and the entire world, which, after all, God created for all humans, appears to be shutting us out," they wrote.[2] The *Kurfürst* was not moved by their plight but was interested in stimulating the stagnant economy. He agreed to accept fifty of the richest Viennese Jews, whom he welcomed for their money and their presumed readiness to help finance his wars. To become his *Schutzjuden* (protected Jews), each had to pay him two thousand thaler (roughly equivalent to ninety thousand dollars today), promise to set up certain industries, and agree "not to establish a synagogue."

Prussia was in dire need of commercial and industrial development. As a result of the Thirty Years War much of it lay in ruins. The population was badly diminished. Berlin alone had lost more than half its population. French Huguenots, another persecuted refugee community, were also allowed to settle in Berlin and for the same mercantilist reasons, but without having to pay. The Huguenots were given "citizenship" and were not prevented from establishing their own church, schools, and judiciary. Nor were their personal and professional rights restricted in any way or proscribed down to the most minute details. Jews were expressly forbidden to farm, own houses, trade in wool, wood, tobacco, leather, and wine, or—with the exception of medicine—practice a learned or guilded profession or craft. The guilds would not have admitted them in any case. Their charters excluded Jews and murderers, punishable manslaughterers, blasphemers, thieves, and adulterers.

The newly arrived Jews were collectively held responsible for one another's misdemeanors, debts, and other obligations. They were specially taxed on every possible occasion—when they traveled, married, or gave birth. Upon the death of a Jew, only his eldest son inherited his "protected" status. Other sons had to prove they possessed an independent capital of at least ten thousand thaler, or leave the city.

Jews were required by law to be recognizable from a distance. In 1710, Frederick William I, the Prussian "soldier king," agreed to abolish the Jews' mandatory yellow patch in return for a payment of eight thousand thaler each. The richest were now allowed to own houses following payment of a special tax. Like most other kings, Frederick William was in constant need of cash. In 1715, he sold his Jews the right to build a synagogue. It had to be of inconspicuous height, however, and thus the floor was laid several feet below street level. In 1722, the king decreed that before a Jew could marry, in addition to first settling "with the military paymaster," he had to purchase a set number of wild boars from the royal preserve.

In their original charter, privileged Jews had been allowed to import their household personnel and a number of teachers, rabbis, gravediggers, ritual slaughterers, and other dependents. By such means the community grew over the years. In 1737, the king became alarmed by their proliferation, which he likened to that of "locusts" bringing ruin to Christians. He decreed that only 120 of "the richest and best" Jewish families could remain in Berlin; all others (some 140 families) were to be expelled within four weeks. "Thank God they are gone," the king noted upon being informed that his order had been carried out. He further issued strict instructions that the dispossessed not be allowed to settle elsewhere in his realm and expressed a pious hope that those still in Berlin would soon die out. Until his death in 1740, Frederick William continued to speak of Jews with utter disdain. His malevolence did not extend to the few he found especially useful. They were mostly minters and entrepreneurs. His official "court Jew," Levin Gumpertz, ran a silk and cotton plant employing Dutch-trained craftsmen. His banker and jeweler, Jeremiah Herz, had inter-European connections and credit lines that Frederick William considered valuable. Both men were exempt from the odious task of paying duty like cattle every time they entered the Rosenthal Gate.

Frederick the Great. Mirabeau said that the king's decrees regulating the lives of his Jews were "fit for cannibals." *Courtesy Leo Baeck Institute, Jerusalem*

Frederick II, the so-called philosopher on the throne, shared his father's contempt for "useless Jews," those not fit to serve as creditors, entrepreneurs, or, in extremis, cannon fodder.[3] The king's aversion to Jews was said to be almost physical. He reproached his sister Ulrike, the queen mother of Sweden, for attending a wedding in the house of one of his court Jews: "Their Hebrew music must have torn your ears!" She did not share his prejudice and told him how impressed she had been by her hosts and by the thorough education they were giving their children: "I felt I was among people of rank and birth."[4]

The king's well-known adage that in his realm every man was entitled to seek salvation "in his own manner" was soon satirized as meaning that in his realm every man might seek salvation "in His manner." Frederick's military and administrative reforms made Prussia the model of a modern militarist state. Strict notions of "duty" and "obedience" were nowhere so savagely or successfully imposed as among his subjects. The harsh discipline was jarring to more refined Germans and foreign visitors. Goethe regarded Prussians as barbarians. James Boswell, a young Scotsman passing through Berlin on his grand tour, was sickened by the way Prussian soldiers were whipped "like dogs" for the slightest misdemeanor. "My ideas of the value of men are altered since I came to this country. I see such numbers of fine fellows bred to be slaughtered that human beings seem like herrings in a plentiful season. One thinks nothing of a barrel of herrings, nor can I think much of a few regiments of men."[5] The Italian poet Vittorio Alfieri, on a visit to Berlin in 1770, thanked heaven for not being born one of Frederick's slaves. Prussia seemed to him one gigantic, loathsome jailhouse.

The Jews who lived in this domain—by now they numbered a few thousand—remained an economic resource to be tapped when needed and evicted when not. The king induced Jews (and Huguenots) to develop new trades, ironworks, and silk factories, increase exports, and compete with those of France and England. Of the forty-six industrial enterprises (mostly silk factories) established in Prussia during Frederick's reign, thirty-seven are said to have been initiated by Jews.[6]

Above all else, Frederick sought to consolidate his many conquests. His wars began with the "rape of Silesia," soon after he took the throne. They continued for the rest of his reign, exhausting his resources and bringing the state close to economic ruin. In response, he ordered several of his Jewish bankers to buy up Austrian, Russian, and other German coins and remint them with greatly reduced silver or gold content. The national wealth of several German and foreign states was thus purloined to finance the king's wars. The king's main instrument in this operation was the Jewish minting and banking firm of Veitel Ephraim & Sons. A popular couplet ran

Outside silver, inside grime
Outside Frederick, inside Ephraim.

Ephraim's rococo town house around the corner from Unter den Linden (it survives to this day) was said to have been a gift from the grateful king. It was the first in Berlin, apparently, with a private bathroom. For services rendered, Ephraim and another Jewish minter, named Itzig, were granted new liberties almost on a par with those of Christian merchants. The lives of the less privileged only grew more difficult during Frederick's reign. In 1750, he issued a "Revised Reglement" for Jews that, according to Mirabeau, was "fit for cannibals." The new list of professional and personal restrictions was even longer than the old. Several categories of "protected" occupations were added but many more were declared out of bounds, including the making of cheese. Those who served in the households of the privileged, at their pleasure, were the

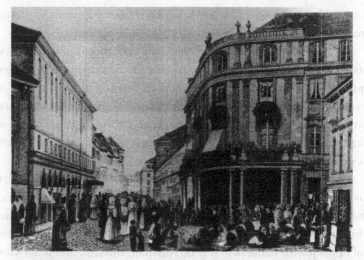

Veitel Ephraim's town house in Berlin. Ephraim helped Frederick II finance his wars by minting coins with reduced silver or gold content. Like most other court Jews, he was exempted from most of the king's repressive regulations. *Courtesy Leo Baeck Institute, Jerusalem*

most vulnerable. When these employees were discharged or died, their widows and offspring were to be stripped of all rights and deported. Although the reglement pertained mostly to poorer Jews and the growing lower middle class, which, in Frederick's eyes, was of little "use," it was so harsh in its formulations, so full of oblique references to reprehensive Jewish morals and other shortcomings, that the rich Jews of Berlin submitted a "most humble and submissive" but ultimately unsuccessful request that the new decree not be made public, even as it was put into effect.

The reglement would remain in force until 1812 and, with minor modifications, in some areas of Posen (Poznan) and Silesia until 1840. When the Royal Porcelain Manufacture, in unsuccessful competition with that of Meissen, fell on hard times, the king decreed that his Jews had to buy five hundred thalers' worth of his porcelain on marrying, three hundred thalers' worth on the birth of a first child, five hundred on the birth of a second, and three hundred on the purchase of a house—this obligation being over and above other duties payable on such occasions. They could not choose the plates or cups they liked or needed but had to take the factory's pick. The factory, of course, used the opportunity to rid itself of unsold merchandise. Moreover, such forced purchases could be resold only outside Prussia. The forced sales continued until Frederick's death and were rescinded by his successor only after payment of forty thousand thaler to compensate him for the lost income.*

Despite Frederick's attempts to rid Prussia of "useless" Jews, the Jewish population under his rule continued to grow as Prussia annexed more and more Jews in the conquered territories. Tens of thousands came under Prussian rule during the two Silesian campaigns (1740–42, 1744–45) and the Seven Years War (1756–63) and later as a result of the final partition of Poland. In Berlin alone the number of Jews grew by 60 percent during this period. In Prussia as a whole, the Jewish population more than tripled. The limited freedoms certain Jews enjoyed in the core of Prussia—Brandenburg, Pomerania, and East Prussia—were not extended to the annexed Jews of Silesia, West Prussia, and Posen. Following the annexation of Breslau in 1742, for example, only twelve privileged Jewish families were allowed to remain in the city. The rest (some ninety families) were forced to roam the countryside in search of a place to live.

Mirabeau said that other states had an army but in Prussia the army had a state. Frederick's calling was war although he also cultivated the muses, French literature, and the company of learned Frenchmen and of dogs. An atheist king "by the grace of God," he was cynical and morose; Rousseau regarded him as a man without principles. Although he was worshiped after his death in absurdly exaggerated ways—in one allegorical engraving Plato, Alexander the Great, and Julius Caesar welcome him into heaven—under his forty-six-year rule Prussia remained outside the mainstream of Western culture and politics. Elsewhere, political parties were born, the idea of a social contract was making headway, rudimentary parliaments came into being, and prime

---

*Moré than half a century later and with the rising antiques market in mind, Heine wrote hopefully that, for the porcelain Jews were forced to buy, their descendants (if they kept it) would recoup a hundredfold. "In the end Israel will be compensated for its sacrifices by the recognition of the world."

ministers were appointed. The divine right of kings was challenged. Against this background Prussia seemed backward, provincial, awkward, even a little comical.

As did the rest of the German states. The German-speaking lands were a cluster of more than one hundred independent states and ministates ruled by an assortment of absolute and minor potentates: kings, dukes, counts, bishops, marquis, margraves, lords, and others. In theory, most were subservient to a "Holy Roman Emperor of the German Nation," who resided in Vienna and also headed the vast Austrian empire. In practice, they were often at war with him and with one another. A few reigning potentates were fabulously wealthy. The landgrave of Hesse was said to be the richest man in Europe, having made his fortune selling or renting excess serfs as cannon fodder to other European rulers. Austria, Saxony, Bavaria, and Prussia were European powers; others, like Hamburg and Frankfurt, were free cities. Most German states were medium-sized or even miniature feudal principalities controlling a few cozy little market towns and a county or two; some were lone castles surrounded by a few hamlets.

Germany was neither a geographic nor even a clear-cut linguistic entity. There were large, cohesive German-speaking communities in distant Russia, on the banks of the Volga and on the shores of the Black Sea in what are today Ukraine, Moldavia, and Romania. There was as yet no hint of a national consciousness anywhere to unite the speakers of more than a dozen local dialects. Nearly every small principality minted its own money. Travelers on the main routes were liable to encounter several roadblocks every day and required to pay customs and other charges.

Jews were by no means newcomers to these regions. No one knows exactly when they first arrived. They seem to have reached the Rhineland and the Danube valley in the wake of Roman legions, long before the establishment of Christianity. In some parts they may have settled earlier than the (later Germanized) Celts, Balts, and Slavs. Long before there were Saxons, Bavarians, or Prussians, Jews lived in what was later known as the German lands. A literate community of ancient renown, in the early Middle Ages they constituted an early urban middle class of traders, surgeons, apothecaries, and craftsmen in gold, silver, and precious stones. The earliest written record testifying to their presence in the Rhineland is the text of a decree of A.D. 321 by the emperor Constantine (preserved in the Vatican Library). It instructs the Roman magistrate of Cologne on relations with the local rabbi.

During the Christianization of Western Europe, they were the only people who retained their religious faith, sometimes at a high price. The first centuries of Christian rule were, by and large, relatively tolerant. For long periods Jews and Germans coexisted peacefully. Prior to the Crusades, Jews were free to own property and practice all trades and professions. Later, their lives were made miserable by the brutality and superstition of the mob, the greed of princes, and the growing intolerance of the Church. By the fifteenth and sixteenth centuries they had become mostly rag dealers, pawnbrokers, money changers, peddlers, and vagrants. The remarkable thing about them was that the poorest men (and some of the women) were often literate, though in Hebrew only.

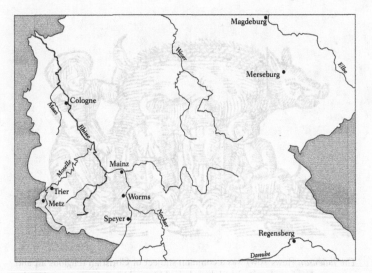

Jews originally settled along the Rhine in Cologne and elsewhere in the wake of the Roman legions. Until the great massacres during the Crusades, they constituted a middle class of merchants, physicians, and other professionals. *Courtesy Leo Baeck Institute, Jerusalem*

In seventeenth-century Prussia, Jews were permitted to live only in the larger cities; elsewhere, these were often closed to them. As petty pawnbrokers, cattle dealers, and peddlers, they were herded into remote outskirts or lived in smaller market towns and villages. Many were on the road all week, carrying their wares on their backs from one hamlet to the next, buying and selling household utensils or used clothes. The daily life of the wandering Jewish peddler made its way into Romantic German poetry, as in Nikolaus Lenau's

> *Wretched Jew, forced thus to wander,*
> *Peddling wares through village and dale,*
> *Poorly fed and shivering cold*
> *Forever hawking: "Goods for sale."*[7]

As a group, the Jews were held together by strict, self-enforced ritual and rigid rules of endogamy. The disdain between Christians and Jews was often mutual but proved in the end more harmful to the Jews

The *Judensau* (Jews' sow) was a common subject of Christian religious art and propaganda, often depicted with bearded rabbis sucking its excrement. Goethe remembered being traumatized as a child by the image of a *Judensau* prominently displayed on the main bridge leading into Frankfurt. *Courtesy Leo Baeck Institute, Jerusalem*

since they had no power. Christians accused them of lacking moral sensibility and cursed them for having denied Christ. Jews, in turn, decried Christianity as a form of pagan image worship. (This contempt predated the Middle Ages. According to the first-century Jewish historian Josephus Flavius, the Roman emperor Claudius saw fit at one point to urge Jews throughout his empire "to use this my kindness to them with moderation and not to show contempt for the gods of others.")[8]

In Prussian and other German records Jews were often referred to as a nation, a term that had as yet no political connotation. Derived from the Latin *natio,* it was originally a genealogical-historical term loosely used by Saint Jerome in his Latin translation of the New Testament to denote non-Christians—that is, "others." Its politicization (as in the French *"la nation"*) came only during the French Revolution. In Berlin "nation" and "colony" were used interchangeably in speaking of the local Jewish or Huguenot community.

There was never a total expulsion of the Jewish "nation" from Germany, as there was from England and Spain, perhaps because there was no unified state and no central power or perhaps because German Jews were so few and impecunious. Local expulsions and massacres occurred every now and again. Jews were occasionally accused of poisoning wells, using Christian blood for sacramental purposes, and stealing Christian babies to circumcise them. The notorious *Judensau* (Jews' sow) was a common subject of Christian religious art and propaganda. Bas-reliefs and cartoons of the *Judensau*—always shown with bearded rabbis who suck and lick its excrement, the scene watched over approvingly by Satan—were displayed in the great cathedrals and domes of Magdeburg, Regensburg, Freising, outside the Schlosskirche in Wittenberg (where Luther posted his ninety-five theses), and in churches and public places elsewhere. Renditions of the *Judensau* legitimized atavistic fears and deadly superstitions and helped perpetuate them from generation to generation. A famous *Judensau* was displayed on the main bridge leading into the city of Frankfurt, affixed there not by some bigoted individual but by "the city government." The city was still paying for its upkeep when Goethe was a child, and he remembered being traumatized by it.

In the early Middle Ages, Jews had been free to live wherever they pleased in Frankfurt and many of the other trading cities. Whatever protected status they enjoyed, however, deteriorated into a form of urban servitude. By 1314, the Jews of Frankfurt were reduced to the status of *Kammerknechte,* "serfs of the Imperial Chamber." Such "protection" as this status implied was worth little but was nevertheless rather costly. At the age of twelve the *Kammerknecht* was obliged to begin paying a sizable poll tax to the emperor's privy purse. As his personal serf, the Jew was stripped of rights and reduced to a commodity, like hay or cattle, which his owner (the Holy Roman Emperor of the German Nation) or his proxy could sell, mortgage, massacre, or give away as a gift. Ludwig I of Bavaria defined the status of his Jews thus: "You are Ours in body and possession. We may make, do, and deal with you as it pleases Us."[9]

Ludwig's successor, Charles IV, used this right in 1349 to mortgage some two thousand Jews (he owned many others) to the free city of Frankfurt in exchange for 15,200 pound heller, roughly equivalent to several million dollars today. Only the wretched and illiterate peasantry—pressed into forced labor or sold as soldiers to fight the wars of local or foreign potentates—were worse off than the Jews. The patience of the oppressed has always been the most inexplicable, as well as probably the most important, fact in all history.

Of the great urban Jewish communities of the Middle Ages, only those of Hamburg, Worms, Frankfurt, and Prague (a German-speaking city) survived into the eighteenth century. Most other German cities had expelled their Jews for allegedly poisoning wells or spreading pestilence and the Black Death: Cologne (where Jews had lived since Roman days) in 1424,* Munich in 1442, Nürnberg in 1499, after which Jews could visit the city only during the day and in the company of a local militiaman. In Bavaria Jews were banned nearly everywhere. Only a handful of protected Jews lived in Leipzig; others were forbidden to enter the city except during the annual fair, when they paid the usual duty imposed on imported animals. Ephraim Moses Kuh, a Jewish poet

---

*As Freud pointed out, Jews had lived in Cologne, a city with the most Germanic of all Gothic cathedrals, long before the Germans.

in Berlin, described a common scene during the seventeenth and early eighteenth centuries:

Collector: Three thalers, Jew, is what you must dole out.
Jew: Three thalers gold? Please, what's this all about?
Collector: You are a Jew! And that's the only reason:
             If you were atheist, or even heathen
             We wouldn't take from you a single sou;
             But you pay through the nose, since you're a Jew!
Jew: Here, take your gold! Are these your Savior's teachings?[10]

Outside Nürnberg, as late as 1800, the scene at the city customs barrier was essentially the same. An anonymous writer described it at the time: "Poor, wretched Israelite, a man like me . . . and yet . . . Forced to stand at customs and be counted, taxed on the head like livestock. A relic from the days of Christ himself."[11]

In the eighteenth century, the independent Hanseatic port city of Hamburg had the largest number of Jews—eight thousand, or 6 percent of the population as a whole. The ghetto had been abolished in 1671. Jews were free to live everywhere in the city. West of Hamburg, Bremen, the nearest self-governing Hanseatic port city, was completely off-limits to Jews, as was Lübeck in the north. Hanover belonged to the English Crown and allowed a handful of rich Jews with princely clients to live there. The university, said to be the most liberal in Germany, banned Jewish students, as did all other German universities. Medical faculties that admitted a Jew or two were notable exceptions. The large number of German universities (compared with only two in England) reflected the political fragmentation and perhaps a more widespread cult of learning. German Jews intent on acquiring a higher education had to go to Holland or farther afield to Italy. Toward the end of the eighteenth century, Kant permitted a few young Jews to attend his philosophy seminars in Königsberg as nonmatriculated students. They could graduate only if they converted.

In the eighteenth century, Frankfurt was perhaps the most oppressive place for Jews in Western Europe. Only Rome and the Papal States treated Jews as harshly. Jewish settlement in Frankfurt—as in Cologne—probably began during the first century, when it was a Roman military outpost. In 1311, Jews were still listed as equals in the citizenship rolls. In 1424, they were struck from the rolls as "enemies of the Cross of Christ" and locked into a walled ghetto. Their cemetery, one of the oldest in Europe, with thousands of tombs stacked one atop the other in five layers, remained intact until it was razed by the Nazis.

At the end of the eighteenth century, Jews were still prevented from leaving the ghetto after dark or on Sundays and Christian holidays. The Frankfurt ghetto consisted of a single dark lane, the Judengasse, foul-smelling and dank, sunless because of its narrowness and its tall, over-crowded houses. Originally established to house some two or three hundred souls evicted from the Christian parts of town, the ghetto soon had to serve a population five or six times larger. The city government rejected all pleas to enlarge it. By 1743, some three thousand Jews (10 percent of the population) crowded into a space originally intended for three hundred in conditions of squalor and congestion unknown elsewhere in the city.

Frankfurt was a city of hard-boiled businessmen, bankers, and wholesale merchants commonly known as "peppersacks" and "barrel-squires." A major European trading center, it was host twice a year to Europe's most important fair. Goethe lamented that the inhabitants of Frankfurt lived in a frenzy of making and spending money. Business opportunities must have been unusual here or the Jewish population would not have grown tenfold over the years. Supply and demand in the limited space drove real estate prices inside the ghetto to absurd levels. In the eighteenth century, the cost of an airless three-room apartment in the Judengasse was higher than that paid by Goethe's father for his airy ten-room town house with garden in the most elegant part of the Christian town. Pale-faced children passed a joyless youth in the congested compound; they had no contact with children outside the ghetto nor were they allowed to enter the public parks and promenades or walk in the nearby countryside.

The ghetto was closed off by high walls and three heavy gates that were locked at night and on Sundays and Christian holidays. Few Christians ever entered it. Goethe, a native of Frankfurt, shared the general prejudice against and atavistic fear of Jews, at least as a young man. In his memoirs he confessed that during his youth, "the cruelties committed by Jews against Christian children" were always in the back of his mind. It took a long time before he ventured inside "the ominous Judengasse." After escaping "the obtrusiveness of so many people untiringly intent on haggling," he did not go back readily. "The confinement, the dirt, the swarm of people . . . made a disagreeable impression, even when observed only from outside the gate. . . . And yet they were also human beings, energetic, agreeable. Their obstinacy in sticking to their own customs, one could not deny it respect. Moreover, their girls were pretty."[12] On another occasion, in conversation with the Prague Jew Simon von Laemel, the poet confessed his "incomprehension as to how this unpleasant people had been capable of producing the world's most memorable book."[13]

Frankfurt was one of several free imperial cities, governed by an oligarchy of patrician merchant families. A general fear of Jewish rivalry must have been a contributing factor to the continuing harshness of the city council's restrictive measures. Jews were allowed to enter the Christian quarters only on business, never for leisure. Inside the Christian quarters, no more than two Jews were allowed to walk abreast, and for some reason they were not entitled to carry walking sticks. Nor could they use the sidewalk. At the cry *"Jud, mach mores"*—roughly, "Jew, pay your dues"—they would have to take off their hats, step aside, and bow. They were banned at all times from the vicinity of the cathedral and could enter the town hall only through a back entrance. Not all these restrictions were enforced and some were observed only sporadically. But until the French Revolution, all public gardens were closed to Jews (as they would be two centuries later under the Nazis). An appeal to end this particular restriction, unparalleled in Germany, was dismissed in 1770 by the city council as one more proof of the "boundless arrogance of this nation."

In the course of the seventeenth century, a tiny elite of privileged court Jews started to separate themselves from the mass of their coreligionists. Court Jews handled the finances of princes, negotiating their loans and supplying them with the luxury goods they craved. The court Jew was a peculiarly German phenomenon. Nowhere in Europe were there as many, and not simply because Germany had so many courts. There was little call for court Jews in France, where the central bureaucracy was more developed, or in Italy, where a more advanced banking system had existed since the Middle Ages. The entry for *"Juif"* in the French *Encyclopédie* of 1751–65 likened Jews to "cogs and nails needed in a great building in order to join and hold together all its parts."

In the relatively backward German principalities, court Jews were products of an absolutist, decentralized, and elaborately ritualized Baroque culture.[14] Local potentates needed to finance their personal, military, and political extravagances. Courtiers had to be furnished with fine cloth, mistresses with jewelry, their cooks with French and Italian delicacies, armies with uniforms, and cavalry horses with fodder. The smaller principalities especially competed with one another in the pursuit of luxuries. The supply of credit was only one of the services court Jews rendered; the procurement of luxuries was another. Communication and the transfer of goods and money were slow and precarious; transportation was difficult. Capital still moved cumbersomely and at great risk on unsafe roads in heavy sacks of gold coin. Through their intimate family links and trusted networks of coreligionists in other countries, court Jews were often better able than others to serve their princes. They belonged to a kind of inter-European monetary aristocracy whose children married one another and who shared a common system of adjudication and tort law. Rabbinical courts throughout Europe and the Near East recognized and enforced one another's verdicts.

For services rendered, court Jews were exempted from the restrictions imposed on their coreligionists. Some were allowed to live outside the ghettos and were entitled to bear arms. They were among the first to discard the traditional long, dark garb worn by their forebears since the early Middle Ages. They adopted the elegant, colorful Spanish and French coats favored by the nobility, along with white stockings and flamboyant silk scarves, and they covered their heads with high white wigs that as Jews, however, they were not allowed to powder.

The majority of Jews were further removed from such privilege or comfort than can now be imagined. Aside from the few bankers, wholesalers, and jewelers most were wretchedly poor, in many areas poorer than the non-Jewish urban and rural populations. Excluded from guilds and crafts, subject to rigorous restrictions, refused residence permits in many towns, by the eighteenth century a great many had been reduced to peddling trinkets, charms, discarded household goods, and used clothes or to begging; it was said of Jewish peddlers that they even hawked trousers "left empty" by the victims of pestilence. Some Jews were petty pawnbrokers and money changers who operated on the peripheries of fairs and market towns. In the larger cities, 15 or 20 percent of all Jews might be money changers; in the smaller towns and villages where most German Jews lived, the figure was very much lower. At midcentury, no fewer than 80 percent of German Jews lived from hand to mouth, at the poorest level of German society.[15]

By far the worst off were the *Betteljuden* (beggar Jews). Since they had no money to buy any kind of "protection," they were mostly homeless or vagrant. Religious strictures did not permit them to become mercenaries, as did the poorest runaway serfs. As one observer noted in 1783, these Jews had no alternatives but to "roam through life as beggars or be rogues." Many were lifelong nomads, descended apparently from several generations of beggars. Born on the road, they depended on theft or charity. Accompanied by their ragged families, they traveled the countryside in swarms, a *Wandervolk* driven from place to place and, like the Gypsies, regarded as outlaws, or *Gauner,* that is, scamps, parasites, rogues, and thieves. In 1712, a traveler reported: "The begging hordes at times make the highways disgusting, particularly when one reaches their encampments where they are sunning themselves in a wood or behind a fence."[16] A rare document from 1773 concerns a fifteen-year-old Jewish girl named Frommet who had been sold by her vagrant parents as a housemaid. She was standing trial in Frankfurt for murdering her employer with a hatchet. The plea submitted in her "defense" stated: "Who does not remember seeing such a horde of wretched creatures, vagrant *Landjuden* [country Jews] with their children, carrying their entire possessions on their humps? And seeing them pass by, who has not promptly noticed the scant difference between them and cattle?"[17]

The cities usually denied the vagrants access; some were admitted for one night only but required to stay in poorhouses maintained by a local Jewish community. Jewish almsgiving afforded some material help. Hospitality was occasionally made available to the needy, especially on the Sabbath. The tradition of solidarity was deeply ingrained among Jews, but the huge increase in homelessness and vagrancy during the eighteenth century was bringing about its collapse.

The existence of the vagrant beggar Jews of the eighteenth century is still largely unexplored. Historians have tended to overlook them, perhaps because of the scarcity of documentary evidence. Several edicts concerning Jewish vagrants survive; a Prussian law, the "Renewed and More Severe Edict" of 1783, ordered all *Betteljuden* expelled from His Royal Majesty's lands." The few documents we have suggest that the beggar Jews were numerous, possibly comprising as much as a tenth of the Jewish population.

Heine, born almost half a century later, missed the *Wanderjuden* at their worst, but had them in mind when he drew the portrait of a Jew deprived of all humanity as though turned by some cursed witch into a wild dog:

> *Dog with doglike thoughts and worries*
> *Slogging on year after year*
> *Through the daily muck and mire*
> *And the urchins' mocking jeer.*

Once a week, on Friday evening, Heine adds (in what may have been a rare lapse into sentimentality), the curse lifts, the dog becomes human, and it celebrates the Sabbath.

Some of the nomads may have been descendants of Jews scattered after epidemics or the expulsions during the Crusades, the Black Death, or later massacres. Others were the younger sons of protected Jews who could not afford to buy them residence permits in the cities of their birth. Stalking the countryside in their rags, they must have appeared as ghosts of Ahasuerus, the mythical Wandering or Errant Jew, condemned after the crucifixion of Christ to walk the earth restlessly. "Errant Jews" were first "sighted" in Germany early in the sixteenth century, then repeatedly over the next two hundred years. "The myth of the Errant Jew has deep roots," Heine wrote, speculating on its origins:

> In a remote, peaceful valley, a mother tells her children the gruesome tale. The little ones gather anxiously around the hearth. It is night. The post horn sounds outside; *Schacherjuden* [Jewish crooks] drive past on their way to the Leipzig fair. We don't realize that *we* are the protagonists of this grisly tale. The white beard, its edge blackened once more by the passage of time—no barber can shave it off![18]

Swarms of vagrant men, women, and children of other faiths, too, were common at the time. Runaway conscripts and serfs, fugitives from justice, prostitutes, failed students, and defrocked clergymen roamed the countryside everywhere. Vagrant Jews often merged with the rest in an early form of assimilation. Schiller did not need to invent much in his play *The Robbers,* which features a mixed band of highwaymen, including a Jewish robber, Spiegelberg, who proposes issuing a manifesto in all four corners of the earth calling on those "who do not eat pork" to move with him to Palestine. "It is rare that a gang of thieves apprehended anywhere does not include one or several Jews," a traveler noted in 1783.[19]

In the eighteenth century, bands of Jewish highwaymen (*havrusse* in Yiddish) were said to infest the countryside in Westphalia, Brandenburg, and Hesse. Some were rumored to maintain a modicum of pious custom, observing a more or less kosher diet, robbing only on weekdays, and resting from their labors on the Sabbath. They became part of the general underworld. German criminal argot of the eighteenth century was filled with Yiddishisms: *ganevenen* (to steal), *gelokachte Sachen* (stolen goods), *Mosser* (informer), *Schmiere stehen* (stand guard).

The integration of Germans and Jews, some might say the symbiosis, flourished on this lowest level, long before reaching the privileged court Jews in their wigs and borrowed manners or Moses Mendelssohn as he started on his pathbreaking career.

2

The Age of Mendelssohn

THE gatekeeper's orders were to keep all Jews with no visible means of support out of Berlin, even if they were only passing through. So it was no surprise that the young Mendelssohn was entering a city in which two-thirds of its roughly two hundred Jewish families were well-to-do; those of more limited means had, over the years, been systematically thrown out. A few families, perhaps half a dozen, were among the richest in town; one Jewish doctor reportedly owned a Rembrandt.

Having passed the interrogation at the gate, the boy made his way to the house of his former teacher, David Frankel, now chief rabbi of Berlin's small Jewish community. Frankel found him lodgings at the house of a neighbor, a money changer by the name of Heimann Bamberger. He was willing to accommodate the boy in his attic free of charge, providing him in addition with two or three meals a week. Hospitality to gifted students was a time-honored tradition.

Mendelssohn enrolled in Frankel's exacting seminary, where the program consisted of unending rote repetitions of early medieval texts, inter-

Moses Mendelssohn, the "German Socrates," here shown in an etching from 1787, was the first German Jew to achieve European prominence. A modern German guidebook to Berlin claims that the history of literature in Berlin began on the day the young Mendelssohn entered the city through the Rosenthal Gate, the only one open to Jews and cattle. *Courtesy Leo Baeck Institute, Jerusalem*

pretations thereof, elaborations of Talmudic law, and copious commentary accumulated over the centuries. There followed years of assiduous learning and extreme poverty. The Talmudic scholar was commonly enjoined to live a life of privation, to "eat hard bread with salt, drink water by measure, sleep upon the hard earth, and busy himself with the Law." For the Sabbath meal a young student might be a guest at his teacher's table. At other times, he might well go hungry. Mendelssohn had an unusually fine handwriting and was able occasionally to earn a few pennies copying texts his teacher was preparing for print. With his few hard-earned coins, he bought bread, often his only diet for days on end. He later recounted that he would mark off seven portions on his loaf of bread to make it last an entire week. Some days he was ashamed to go out because his shirt was ragged or filthy. A "great joy," he remembered, was the day he found twenty pennies in the street, which he used to buy himself a new shirt.

In addition to his religious studies, Mendelssohn taught himself German as well as Latin, Greek, French, and English. He read every book he could find. He was careful to do this secretly, in his attic or some other safe place: secular studies were frowned on at the seminary. Mendelssohn was fortunate in that his landlord was "too upright or too phlegmatic" to suspect his covert reading. Religious scholars spoke Yiddish or *Judendeutsch* only and condemned as heretics all who attempted to acquire a secular education. Mendelssohn's mentor may have been more open-minded than most but only up to a point. Had Mendelssohn been caught reading a German book, he might have lost Frankel's sponsorship and been expelled from Berlin as a penniless foreign Jew. Under Prussian law, the Jewish wardens of the poor had the power to enforce eviction and only in rare cases would the Prussian magistrate revoke such orders. The mere possession of a German book was enough to send someone away. Indeed, three years after Mendelssohn's arrival in Berlin, the warden caught a fellow student named Bleichröder carrying one of Mendelssohn's German books in the street. The warden screamed, "What have you got here? Not a German book, I hope!" The warden, Bleichröder later wrote, "tore the book out of my hand and dragged me to the bailiff. He ordered the bailiff to evict me from the city. Mendelssohn learned of my fate. He did his best to secure my return, but in vain."[1]

Intellectually, German Judaism was at a low point, even in Berlin. Piety was often reduced to the mechanical repetition of ritual. With few exceptions, German Jews were no longer producing outstanding religious thinkers; most clerical posts were occupied by parochial rabbis from Poland and points farther east, where conditions had prevented any form of acculturation and modernization. A few sons of wealthy Berlin Jews were already attending a *Gymnasium,* a German high school. The poor and unprivileged, like Mendelssohn, had as little access to the riches of secular thought and culture as to the comforts of prosperous living.

Social intercourse with non-Jews was difficult and in some eyes unthinkable. Non-Jewish sources of information were closed or even forbidden to him. Nevertheless, Mendelssohn became fluent in German—we do not exactly know how—within a remarkably short time. His talents were noticed by several wealthy young Jews, sons of well-to-do families who dabbled in secular studies undisturbed by wardens and magistrates. One of them, Moses Salomon Gumpertz, who later became the first Berlin Jew to graduate from a German university as a medical doctor, took a liking to Mendelssohn. He helped him with Latin (he himself had taken his first Latin lessons, perhaps surreptitiously, from a friendly Huguenot). Another young man sparked

Mendelssohn's interest in mathematics. A third introduced him to the philosophy of Leibniz and lent him Locke's *Essay concerning Human Understanding* (in Latin); Mendelssohn read it with the help of a dictionary. The book opened his eyes to unimagined intellectual marvels. The little philosophy taught at Frankel's seminary was Maimonides' *Guide to the Perplexed,* which had recently become available again, having long been banned by the zealots for its attempt to reconcile Aristotle with Jewish theology. (Like many other twelfth-century Spanish Jews, Maimonides had shared the intellectual heritage of his non-Jewish neighbors to an extent that was still practically nonexistent among German Jews.) The help Gumpertz and his friends were able to give Mendelssohn was necessarily only marginal. Almost everything he learned beyond the sacred religious texts was entirely self-taught. "I never attended a university," he wrote later, "and have never participated in a seminar."[2] In any case, there was no university in Berlin at the time. If there had been one, he would not have been allowed to attend it.

In 1750, Mendelssohn's studies with Frankel came to an end. He was twenty-one and might easily have been ordained as rabbi, but he decided to pursue a different career. A wealthy Berlin silk merchant, Isaac Bernhard, agreed to hire Mendelssohn as a tutor for his young son and was able to extend Mendelssohn's residence permit as an indentured member of his household. He took a liking to his son's new tutor. Certainly, he must have known what he was doing when he hired the well-read, multilingual Mendelssohn rather than a traditional Talmudist who spoke only *Judendeutsch* and Hebrew and regarded secular studies as an abomination.

Mendelssohn's standard of living improved. For the first time in his life, he was able to buy books. His reading now ranged to Spinoza, Cicero, Euclid, Aristotle, Plato, Newton, Montesquieu, Rousseau, and Voltaire. For the next four or five years he was as much his own teacher as the young Bernhard's. He taught his pupil German and mathematics and himself philosophy and German, Latin, French, Italian, and English literature.

In the enlightened atmosphere of Bernhard's household, Mendelssohn's social life expanded to include a few leading non-Jewish intellectuals. Thus he came to know two remarkable young men his age, Gotthold Ephraim Lessing, a budding playwright and journalist for the local *Vossische Zeitung*, and Friedrich Nicolai, a bookseller and leading liberal publisher. They became friends, remaining close for the remainder of their lives. Together they founded what was later known as the Berlin literary school, perhaps the most prominent such group in Germany until the arrival of Goethe and Schiller. Inhabiting a milieu where literature and philosophy overlapped, the three friends had a great deal in common, being rationalists in philosophy and religion and cosmopolitans in politics. They were good-natured men of the world, urbane and kindly; Lessing spoke for all three when he said that patriotism was a heroic but useless human weakness. Ethically motivated, with little urge to build comprehensive systems, they were freelance intellectuals, living by teaching and writing, independent of institutional and academic structures. None drew funds from any public purse.

Their commitment was to the Enlightenment, which Kant famously defined as the "liberation of man from his self-incurred immaturity." Man's immaturity was his inability to think for himself. *"Sapere aude! Have the courage to employ your own mind!"* The spirit of the Enlightenment had come to Germany first from England and more recently from France. In England, Enlightenment thought was mostly concerned with the economy; in France, with liberalizing the political system. In Germany, which had been devastated during the Wars of Religion, the Enlightenment focused on ensuring freedom of faith; unlike in England or France, it was not, or not yet, rooted in a political class. The German middle class, such as it was, remained mired in deeply ingrained habits of discipline and servility. Mercantile cities like Frankfurt, Hamburg, and Nürnberg were politically inactive. The newly emerging middle class of Berlin largely consisted of well-to-do Jews who lacked citizenship rights or the courage to demand them. Their toleration could be abrogated at any moment.

If Kant was the philosophic spokesman of the Enlightenment in Germany, Lessing was its main literary herald. In his journalism and his plays, Lessing preached tolerance and the rule of reason. The son of a Lutheran pastor, he was an early freethinker. There are few writers to whom German liberalism owes so much. Goethe, Schiller, and many others acknowledged their debt to him. His work prepared the ground for a succession of writers who would gain Germany a leading role in European culture. Lessing's prose was pure and precise to a degree hardly seen in German letters until then. His plays were landmarks in the history of German drama, which until then had been largely imitative of the French. Lessing turned the stage into a pulpit and art into a new secular religion. He was the first popular German writer to concede that Jews possessed "virtue" like other humans, a view that caused a sensation at the time. In *The Jews,* one of his early plays, written before he met Mendelssohn, an elegant young traveler saves a German nobleman and his lovely daughter from a pack of thieves. The traveler wins the father's gratitude and his daughter's heart but graciously declines to accept her hand for, as he reveals to her father's astonishment, he is a Jew.

The Daughter: What difference does it make?
The Governess: Shush, Fräulein, shush, I'll tell you later what a big difference it makes.

Soon after meeting Mendelssohn, Lessing wrote that he expected him to become "an honor to his nation"—if his fellow Jews would allow it, Lessing added, for they tended to persecute such people. Lessing was alluding to the excommunication of Spinoza a century earlier. In later years, the two men wrote very warmly of each other. It is not difficult to see why Lessing was so attracted to Mendelssohn. In the first place, he admired Mendelssohn's autodidactic gifts. Apart from his other qualities, Mendelssohn was living proof of one of the Enlightenment's major tenets: he had "become what he was by the force of his *own* thinking, with the help only of a few books." Mendelssohn later said that everything he had done or written in his life had been with Lessing in mind as inspiration and judge. Lessing had formed his soul, he wrote.

Nicolai, the third of the trio, was the son of a bookseller and, like Mendelssohn, an autodidact. He became Lessing's and Mendelssohn's devoted publisher and edited several influential literary reviews that published Mendelssohn's book reviews, his studies in semantics, aesthetics, and art, and his translations of English and French poetry. Heine said that Nicolai tried hard to achieve in Germany what the encyclopedists achieved in France—the eradication of the heritage of the Dark Ages. In this he could not succeed, Heine added, because the old ruins in Germany were still too solid and too haunted by ghosts, making a mockery of his efforts.

Lessing, Mendelssohn, and Nicolai met almost every day, often in Nicolai's pleasant garden, to discuss literature and philosophy. Lessing recalled that Mendelssohn often "played the role of the chorus in ancient Greek drama. . . . When we still thought ourselves far from any conclusion, he would sum everything up in a few striking words that left us all content."[3] Johann Georg Hamann, the reactionary opponent of the Enlightenment, who after leading a rather debauched life had embraced Christian piety, also met "the Jew Mendelssohn" (as he put it) at this time. He and Mendelssohn disagreed on almost everything, but pleasantly and lightheartedly, in a spirit of mutual tolerance. The encounter encouraged Mendelssohn to feel that Jews and Germans were on the threshold of a new, more liberal age, confirming his fondest hopes for dialogue.

Throughout this period in his life Mendelssohn continued his strict observance of Jewish ritual and dietary laws. Thus he probably never accepted any cooked food and perhaps not even a glass of water at Lessing's or Nicolai's home. If his strictness taxed their friendship, neither ever complained. Mendelssohn spoke of it with good-natured self-irony. The others, of course, enjoyed wholesome meals in Mendelssohn's house. Later, as a married man, when his friends visited him on a Friday afternoon, Mendelssohn would excuse himself an hour before sunset, declaring: "Ladies and gentlemen! I am only going to the next room to receive my Sabbath and will soon rejoin you; in the meantime my wife will enjoy your company even more," or words to that effect. To Lessing he once wrote: "Tomorrow is Saturday so I cannot come to you. . . . If you, who do not have to celebrate the Sabbath, are able, do come here."[4]

In 1755, Lessing brought Mendelssohn a book by the English philosopher Anthony Ashley Cooper, 3rd earl of Shaftesbury. Soon after, he asked him what he thought of it. "It is quite good," Mendelssohn replied. "But I, too, could do this kind of thing." "Is that so?" Lessing said. "Then why don't you go ahead and do it!"[5] Some time later, Mendelssohn handed him a manuscript of *Philosophical Dialogues*. Several months passed. Mendelssohn asked him whether he had read it. Lessing surprised Mendelssohn with a printed, bound copy; the book had just been published by Nicolai's press. It launched Mendelssohn as a German author. Several other books followed in quick succession. His *Letters on Sentiment* (1755) virtually founded German philosophic-aesthetic criticism. In 1767, Mendelssohn's *Phaidon, or The Immortality of the Soul in Three Dialogues* appeared. A charming adaptation of Plato's dialogue on immortality, it established Mendelssohn as among the best-known German writers; the book was lauded for the lucid elegance of its style, uncommon at that time in a German philosophical text. An attempt to prove the existence of God by reason alone, without recourse to revelation, *Phaidon* articulated one of the main dogmas of natural religion. Reason itself was divine and thus held a promise of immortality. "He who is robbed of the hope of attaining immortality is the most abject creature on earth. To his profound misfortune, he is forced to brood on his condition, to fear death, and to despair."[6]

Phaidon was what we today would call an instant best-seller. It was said to be the most widely read book of its time in Germany. Pirated editions were printed in Hamburg and Leipzig. It was quickly translated into several European languages and did more than any other contemporary book before Kant to enhance the reputation of German philosophic thought. Mendelssohn became a European celebrity, the so-called German Socrates. For the first time since Spinoza, a Jew had crossed a line to emerge a prominent figure in the majority culture. Curiosity about this strange Jew spread through Germany and elsewhere. Catholic monks wrote to him from their monasteries asking for theological instruction. The duke of Brunswick wished to offer him a ministerial post. The Prussian Academy of Sciences elected Mendelssohn a member. It was not the first time Mendelssohn had come to the academy's attention. Three years earlier the academy had awarded him first prize for an essay entitled "On Evidence in the Metaphysical Sciences" (Immanuel Kant came in second).

The academy happened to be Frederick II's hobbyhorse. Voltaire was its genius loci; as its president, the king had imported the French mathematician Pierre-Louis Maupertuis. The academy was not free to act on its own: the monarch had to ratify each election. Frederick chose to ignore the unanimous vote electing Mendelssohn. Maupertuis resubmitted the proposal to make Mendelssohn a member. The king vetoed it. Nobody dared ask him why.

There the matter rested. Maupertuis observed that in order to join the academy, Mendelssohn lacked only one thing: "a foreskin." Mendelssohn took the rejection lightly, remarking that it was more creditable to be honored by an academy and vetoed by a king than the other way around.

Long after Mendelssohn's reputation had been established throughout Germany and Europe, Frederick II still pretended he did not exist. The two men never met. A few weeks after the king's veto, a prominent foreign dignitary, the Saxon minister von Fritsch, was the king's guest at Sans Souci, the royal retreat on the outskirts of Potsdam. Fritsch mentioned that he planned to call on Mendelssohn on his way home. The king ordered his adjutant to summon Mendelssohn to Sans Souci. Mendelssohn drove out and met with the Saxon minister. The king remained out of sight.

Following this visit, an anecdote made the rounds. The curt summons issued by the king's adjutant had reportedly ordered "the famous Herr Mendelssohn" to present himself at Sans Souci at noon the following day. Upon Mendelssohn's arrival at the palace gate, the guard asked, "Where is the Jew going?" Mendelssohn handed him the summons. The officer studied it and, addressing him in the third-person singular, as he would a servant, asked, "What is he so famous for that His Majesty summons him here?" Mendelssohn answered coolly, "I am a famous sorcerer." "Is that so?" said the officer. "Well, go, in God's name, go!"[7]

In the meantime, Mendelssohn's pupil, Bernhard's young son, had grown up. No longer needed as a tutor, Mendelssohn became Bernhard's bookkeeper. This meant that he now spent long days at Bernhard's dusty warehouse, where some sixty looms were producing cotton and silk fabrics and buyers and porters were coming and going. In a

Fromet Mendelssohn. *Courtesy Leo Baeck Institute, Jerusalem*

letter to Lessing he complained of the humdrum activity and useless talk going on around him all day. He had so many tiring chores, he wrote, that he pined for the evenings when he might finally be able to converse with intelligent human beings. His responsibilities at Bernhard's firm grew and his salary rose to twenty-five thalers a month (roughly equivalent to five hundred dollars today). His many admirers wondered at the incongruity of his routine, one part spent in the bustle of workers, porters, storekeepers, buyers, and suppliers and another in an atmosphere of refined literary culture with Nicolai, Lessing, and other friends. His ability to combine the two worlds with good humor was considered heroic. Few were aware that his daily routine encompassed yet another world, that of Hebrew letters and the subtle interpretation of arcane aspects of Talmudic texts.

Mendelssohn became an attraction for visiting intellectuals from all over Europe. They reported meeting "the Jew Moses" in his "counting-house," busy with silks and account books, signing bills of sale and totaling cash receipts. They found him affable, always hospitable, in good humor, and—between processing one bill of lading and the next—able to engage in brilliant philosophic conversation. Some were shocked to see him "surrounded by common merchants, money changers, and hagglers," noting how little his external circumstances corresponded with his talents.[8]

He also married. He first saw Fromet Guggenheim on a business trip to Hamburg. "I visited the theater, met scholars, . . . and committed the folly of falling in love in my thirtieth year," Mendelssohn wrote to Les-

sing. "The woman I want to marry has no means and is neither beautiful nor learned."[9] She was twenty-four, blue-eyed, and a head taller
than the bridegroom. It was a love match, rare at a time when most Jewish marriages were arranged through matchmakers and negotiated by
relatives. The bride's father was not in Hamburg when the two first met
and secretly became engaged. Mendelssohn was presented to him only
several months later.

Though still the indentured household servant of a protected Jew,
Mendelssohn was prominent enough to secure his prospective wife a
Prussian residence permit fairly quickly. With heavy irony he wrote to
Fromet that henceforth she must show only enthusiasm for Prussia and
its allies and contempt for its many enemies. On the occasion of his
marriage he was, like all other Jews, compelled to purchase a few hundred thalers' worth of Royal Porcelain—not the soup bowls or cups that
might come in handy for the newlyweds but the flawed or unsellable
items chosen by the king's factory. Thus Mendelssohn came into possession of twenty life-sized, monstrously ugly, garishly painted porcelain monkeys that would remain in the family for several generations.
His grandson, the composer Felix Mendelssohn-Bartholdy, kept one
such monkey in his study and pointed it out to visitors.*

---

*In 1978, the West Berlin Senate nostalgically decided to stage an extravagant exhibi-
tion called *Preussen—Eine Bilanz* (Prussia—Taking Stock). One member of the advi-
sory board, Walter Grab, suggested that in addition to the usual knickknacks (Frederick
the Great's gloves, riding boots, pistols, snuffboxes, cuff links, portraits, and statues) the
exhibition include also one of Mendelssohn's porcelain monkeys. Grab had tracked one
down in the Hamburg Museum of Arts and Crafts. It would illustrate, he said, the discrimination and lack of freedom in Frederick's reign. Grab's proposal was rejected on
grounds of the monkey's ugliness. Grab argued that the repulsive monkey was a symbol,
the embodiment of the Jews' humiliation under Frederick. The curators preferred dis-
playing a far prettier porcelain monkey, which they had found on the shelves of the
Hohenzollern Museum. That particular monkey was altogether too attractive and
missed the point entirely, but Grab was overruled. The attractive monkey went on display, appearing also in the exhibition catalog (see W. Grab, in *Jüdischer Almanach*, Leo
Baeck Institute, Jerusalem, 1994, pp. 49–54).

Soon after his marriage Mendelssohn ran afoul of the Prussian censors. He was accused of having defamed Christianity in the pages of Nicolai's literary magazine. The magazine was shut down. Mendelssohn was interrogated by the *Generalfiskal* (attorney general), a powerful man whose duties included making sure that "protected Jews" conformed to the terms of the royal edict. "How dare he write against Christians?" he barked, but failed to cite a specific text. Mendelssohn assured him that he had been misinformed.

> **Attorney General:** Ah, he denies! But we know better. We will get to the bottom of his tricks. What he has done is a violation of the *Judenprivilegium*—he has forfeited his protection.
>
> **Mendelssohn:** But I have no protection to forfeit. I am the bookkeeper of the protected Jew Bernhard.
>
> **Attorney General:** So much the worse! The mildest punishment for his wickedness will be his expulsion from the country.[10]

The summons turned out to be the result of an anonymous denunciation and the matter was cleared up within days. But Mendelssohn and his friends realized how vulnerable he was as an indentured servant. An admirer, the French marquis Jean-Baptiste d'Argens, a member of the academy and one of the king's resident philosophers, urged Mendelssohn to petition Frederick directly for a change of status. He promised to place the petition on the king's desk himself. Mendelssohn was reluctant to beg for what he considered his natural right but his friends insisted. In the interest of his growing family and his literary projects, he eventually agreed. The letter was couched in the inevitable obsequious terms necessitated by the circumstances. Mendelssohn appealed *alleruntertänigst* (in the utmost obedience and submissiveness) to the *allergnädigst* (most merciful) king to "most graciously" deign to designate him and his family protected Jews even though they lacked the required capital. He promised to make up for this lack by his "scientific efforts."[11]

D'Argens put the letter on the king's desk. The king ignored it.

Mendelssohn soon regretted having written the letter in the first place although he did not complain to d'Argens. Months later, d'Argens learned indirectly that Mendelssohn had received no reply and reproached the king, who claimed never to have received any such letter. D'Argens pleaded with Mendelssohn to submit a second petition and added a note of his own to this document—in French: "One philosopher who is a lapsed Catholic urges another philosopher who is a lapsed Protestant to grant a Letter of Protection to a third philosopher who is a lapsed Jew. There is too much philosophy here for reason not to be on the side of this appeal."

The appeal was only partially successful. The king agreed to grant protected status to Mendelssohn but not to his wife and children, who risked expulsion in the event of his death. The king's largesse also came at a price. The royal treasury demanded a fee of one thousand thalers (the equivalent of twenty thousand dollars today). Mendelssohn, whose monthly salary was twenty-five thalers, could not possibly raise such a sum. He submitted another "most submissive and obedient request" asking that the fee be canceled. The treasury held back, afraid of establishing a precedent. Mendelssohn's friends intervened, emphasizing the supplicant's exceptional qualities. The negotiations lasted almost a year and the fee was finally waived. Mendelssohn was officially recognized as an "exceptional," that is to say, as an un-Jewish Jew, a fabled animal heard of perhaps but rarely seen, a kind of human unicorn. The episode confirmed the limitations of eighteenth-century tolerance. Goethe was among the few who recognized them, remarking that "tolerance" had to be only a temporary state leading to acceptance. "To merely tolerate is to insult. True liberalism means acceptance."[12]

A contemporary engraving celebrating the author of *Phaidon* illustrates the lack of acceptance. It reproduces Mendelssohn's refined countenance with the inscription "Behold an Israelite . . . in whom there is no guile." The quotation refers to the "good" Jew Nathanael, who acknowledged Christ as the Son of God in the Gospel of St. John (1:47). Mendelssohn was expected to make a similar gesture. The missionary who took upon himself the "sacred" task of converting Mendelssohn to Christianity was a zealous Protestant deacon in Zurich named Johann

The physiognomist Johann Caspar Lavater, Moses Mendelssohn, and Gotthold Ephraim Lessing (standing) in a contemporary French lithograph by S. Maier. *Courtesy Leo Baeck Institute, Jerusalem*

Caspar Lavater. He believed that the "conversion of the entire Jewish nation to Christianity" was imminent and would herald the Second Coming of Christ.[13] What could be more auspicious than the conversion of the "German Socrates"?

In addition to being an eager proselytizer, Lavater was an ardent disciple of physiognomy, a pseudoscience according to which a man's character and talents—as well as his fate—were indelibly imprinted in the lineaments of his face. Physiognomy was like astrology, except that signs found in the sky were now visible in the shape of a man's head, ears, nose, cheeks, chin, and brow. Wisdom and good character, but also stupidity, resided in the forehead (especially the upper part), avarice and duplicity were reflected in the shape and position of the eyes, and so on. Before Lavater, interest in physiognomy had generally been on the wane in Europe; in England, Parliament had outlawed it as quackery. Lavater's eloquence, however, gave physiognomy—he called it the "divine science"—a new lease on life. The author of several weighty treatises on the subject, he propagated its eternal truths with the passion of the true believer, and his renown as a physiognomist spread throughout Switzerland, Germany, and France.

Lavater had read Mendelssohn's recent books. After briefly meeting him in Berlin, he spent many hours poring over engravings of his hero's features, which he considered unusually noble. From the shape of Mendelssohn's forehead alone, Lavater concluded that Mendelssohn was a likely convert, willing and ready to see the light. The evidence was clearly imprinted in his face, he wrote. Lavater had just translated a book by the Swiss philosopher and naturalist Charles Bonnet, *Philosophical Palingenesis or Ideas on the Past and Future States of Living Beings,* which purported to prove the truth of the Christian faith scientifically. Without consulting Bonnet, Lavater provocatively dedicated his translation to "Herr Moses Mendelssohn in Berlin." In an open letter attached to his translation, he challenged Mendelssohn to "disprove" Bonnet or, if he could not, convert on the spot: "Do what sagacity, love of truth, and honesty would naturally dictate, what Socrates would have done had he read this treatise and found it irrefutable."[14]

In his challenge to Mendelssohn, Lavater was supported by a phalanx of disciples, professors, and pious ladies in Zurich and Geneva, and country parsons in northern Germany. All were eager to save the famous philosopher's soul, the sooner the better. They had thoroughly misunderstood Mendelssohn's position. Mendelssohn respected Jesus as a historical figure, a critical first-century Jewish rabbi who, unlike his disciples, never rejected Judaism or proclaimed his divinity. In Mendelssohn's view, no religion, including Judaism, was free of harmful man-made features, of hypocrisy and superstition. Yet of the "essential core" of his own religion Mendelssohn was as sure as Lavater and Bonnet were of theirs. Judaism, in Mendelssohn's view, was a faith of reason. He could never abandon it for Christianity, whose revealed dogmas, in his view, contradicted reason. Judaism may have become overly inbred and disconnected from the surrounding world, but Christianity's dependence on miracles was thoroughly alien to him. Mendelssohn said as much in a brief and dignified response to Lavater's open letter, adding: "On this occasion, I declare myself a Jew. I shall always remain a Jew."

The calm tone of Mendelssohn's answer was deceptive. Lavater's provocation had deeply embarrassed and angered him. Lessing and others urged him to deliver a fierce theological counterattack. Nothing was further from his mind. He saw no point in engaging in a useless debate reminiscent of the notorious public disputations between rabbis and monks staged in the Middle Ages more for the entertainment of bored courtiers than for real enlightenment.*

The affair prompted a considerable stir and produced a small library of pamphlets. Lavater's challenge and Mendelssohn's reply were published and republished. Lavater had second thoughts even before receiving Mendelssohn's response and wrote Mendelssohn to apologize, asking what he might do to remedy his faux pas. His apology arrived too late; Mendelssohn had already published his riposte. Intellectual opinion was divided but, in keeping with the liberal spirit of

---

*In Heine's parody of a medieval disputation a famous rabbi and a renowned friar meet to dispute each other's religion. They arrive in the arena with trains of enthusiastic disciples equally sure of their champion's victory and the imminent conversion of his rival. The Jews are hopefully sharpening circumcision knives; the Christians are readying the baptismal font. After hours of mutual condemnation, the king turns to his queen: "Who is right and who is wrong?" She answers:

> Which is right I do not know
> On the whole I tend to think
> That the rabbi and the friar
> That they both—forgive me—stink.

the time, by and large on Mendelssohn's side. The prominent mathematician-astronomer and aphorist Georg Lichtenberg attacked Lavater in a biting satire entitled "Timorus: The Defense of Two Israelites Who, Overwhelmed by Lavater's Proofs and the Taste of Pork Sausages, Converted to the Only True Faith." Goethe was incensed by Lavater's impertinence and dismissed him as a hypocrite and villain. (He, too, would eventually fall victim to Lavater's missionary zeal and would

Moses Mendelssohn's silhouette as published in Lavater's book *Physiognomic Fragments.*

attempt to put an end to it by bluntly informing his torturer, "I am not a Christian.")[15]

Lavater continued to rant about Mendelssohn's facial features. In his *Physiognomic Fragments,* published after Mendelssohn's death "for the advancement of human understanding and love," Lavater reprinted another fine silhouette of Mendelssohn. The gushing text "converts" Mendelssohn posthumously, together with Plato and Moses, to the one true faith:

> You probably know this silhouette. It is very dear to me! It speaks volumes! I marvel at its contours! My gaze runs from the marvelous arch of the forehead to the sharp bones of the eye. In these depths resides a Socratic soul. Mark the wonderful transition from nose to upper lip . . . how all this combines to make the divine truth of physiognomy palpable and visible. Yes, I see him, Abraham's son, who—together with Plato and Moses—will surely recognize and worship the crucified Lord of Splendor![16]

The four volumes of this work, richly illustrated and written in an ecstatic style, further enhanced the popularity of physiognomy, a popularity that, in Germany especially, it has since never quite lost.[17] Lichtenberg's vociferous attacks on Lavater—men, he said, must not be judged by their exteriors like dogs and horses—and on other popular charlatans did little to counter the renewed fascination with this pseudoscience. Lavater's silly idiosyncrasy was relatively harmless compared with what would come later. Race was not a factor in Lavater's pet project and he insisted that the "perfect physiognomist" be above all a sympathetic man: "Love must open his eyes and sharpen his gaze."[18] The physiognomists who came after him largely joined forces with racial theorists; love was replaced with hatred. The first "learned" discourse on the grimace, "The Mien of the Jew: Ideas for a Physiognomic Anthropology," by one Johann Grohmann, appeared in Leipzig in 1791, the progenitor of a long line of hate-mongering works that culminated in the anti-Semitic caricatures of the nineteenth century and the Nazi organ Der Stürmer.

LAVATER's challenge had no adverse effect on Mendelssohn's growing renown. If anything, it enhanced it. Prominent intellectuals continued to express admiration for his work. Soon after the Lavater affair, the hereditary prince of Mecklenburg, on a visit to Berlin, demonstratively "paid his respects to the celebrated Herr Moses Mendelssohn" by inviting him to his palace, the Berlinische Zeitung reported. There were many other public shows of respect and admiration. Goethe came to Berlin in May 1778 and "waited upon no other poet but sought Mendelssohn's company."[19]

Nonetheless, the affair marked a turning point in Mendelssohn's life. Before the confrontation with Lavater, Mendelssohn had been content to be a litterateur interested mostly in philosophy, language, and modern European letters who kept his Jewish passions out of the public eye. After the affair, he vigorously engaged in Jewish reform, increasingly aware of the fragility of his own position and that of his coreligionists. Before the affair, he had been more prominent in German than in Jewish literary life. Nearly everything he published during the remaining seventeen years of his life, in German or Hebrew, aimed at promoting civil and cultural reform of Jewish life in Germany. In *Jerusalem, or Upon Ecclesiastical Power and Judaism* (1783), written under the impact of the affair, he tried to show that his version of Judaism, born of reason, was in harmony with the leading ideas of the Enlightenment. One could be both a practicing Jew and an enlightened German—there was no contradiction. Upon publication, Kant wrote to congratulate him for exercising a freedom of consciousness that no other religion permitted and that heralded a great reform.[20] Kant expressed the wish that Christian churches might soon follow suit. Elsewhere, he wrote that few men were so fortunate as to think for themselves and for others simultaneously and to choose a style appropriate to all. "There is only one Mendelssohn!"

A radical reformer in the guise of a conservative, Mendelssohn remained personally committed to strict traditional observance even as he was convinced that without change Judaism would degenerate into sentimentality or dissipate entirely for all but a diminishing minority. Judaism was becoming ossified, losing its creative impulse and turning to the passive virtues of prayer, self-pity, and suffering rather than to action. He was as tough on Jews as on their detractors. He urged the former, "Adopt the habits and constitution of the land in which you live but retain the religion of your forefathers," and berated the latter, "You tie our hands and complain that we do not use them." Jews were a religious and cultural community, he believed, not a national one. Differences in speech and dress, which caused so much suspicion and misunderstanding, were only exterior manifestations and should disappear. Above all, he called for a limit to the power of the rabbinate. True faith, he wrote, "knows no force but that of logical persuasion. . . . Rational argument is the path to bliss."[21]

Implied in this was a critique of the Jewish religious establishment, which, he feared, was responsible for the widespread neglect among Jews of secular knowledge. There had been no such neglect during the Middle Ages; it had increased with every century and now reached a dangerous level. Through their obsessive cultural introversion and fear of anything new and different, German Jews were contributing to their oppressive isolation. They differed in this respect from Jews in Italy and Provence, whose dress, language, and cultural openness continued the rich tradition of Jewish participation and prominence in the Hellenistic and Mediterranean world and in medieval Spain. In Germany, on the other hand, zealous schoolmasters from Poland—by 1780 there were few others—were driving young Jews to cultural self-immolation. In Italy and Provence, secular poetry was still written in classical Hebrew. In Germany and in Eastern Europe the language was essentially dead. Even Scripture was rendered into *Judendeutsch,* the uncouth vernacular that distorted the poetic beauty and depth of the Hebrew original and often gave the text a narrow, misleading interpretation.

As a first step, Mendelssohn advocated the revival of classical Hebrew and the use of High German as the secular day-to-day language. Jews able to speak German were often illiterate in that language. To make German more accessible, Mendelssohn embarked on a new, authoritative German translation of the Pentateuch and Psalms. Luther's translation was, understandably, suspect. Mendelssohn's new German text, printed (like *Judendeutsch*) in Hebrew letters next to the Hebrew original, would, he hoped, help replace the vernacular with High German as the everyday language. The vernacular was primitive and debased and greatly contributed, in Mendelssohn's view, to what he called the *Unsittlichkeit* (ignorance and bad manners) of the "common Jew."[22] Because of this debased language, German Jews often had a distorted sense of form and aesthetic feeling. He would help them speak pure German and pure Hebrew. Without fluency in Hebrew they would cease to be a cultural community; without fluency in German they would remain foreigners forever.

Mendelssohn's translation, then, had a definite *political* dimension. He was well aware that, beginning in antiquity, specific translations of the Bible had often been seminal in the history of Judaism—the early translations into Aramaic, the Septuagint (to serve the prominent Hellenistic Jewish population of Alexandria), Saadiah Gaon's translation into Arabic during the golden age of Jewish integration in Moorish Spain. In his task, Mendelssohn was also inspired by personal motives. His own children balked at reading Hebrew. In the past, he had often tried to make the Hebrew Bible more accessible to them by translating for them certain especially beautiful passages. After the Lavater affair these sporadic renderings became a concerted and systematic effort.

The truth was that among German Jews the Bible, both as poetry and as the original source for sacred law, had fallen into neglect. Lifeless interpretations and pedantic reinterpretations had become more important. With his new translation, Mendelssohn hoped to render a service not only to his own children but to "a good part of my nation as well." It would be "the first step toward obtaining the *Kultur* from which my nation has been kept so removed that one despairs of the notion that any improvement is possible."

Mendelssohn's translation of the Psalms and the Pentateuch (the final volume came out together with *Jerusalem* in 1783) often closely follows Luther's; other passages are entirely original and nearly always wonderfully clear and precise.* The tetragrammaton, which Luther had rendered as "the Lord," seemed too static; to suggest the timelessness of the Hebrew *Yehova,* Mendelssohn favored "the Eternal." At the same time as he worked on German translations, he wrote more and more frequently in Hebrew. In his view, the Psalms and many other biblical texts were superb examples of the lyrical poetry of the ancient Hebrews whose clear meaning had for too long been obscured by mystical interpretations of Scripture. He aspired to bring about a renaissance of Hebrew poetry, philosophy, and biblical commentary, all of which had virtually died out among the Jews of Germany. In many ways he succeeded, setting in motion the nineteenth-century revival of Hebrew poetry and belles lettres, the so-called Hebrew Enlightenment, which secularized the Hebrew Bible as a literary jewel and legitimized cultural assimilation by radicalizing the old Maimonidean contention that secular studies must be recognized as an essential part of the education of a Jew. Maimonides had been the first to claim that where the Pentateuch conflicts with reason it need not be taken literally, a view for which he was banned by the zealots. Mendelssohn went a big step further. Heine was perhaps too exuberant in his claim that just as Luther had overthrown the papacy so Mendelssohn had overthrown the Talmud ("a Gothic cathedral burdened with naïve embellishments

---

*Schubert set Mendelssohn's translation of Psalm 23 to music. Mendelssohn's grandson Felix preferred to intone Luther's version.

that nevertheless fills us with awe through its sheer heaven-aspiring grandeur") and proclaimed the Bible as the fountainhead of religion; yet there is no doubt that Mendelssohn paved the way for Reform Judaism and the science of Judaism, which made the religion the object of modern critical study.[23]

Given the vehemence of Mendelssohn's reformist vision, it is hardly surprising that many people wondered whether his continuing strict observance was not a tactic to retain the confidence of his more conservative coreligionists. Indeed, following the publication of *Jerusalem* and his new translation of the Pentateuch, Mendelssohn risked incurring the fate of Spinoza, whom the rabbis had excommunicated a hundred or so years before. The printing of Mendelssohn's "profane" German text of the Pentateuch on the same page as the original Hebrew scandalized the zealots. Rabbis promptly denounced Mendelssohn for violating the sacred. His new "Berlin religion" (as it was derogated) was condemned from many pulpits. Prominent rabbis in Prague, Hamburg, Fürth, and Frankfurt considered banning Mendelssohn as a heretic. In Frankfurt and Hamburg-Altona they were restrained by the secular authorities; elsewhere in Germany the old weapon of excommunication was too worn out to be effective. In Berlin there was a halfhearted attempt, foiled by the Prussian government, to hurt Mendelssohn indirectly by ordering Hartwig Wessely, one of his close collaborators on the translation, expelled for his liberal views. In Posen and, farther east, in Lissa, Mendelssohn's Pentateuch was publicly burned.

Mendelssohn's new translation was sold by prior subscription and widely distributed everywhere. It had a catalytic effect on Jewish opinion, perhaps comparable to the influence Diderot's *Encyclopedia* had exercised in France. In Berlin, twice as many prior subscriptions were sold as in any other German town.

THE entrenched power of the religious establishment, even in Mendelssohn's Berlin, was exemplified in 1778 by the treatment of an eccentric young genius named Salomon Maimon from Polish Lithuania. Poor and ragged, Maimon arrived on foot at the Rosenthal Gate, making a futile attempt to settle in Berlin as a student. A budding philosopher, he wanted only to "learn, learn, learn," much as Mendelssohn had thirty-five years earlier. Unlike Mendelssohn, however, Maimon had no personal references and was confined to the Jewish poorhouse for further examination. Closely interrogated by one of the wardens, Maimon innocently revealed his most precious possession, a copy of Maimonides' *Guide to the Perplexed*. Maimonides—Mendelssohn's idol—was no longer proscribed by the rabbis for his rationalism, but Maimon's open disclosure of admiration for the Spanish sage was enough for the warden to order his expulsion as a potential troublemaker.

Maimon's second attempt to enter Berlin, in 1781, this time by coach, proved more successful. He was able to find quarters in the city. Still, as he wrote in his autobiography, his troubles were far from over:

> The Jewish police officers . . . made a daily circuit of the hotels and other houses designed for the reception of strangers, inquired into the quality and occupation of newcomers as well as the probable length of their stay, and allowed them no rest till they had either found some occupation in the city or were out of it again. . . . The Jewish police officer L. M. came and examined me in the strictest manner. I told him that I wished to enter into service as a family tutor in Berlin. . . . I appeared suspicious to him; he believed he had seen me before, and evidently looked on me as a comet which comes nearer earth the second time than the first and so makes the danger more threatening. But when he saw I had a Mill ha-Higgayon, or Hebrew Logic, composed by Maimonides and annotated by Mendelssohn, he went into a perfect rage. "Yes! Yes!" he exclaimed, "that's the sort of book!" He turned to me with a threatening look and said, "Pack! Out of Berlin as quick as you can, if you don't wish to be led out with an escort!" I trembled and knew not what to do.[24]

In the event, Maimon found someone to intercede on his behalf and was allowed to stay for a limited time. He met Mendelssohn, who received him warmly. Like everyone else, Mendelssohn was impressed by Maimon's scholarship. He introduced him to other scholars and to some of the wealthy protected Jews.

Although Maimon wrote several original books of philosophy (some are admiringly cited to this day), he is remembered mostly for his remarkable autobiography. The genre often serves to reveal more about other people than about oneself. This cannot be said about Maimon's memoir, which bears comparison with Rousseau's *Confessions* for its severe and frank self-examination. Maimon portrays himself as a reckless bohemian, womanizer, thief, rogue, gambler, and drunkard. He describes his impoverished upbringing in Lithuania and Poland, where he wandered with his homeless parents through the violent countryside in winter, "like the Israelites in the Arabian desert." When he was eleven, his parents forced him to marry an even younger child. He became a father at fourteen.

Despite the wretchedness of his circumstances, Maimon apparently was so brilliant a Talmudist that he was ordained a rabbi while still a teenager. At twenty-two he unscrupulously abandoned his wife and children, leaving "nation, fatherland, and family" to free himself, he writes, from the shackles of poverty, superstition, "Talmudic darkness," and the arid scholasticism that governed the teaching and practice of the Jewish religion in Eastern Europe. He had grown tired of the sterile dialectics of endless speculation on "how many white hairs a red cow may have and still be a red cow" or whether the high priest must first "don his shirt and then his pants or vice versa": "I can barely hold onto my pen recalling how I—together with several of my peers, all in the prime of life—was forced to stay up nights, bent over this mind-killing business of attempting to create meaning where none existed, expending our wits raising contradictions where none appeared, and sharpening those we could discern. We spent endless hours quibbling our way through long chains of conclusions, chasing after shadows, and building castles in the air."[25]

So Maimon became a *Betteljude*, a mendicant, a wandering scholar "in search of truth," at once a genius and a wretch. He took up the study of cabala, Jewish mysticism and magic, imagining himself as a Jewish Faust conjuring up spirits and deeper wisdom. The wildest flights of the Jewish and Germanic imaginations were rarely combined so richly as in this restless wanderer between religions and cultures. A brief attempt to convert to Christianity during a stay in Hamburg in the hope of improving his "material circumstances"—as he openly admitted—was foiled by a Protestant priest to whom he had turned for help. He recorded their dialogue:

"But," said the pastor, "do you not feel any inclination of the soul to the Christian religion, without reference to any external motives?"

"I should be telling you a lie if I were to give you an affirmative answer."

"You are too much of a philosopher," replied the pastor, "to be able to become a Christian. Reason has taken the upper hand with you, and faith must

Salomon Maimon, reckless bohemian, womanizer, rogue, gambler, and autodidact. Kant was impressed by his philosophic gifts. *Courtesy Leo Baeck Institute, Jerusalem*

accommodate itself to reason. You hold the mysteries of the Christian religion to be mere fables, and its commands to be mere laws of reason. For the present I cannot be satisfied with your confession of faith. You should therefore pray to God, that He may enlighten you with His grace, and endow you with the spirit of true Christianity; and then come to me again."

"If that is the case," I said, "then I must confess, Herr Pastor, that I am not qualified for Christianity. Whatever light I may receive, I shall always illuminate it with the light of reason. I shall never believe that I have fallen upon new truths if it is impossible to see their connection with the truths already known to me. I must therefore remain what I am, a stiff-necked Jew."[26]

Maimon's autobiography combines personal reminiscence with brief essays on social conditions, education, mysticism, and religion among Jews in Poland and Lithuania. In his descriptions of the sheer poverty and backwardness of daily life, he cannot have exaggerated much. Fifty years later, after a journey to Poland, Heine described the same countryside as one of the saddest places on earth, the people still living in mud kennels like beasts.[27] Maimon vividly narrates the uneasy, conflict-laden coexistence between mostly illiterate Poles and literate but by and large equally superstitious Jews. Descriptions of natural disasters, looming pogroms, and devastated landscapes alternate with discourses on Kant's philosophy seminar in Königsberg, which he attended, and on Mendelssohn's exquisite kindness.

Maimon's critique of daily Jewish life in Poland and Germany during the second half of the eighteenth century remains unparalleled. He was one of the first of the *Ostjuden* to leave home to make their fortune in the West because life was too impoverished and constraining, only to run into trouble with their coreligionists in Germany. A lapsed Talmudist in search of secular culture, he was emblematic of many others. Over the next 140 years, tens of thousands like him would flock west to German schools and universities in a similar quest. Throughout the nineteenth century, Polish and Lithuanian Jews often equated civilization with German manners, technology, language, and *Kultur*. Maimon's bleak view of conditions in the East and his bitter condemnation of the backward atmosphere of Jewish orthodoxy would be echoed by many others, from Chaim Weizmann to Franz Kafka and Isaac Bashevis Singer.

Published in 1791, Maimon's book was hailed as a masterpiece. Goethe, Schiller, and Kant, among many others, were impressed by the author's literary gifts and philosophic insights. Kant recognized Maimon as his most important interpreter—and critic; nobody, Kant said, had understood him so well. Goethe wished that Maimon would move to Weimar and become part of his intimate circle. In the eyes of his admirers, Maimon's intellectual achievements, like Mendelssohn's before him, once again confirmed one of the axiomatic assumptions of the Enlightenment, that the "sheer power of thought" could lift man out of the most pressing external circumstances.[28] Readers marveled at Maimon's colorful descriptions of Jewish life in "darkest Lithuania" and at his success in rising unaided and entirely self-taught from what was rashly regarded as a state of primitive ignorance to a pure realm of philosophic knowledge. Their views reflected the bias of their time and place. Heinrich Graetz, the leading nineteenth-century Jewish historian, expressed the same prejudices. His only regret was that Maimon's ruthless descriptions of primitive "Polish Jews" might be attributed to Jews elsewhere.

Maimon spent his last years alone on the estate of a philosophically minded Prussian count, comforted only by his dog, Beline. He died at forty-six of apparent alcoholism. "I have not yet achieved peace," he wrote in the concluding line of his autobiography, but *"quo nos fata trahunt retrahuntque sequamur"*—where fate takes us we must follow.[29]

SHORTLY after Maimon's second attempt to settle in Berlin, Christian von Dohm, a Prussian civil servant, caused a sensation by publishing a call for the civic and political emancipation of Germany's Jews. Nobody had done so before. For Dohm to do so was an act of courage: he was, after all, a relatively lowly bureaucrat in Frederick's administration. A former history teacher and university lecturer and a close friend of Lessing and Nicolai, Dohm frequently attended Mendelssohn's intellectual soirees. He had been talking about his project with Mendelssohn for several years. Indeed, it may have been at Mendelssohn's instigation that he finally collected his thoughts in a book. Published in October 1781, it was entitled *On the Civic Improvement of the Jews.*[30]

As a political treatise on Jews, Dohm's work was the first in Germany to eschew all religious argument. Animated by a combination of humane and political considerations, Dohm focused on social, economic, and moral issues only. Emancipation was correct from a moral point of view, and it was imperative in the general interest as well. Once freed of their restraints, Jews (Dohm referred to them as his "circumcised brethren") would be "happier" and more "useful to our states."[31]

Dohm's ideas came partly from France and partly from the new United States, whose Declaration of Independence offered a powerful model. Dohm was ready, for the sake of argument, to concede that Jews "might be more *verdorben* [morally corrupted] than other nations and even guilty of relatively more misdemeanors than Christians."[32] Moreover, their religious prejudice might make them "intensely clannish and unsociable." Such views later garnered him accusations of anti-Semitism. But Dohm also argued that the Jews' clannishness was a natural consequence of the oppression they had suffered for centuries at the hand of Christians. Since their degraded condition was a result of their deliberate exclusion from all productive occupations, the Christian state was duty-bound to lift these restrictions. It must gradually, step by step, grant Jews full and equal civic rights.

The Christian state, in Dohm's view, was guilty of "barbarism" for its incapacity to "wisely mitigate the divisive principles of religion" and for its failure to promote a common sense of citizenship among Christians and Jews. Jews were "unfortunate refugees from Asia," driven by the disasters and vicissitudes of history to live in foreign lands. They must be allowed to engage in all trades and occupations, including farming. They should be given public land for cultivation and allowed to practice their religion freely.

Dohm's book produced no immediate practical results. Frederick II merely acknowledged its receipt. "More was not to be expected," Dohm observed dryly many years later in his memoirs. Frederick was too committed to prejudices, Dohm wrote. The book of a lowly bureaucrat like himself, especially one written not in French but in German—a primitive language in the king's view—was not a sufficient incentive for Frederick to "rethink" his position. Mirabeau, in a conversation with the king, praised Dohm's book but also elicited no response.[33]

Nevertheless, *On the Civic Improvement of the Jews* created a stir in Germany and Western Europe. Even Lavater took time off from his missionary preoccupations to laud the "wise and humane Dohm! Hail thee for engaging yourself so sincerely on behalf of the despised!"[34] Within a few months, Dohm's treatise spawned numerous laudatory and critical tracts and brochures. A French translation appeared the following year. Mirabeau and the Abbé Henri-Baptiste Grégoire, who led the campaign for the civic emancipation of Jews in France, adopted Dohm's arguments almost word for word.

In Germany, the voices in support of Dohm by and large outnumbered those against. It is difficult to categorize the responses neatly since several of the most ardent publications both agreed *and* disagreed with him. Mendelssohn had always been convinced that Jews should steer clear of such controversies. But having indirectly contributed to this one, he joined it with gusto. He was disturbed by Dohm's formulations about the moral depravity of Jews and objected to the term *civic improvement*; he would have preferred *civic acceptance*. At the same time, he rejoiced at Dohm's initiative. Dohm's most prominent public critic was the Protestant theologian Johann David Michaelis. A professor of Oriental studies at the University of Göttingen, Michaelis had crossed swords with Lessing over his play *The Jews*. A noble Jew was "a poetic impossibility," according to the professor; Gypsies would sooner become "human" than Jews would. Michaelis was not against integrating Jews into civic society—if they gave up their pernicious religion and became Christians. His reasons were both theological and practical. "A people that cannot eat and drink with us [because of dietary prohibitions] remains forever a people apart in its own eyes and in ours," he argued, harking back to Tacitus and the ancient Greeks, who had made similar accusations. "Add to this the national pride of the Jews and it becomes simply unbearable, at least for Germans and Englishmen, to accept them as overlords!"[35] As for allowing Jews to engage in agriculture, Michaelis would settle them as "colonists" in "deserted regions" where they could do no harm to authentic Germans.

Dohm's book was soon followed by the first German tract in favor of women's rights, Theodor von Hippel's *On the Civic Improvement of Women* (1782), whose title and content may have been inspired by Dohm's. Dohm's book also coincided with the "Edict on Toleration" issued in Austria by Joseph II in which the emperor formally recognized Jews as fellow human beings. In distant Hamburg, the German poet Friedrich Klopstock hailed the emperor exuberantly for removing "the rusty irons from the wounded arms of the Jews."[36] Klopstock's description of the emperor as a "savior" was hardly warranted; Joseph had openly declared his hope that the edict would lure Jews into the bosom of the Church. Moreover, the emperor's edict retained all existing limits on the number of Jews allowed to reside in various localities, especially within Vienna. He expected to reap profits by taxing his Jews for their newly acquired "tolerance"; their children would have to pay the tax all over again. The tolerated would still be denied full citizenship unless they converted to Christianity. They could not become public servants. In Vienna they were still forbidden to own houses or build a synagogue. On the other hand, they were finally free to practice any trade or profession and to enroll in universities.

However limited these concessions, the Prussian and other German authorities would not even consider emulating them. In Austria itself, the high hopes initially generated by the edict quickly dissipated as even its most minimal provisions were implemented only erratically.

MENDELSSOHN had foreseen this outcome. His reputation was now more exalted than that of any other Jew in Europe. A new play by his friend Lessing, *Nathan the Wise*, enhanced his reputation even more. The play's protagonist, "the wise and noble Nathan," was modeled on Mendelssohn. The German premiere took place in Berlin in 1783. In Vienna and Frankfurt the play was banned.

Lessing's Nathan is the antithesis of Shakespeare's Shylock. The play boldly attacks all religious and national prejudice; the idea of a "better god" is absurd, the propagating of the idea a cause for "pious rage." Not faith but moral behavior is the essence of all religion. In beautiful blank verse, Lessing restates the finest ideals of the Enlightenment—tolerance, brotherhood, and love for humanity. Set in Jerusalem during the Crusades, the play builds to a high point with Nathan's parable of three miraculous rings given by a father to his three sons. Symbols of Christianity, Judaism, and Islam, the rings assure each son the love of God and men if he but wears his in good faith.

The play annoyed and insulted a great many, who felt offended by it as "Germans" and as "Christians." Voltaire's *Candide* never incurred as much ill will as Lessing's *Nathan the Wise*. But generations of German Jews, throughout the nineteenth century, saw in Lessing's play their Magna Carta, unmindful in many cases that it was a product of poetic imagination and not the upshot of a popular referendum, unmindful too that Lessing, a pastor's son, stopped short of condoning mixed marriages between equals—that is, without the conversion of one partner to the majority religion.[37]

Mendelssohn was acutely aware of the disparities. He sensed the contrast between the widespread respect for him personally and the general disrespect, to put it mildly, toward his coreligionists. Physically, he still cut a slightly grotesque figure, humped and stuttering. On a visit to Dresden, the renowned German Socrates was recognized even by the gatekeeper but was charged the usual customs duty. As soon as the local authorities heard about it, the money was refunded with an apology. But the incident left its mark. Mendelssohn's wife, Fromet, enjoyed the high regard in which her husband was held but the slights frequently endured by others elicited her favorite (polyglot) expression, *"Wie mies ist mir vor tout l'univers!"* (How wretched the whole universe is before me).[38] As the couple entered a Berlin concert hall one evening the audience rose in the stalls to applaud. Mendelssohn was well aware that the audience was not necessarily in favor of acceptance or even tolerance; it was applauding its own prejudice by recognizing him as an *exceptional*, that is to say, a noble, "un-Jewish" Jew. Not long afterward, a young Jew applied to the Berlin *Singakademie* and was rebuffed as it was "mathematically impossible that a Jew could compose music."[39] To the Benedictine monk Maurus Winkopp, Mendelssohn wrote: "Throughout this so-called tolerant land I feel hemmed in; my life is so restricted on all sides by genuine intolerance that for the sake of my children I have to lock myself up all day inside a silk factory, as you do in a monastery."[40]

It was becoming common even among enlightened authors to cast excessively noble, charitable Jews in their works of fiction, thereby, perhaps unintentionally, reconfirming the cliché that to be good a Jew had to be better than most mortals and cease being himself. Johann Gottfried von Herder echoed the idea when he wrote that, in their philosophies, Spinoza and Mendelssohn did not seem to him "Jewish." The young Goethe fell into the same trap. He was thrilled one day to come upon a slim volume of poetry by one Isachar Falkensohn Behr, entitled *Poems of a Polish Jew.* Surely a man such as this Jew, born under a "strange and bleak sky who suddenly enters our world," Goethe wrote, must have a fiery spirit and something truly poetic and important to say. He was disappointed to discover that Behr's poetry was not superior to that of any ordinary Christian *"étudiant de belles lettres."* It was downright "mediocre," Goethe complained, and he was undoubtedly right. But why did he assume that Behr's Jewish background guaranteed some extraordinary artistic effort?

Throughout the nineteenth century, generations of hopeful German Jews would celebrate Mendelssohn as their patron saint; like Mendelssohn, they sought a larger community of rational men beyond the stagnant confines of religious identity. Kant, philosophically

Mendelssohn's most competent contemporary reader, sensed this quest early on and thought he understood Mendelssohn's deepest purpose. So did Lessing. Shortly before his death, he sent Mendelssohn a Jewish acquaintance whose one desire was to emigrate. The man had been "treated very badly by our people, after they were stirred up by yours. He doesn't want anything from you, dear Moses, except for you to point out the shortest and safest route to whatever land in Europe has neither Christians nor Jews. I'm loath to lose him, but as soon as he is happily arrived there I'll be the first to follow in his footsteps."[41]

Lessing died before Mendelssohn could reply. Would Mendelssohn have followed him to that mythical country? Both believed in the brotherhood of man. They believed—erroneously, we now know—that it should be "enough," politically speaking, to be "a Mensch," that is, a decent human being, to be recognized as an equal. The idea of a common humanity permeated eighteenth-century idealism from Rousseau through the encyclopedists to Mozart's Magic Flute. It was the leitmotiv of Lessing's plays The Jews and Nathan the Wise. Nathan wants to be known only as a decent human being. When the sultan Saladin asks his identity, Nathan answers: Ich bin ein Mensch—I am a human. To this day, his answer provokes audiences to applaud.

It is possible that in modeling Nathan on Mendelssohn, Lessing misunderstood his friend. We know today that Nathan's famous reply— if it really reflected Mendelssohn's thinking—was "nothing but a grotesque and dangerous evasion of reality," Hannah Arendt observes.[42] In the real, as against the mythical, world, insisting that one was first and foremost a Mensch was never enough to ensure respect for one's human rights. To be a Mensch was a private, not a political, quality. In the real world, it was only as political creatures that minorities were able to demand and, if they were lucky, win acceptance of diversity and eventually gain equality, too. Politically, when they insisted that they were nothing but Menschen, they were, in Arendt's words, already lost.

3

Miniature Utopias

During the final decade of his life, Mendelssohn witnessed the rise of a young generation closer in spirit to the general culture than any German Jewish community had been since the Middle Ages. And, in most cases, its members were regarded as Jewish by all but the most rigidly traditional. Traditions were crumbling; tolerance was seeping in through the cracks. The walls of segregation were first breached in Berlin, where more than one or two "exceptional" Jews were now permitted to assimilate and live, like Mendelssohn, in two worlds. Those who most benefited from this shift were the sons and daughters of the wealthier, privileged upper middle class. They had taken seriously Mendelssohn's injunction to master German language and culture. Their parents engaged tutors or sent them to German schools. Elsewhere in Germany such openness was still almost unheard of.

In the eyes of the young, the key to integration was through the cult of *Bildung*, as defined in Goethe's novel *Wilhelm Meister:* the refinement of the individual self and character in keeping with the ideals of the Enlightenment. Even as they remained Jews, *Bildung* and *Kultur* would make them 100 percent German. Their commitment to this ideal of self-improvement and refinement allowed these spirited young men and women—all born of devout Jewish families—to accomplish in two or three decades a journey that their peers elsewhere, especially in Eastern Europe, would take much longer to complete: from a hermetically closed system centered on divine sacraments to an emancipated agnostic culture centered on man.

Prominent among them were Mendelssohn's own children—three sons and three daughters—and his closest and best-known associates in the Hebrew revival and Bible-translation project. One of these associates, the scholarly merchant prince David Friedländer, was widely expected to be Mendelssohn's successor at the intellectual vanguard of German Jewry. But while Friedländer was able and devoted, he lacked Mendelssohn's passion to combine both cultures. One of many who suspected that Mendelssohn's religious orthodoxy had been a tactical step designed to make his ideas more palatable to the traditionalists, Friedländer had given up strict practice while Mendelssohn was still alive. Mendelssohn's own children were less drawn to the old faith than to the promise of emancipation. They were essentially deists and regarded traditional Judaism as a relic from the stone age of religion.

Mendelssohn cannot have been entirely ignorant of such sentiments among his children and associates. In some ways, he may even have been partly responsible. Before his death in 1786, he seems to have accepted the fact that his eldest son had given up Hebrew studies and, like Friedländer, was no longer strict in his religious observance. Mendelssohn appointed Friedländer as his literary executor and dedicated his last book to him, saluting Friedländer as a "beloved helper and supporter."

A civic-minded man, Friedländer saw as his main task the promotion of religious reform. Born in Königsberg to a wealthy family, Friedländer had married in 1771 into the family of David Itzig, one of Frederick II's privileged court Jews. At Mendelssohn's urging, Friedländer translated the traditional Jewish prayer book into High German and founded the first Jewish *Freischule* (Free School) to enable impecunious young men—not only the privileged rich—to read and speak German, acquire a general education, and mix with non-Jewish students. The example of Friedländer's Free School was soon emulated in a dozen other German cities, including Dessau, Hamburg, and Frankfurt.

By 1790, Friedländer had become the main spokesman for the Jews of Prussia. During the reign of Frederick II, there had been little hope for civic reform. Under his successor, Frederick William II (1786–97), Prussian Jews expected to fare no better. The king was inclined to show favor only to a few well-connected individuals, including Mendelssohn's widow and six children, whose residence permits in Berlin were in danger of expiring. But he rejected Friedländer's pleas to annul the notorious reglement of 1750 and initiate civic reforms along the lines proposed by Dohm.

The laws governing the Jewish minority were now a contradictory mix of arbitrary general rules and special dispensations. Twenty-one prominent businessmen, including Friedländer, received Prussian citizenship. The rest—more than a hundred thousand—fell as before under the oppressive rules of the old edicts. Popular prejudice, however, seemed to be diminishing, at least among the educated classes. An anonymous "Traveler through the Royal Prussian States" in 1779 lauded the high level of civilization and manners among the Jewish residents of Berlin. "They socialize a good deal with Christians, participating together in innocent pastimes. . . . They love reading more than ever. They pay equal attention to the weekly journals and the theater, and in this way nourish poetic sense and aesthetic sensibility. The mania for novels has proven particularly contagious . . . but they love the theater above all else, and on Saturdays take up most of the seats in the parterre.* When the weather is good they come out in droves to promenade around the Tiergarten or along Unter den Linden.[1] Jewish women were praised especially for their devotion to the arts. They were said to read all the new books. And, wrote the author, "there are real beauties among them." No such report has survived from that time anywhere else in Germany or Europe.

---

*The theater was the main platform for progressive social ideas in eighteenth-century Germany.

In 1786, Friedrich Nicolai's guide book to Berlin reported the prevalence among Berlin Jews of scholars, men and women of good taste, and lovers of literature. In 1788, Shakespeare's *Merchant of Venice* was performed at the Berlin National Theater. Before the curtain rose, the lead actor appeared onstage and reminded the audience "that intelligent Berliners are now beginning to show a higher regard for the coreligionists of the wise Mendelssohn."[2] He urged the audience not to deduce from Shylock's character conclusions about Jews in general. In September 1789, the *Vossische Zeitung* reported matter-of-factly that with the *"allerhöchste Bewilligung"* (highest approval, that is, from the king) a certain cattle and retail market in Berlin would be postponed for two days because of the Jewish Feast of Tabernacles. A few years later, the journalist K. A. Böttiger hailed the guiding role played by Jews in Berlin, "so much so, indeed, that in matters of taste and philosophy the Christians feed their meager little lamp with the oil supplied by the Jewish brokers of enlightenment."[3] (The motives behind such a generalization must have been varied and complex.)

Popular Jewish poets emerged at the same time. As Friedländer remarked, they could be as banal as any Teutonic versifier:

The Drunkard

That one could truly drink one's fill
Is not as clever as it seems
The sea drinks from a thousand streams,
Yet drunk or sober, who could dream
Its thirst might ever once be stilled.

Ephraim Moses Kuh[4]

Another contemporary found it noteworthy that among the Jews of Berlin "even tradesmen, forwarding agents, and money changers are endowed with unexpected insights."[5] Of course, there could also be too much of a good thing. The poet Heinrich von Kleist wrote his sister that he would prefer the company of Jews "if they were not so ostentatious about their education."[6]

THE new tolerance, however limited or relative, was nowhere as manifest as in the sudden blossoming in the late 1780s and early 1790s of literary salons on the French model. There had been a "mixed" Monday Club before, but for men only; attended by Lessing, Mendelssohn, Nicolai, and others, the club fanned the first glimmers of the Enlightenment among the literati in Berlin. The new literary salons broadened that free space considerably by including, for the first time, members of leading aristocratic families and by granting a prominent role to women. In France the inclusion of women had been routine for decades; in Prussia it was an unheard-of novelty. Court society in Berlin was predominantly male and notoriously boring. Frederick II's queen lived apart from her husband (who preferred the company of men and greyhounds). As a rule, women were not welcome at scholarly gatherings and in literary cafés. For young Jewish women to break this rule was doubly daring as they usually suffered even greater restriction and regimentation than their Christian counterparts. Then, too, it was one thing for a French duchess or haute bourgeoise to run a salon and another for the unmarried young daughter or occasionally the wife of a disenfranchised money changer or silk merchant to do so. The Berlin salons stood outside the Christian class system, a free arena where willful or eccentric Prussian aristocrats could mingle informally with middle-class poets, writers, actors, and young Jewish women and men they were rarely, if ever, able to meet at home. On a visit to Berlin, Madame de Staël observed that the Jewish salons were the only places in the whole of Germany where aristocrats and bourgeois met freely and that did not reek of beer and smoke.

The new Berlin salons briefly linked the cause of Jewish emancipation with that of women. But on the whole, these gatherings, unlike their French counterparts, were apolitical, concerned almost exclusively with promoting the arts and the Romantic cult of friendship. With their pronounced sentimental eroticism, they were for a time a kind of freemasonry, a conspiracy of the heart, and a safe haven for nonconformists. From their first days on, they were attended by Mendelssohn's daughters Dorothea and Henriette, David Friedländer, the Humboldt brothers (Alexander, the naturalist and future explorer of Latin America, and Wilhelm, a prominent liberal educator), the sculptor Johann Friedrich Schadow, the innovative Lutheran theologian Friedrich Schleiermacher, the early Romantic poets Heinrich von Kleist, Johann Tieck, and Friedrich Schlegel. All were brought together by curiosity, the Romantic celebration of feeling, and a common passion for literature, especially the new literary style of Sturm und Drang. Indeed, the Jewish *salonnières* are credited with having inaugurated a Goethe cult throughout Germany. They and most of the other habitués were in their early twenties. All made a fetish of sharing their most intimate thoughts, exchanging gifts and coded letters, and, presumably, secret kisses.

French frivolity made its entrance into the salons together with the latest German books. Prudish Jewish historians, in the Victorian and more nationalistic atmosphere of the 1860s, assaulted the young women who ran these salons for promoting "moral depravity." In his monumental *History of the Jews,* Heinrich Graetz complained that the charged atmosphere of the salons violated the sacred chastity of Jewish women. He likened the *salonnières* to the Midianite whores: "If the enemies of the Jews had designed to break the power of Israel, they could have discovered no more effectual means than infecting Jewish women with moral depravity, a plan more efficacious than that employed by the Midianites, who weakened the men by immorality."[7] Graetz had equally harsh things to say about David Friedländer, whom he accused of self-hatred and of coveting the honor of joining the "haughty Christians" instead of avoiding them.

In the stiff ambience of Prussian social life, the informality of the salons was their strongest attraction. There was as yet no university in Berlin. Court life under Frederick William II continued to be insufferably dull. The cultural horizons of the rising Christian middle class were still limited. In the salons, on the other hand, the spirited Jewish hostesses cultivated witty conversation and good fellowship. The result was a camaraderie among young Jews and like-minded Prussians of both sexes, that would have been unthinkable twenty years earlier. It went far beyond the modest beginnings in Mendelssohn's days. The young poet Ludwig Levin, visiting Amsterdam in 1801, informed his sister Rahel that in Amsterdam "Jews and Christians are scandalously separated. *Il n'y a qu'un seul Berlin!"*—There is only one Berlin. For a decade or two, the salons made Jews all over Europe turn their eyes enviously toward Berlin.

In their families' large and comfortable homes, the first *salonnières* entertained their guests in the early evening hours on a mixed fare of poetry readings, canapés, and drinks. In France, where wealth and rank often went hand in hand with intellect and culture, such gatherings would not have surprised anybody. In Berlin they were anomalous. The surprise was not that there were so many well-to-do Jewish families in Berlin whose daughters could afford to run a successful salon—poorer families had been systematically thrown out over the years. What was unusual was that these families, or at least their younger members, were so deeply interested in the arts. The Rothschilds (in Frankfurt), the Warburgs, and Oppenheims (bankers in Hamburg and Cologne, respectively), were not.

Mendelssohn's eldest daughter, Dorothea, had often been present at her father's Saturday afternoon open house. She now became one of the leading spirits of the new sociability, a driving force in the first salon, that of her close friend Henriette Herz. A young woman married to a physician twenty years her senior, Henriette had grown up with Dorothea and some of the other *salonnières;* they shared tutors and a common interest in modern letters. While Dorothea was rather squat and plain-looking, Henriette was tall and statuesque. She was said to be the most beautiful woman in Berlin. A bust sculpted by Schadow in 1784, soon after she launched her salon, shows her strikingly good looks: sensuous lips, high cheekbones, long curly hair, and a near-perfect Greek profile. Henriette's husband, Marcus Herz, a doctor, had studied medicine at the University of Königsberg (one of only three that accepted Jewish students although only in its medical faculty). In Königsberg Herz had become Kant's admirer and friend, and in Berlin he helped spread the philosopher's fame. In his spacious home in the Neue Friedrichstrasse, the doctor held formal seminars on science, literature, and philosophy that attracted noblemen, senior bureaucrats, writers, Mendelssohn, David Friedländer, and other interested Jews and Christians.

After a few years, Herz's salon split in two. The doctor conducted his

Henriette Herz, in an engraving based on a painting by Salomon Pennet. Her salon was the prototype of several others, "miniature utopias" where, for the first time, prominent Germans and Jews met socially on almost equal footing. *Courtesy Leo Baeck Institute, Jerusalem*

science seminars in one room; Henriette entertained her literary friends in another. Asked once to interpret a new poem of Goethe's, the doctor referred the questioner to his wife in the next room: "That's her department. She understands such things." (Although according to another version he said, "She interprets such nonsense.")

The doctor's science seminars were soon overshadowed by Henriette's livelier literary gatherings, which met on Tuesdays. The guests were younger and more socially prominent. "The mind is the great equalizer," she wrote many years later in her memoirs, recalling the heyday of her salon. "The Christian homes of Berlin . . . offered nothing comparable in intellectual sociability." Prominent Berliners, "despite the prevailing prejudices, eagerly availed themselves" of the scintillating company offered in Jewish homes. There was "no man or woman who later distinguished himself in some form" who "did not belong to these circles, . . . [including] the genial Prince Louis-Ferdinand of Prussia" (a nephew of Frederick the Great), she wrote.[8]

Mirabeau, on a secret French embassy to Berlin, and other distinguished foreign visitors made a point of attending Henriette Herz's salon. Alexander von Humboldt was a frequent guest. Henriette gave him Hebrew lessons, and on several occasions they exchanged love letters in that language. In one letter to Henriette from his family's feudal estate, Humboldt called it Schloss Langeweile (Boredom Castle). Schleiermacher was another regular at Henriette's salon. He preached a religion of "feeling and of the heart" and brought a lot of both into Henriette's circle.

For her Jewish guests, Henriette's salon was a "miniature utopia," as the modern-day writer Deborah Hertz aptly puts it.[9] Surrounded by luxurious comforts and social luminaries, David Friedländer, Ludwig Levin, and other enlightened young Jews were able briefly to forget that elsewhere they were still outcasts as for centuries their ancestors had been. As Henriette welcomed her guests with an inclination of her pretty head that best displayed her fine classical profile, it was quite understandable that Friedländer and others should view the future with some optimism.

IN 1799, Friedländer made a radical proposal. His immediate motive may have been concern over a recent wave of conversions. The reasons for such conversions were usually opportunistic and pragmatic. Nonetheless, Friedländer disapproved of them. He was no opportunist and he could not accept the "surrender" of individual Jews to the religion of the majority. Instead he sought a broad political solution for the entire collective. Together with other "Jewish householders in Berlin," he addressed an open letter—a *Sendschreiben,* a term reminiscent of Luther—to Wilhelm Teller, the leading Protestant provost in Berlin. They would be ready, Friedländer wrote, to join the Lutheran Church if it enabled Jews to enter on the basis of shared moral values, without having to recognize the divinity of Christ

David Friedländer. His suggestion that Jews undergo "dry baptism"—embracing Lutheranism without recognizing the divinity of Christ—was rejected. *Courtesy Leo Baeck Institute, Jerusalem*

and without formally undergoing baptism. In return, Judaism would abandon some of its purely ceremonial features.

Friedländer's proposal for a "dry baptism," as it came to be called, essentially envisioned the establishment of a confederated unitarian church-synagogue. The universal rationalist religion postulated by the Enlightenment might yet unite Christians and Jews, he hoped. His decision to address Teller was no accident. Teller was perhaps the most open-minded Protestant theologian in all of Germany. The Christianity he preached was rational and enlightened. In the past, he had been close to Mendelssohn. The two had once exchanged lighthearted doggerel in which Teller asked Mendelssohn why, since he believed in God the Father, he refused to believe in God the Son. Was it not a time-honored custom among Jews that sons were given their patrimony, or at least were credited for it, long before their fathers' deaths? Mendelssohn answered Teller in the same vein. How could this son ever receive the patrimony, given that the father is eternal?* Similar good-humored exchanges continued for some time between the two men.

Teller later made a name for himself as a militant for a reformed Lutheran Church. He was the author of the revolutionary *Manual of Christianity*, which made no mention of the Trinity and other basic Christian dogma. According to Teller, an "age of religious maturity" had recently dawned: "many things that had validity during the childhood of religion must now change."[10] Friedländer had reason to believe that Teller would not reject his proposal outright. And if accepted, it might enable Jews to gain the civic and political rights still denied them without their having to endorse Christian dogma hypocritically, as most

---

*Teller: You believe in God the Father—
                Add His Son and let it rest:
                You advance your own sons' credit
                Long before their fathers' deaths.

Mendelssohn: But how would he pay back the loan
                Unless he comes into his own?
                And how can he inherit from
                God immortal, God the One?

converts did. Friedländer's initiative surpassed anything Mendelssohn had conceived. In his books, Mendelssohn had described Judaism as a rational religion, but he never questioned the validity of ritual practice. Any call for a union of all faiths would have seemed to Mendelssohn intolerance in disguise.

Teller's response to Friedländer's *Sendschreiben* was convoluted but ultimately negative. As a philosopher, Teller may well have been sympathetic to Friedländer's unitarian offer; as provost of the Berlin cathedral, he disdained it. The language of his reply was unctuous and condescending. He could forgive Friedländer's ancestors for their rejection of Jesus Christ but not Friedländer's apparent refusal to acknowledge him as the savior. Friedländer and his fellow householders in Berlin must recognize Christianity as the better moral religion, far superior, as Teller saw it, to the largely ceremonial religion of the Jews.

In years to come, Jewish comment on Friedländer's initiative would be overwhelmingly hostile ("a dishonorable act," an attempted "desertion" to the enemy camp, etc.). The nineteenth-century historian Heinrich Graetz would go so far as to call Friedländer an "ape." Heine would joke that Friedländer had tried to cure a "skin abscess" by "bloodletting." At the time, however, Jewish reactions were calmer and, at least in Berlin, tacitly supportive. Not a single voice of criticism seems to have been raised against the proposal publicly. The strict traditionalists did not react at all. Soon afterward, Friedländer was elected head of the Jewish community of Berlin.

By contrast, Protestant spokesmen almost unanimously condemned Friedländer's overture. Their language was harsh, and the agitation over Friedländer's "insolence" did not abate for months. Friedrich Schleiermacher, who had met Friedländer at Henriette Herz's salon, protested that Jesus was not just another Jewish rabbi or prophet, as Friedländer seemed to suggest. Christianity must not be "Judaized." Christians must beware, he warned, of "inoculating" themselves with such a "disease." Schleiermacher then returned to Henriette's salon, where Friedländer, of course, was a frequent guest, as though nothing had happened. After the death of her husband, Henriette came under Schleiermacher's powerful influence and converted. Schleiermacher had convinced her that Judaism, once a living faith, was now practically dead. "Those who wear its livery only sit lamenting around its mummy."

LITERARY-minded Jewish ladies found themselves much in demand, not just in Berlin but also in the capital of German letters, Goethe's Weimar. "Jewish women possess the gift of being the most sensitive audience," commented Goethe's secretary, Friedrich Riemer. "Goethe liked to recite his literary creations to them."[11] The unexpected prominence of literary or philosophically minded Jewish women was quickly the subject of satire. The caption of one newspaper cartoon had a Jew on a park bench saying to another: "Since I have begun teaching my Rahel the Cakagoric Amberatif, you've no idea how charming she has become. . . . She's becoming positively transcendental."

The lead set by Henriette Herz was soon followed by Marianne and Sara Meyer, granddaughters of Veitel Ephraim, the mintner who had helped Frederick II win the Seven Years War. Marianne and Sara corresponded with Goethe, and both later married Prussian aristocrats. The most famous salon and probably the liveliest and most influential, however, was launched in 1791 by Rahel Levin, an unmarried twenty-year-old. She was not remotely as beautiful or "exotic" as some of the other Jewish hostesses—of medium height, with pitch-black hair and clear eyes, she had a puffy face and her chin was overlong. Nor was she rich. Her father had died a few years earlier, leaving her in straitened circumstances. Her salon was held not in an elegant mansion but in the garret of her late father's home in the Jägerstrasse. Here she held an open house several times a week. The guests gathered in the late afternoon under a portrait of Lessing and were served nothing but weak tea and pretzels. The main attraction was Rahel's personality, her tenderness and conversation. She was a woman of rare sensibility and intellect whose many admirers included Henriette's friends—Schleiermacher, the Humboldt brothers, Kleist, Schlegel, and Tieck—along with several budding Jewish poets and playwrights and a number of prominent Prussian noblemen and officers like Friedrich von Gentz (Metternich's future right-hand man). There were also opera singers, foreign diplomats, and the Polish prince Anton Heinrich Radziwill, who was married to Frederick II's niece, and Frederick's nephew Prince Louis-

Ferdinand—both amateur composers. Louis-Ferdinand, according to his biographer, was "handsome, spoiled, a bit of a revolutionary, and perpetually in debt; rebellious toward his family and his class, talented, but confused, sad, and, in addition, usually drunk by early afternoon."[12] Yet Louis-Ferdinand best described what Rahel Levin meant to her many friends in a letter he sent her:

> "Je serais cet après-midi entre six et sept heures chez vous, chère et aimable Mademoiselle Levin, pour raisonner et déraisonner avec vous pendant deux heures. As I told Gentz, you are a moral midwife and you accommodate one so gently, so painlessly, that even the most distressing ideas leave behind a pleasant feeling."[13]

The poet Jean Paul wrote that scholars, Jews, officers, Prussian bureaucrats, noblemen, and all others who elsewhere "were at one another's throats" contrived to be "friendly at [Rahel Levin's] tea table."[14] Even Goethe paid a visit. Of course, the conversation was not always exalted. A witness described Gentz's arrival one afternoon: "Unexpectedly Gentz . . . rushed into the room and, without taking the least notice of us, threw himself on the sofa and called out: 'I cannot bear it any longer. . . . I spent the entire night writing, worrying! At 5 A.M. the goddamn creditors! Wherever I turn they are confronting me; they are hounding me to death. Nowhere is there calm and rest!' "[15]

Rahel Levin in 1800, aged twenty-nine. "The truest, purest German *Frau*," according to Napoleon's niece. Rahel's salon, attended by poets, philosophers, noblemen, and diplomats, was in the garret of her parents' house. *Courtesy Leo Baeck Institute, Jerusalem*

Rahel—she was widely known by her given name alone—was an early feminist, a willfully independent woman who set out to build her life on her own terms. She had many lovers, some of whom, like Friedrich von Gentz, remained enchanted with her into old age. In 1803, he wrote her: "Do you know, my love, why our relationship is so grand and so perfect? You are an infinitely productive, I am an infinitely receptive being; you are a great man; I am the first of all women who ever lived. I know this: that had I been physically a woman I should have brought the globe to my feet. . . . [Ours is] a physical relationship between people whose inner selves are reversed in each other."[16] Although Gentz was older than Rahel, nearly all her other lovers were considerably younger.

More than just a renowned socialite, Rahel was also the most important German woman of letters of the nineteenth century; Gentz called her the very first Romantic. Entirely self-taught, she left no conventional oeuvre but was an astonishingly prolific letter writer. Intensely personal and introspective, her correspondence (more than six thousand letters survive of an estimated ten thousand) reveals her impatience with the superficialities and hypocrisies of the elegant world in which she lived. She had a rare ability to portray herself with utmost sincerity; it was said that her heart's blood was contained in every envelope she posted. Since her handwriting was difficult to read, her friends had her letters copied so they could pass them around. The letters touch on all aspects of literature and art; remarkably, politics and the extraordinary historical events of her lifetime (the French Revolution, the Napoleonic wars) are rarely if ever mentioned. The cult of *Innerlichkeit* (intense introspection) so dear to the Romantics predominates.

A thoroughly assimilated Jew, Rahel was credited with having inaugurated the so-called symbiosis between Germans and Jews. Jenny von Gustedt, Napoleon's niece, was quoted as saying that she was the "truest, purest German *Frau*" she had ever met.[17] Perhaps this was an exaggeration, but certainly Rahel deeply disdained her background. In 1793, she wrote her Jewish friend David Veit, a young medical student: "Imagine! Yesterday . . . on the Jewish Sabbath at half past two and in broad daylight I drove in a royal carriage [presumably Louis-Ferdinand's] from the opera rehearsal; no one saw me and I would deny it to anybody . . . [even] if he helped me out of the carriage." Veit responded with a reprimand. If she drove on the Sabbath she must not deny it or he would believe that she did "not want to help in the reformation of

Judaism," as Veit felt she should. But Rahel was not interested in Jewish reform; she yearned for integration into the German world. She was revolted—the word is not too strong—by her observant relatives. Mendelssohn's version of Judaism hardly appealed to her more; it was too dry and sterile in its rationality. She worshiped feeling, not reason. Her religiosity was of the heart and, like that of other Romantics, couched in the mystical imagery of Christianity: Christ's Passion and the Mother of God. Compared with such profundities, *Vernunft* (reason) was mere *Vernünftelei* (humbug); she disliked people who spoke familiarly of God "as of some county magistrate."

Rahel's rejection went beyond religiosity. She hated her Jewish background and was convinced it had poisoned her life. For much of her adult life she was what would later be called self-hating. Her overriding desire was to free herself from the shackles of her birth; since, as she thought, she had been "pushed out of the world" by her origins, she was determined to escape them. She never really succeeded. In 1810, she changed her family name to Robert, as her brother Ludwig, the poet, had done earlier. And in 1814, after her mother's death, she converted. But her origins continued to haunt her even on her deathbed.

Rahel's supreme desire was to live life as though it were "a work of art." Such a life demanded a "great love." And indeed, she gave herself to love unreservedly. Yet her affairs (including a secret engagement to Count Karl Finck von Finckenstein) ended rather badly. Several Prussian aristocrats and one flamboyant Spanish diplomat eventually backed away or were forced by their families to refuse a misalliance. It is difficult today to determine which element—class or Judeophobia—was decisive. Probably both were. Rahel herself attributed her failure to marry Count Finckenstein, the first man "who wished me to love him and seduced me with his love," to his flawed character (he was a "swindler caught in the act") but also to her "erroneous" or "infamous" birth. She considered her origins "a curse, a slow bleeding to death. By keeping still I can delay it. Every movement is an attempt to stanch it— new death; and immobility is possible for me only in death itself. . . . I can, if you will, derive every evil, every misfortune, every vexation from *that*."[18]

The idea that as a Jew she was always required to be exceptional—

and go on proving it all the time—was repugnant to her. "How wretched it is always to have to legitimize myself! That is why it is so disgusting to be a Jew." She was one of the first of a new breed more common later on, always self-conscious, always looking over her shoulder. She was denied, she felt, what was readily granted to the simplest peasant woman—an easy sense of identity.

Exquisitely sensitive, Rahel would have registered the subtle divisions that existed even in the free space of the salons. Her many admirers and guests rarely if ever returned her invitations. The Finckensteins and the Humboldts had fine town houses in Berlin and grand villas in the near countryside; from all we know, she never entered any of them. Finckenstein kept his three-year liaison with her secret from his family. The Humboldt brothers, too, for all their liberalism, were hardly less prejudiced. In one of Wilhelm von Humboldt's letters to a friend, he referred condescendingly to the thirty-nine-year-old Rahel as "the little Levy," and in addition misspelled her surname. Humboldt later played an important role in the battle for Jewish emancipation, yet he told his wife, "I love the Jews only en masse; the individual I avoid."[19] On almost the same day that Gentz praised Rahel for being the finest being in the world—no one loved as well as she—he remarked to a friend, "Never has a Jewess—without a single exception—known love."

Rahel spent almost all her life in this twilight between acceptance and rejection. She was the first German Jew to articulate what it meant to be enclosed in the haunted circle of favor and misfortune that Heine, Rahel's close friend and admirer, called the thousand-year-old Judenschmerz. Rahel called it "the text of my offended heart."

Her salon in Berlin did not survive the Franco-Prussian War of 1806, nor did those of the other Jewish salonnières. In the nationalist frenzy that seized Germans in the war's aftermath, the Jewish salons simply ceased to exist. They owed their success not to money or social status but to a climate of tolerance, which, however short-lived or limited, had never existed in Germany or any other European country before. They owed it as well to the rare social talent of a number of extraordinary personalities.

Rahel, the most extraordinary personality of all, was the first to close her salon. New venues sprouted up in the Berlin homes of Christian aristocratic nationalists, but these were, in effect, secret patriotic societies. Many of Rahel's friends, including Kleist, Schleiermacher, and Humboldt, frequented the new gatherings. Rahel was no less patriotic, but she and other Jews were simply not welcome. Humboldt wrote his wife in 1808 that Rahel had become quite isolated. The outsiders dispersed. Louis-Ferdinand fell on the battlefield. "What happened to the time when we were all together!" Rahel lamented in retrospect. "It sank in 1806. Sank like a ship, carrying the most beautiful gifts, the most beautiful pleasures of life."[20]

THE rise and fall of the Jewish salons coincided with the first wave of Jewish conversions to Christianity. Reliable numbers are not available, partly because conversions were not necessarily registered. Minors were baptized together with their parents and not always counted. But there is no doubt the figures were high, the highest in Europe since the fifteenth century, when some 60 percent of the Jews of Spain reportedly converted to Christianity. One rabbi in Breslau spoke of an "earthquake." Its epicenters, apart from Breslau, were Berlin and Königsberg. The historian Heinrich Graetz claimed that, in Berlin alone, no less than half the Jewish community converted, including four of Moses Mendelssohn's six children. A pastor in Königsberg estimated that the entire Jewish community in that city was about to disappear.

Nineteenth-century Jewish historians, understandably, viewed conversion very harshly; in their opinion, it degraded Jews in the eyes of the very government that encouraged it. For this reason alone, it was morally reprehensible. There was talk of an "apostasy en masse," an "epidemic," a "mania," a "countrywide plague." After the Second World War, some exerted themselves in an effort to prove that the extent of conversions had been exaggerated. Toward this end, even the resources of the Nazi Reichsstelle für Rassenforschung—which kept records of suspected "false Aryans"—were combed and presumably exhausted. Zionists, for their part, regarded converts as traitors, and stupid traitors at that, since conversion would inevitably prove to provide little protection or advancement.

German Jews usually converted on their own initiative, not in response to proselytizers. Some conversions were sincere; most were motivated entirely by pragmatic considerations. The act was undertaken, more or less casually, to conform, escape stigma, gain professional rights, bolster social status, win a government or academic post, marry. Before conversion most converts were nonpracticing Jews; after conversion, they were nonpracticing Christians. The young, if they were ambitious and talented, pursued conversion much as today's ambitious and talented youth the world over eagerly learn English, the "global language" (and with considerably more pain and effort). In a Eurocentric age, Christianity was the "global religion" and the established religion of Germany. Adopting it was a way to confirm one's political identity.

By the repetition of a formula—for many no more than empty words—men and women hoped to radically change the basic conditions of their daily lives. The well-known philologist and convert Fritz Mauthner claimed that, while it was not impossible that an educated Jewish man might convert out of conviction, he himself had never met one. "Expediency brought the overwhelming majority of adult converts to profess their belief in Christianity."[21]

The facile, almost casual character of conversions is illustrated by Karl Marx and his parents. The Marx family was baptized in 1824 by a Protestant pastor in a brief ceremony without, apparently, any prior instruction or preparation. Karl was six years old. Afterward, the family continued to attend Sabbath lunches at the home of an uncle who happened to be the chief rabbi of Trier. Family ties were more powerful than religious solidarity.

Heine famously called the baptismal certificate "the entrance ticket to European culture." It promised equality, if not immediately—because of continuing prejudice and the rigid class system—then at some point in the future. Many pragmatic converts soon discovered that their social or professional dreams did not materialize as they had thought. Only much later did the general realization sink in that baptism, however tempting, could not begin to solve the complex problems generated by centuries of prejudice, legal restrictions, and enforced but often also self-imposed segregation.* Nor was agnosticism a sufficient solution. Even after legal differences were diminished, unfathomable differences remained between agnostic Jews who had abjured their faith and Christians who had done the same. Judaism was always seen as something more than simply a religion—even before "race" became a factor—although that something defied clear definition.

Conversion was mostly a middle- and upper-middle-class phenomenon. The richest, most talented, successful, and cultured men and women were often the first to convert. The rich hoped to enter the aristocracy. Intellectuals rationalized their conversion as bringing them a step closer to the Kantian ideal of universal religion. They found their new faith was less demanding than the old, especially as casual observance of religion was spreading among Protestants as well. Enlightened Christians, including some of the more liberal pastors, did not expect the converts to actually "believe" in dogma that they themselves were beginning to doubt. Certainly, a few converts fully embraced their new identity as Christians. Felix Mendelssohn-Bartholdy became the foremost composer of Christian religious music. (A contemporary wit quipped that "the most *Jewish* thing Felix ever did was to become a Christian.") Whatever their attitude on becoming Christian, converts rarely saw themselves as traitors to the faith; tribal or national bonds—what is now called "ethnic survival"—did not count for much. If, occasionally, the converts had qualms, these were easily dispelled. They could cite Spinoza's statement in the *Tractatus Theologico-Politicus* that there was nothing "marvelous" in the mere survival of the Jewish nation for so long after its dispersion and loss of empire (3:55). They could also draw comfort from the encouragement offered by the governments of the various German states—the king of Prussia readily stood as godfather at the baptisms of children of prominent court Jews; he sent those whose baptisms he didn't attend a gift of ten ducats. Karl Marx's father is said to have claimed that conversion was in the best Jewish tradition

---

*Some converts found themselves rejected by both Jews and Christians; their descendants married other converts or the descendants of converts, in a pattern that sometimes continued over two or even three generations.

and must have been widespread at all times or there would have been at least a hundred million Jews in his day.

Nonetheless, family and community disapproval caused some shame to be attached to the act. A number of baptized Jews went to great lengths to hide their conversions even from their families and friends. Many sought out country preachers far from home; some went abroad, preferably to France. The young often delayed conversion until after their parents had died. Many announced the fact to friends and relatives only after they had officially been converted.

A few among the rich and prominent resisted. In 1816, Carl von Rothschild, a handsome young man, arrived in Berlin. He was the third son of a new Frankfurt banking dynasty that had accumulated vast fortunes during the Napoleonic wars. The Rothschilds were sufficiently rich or important to have been granted Austrian titles of nobility without first converting to Christianity. Carl Rothschild's father, on his deathbed four years earlier, had exhorted his sons to remain loyal to the Jewish faith and Carl was resolved to follow his injunction. An unusually good catch, Carl was much sought after and entertained during his stay in Berlin. But though he remained for several weeks, he was not interested in any of the women he met. "I could marry the most beautiful and richest girl in Berlin," he wrote his brothers. "But I would not do it for all the treasures in the world. Here in Berlin, if a young woman has not herself converted, then certainly a brother or a sister-in-law has. . . . We have made our money as Jews, and we want nothing to do with such people."[22]

For rich Prussian Jews, though, the rewards, often titles of nobility, were compelling. A Prussian military contractor named Jonathan Jakob Moses became the Baron Delmar soon after converting in 1806.* A certain Moritz Levi became Johann von Oppenfeld. First names were often changed upon conversion, in some cases at the instigation of the priest; popular choices were Christian and even Fürchtgott (God-fearing) or innocuous but un-Jewish names like Wilhelm and Friedrich.

---

*Delmar (or *del mare*, meaning "out of the sea") seems to be a translation of the name Moses, which the Hebrew Bible suggests means "drawn out" of the water (Ex. 2:10).

David Mendel was baptized August Neander ("new man") and became a leading Protestant theologian. The poet Chaim (Harry) Heine became Christian Johann Heinrich Heine. The liberal polemicist Loeb Baruch became Ludwig Börne. The prominent Prussian ideologue Friedrich Julius Stahl was born Joel Golson, the son of a Bavarian Jewish cattle dealer.

The new Christians, inevitably, became the subject of caricature and satire. "Waterproof Jews" was the sobriquet applied to those "not yet baptized." Ludwig Börne, himself a "pragmatic" convert, ridiculed other converts, including the daughters of Israel who promenaded along the streets of Berlin, crosses hanging from their necks, "longer even than their noses and reaching down to their navels." As for the men, Börne wrote, there was a time when circumcision cut deeply into the flesh and affected the soul; nowadays, the only marks it left were skin-deep.[23] In a brief sketch, "The Baths of Lucca," Heine parodied a well-known Hamburg businessman named Gumpel (the newly created Marchese Christoforo di Gumpelino), who addresses the author with the following words: "Herr Doktor, enough of the old Jewish religion. I wouldn't wish it on my worst enemy. It brings nothing but shame and abuse. I tell you, it's not a religion at all. It's a calamity! I avoid everything that reminds me of it."[24]

While pragmatism was the dominant motive among male converts, it could not account for the high rate of registered conversions among Jewish women, which between 1780 and 1840 was double that among men. Politically or professionally, women had much less to gain by conversion than men: women of all faiths were denied the vote and remained barred from university and civil service posts. While some women probably converted in the hope of social advancement, many apparently did so in order to marry the man they loved. There was no civil marriage before 1860; to marry a Christian one had to convert, and conversion to Judaism was illegal.

More than a few Prussian and other aristocrats came to speculate on the thriving Jewish marriage market in the hope of improving their financial position. Well-to-do Jewish brides were sought by impecunious aristocrats, debt-ridden army officers, and other fortune hunters. The Prussian landed aristocracy was largely impoverished; ancient estates were heavily in debt. Since Jews were not allowed to own real estate, their assets tended to be liquid. A few opportunists actually married the daughters of their creditors or met their brides through them. Heine ridiculed in turn the parvenus who bought their homely daughters handsome Christian husbands:

> *You sly dog, Jacob, how much did you pay*
> *For that fine strapping Christian man*
> *To take your little daughter's hand,*
> *And she a bit rusty, if I may say?*
>
> *Was it sixty thousand? Or sixty-six?*
> *Did seventy thousand marks do the trick?*
> *For good Christian flesh that's not too dear,*
> *And she a bit cheeky, as I hear.*[25]

Benjamin Ephraim, of the enormously rich family of Berlin court Jews whose palace stood around the corner from Unter den Linden, the city's main boulevard, noted that Prussian officers and other noblemen continuously importuned him with blunt questions about his daughters and the dowries he was prepared to give them. "They never bother to inquire about other circumstances and characteristics important in marriage," he complained.[26]

On the other hand, Christian fortune hunters were warned early on that they might be miscalculating. Two famously rich Jewish heiresses who converted in order to marry Prussian noblemen lost their promised inheritance as a result. Their father had stipulated in his will that his heirs must remain loyal to the faith or lose their share. The king intervened in favor of the two young women. In a series of lawsuits, they first won and then lost their case; the Prussian appellate court overruled the king and upheld the father's will.

Not all unions were venal, of course. Among Jewish intellectuals and artists, in particular, intermarriage was common and sometimes the result of deep emotional and intellectual affinity. Later historians blamed the leading *salonnières* for sponsoring such mixed marriages.

Graetz, for example, vilified Rahel and her ilk as decadent women misled by their vanity and intent on misleading others; he accused them of actively persuading their friends to convert. The young Christians who frequented their salons were cynical and licentious fortune hunters, he claimed, attracted by the darkly "exotic" eroticism of their hostesses. The assertion is hard to believe: Rahel was downright plain, as was the squat, red-haired Dorothea Mendelssohn. Dorothea's sister Henriette was physically deformed, like their father. Several *salonnières* were blond. Only Henriette Herz was beautiful, but she was not a social climber; she turned down the marriage offer of at least one prominent, well-to-do Prussian aristocrat.

The atmosphere in the salons certainly set a permissive tone. Though some of the more prominent Jewish converts may have met their future spouses at one of them, the impact of the salons on the rate of conversion was marginal at best. Of the eighteen best-known hostesses of Berlin salons, seventeen eventually converted, in most cases long after their salons folded. (These "sinful Jewish women did Judaism a service [by converting]," Graetz wrote contemptuously.) And while the young Christian men were attracted to the salons by their hostesses' vivid personalities and occasional good looks, few marriages resulted. There were no fortunes to be had with either Rahel Levin or (after the early death of her husband) the beautiful Henriette Herz. Mendelssohn's eldest daughter, Dorothea, was the exception. She met her second husband, the Protestant writer Friedrich Schlegel, at Henriette's salon and converted in order to marry him.

Dorothea was forty-one at the time of her second marriage; Schlegel was nine years younger. When the two met, Dorothea was still married to Simon Veit, a dull "philistine merchant," according to Henriette Herz, and the mother of two small children. It had been a loveless marriage, arranged without her consent early in Dorothea's life. Dorothea was a passionate, emotional, impulsive woman. Like Schlegel, she believed that great love must strike as a bolt from out of the blue; in this case it did. Dorothea left her marriage abruptly but with her husband's consent. "I will thank God forever," she wrote him some years later, "that you *blessed* where others might have *cursed*."[27] By all indications, her second marriage was a happy one. Dorothea wrote a notable novel.

She converted a second time when, together with Schlegel, she became a Catholic. Her ex-husband, Simon Veit, granted custody of their two young sons to her. When they, too, converted to Catholicism, Veit wrote to console them (and himself) that, even though they now belonged to different religions, they nevertheless remained as one in their moral principles.

Converts often rationalized their conversions as a step undertaken for the sake of their children. When, after years of painful hesitation, Rahel Levin's younger brother, Ludwig Robert, finally decided to convert, he gave as his reason that it was unfair to place so heavy a burden as Judaism upon one's children. The story of Moses Mendelssohn's eldest son, Abraham, was less tortured. Long before he himself decided to convert, Abraham Mendelssohn brought his children up in the Protestant faith. He did so discreetly, not wanting to hurt his mother's feelings. But he had qualms: What about his father's legacy of enlightened Judaism? Had he not betrayed his father's memory? Abraham's brother-in-law successfully put these doubts to rest:

> You say *that you owe it to the memory of your father*; but do you think you have done something wrong by giving your children the religion which appears *to you* as the best? It is the most honorable and just homage any of us could pay to the efforts of your father to promote true light and knowledge; and (if he lived today) he himself would have acted as you have for your children and as I have for mine.[28]

Abraham convinced himself that there was little sense in being fussy about religious details. God the Father was the same for all and his son had, after all, been a Jew. In this day and age, he thought, it was best to conform to the religion practiced by the majority. As for Abraham's children, their success seemed to him to confirm the wisdom of his decision: one of his sons was the composer Felix Mendelssohn-Bartholdy. (Abraham used to say, "I was once my famous father's son; now I am my famous son's father.") Abraham's daughter Fanny was confirmed in church in 1820. On that occasion he wrote her a long, fatherly letter that shows to what lengths he was ready to go to internalize and adopt the reigning Prussian ethos:

We, your mother (her whole life is devotion, charity, and love) and I, were born and brought up by our parents as Jews. Without being obliged to change our religion we have been able to follow the divine instinct in us and in our conscience. We have educated you and your brothers and sisters in the Christian faith because it is the creed of most civilized people today. It contains nothing that can lead you astray from what is good, and much that guides you to love, obedience, toler-ance, and resignation.[29]

Two years later, in Paris, he too embraced Christianity, together with his wife.

Other converts felt that Christian spirituality best suited their tem-peraments. Rahel Levin craved a religion of feeling; her conversion seemed to serve a deep spiritual need. In her eyes, Christianity was a religion of compassion "uniquely aimed at those who suffer," as she did.[30] Even so, she delayed her conversion until relatively late in life, on the eve of her marriage to August Varnhagen von Ense, a Prussian diplomat and man of letters. Varnhagen adored his wife. Fifteen years her junior, he survived her by more than two decades, which he spent editing and publishing her writings. Were it not for his dedication she would be unknown today. He stylized and perhaps overdramatized the last moments of her life to endow them with wider meaning. Rahel died, he wrote, not of old age but because the world had refused to improve and she could not bear to wait any longer. Her last words, according to Varnhagen, confirmed her mystic faith in the healing pow-ers of Christ. And yet, for all the pain her "cursed" birth had caused her, he said, on her deathbed she was grateful for having been born a Jew, crying out:

> What a history!—A fugitive from Egypt and Palestine, here I am and find help, love, fostering in you people. With real rapture I think of these origins of mine and this whole nexus of destiny, through which the oldest memories of the human race stand side by side with the lat-est developments. The greatest distances in time and space are bridged. The thing which all my life seemed to me the greatest shame, which was the misery and misfortune of my life—having been born a Jewess—this I should on no account now wish to have missed.[31]

Indeed, her "misfortune" only brought her life closer to Jesus Christ's. "Dear August," she exclaimed, "my innermost heart is revived. I have thought of Jesus and have cried over his suffering. I feel, I feel for the first time that he is my brother!"[32]

Her real brother, Ludwig, voiced similar thoughts. He was both Jew and Christian, he insisted. As one already condemned to slavery in his mother's womb, he was a Jew who knew that he would always remain one. This was his cross to bear; God was testing him to bear it humbly. For this reason, he wrote, "I may also say in all honesty, I am a Christian."[33]

One outcome of this first wave of conversion among German Jews has rarely been commented on by historians. At the very moment when the new Jewish middle class was beginning to enter German society and German politics, conversion deprived German Jews of their social and intellectual elite. The most influential segments of the middle and upper middle class abandoned the poor and petite bourgeoisie to their fate. This failure of solidarity would have consequences later on.

A few hours after Prussia's military defeat in October 1806, the philosopher Hegel looked out his window in Jena and watched Napoléon himself triumphantly ride into town. Hegel felt he was witnessing nothing less than the "end of history."

For serfs, Jews, and most other disadvantaged people in Prussia—"Europe's most enslaved country," in Lessing's phrase—history was only now beginning. Napoléon mercilessly reduced Prussia to what it had been prior to Frederick II's extensive conquests. For almost half a century, Prussia had been a great European power. Now all that remained was a rump state. Prussia lost much of its revenue, half its population, and almost half its land. Most Prussian Jews suddenly found themselves part of the newly created Grand Duchy of Poland. Those who remained inside the reduced Prussian state expected to be finally granted civil rights. Liberal Prussians led by Karl August von Hardenberg, the new chancellor (a friend and protector of David Friedländer's), were finally gaining ground. They induced the reluctant king to free the serfs, abolish medieval guilds, annul corporal punishment, and pass more tolerant municipal ordinances. The king still balked at ceding full citizenship rights to Prussian Jews. Two years after the great defeat, a new ordinance gave the richest of the Jews of Berlin equal municipal but not full citizen status. Only a small minority of Jews benefited.

Elsewhere in the German lands, in the territories annexed by metropolitan France, and in the new French vassal states, Jews were finally emancipated and granted full political rights. Düsseldorf became a French *arrondissement*. Heinrich Heine recalled the dramatic changes in his native city. The old hereditary ruler (his crown "grew firmly on his head, at night he pulled his nightcap over it") was deposed.[34] The new ruler, Napoléon's brother-in-law Joachim Murat, introduced the French civil code, which abolished all discrimination and inherited privilege. Heine's father gained a commission in the local civil guard. No Jew, apparently, had held a similar office anywhere in Germany since the early Middle Ages. On the day that Heine's father donned his blue-and-red uniform and took charge of security in the city's streets, he treated his fellow officers at headquarters to a barrel of good wine.

As poets often do, Heine articulated some of the most pertinent emotions of the time. A nine-year-old boy with a pounding heart, he watched the French troops march in. He was thrilled—his mother less so—at the prospect of having the French drum sergeant quartered in his home. He observed Napoléon, in his pale green uniform and "world-famous little hat," ride into town and through the city park, where riding a horse was strictly *verboten* and subject to a penalty of ten thalers, payable on the spot. No Prussian policeman dared bar Napoléon's way or collect the fine. "A smile that warmed and reassured every heart played over the emperor's lips, yet everyone knew these lips had only to whistle and Prussia would cease to exist. These lips had only to whistle and the clergy was finished. These lips had only to whistle and the entire Holy Roman Empire of the German Nation would dance to his tune."[35]

Düsseldorf was a picturesque little city on the banks of the Rhine with some 6,000 inhabitants, including 570 Jews. It was surrounded by vineyards and forests and cozy little villages nestling around old church towers. As an adolescent, Heine felt perfectly at home there. Few German Jews have written so warmly of home and native ground, in terms so intimate, colorful, and concrete: "Düsseldorf is very beautiful; thinking about it when you're far away can move you in a strange way. I was born in that city, the very notion of it makes me feel compelled to go home at once, by which I mean the Bolkerstrasse and the house where I was born."[36] In Heine's lycée, even German history was now taught in French, by the abbé d'Aulnoi, an émigré who had written several French grammars and wore a red wig. The philosophy teacher was a Catholic priest who was a freethinker on weekdays in class and celebrated Mass in chapel on Sundays. Heine was soon in trouble over *la réligion*. D'Aulnoi had to ask him at least six times, "Henri, what is the French word for *Glaube* [faith]?" Heine's replies, each time more tearful, were *"le crédit,"* until the abbé, furious, screamed, *"La réligion!"* and gave Heine a beating while all his schoolmates laughed.* Since that day, Heine claimed later, he could not hear the word *religion* without considerable unease. In truth, *le crédit* had always proved more useful to him in life than *la réligion*.

Heine spent weekdays at the lycée, where he learned German, French, Latin, and Greek, and the Sabbath at home studying Hebrew with a private tutor. He was one of the first German Jews to grow up as a free man. In French eyes, he was certainly as German as any of his schoolmates. When he balked at an assignment to write a poem in French, he was scolded by the abbé d'Aulnoi as a barbarian from the Teutonic forests. The principal, himself a deist, advised Heine's mother that he should seek a career in the French army or even in the Church. He was aware, of course, that Heine was a Jew but since, in his opinion, there seemed little difference between religions, there was no point in being fanatical. One day, Heine asked his father who his grandfather had been. "A little Jew with a long beard," Heine's father replied. Heine rushed to convey this intelligence to his classmates. It produced a commotion. The boys jumped up and down on their desks, shouting, "A little Jew with a long beard." Heine was blamed for the disturbance and punished with the cane. He never forgot his punishment or the clergyman who administered it.

THE French also decreed full citizenship and civic rights in the northern Hanseatic towns of Lübeck and Bremen (where for centuries reli-

---

*In German the same word, *Gläubiger,* is used for "believer" and "creditor."

Napoleon frees the Jews. Allegorical etching showing the emperor, like Moses, holding the Tablets of the Law in his right arm. As a boy, Heine thrilled to see Napoleon on horseback in the Düsseldorf city park, where riding was strictly *verboten* but no Prussian policeman dared stop him. *Courtesy Leo Baeck Institute, Jerusalem*

gious prejudice, coupled with commercial rivalry, had scarcely allowed Jews to breathe). All professional, commercial, educational, residential, and other restrictions were lifted. In Hamburg, several Jews were elected to seats on the city council. Only Frankfurt managed somehow to remain segregated. Try as they might, Jews in Frankfurt were less successful in promoting their civic interests than Jews elsewhere in French-dominated Germany. With Frankfurt in mind, Heine wrote:

> *Malice and stupidity*
> *Like street dogs used to mate*
> *Their brood can still be recognized*
> *By their sectarian hate.*[37]

While in 1792 the troops of the French Revolution had been welcomed as liberators in nearby Mainz, in Frankfurt, which they briefly occupied, they were booed by both Jews and Gentiles. Goethe's mother could afford to be more enlightened; with the equanimity of an eighteenth-century patrician vis-à-vis the "barbaric" new nationalisms, she wrote her son that she preferred to live in Frankfurt under the French yolk rather than under the "wooden" Prussian one. But the Jews of Frankfurt, thoroughly cowed and demoralized, demonstrated (or feigned) nothing but love for the city that had humiliated and oppressed them for so long. Inside the ghetto, Jews met the first French troops with cries of "Down with the French!" When, a few weeks later, the small French garrison was forced out by Prussian troops, the ghetto erupted with cries of "Long live the king of Prussia!" The French commander went so far as to claim that one of the reasons for his capitulation was the hostility shown to his troops by the Jews of Frankfurt. Four years later, during the next French attack on the city, the ghetto was badly hit and burned almost to the ground; for the first time in centuries, Jews were allowed to live everywhere in the city. The parks and promenades, though, remained closed to Jews as before until, in 1804, a visiting French citizen named Cohn was roughed up by the local militia for entering the segregated promenades. The French commander at Mainz demanded immediate amends on behalf of the French republic: *"C'est une satisfaction que je demande pour la nation française."*[38] The offending militiamen were arrested and made to apologize publicly to the victim. Since it was impossible to distinguish between French and German Jews by their looks alone, the promenades were finally opened to all. It was characteristic of Frankfurt—a city ruled, in Schiller's words, "by money, the god of this world"—that when, under renewed French pressure, it finally emancipated its Jews in 1811, they were required to pay a ransom for their freedom, a lump payment of 400,000 gulden (approximately 28,000,000 dollars today). The Frankfurt treasury declared that it had a right to be compensated for the loss of potential income from the special Jewish tax. The community borrowed half the amount from the Rothschilds. The reigning grand duke of Frankfurt (appointed by the French) required an additional fee.

Meanwhile, in the newly truncated Prussia, where most German Jews lived, a number of liberal civil servants continued to draft reforms aimed at making Jews full Prussian citizens. Draft after draft was rejected by the king, Frederick William III. Finally, in 1812, he relented and approved an edict of emancipation that annulled most of the existing restrictive laws and recognized Jews, at least in theory, as full citizens. The liberating act was the result not of a popular revolution, as in France or the United States, but of a command from above. The difference would prove crucial. Through their vague and contradictory language, paragraphs 8 and 9 of the emancipation decree still enabled the exclusion of Jews from government positions and from teaching posts in public schools and universities pending future decisions by the king. Few German liberals of the time saw anything wrong in that; like the conservatives, they felt a need to preserve the nation's Christian character. An immediate result of the decree was a sharp increase in the number of conversions, which more than doubled between 1812 and 1819.[39] In any event, the edict of 1812 was short-lived; it was suspended a mere three years later upon Napoleon's defeat.

While their relative freedom lasted, Prussian Jews gave ample proof of their unwavering patriotism. A disproportionately large number of Jewish volunteers in the German war of liberation against Napoleonic France saw active service in the Prussian army. David Friedländer and other elders urged young Jews to volunteer for army service, for it was indeed "a heavenly feeling to possess a fatherland! What rapture to be able to call a spot, a place, a nook one's own upon this lovely earth. . . . Hand in hand with your fellow soldiers you will complete the great task; *they will not deny you the title of brother for you will have earned it.*"[40]

Rahel Levin wrote that among contributors to patriotic charities, Prussian Jews "topped the lists." Jewish women were said to be even more ardent patriots than their men. Freed of the burden of running a prominent salon, Rahel volunteered in 1813 to tend Prussian soldiers wounded in battle. Fanny Arnstein, a Berlin Jewish woman married to a prominent Viennese banker, was reported by the Austrian secret police to be making absolutely scandalous remarks "against Austria and its august monarch for not being more supportive of Prussia."[41] Dorothea Mendelssohn Schlegel was again the exception. On account of her "Asian" extraction, she said sarcastically, she "hoped that Germans will forgive me if I don't display more passion for my fatherland."[42] At Friedländer's Free School in Berlin, Jewish and Christian

Contemporary woodcut of a Jewish volunteer taking leave of his parents during the German war of liberation against France. Unlike Christian volunteers, Jewish soldiers were not eligible after the war for government positions, nor could their widows receive pensions. *Courtesy Leo Baeck Institute, Jerusalem*

boys joined to sing patriotic songs; at prayers they stood "together, some with covered heads, others with uncovered. All prayed to our common creator and father in heaven," according to a report in an 1807 issue of the Jewish family magazine *Sulamith*. The magazine would eventually drop the words *Jewish Nation* from its name, calling itself "A Magazine for the Promotion of Culture among the Israelites." They were citizens now, the editors wished to stress, no longer a "nation"; henceforth they would simply be Prussians of the Israelite—or, better yet, "Mosaic"—persuasion. For all her protestations of patriotism, Rahel Levin was considerably more cautious than many others. How much easier it would be to love one's country, she wrote, if it would only love one back a little bit!

Support for emancipation—never widespread—seemed, in fact, to have weakened since it was first mooted by Christian von Dohm thirty years earlier in his pathbreaking *On the Civic Improvement of the Jews*. In the intervening years, the Enlightenment had given way to Romanticism, the cult of reason to blind nationalism. The new nationalism harked back to the Middle Ages and its sacred union of church, people, and state. It worshiped homogeneity and appealed to tribal instincts. Linked to Christianity, German nationalism aspired to a mystical union between tribe and state that, almost by definition, excluded Jews and other allegedly alien elements. It was one of the ironies of history that the new nationalism first took root in Prussia, where the population was predominately Slav.

Opposition to emancipation was growing among refined intellectuals as well as uncouth "Teutomaniacs." The term was coined by a Jewish liberal named Saul Ascher in a pamphlet published in 1815 that precipitated an avalanche of counterattacks and self-righteous protests. Two basic lines of patriotic "reasoning" emerged. The first upheld the essentially Christian nature of the emerging German state, something that Jews were said to be genetically incapable of sharing. The second postulated an immutable Jewish "mentality"—an amalgam of religion, psychology, ethnicity, race, history, and tradition—that made integration and assimilation both undesirable and illuscry.

The changing fate of one anti-Semitic diatribe illustrated the new mood. *On the Physical and Moral Constitution of Today's Jews: The Voice of a Cosmopolite* was first published anonymously in 1791. Almost nobody read it at the time. The author, Karl Wilhelm Grattenauer, a distinguished Berlin jurist, had taken care to hide his identity, afraid perhaps of exposing himself prematurely in a city considered friendly to Jews. Reissued in 1803, this time with the author's full attribution, the same pamphlet almost immediately became all the rage in Berlin and elsewhere in Germany. Grattenauer may, in fact, have been the first to introduce the concept of a Jewish race. As he put it, "that the Jews are a very singular race no historian or anthropologist can deny. . . . Why suffer among us a horde of people whose character is a mix of all the evils and failings that exist in humanity and who multiply like locusts?"[43] Grattenauer also attacked the appropriation by Jews of *Kultur* and the cult of *Bildung* (self-improvement through education): they thereby threatened the very survival of German nationhood and culture, he insisted. More than sixty pamphlets for and against Grattenauer appeared within the same year. Intimidated by the heated debate, the Prussian authorities banned all further publications on the subject. Elsewhere in Germany they continued to appear.

The time seemed to have been ripe for such diatribes. Instead of trying to build bridges in the name of a common humanity, as the main spokesmen of the Enlightenment had done, the Romantics emphasized national uniqueness and seemingly unbridgeable differences of "race." A new kind of Jew hatred (the term *anti-Semitism* was coined much later in the century) emerged in Berlin after Prussia's defeat in 1806, mixing religious and "racial" sentiment with attitudes that were vaguely anti-modern, anti-French, and anticapitalistic. Jews were decried as parvenus yet also lumped together with the old feudal aristocracy. Shortly before his death, Moses Mendelssohn seems to have sensed the direction in which things might be heading. The new Romantic movement made him uneasy. He approached it with incredulity and fear. In the long run, he warned, it would prove a dangerous irrational uprising against the values of the Enlightenment.

The new Jew hatred resulted not from ignorance, as in the Middle Ages, but from increasing familiarity; its targets were not the alien-seeming traditionalists but the new, recently assimilated Jewish middle class. In the past there had been fear and sometimes blind hatred of an unknown, mysterious entity. Now there was a dislike of people one thought one knew only too well. These Jews spoke and wrote the common language, sometimes better than their Christian countrymen, and lived not segregated from other Germans but among them.

Johann Gottlieb Fichte, the leading philosopher of the moment, otherwise a sensible man, gave voice to the new phobia. He defined nations in organic terms, as born of a common "mystical experience of the soul." The intellectual elite, including Rahel Levin and her friends, attended his public lectures in Berlin, and he enjoyed great popularity. Fichte postulated an ideal German nation, homogeneous and without classes, guilds, or nobles—and especially without Jews. "I see only one way to grant them civil rights," he wrote. "Cut their heads off one night and plant new ones on their shoulders that contain not a single Jewish idea. To protect ourselves from them, there is no other means but to conquer their Promised Land and banish all Jews to there."[44] An otherwise staunch defender of democratic ideas, Fichte had no compunctions about excluding Jews. His hyperbole about cutting off heads need not be taken literally but it is clear that he wanted to see Jews quarantined and removed, as though they were infested with plague. Even Goethe was caught up in the fervor. In 1809, he vented his anger at the "unctuous humanitarians" who had come out in favor of Jewish emancipation. A few years later, he was "furious" upon hearing of a new law in his beloved Weimar aimed at legalizing marriage between Christians and Jews. He suspected the "all-powerful" Rothschilds of being behind this plot and warned that it would undermine all "moral" feeling.[45]

The erosion of support for emancipation within the intellectual elite was reflected in the emergence in Berlin of the new Christian German Eating Club. Excluded from membership were "women, Frenchmen, Philistines, and Jews" (including converts, down to the third generation). The lumping together of these groups paralleled the amalgam of misogyny, xenophobia, and Jew hatred in the mental makeup of the new patriotic elite. The exclusion of women seemed a deliberate stab at Rahel Levin, Henriette Herz, and the other former hostesses of salons. "Philistine" was code for cosmopolite: Jews and Frenchmen were often referred to as cosmopolitan "reason mongers."

The club members included nearly the entire non-Jewish intellectual elite of Berlin and its new university: Fichte; the diplomat Friedrich von Gentz (Rahel's ardent admirer); the poets Heinrich von Kleist, Clemens Brentano, and Achim von Arnim; the political theorist Adam Müller; the legal philosopher Karl Friedrich von Savigny; the architect Karl Friedrich Schinkel; the military historian Carl von Clausewitz; and even, for a while, August Varnhagen von Ense, Rahel's future husband. Club members met once a week for lunch and speeches in a pub, where the refreshment was beer rather than the weak tea served in Rahel's salon. The topics of discussion would have been unthinkable in Mendelssohn's day. On one occasion, Achim von Arnim, perhaps the central literary figure of the early Romantic movement, lectured on the moral depravity of Jews and their disgusting physical characteristics (distinctive body odors, genetic diseases, excessive flatulence, and other physical failings). The audience "roared, beside themselves with enthusiasm."[46] Arnim appealed to club members to be on the lookout for secret Jews who might try to penetrate their ranks. As a preventive measure he suggested that a Jew be skinned to determine his unique "chemical composition." Perhaps a model of a Jew could then be assembled to make it easier to uncover secret ones. Brentano followed suit with a diatribe on the "Philistine Before, In, and After History": Philistines were people who showed little respect for national distinctions and traditions. Brentano's speech was so well received he reprinted it in his collected works.[47] After other such offerings, club members usually practiced the new patriotic art of singing German folk songs in chorus. From here, according to Hannah Arendt, grew the singular, slightly comical German combination of patriotism and male singing clubs.

Rahel and her like-minded friends must have wondered how the emancipation of 1812 might have fared had it been enacted a generation or two earlier, in the heyday of the Enlightenment, as it had in America. The fact that the 1812 edict—imposed from above—coincided with the new nationalism rising from below was fatal to both Germany and its Jews. For more than a century, the new nationalism would bedevil Europe as well. It would condemn German Jews to continue living in a twilight of favor and misfortune, forever straining to be (and not to be) themselves, Germans, Jews, equals, free.

4

Heine and Börne

In early August 1819, a sudden wave of riots struck the Bavarian city of Würzburg. For two or three days, frenzied mobs ran through the streets looting and demolishing Jewish homes and shops, screaming *"Hep! Hep! Jude verreck!"* (Death to all Jews!)* The rioting began at the local university. During an academic ceremony, an aged professor who had recently come out in favor of civic rights for Jews had to run for his life as angry students assaulted him. The riots then spread to the streets. The students were joined by shopkeepers, artisans, and unemployed workers. Two people were killed and some twenty wounded. The material damage was considerable. With cries of *Hep! Hep!*—an acronym of the Latin *Hierosolyma est perdita* (Jerusalem is lost)—the mob broke into shops and homes, wrecking doors and furniture. The army was

---

*The German verb *verrecken* is generally used for animals only.

called in, preventing a massacre. The Jewish population fled the city and spent the next few days in tents in the surrounding countryside.

From Würzburg the riots swept through other Bavarian towns and villages and from there to central and southwest Germany—to Bamberg, Bayreuth, Darmstadt, Karlsruhe, Mannheim, Frankfurt, Koblenz, Cologne, and other cities along the Rhine—and as far north as Bremen, Hamburg, and Lübeck. In Franconia, Jews were chased out of their homes. In Hamburg, hundreds fled the city to seek refuge across the nearby Danish border.

The riots appeared to be entirely spontaneous. Some thought they had been triggered by economic crisis. The year 1816 had been one of drought and hunger, rising bread prices and widespread unemployment. Others claimed that Jews were scapegoats for oppressive reactionary regimes of the post-Napoleonic era. Why Jewish residents of Würzburg or Koblenz would have been held responsible for unemployment or the arrests of liberal militants was unclear. The search for "rational" reasons was widespread and, of course, useless. Some 90 percent of German Jews were poor or very poor; 10 percent of the latter were said to be beggars. More rich Jews lived in Prussia than anywhere else, yet in Prussia there were no riots at all.

Nothing similar had been seen since the Dark Ages. On August 18, after witnessing one of the riots, Friedrich Schlegel wrote to his wife, Dorothea, that they were a return to the "wrong end" of the Middle Ages.[1] Johann Heinrich Voss, the aged Enlightenment poet, wrote that one might have thought one was living in 1419, not 1819. The rabble, it seemed, had simply been waiting for a pretext. A shocked English traveler remarked that for some reason Jews seemed to inspire a mysterious horror almost everywhere.

In some places, the police and militia appeared on the scene too late or stood by idly while the mob raged through the streets. In towns where the militia arrived promptly, the riots were put down relatively quickly. In Heidelberg the police were tardy in their response, but two liberal professors and their students, "humanized, perhaps by contact with France," according to one historian, took the law into their hands and prevented a bloody pogrom.[2] They restrained the culprits and made citizen's arrests.

For the first time, "intellectuals" joined the rioters. The women in this engraving by Johann Michael Voltz depicting the *"Hep! Hep!"* riots in Frankfurt in 1819 resemble the thugs common in engravings of previous anti-Semitic riots. Here they are joined by an elegant man, perhaps a pharmacist or a schoolteacher.
Courtesy Leo Baeck Institute, Jerusalem

Nearly everywhere, the authorities were taken by surprise. With the exception of Heidelberg, townspeople generally remained passive bystanders. The battle cry of the rioters was the same everywhere—*Hep! Hep!*—variously attributed to Roman soldiers during the siege of Jerusalem in A.D. 70 and to rioters in the Rhineland during the Crusades. The choice of Latin suggested its origins were among the educated. "It is remarkable!" Ludwig Robert, Rahel Varnhagen's younger brother, wrote to his sister on August 22, 1819, from Karlsruhe, where the *Hep! Hep!* riots had just broken out. "How come the common people are using this phrase? They could not be familiar with its origin. It must be a *learned* mob that started the whole thing."[3]

In several cities, members of the "respectable" bourgeoisie, students, and even university professors were among the instigators. Since the *Hep! Hep!* of poets and professors had preceded by almost a decade the *Hep! Hep!* of the mob, this was hardly surprising. One of the leading patriotic poets, Ernst Moritz Arndt, well known for his anti-French poem "The God Who Bade the Iron to Grow," was equally known for his harsh words against Jews. They infested the fatherland with their "smut and pestilence. . . . Cursed be their vaunted humanism and cosmopolitanism!" he wrote.[4] Jakob Friedrich Fries, a professor in Heidelberg, had recently preached a similar gospel. His diatribe *On the Endangerment of the Prosperity and Character of the Germans by the Jews* was confiscated by the authorities in 1816 but nevertheless found many readers. Fries lamely excused himself after the riots, saying that in his pamphlet he had merely called for the extermination, "root and branch," of "Judaism," not of Jews themselves.[5] In his report on the riots, the Koblenz police chief noted that intellectual and religious incitement had become so general that many now saw it "as meritorious to mistreat Jews."[6]

A contemporary engraving (1819) of the riots in Frankfurt has survived and reflects this climate. In this truly remarkable social document (by one Johann Michael Voltz), two rough-looking peasant women are assaulting a falling Jew with pitchfork and broom. The women resemble the thugs in a 1617 engraving by Matthäus Merian the Elder depicting a notorious pogrom inside the Frankfurt ghetto. In the 1819 engraving, the women are joined by a rioting gentleman—perhaps a pharmacist, a landowner, or a schoolteacher—wearing spectacles, tails, a white (silk?) scarf, and a fine six-button waistcoat. With one hand he grabs the fat, ugly little Jew by the throat; in the other, he wields a truncheon, about to club him down.

LUDWIG Robert was in Karlsruhe at the time, visiting his fiancée. Only a few weeks earlier, Robert had finally converted to Christianity. And now this! He was a man of principle and ideals who did not act lightly. During the recent wars, he had been beyond military age but his refusal to join the army as a volunteer had infuriated his friend the superpatriotic Baron Friedrich de la Motte Fouqué, who threatened never to speak to him again. The baron, himself a volunteer at age thirty-nine, believed that it was the noble thing to do. Robert objected. The Prussian emancipation edict of 1812 had come so late, he said, and was still so incomplete, he saw no reason to exert himself for a dubious fatherland. It was nice that Fouqué wanted him to act like a Prussian nobleman, but after being a Jewish outcast for the first thirty-five years of his life, he simply could not now, at thirty-seven, generate enough enthusiasm to volunteer for the army. He would gladly give up all his comforts to achieve a great goal, even suffer an amputation, he wrote, "but to become a cog in the wheels of a death machine? No!"[7]

Robert was a successful playwright, librettist, and translator from the French. His play *The Power of Circumstances*, based on an anti-Semitic incident in Berlin a few years earlier,* had been a recent hit in Berlin and elsewhere.

As Robert sat down in Karlsruhe to give his sister an eyewitness account of the rioting, the streets were still strewn with rubble and patrolled by mounted troops. He was in a state of shock. He felt like committing a murder himself. What struck him most was the fact that so many people were indifferent or openly sympathetic to the rioters. The attacks seemed to have been sanctioned at least implicitly by large segments of the population. Flyers pasted on walls in the city threatened a massacre. For two days, Robert heard the cries in the streets:

Hep! Hep! Death and destruction to every Jew!
If you don't flee, then you are through!

As he wrote, some of the rioters were still at large. Late in the evening of the second day, the police finally arrested or dispersed most of them. Police and cavalry patrols were urging the crowds to go home. Even so, "as soon as the patrols moved on," Robert noted, *Hep! Hep! Jude verreck!* Rang out again "amid loud laughter, more amused than fanatically wild." Of his own walk through the streets, he wrote:

I didn't want to stay in one place for fear of being arrested, so I walked all the way to the Waldhorngasse. There I caught sight of the commandant of the city, General Brückner, on horseback, and as there was still

---

*An arrogant Prussian nobleman had offended the family of a young Jew named Hitzig, who challenged him to a duel. The nobleman refused: to give satisfaction to a Jew was beneath his dignity. Thereupon, Hitzig publicly thrashed him with his walking stick. Tried for assault, Hitzig was let off lightly by a sympathetic judge. "Public" opinion was said to be on Hitzig's side. It increased considerably after Hitzig fell in battle against Napoleon while the nobleman remained closeted at his country estate.

sporadic shouting, he told his patrol: "Let the bastards shout away if they insist, but the minute they do something dumb, let them have it!" Everyone in town was standing at their open windows, and I went back slowly, close to the buildings, so that I could hear what was being said and assess the mood.

Children were playing in front of the doorsteps, laughing and giggling; they told about the day's events with childish interest. But none of the men or women admonished them or even engaged them in serious conversation. And there was even less chance of seeing a priest, even though in my opinion this was truly where they ought to have been, as teachers of the religion that holds love in such esteem.

Too many made light of the events, Robert complained. "How corrupt people really are and how inadequate their sense of law and justice— not to mention their love of humanity—is clear from the fact that there was no indignation expressed at these incidents, not even in the official papers. . . . The townspeople are said to have been angry with Brückner for closing the taverns right away. They threatened to tear him off his horse."[8]

On the third day, the infantry was called in and cannons were deployed in the streets of Karlsruhe. New flyers challenged the old: "Emperors, kings, dukes, beggars, Catholics, and Jews are all human and as such our equals." The grand duke of Baden, a humane man of liberal sentiment, left his castle and demonstrated his solidarity with the threatened Jews of his capital by taking up residence at the home of a prominent Karlsruhe Jew. After this, calm was restored.

JEWISH reactions to the riots were remarkably restrained. Many Jews were either too cowed or too trusting in the rule of law and order. The detachedness and lack of personal identification with the victims on the part of the Jewish upper middle class is an indication that the rich and the largely converted intellectual Jewish elite were turning their backs on the poor and petite bourgeoisie. The Jewish family magazine *Sulamith* did not mention the riots at all. Rahel's reply to her brother's letter is exceptional for its recognition that the riots were more than a temporary aberration. "I am infinitely sad on account of the Jews," she wrote, "in a way I have never experienced before. . . . What should this mass of people do, driven out of their homes? They want to *keep* them only to despise and torture them further."[9] Like her brother, she referred to "the Jews" not to "us Jews." Still, she did not distance herself from their tragedy; it was *her* tragedy, too, but as a German. She vowed to stand by the "unhappy remnant" in its hour of need, this "great and gifted nation, far ahead of others in its knowledge of God."[10] Nothing could console her. Nor could cosmetic remedies disguise the truth, not even if applied with "paintbrushes."

Her tone was bitter and sarcastic. The *Hep! Hep!* riots were a result not simply of religious prejudice but of a deeper malaise. The riots did not surprise her, she assured her brother: "Vileness never does." She was used to it. Germans seem to be in desperate need of their Jews, she maintained, as scapegoats to be hated freely:

> I know my country. Unfortunately. For the past three years I've said the Jews will be attacked. I have witnesses. The Germans wax bold with indignation, and why? Because they are the most civilized, peace-loving, and obedient people. . . . Their newfound hypocritical love for Christianity (may God forgive my sin) and the Middle Ages, with its poetry, art, and atrocities, incites the people to commit the only atrocity they may still be provoked to: attacking the Jews! All the papers have been insinuating it for years—Professors Fr [ies] and Rü [hs] or what-ever their names. . . . Their hate does not stem from religious zeal: how can they hate other faiths when they don't even love their own?[11]

She wondered why the riots had yet to reach Berlin and feared they soon would. In Berlin most young Jews had served in the army, and half were baptized and married to Christians, she wrote.

AT the time of the riots, Germany consisted of thirty-six independent states and a number of free cities. The status of Jews varied from state to state. Some states had bluntly abrogated the emancipation edicts passed during the Napoleonic era; others retained them in theory but ignored them in practice. Once again Jews were excluded from posts in the public administration and the army and forbidden to hold teaching positions in schools and universities. Though they enjoyed near equality in a few of the smaller states, in most there was still full or partial segregation.

In some places, attempts were made to return them to their old medieval status. The free city of Frankfurt reinstated parts of the medieval statute that restricted the rights of Jews. As in 1616, only twelve Jewish couples were allowed to marry each year. The 400,000 gulden the community had paid the city government in 1811 in return for its emancipation were declared forfeited. In the Rhineland, which had reverted to Prussian control, Jews lost the citizenship rights they had been granted under the French and were no longer allowed to practice certain professions. The few who had been appointed to public office before the war were summarily dismissed.

Prussia did not formally abrogate its emancipation edict of 1812; the edict was simply circumvented as much as possible by administrative means. Thirteen hundred Prussian Jews had served in the army during the war; seventy-one had won the Iron Cross for valor. All had been promised government jobs or promotions after the war but only one, an artillery lieutenant named Meno Burg, was even considered—briefly— for advancement. The Prussian minister of justice, Friedrich Leopold Kircheisen, claimed that in the case of Jewish servicemen "temporary bravery did not preclude a lower degree of morality."[12] With regard to Burg, Frederick William III ruled: "I cannot promote . . . Burg . . . to captain in the army. But I am confident that as a well-educated man he will see the truth and salvation of the Christian faith" and thus "clear away any obstacle" to his advancement.[13]

Jews continued to be admitted as students, though not as professors, to Prussian faculties. They could study law but not teach or practice it. The fact that so many still enrolled in the law faculties reflected their conviction that the restrictions would not last. A good number of law and philosophy students ended up as journalists, and journalism came to be regarded as a largely Jewish occupation. Medicine was the only academic profession they were able to practice freely.

The 1812 emancipation edict, even in its diluted form, did not extend to the large territories in the east that Prussia had been allowed to repossess after the war and that tripled the number of Jews under

Prussian rule. The result was that the ninety thousand Jews of Posen and Silesia were subjected to some thirty different sets of near-medieval restrictions and limitations.

In Berlin, many Jews had kept their part of the understanding implied by the edict—that they would become equal citizens if they abandoned particularities of language, dress, and custom. Even those who had converted to Christianity understood that they were still, so to speak, on probation. They had assimilated, but the rewards of emancipation continued to elude them.

Rahel Varnhagen was a notable exception. In 1819, after a few years in Karlsruhe, where August Varnhagen served as Prussian chargé d'affaires, the couple settled again in Berlin. August seems to have been suspended from his post for his overly liberal politics. Rahel, now the wife of a retired Prussian diplomat, revived her old salon. Much had changed. The gatherings no longer took place in a "garret" but in an elegant apartment on the Französische Strasse. Her friends returned her invitations. Among her guests were the philosopher Hegel and the historian Leopold von Ranke (who called her the greatest woman of her time). There were fewer noblemen in attendance and no members of the royal family; the Varnhagens, because of their liberal sympathies, were considered vaguely subversive.

Another Berlin Jew in no need of legitimizing himself was Mendelssohn's grandson, the famous musical wunderkind Felix Mendelssohn-Bartholdy. Even he was subject to some mild ridicule. With Felix in mind and in a mixture of German and mock Yiddish, Goethe's friend Karl Friedrich Zelter wrote the poet that it would really be *"eppes rores* [something rare] if a Jew boy were to become an artist."[14] For his part, the gifted boy assured Goethe that his greatest joy was to be "a German and alive now."[15] Goethe invited him to Weimar, where every morning and afternoon "the author of *Faust* and *Werther* gives me a kiss," Felix reported to his mother, "and says, I haven't yet heard you today, make a little noise for me."[16] Felix would play the piano for two hours. One afternoon, ravished by the music, the old poet told Felix the biblical story of the mad King Saul and young David. When the "evil spirit" came upon Saul, David had to play the harp to soothe him. Driven by murderous envy, Saul smote David with his spear. Goethe added: "You are my David: if I should fall sick or be sad, chase away the bad dreams with your playing. Unlike Saul, I promise I'll never throw a spear at you."[17]

Commenting on this incident more than a hundred years later, the German Jewish author Adolf Leschnitzer wrote that a great poet's word "occasionally contains meanings that he himself barely surmises and that are fully revealed only to later generations."[18] Goethe's lighthearted remark to Moses Mendelssohn's grandson, coming as it did at the dawn of the modern German-Jewish encounter, proved to be tragically poignant.

A few weeks after the *Hep! Hep!* riots, three remarkable young men—Eduard Gans, Leopold Zunz, and Moses Moser—met in Berlin to discuss the situation. Was there anything they could do to reduce the rampant Judeophobia? They decided to found a Society for the Culture and Science (*Wissenschaft*) of the Jews. Its purpose was to bring ordinary Jews into the orbit of German *Kultur* and at the same time reinforce their Jewish identity by bridging the gulf between secular and religious education.

The term *Wissenschaft* stands for much more than science and empirical research. It implies knowledge, learning, understanding, with a hint of philosophy and speculation. *Wissenschaft,* then, was to reconcile Jews and Germans. Committed to a view of Judaism as both secular civilization and religion, the three young men were eager to spread knowledge about the former and help young Jews to remain Jews even as (like many young Christians) they lost some of the latter. In Spain, Holland, Italy, and elsewhere, Jews had once made important contributions to philosophy and the natural sciences. The new society would strive to enhance modern appreciation of this heritage through the "scientific" exploration of liturgy, literature, music, poetry, philosophy, and the natural sciences.

Two of the founders, Gans and Zunz, were outstanding graduates of the universities of Berlin, Heidelberg, and Halle. They were among the first German Jews to earn doctorates in jurisprudence and philosophy. Their social backgrounds, however, could not have been more different. Eduard Gans, president of the new society, was the pampered twenty-two-year-old son of a rich Berlin family of court Jews. His father had been one of the founders of the Berlin stock exchange, a protégé of the Prussian chancellor Karl August von Hardenberg. His mother had been the queen of Prussia's maid of honor at her marriage to the crown prince, an unusual distinction for the daughter of a practicing Jew. Like others of his class, Gans attended the elite Gymnasium zum Grauen Kloster in Berlin. At the University of Berlin he was one of Hegel's star pupils. His great ambition was to specialize in the history of jurisprudence and teach it at the university.

Leopold Zunz, by contrast, had spent his early years in the poverty, neglect, and disorder of a cramped, oppressive religious Jewish orphanage in the small town of Wolfenbüttel. The children were strictly forbidden to read German. The sole subject of instruction was Talmud, taught, he remembered, in "the most frightful" Yiddish dialect.[19] In 1807, the oppressive atmosphere changed almost overnight with the appointment of an enlightened young man named Samuel Meyer Ehrenberg, a disciple of Moses Mendelssohn, as director. Ehrenberg moved swiftly to modernize the curriculum. Zunz became aware, for the first time in his life, of the culture and language of the country in which he was living. Later, at the new University of Berlin, Zunz studied ancient and biblical history. Like so many other young Jews, Zunz toyed at one point with the idea of baptism, but he changed his mind and decided that conversion was degrading.[20] Twenty-six when he helped found the society, Zunz had as his great ambition the establishment of a department of Jewish studies at one of the German universities.

The third founder, Moses Moser, was a young banker and a secular man of great learning and sensibility. "If you are able to pray, pray for me too!" he told a friend on the eve of a Jewish high holiday. "For my part, I'll study philosophy for you."[21]

The three men threw themselves into the work of the society, convinced there was nothing more wonderful than "an intellectual life in the company of friends filled with the same enthusiasms!"[22] The society would link Jews to their past, show them a way out of the ghetto, and help them arrive at the point "that the rest of Europe has already reached."[23] It preached the current ideal of *Bildung*, as enunciated by

Goethe—self-improvement and refinement through literature, philosophy, and the arts. But first certain changes would have to be made. The society was born in a flurry of anticlericalism. Zunz was convinced that unless "the Talmud is overthrown there is nothing one can do."[24] He occasionally led the service at a new nontraditional synagogue in Berlin where prayers were read in German and accompanied by organ music. Traditional rabbis attacked him for his sermons. As the attacks on Zunz mounted, Ehrenberg, his one-time "liberator" at the orphanage at Wolfenbüttel, urged him to stand firm. "Carry on," he wrote to Zunz. "Become a Luther!"[25]

Ehrenberg loved his former pupil but he overrated him. Zunz never became a Luther. He was not a charismatic figure and lacked the powerful inner force to impose himself on his time. Reform Judaism would be founded by others several decades later. At this early stage, in any event, the first nontraditional temple in Berlin was forced by the government to close; nontraditional prayer services could be conducted only in private homes. The king opposed all innovation in Jewish synagogue observances, fearing that a reformed Jewish service might keep Jews from converting to Christianity, possibily even attract Christians to Judaism, and encourage reform in the Lutheran church.

The society, on the other hand, was tolerated. It soon had a membership of some fifty prominent people, including the aged David Friedländer, still firm in his belief that Jews and Christians could become brothers in faith if only they trimmed their outdated doctrines and rituals. Zunz, who became secretary and one of its most active members, wrote the charter. It declared the society's most ambitious aim—to give German Jews their first modern intellectual center. When, in later years, other reformers looked back on these modest beginnings, they recognized Zunz's charter as "brilliantly designed" and Zunz as a man "who had taken upon himself one of its most difficult tasks."[26] The society held weekly sessions; minutes were kept and are still extant. Although the discussions were all too often couched in Hegelian abstractions, the resolutions were practical and concrete. First and foremost, the members vowed that they would never convert. They would always remain Jews. And since their main task, as Gans, Moser, and Zunz saw it, was to help break the cultural and social isolation of

Jews in German society, the society resolved not only to combat prejudice but to become a movement of Jewish self-criticism.

At one of the very first sessions in December 1819, Zunz presented an outline of the so-called *Judenübel*—the failings or flaws of the Jews.[27] He distinguished between flaws rooted in Judaism itself and those that had accumulated over centuries of oppression and isolation:

Outline of Matters in Need of Improvement among Jews

THE INNER WORLD OF IDEAS

1. Religious concepts, especially God's love and exclusive favoring of the Jews
2. Conceit
3. Superstition
4. Intolerance of other viewpoints
5. Neglect of decent manual labor in favor of ascetic idleness or overly literal observance of ceremonies
6. Huckstering
7. Avarice
8. Greed
9. Contempt for science; all this leading to
10. The persistent delusion, contrary to law, that it is permissible to cheat non-Jews

THE CULT

1. Synagogue services
2. Forms of prayer
3. Obsolete, harmful, senseless customs
4. Overemphasis of ceremonial law

INNER CONSTITUTION OF THE COMMUNITIES

1. Tyrannical rabbis—their power, fanaticism, and uselessness
2. Lack of authority, hence anarchy, misuse, such as
3. Alms wasted on idlers
4. Bad schools or none at all

EDUCATION

1. Effeminate children, therefore
2. Cowardice
3. Harmful examples in parents' home
4. Ignorance, immorality, uncouth Talmud students
5. Disparity between the teachings of the Law and its observance at home
6. Faulty and useless instruction at school: Talmud but no instruction in languages and science
7. No appreciation of learning is evoked among pupils
8. Badly paid and substandard teachers
9. Neglect of mother tongue
10. Neglect of (discrimination against) females

JEWS IN CHRISTIAN SOCIETY

1. Only trade, mostly petty commerce or peddling, no artisans
2. Shunning physical labor, no farming
3. Neglect of self
4. No physical activity
5. Little desire to improve situation
6. No class distinctions
7. Superficial cleverness, hence misinformation
8. Lack of thorough, concentrated study
9. Sham interest in enlightenment
10. Apostasy
11. Withdrawal from or forcing themselves on Christians
12. Uncouth language, comportment, social intercourse, manners

Much of this compilation of "needed improvements" will strike modern readers as evidence that Zunz had internalized anti-Semitic stereotypes. Yet at the time Zunz's list would have been seen more as a blueprint in the prevailing spirit of *Bildung*, or self-improvement. As an exercise in Jewish self-criticism it anticipated the Zionists by almost a century. Its main purpose was to make Jews emerging from the ghetto more acceptable to their neighbors by eliminating external differences—only the "disturbing, entirely self-centered isolation should be eliminated," Zunz explained.[28] He wanted Judaism to thrive as a secular and religious civilization but also to "merge with" and become subsumed by Europe—as indeed it successfully did over the next 180 years. According to Zunz, the voluntary self-segregation of many Jews was a remnant of the Middle Ages, when, in the aftermath of massacres, Judaism had closed in on itself. Now that "high culture" was becoming an integral part of being German, such isolation was no longer necessary. Jews needed not only to discard their medieval garb and unlettered dialect but to become modern European men and women in the fullest sense.

Gans remonstrated with Zunz. Only a few centuries earlier, he argued, the customs Zunz was now criticizing so mercilessly would rightly have been considered virtues. While it might seem "ridiculous for Jews to consider themselves the chosen people, from the perspective of an oppressed community that survived only through inner strength" it was "a truly great idea!" Even the Jews' alleged greed, Gans claimed, was a consequence of oppression, a vestige of a time when they were able to find their "political footing only in commerce and nowhere else."[29] Still, Gans agreed that times had changed: Zunz's critique might well be justified in the present.

The society established a research institute, a library, and an archive. It opened another Free School in Berlin where young Jews from the eastern provinces were given instruction in the German language and culture. The newcomers were encouraged to seek careers, wherever possible, in agriculture and as artisans. The society also engaged in a correspondence with Mordecai Manuel Noah, a bizarre former United States consul to Tunis, sheriff of New York, and, as he described himself, "by the grace of God, Governor and Judge of Israel." Noah was planning to establish a colony for persecuted European Jews on an island in the Niagara River near Buffalo. This place of refuge, not surprisingly, was to be called Ararat, after the mountain on which the biblical Noah safely landed the ark after the flood. Zunz's correspondence with the American Noah was quite fantastic. Noah grandly appointed Gans and Zunz his "ministers plenipotentiary" for Europe. It was never clear whether he was a genuine idealist or an ambitious real estate developer. Perhaps he was both. In any case, his big plan came to naught but cost Zunz, as he put it, a lot of postage.

The society also published a short-lived magazine. The first issue was blocked by the Prussian censors, who suspected (perhaps because of the word *science* in the title) that it was the organ of a new religious sect. To overcome the censors' apprehensions, Zunz and his friends had to renounce publicly any interest in generating "Christian support for Jews and Judaism" and promise that their magazine would circulate exclusively among their coreligionists.[30]

While these negotiations dragged on, Gans lived through an agonizing personal drama. In the fall of 1819, upon receiving his doctorate in jurisprudence, Gans bravely applied for a teaching position on the law faculty of the new University of Berlin. He attached a legal brief citing the 1812 edict of emancipation. Even though the king had not yet decreed specific rules, Gans tried to force the issue by citing paragraph 8 of the king's edict, which made Jews fully eligible for academic positions.

The application went back and forth between the law faculty, the Prussian chancellor, and his minister of education. The chancellor recommended that Gans be hired. The minister demurred. The faculty was opposed. In mid-1820, the faculty wondered whether Gans, "who belongs to a well-known Jewish family, had indeed joined the Christian Church and, if not, whether this might not impede his appointment."[31] They knew very well that Gans had not converted.

The matter was tossed around for another year. The chancellor wrote to his minister of education several times in support of Gans's application. The minister responded in increasingly evasive terms. In his opinion, the Christian character of the state precluded the employment of Jews as teachers of the young, except in medicine or in the natural sciences. The chancellor did not insist.

In May 1822, Gans grew desperate. In a final appeal to Chancellor Hardenberg, his late father's protector, and to the minister of education, Gans complained that he was the victim "of two years of oppression, insult, and humiliation. . . . I belong to that unhappy class of men who are hated for having no education and are persecuted for trying to obtain one."[32]

The letter spoke for an entire generation of young Jewish university graduates who, ten years after the supposed emancipation, still found themselves at a dead end. Gans's final appeal to Hardenberg was futile.

The government now retroactively legitimized its stonewalling by issuing a new royal decree. Widely known as "Lex Gans," it supplanted the famous paragraphs 8 and 9 by explicitly outlawing the employment of Jews in universities and in the public sector. Gans had no further recourse. As a consolation, the government offered him a "travel grant" of five hundred thalers from the royal purse, with an admonition to use it well, that is, to "train himself for another occupation with diligence and assiduity" since a position at any of the "royal universities, in any of the faculties, was not to be expected."[33]

The defeat of Gans's efforts cleared the air of any illusion. A man of independent means, Gans settled down to complete the first of two volumes of a comparative history of European inheritance law. Disillusioned, the society once again focused its energies on emigration. Correspondence with the American Noah resumed; there was even talk of establishing a "Ganstown" on Ararat. More and more poor Jews from the eastern provinces were passing through Berlin. Early one morning, the poet Adalbert von Chamisso observed Jews waiting for alms outside Abraham Mendelssohn's house. Their predicament moved him to write:

> *From here I must depart,*
> *My wandering staff in hand,*
> *To Holland or to England,*
> *In search of a free land.*[34]

AT about this time, an unusual newcomer began to make his presence felt in the inner circles of the society. Heinrich Heine was an enormously gifted young poet, slight, pale, with dreamy blue eyes and long, wavy blond hair. He wore velvet jackets, dandyish, open Byronic collars, and a fashionable wide-rimmed high felt hat known as a Bolivar. Heine had arrived in Berlin in the summer of 1821 to study law at the university and attend Hegel's seminar on aesthetics. Barely twenty-four years old and on the strength of only a few publications, he was already a fairly well-known literary figure, listed in Friedrich Rassmann's *Pantheon of Living German Poets*.

As a poet he was destined to leave an indelible mark on German culture, one that even the Nazis, try as they might, were unable to erase. The lyricism of his poetry was as remarkable as the scathing wit of his prose. The literature on Heine is vast but there has not been an outstanding biography, perhaps because Heine was so many different people at one and the same time. Lion Feuchtwanger said of him that he could be peeled like an onion: beneath every layer was another.

Heine's imagery was drawn from the store of both German and Hebrew mythology. No other writer has ever been so German and so Jewish and so ambivalent and ironic about both. Jews and Germans, he once wrote, were Europe's "two ethical peoples," who might yet make Germany "a citadel of spirituality." The opposite, he insisted, was just as possible. Germans "bow to none, when there is hatred to be done," and they could yet bring untold ruin upon Europe. Jews, on the other hand, had come out of Egypt, "the fatherland of crocodiles and priesthood, and along with its skin diseases and its stolen gold and silver vessels, they also brought what came to be called a positive religion, and what came to be called a church, a scaffolding of dogmas in which you had to believe, and of sacred ceremonies you had to perform, a model for subsequent state religions."[35]

In his own fanciful way, Heine anticipated Freud's view of religion as a form of neurosis. At his most sober, he had few illusions about Germany or about himself, a Jew living and writing in Germany who scorned "*all* positive religions." Along with his family, Heine had been granted full civic rights in Düsseldorf during the Napoleonic era and had lost them overnight with the restoration of Prussian rule. Heine was the first German Jewish writer to proclaim in 1820—as would many others after him—that his true fatherland was the German language, "our most sacred possession, . . . a fatherland even for him who is denied one by malice and by folly."[36]

Heine wrote these lines at the age of twenty-three, a few months after witnessing the *Hep! Hep!* riots. Just before moving to Berlin, he attended the universities of Bonn and Göttingen. Older than most of his fellow students by two or three years, he was allergic to the alcohol, nicotine, and "patriotic" politics they indulged in so boisterously. His distaste for alcohol persisted; he is said to have claimed that the Jewish contribution to the new German patriotism was "the small glass" of beer.

While a student in Bonn in 1820, he wrote the verse tragedy *Almansor*. A parable about early-nineteenth-century Germany, *Almansor* is set in the sixteenth century during the Christianization of Spain. Its main characters are Moors tortured into converting to the dominant Christian culture. An auto-da-fé takes place and the Koran is publicly burned in the marketplace of Granada. Summing up the scene, Heine warns: "Wherever they burn books they will also, in the end, burn human beings."[37]

Heine was alluding to a recent book burning in Germany that had caused a sensation all over the country. On October 17, 1817, during the anniversary celebration of the victory over Napoleon at the battle of Leipzig, German student fraternities had convened in the historic Wartburg castle where Luther had translated the Bible three hundred years earlier. On this occasion, the students burned several "subversive" books, emulating Luther's public burning of the papal bull. The offending volumes included the French civil code and Saul Ascher's pamphlet against the "Teutomaniacs." To the accompaniment of fierce speeches against "foreigners," "cosmopolitans," and "Jews," among others, the books were solemnly thrown into the flames. "Woe to the Jews who hold on to their Jewishness while mocking and reviling our own national character, our Germanness."[38]

At the University of Göttingen later in 1820, Heine's distaste for patriotic student movements deepened. Watching rowdy fraternity students in a local beer cellar one night, he pondered what they might do if they came to power. They would condemn to exile "Frenchmen, Jews, and Slavs, down to the seventh generation," he decided.

The students in Berlin were no

Heinrich Heine. No other writer was so German and so Jewish—and so ambivalent and ironic about both. Lithograph after a portrait by Jules Sière. *Courtesy Leo Baeck Institute, Jerusalem* improvement over those he had known in Göttingen and Bonn. Mired in a "swamp of nationalist narcissism," they irritated him with their "ur-Teutonic beer bass." But soon after his arrival in the Prussian capital, a local publisher issued a book of his recent poetry. The slim volume spread his fame among the literati and the patrons of intellectual salons. The leading hostesses readily adopted him. They were charmed by his wit and his shy flirtatiousness. Elise von Hohenhausen, a prominent *salonnière*, proclaimed him the German Byron. Friedrich von Gentz, alerted to Heine's existence by Rahel Varnhagen, confided to her that he was bewitched by the sheer "magic" of Heine's poetry. Abraham Mendelssohn and his wife, Leah, entertained him in their fine new villa off the Wilhelmstrasse, where on special evenings the thirteen-year-old Felix astounded the guests, playing his own compositions on the pianoforte.

Heine was a regular at Rahel Varnhagen's newly revived salon. Twice Heine's age, she recognized his genius and was full of "restless apprehension for his future," as she wrote to Gentz. Heine, for his part, was deeply grateful to the "little woman with the great soul." Rahel was perhaps the only person in his life about whom he never wrote a single sardonic line. "I think of Frau von Varnhagen, *Ergo sum*," he told her husband. He was ready to put on a dog collar with the inscription *J'apartiens à Mme. Varnhagen*—I belong to Mme. Varnhagen.

Ludwig Robert's estranged friend the poet Friedrich de la Motte Fouqué sent Heine a warm letter and even dedicated a "beautiful" poem to him. "When he looks more closely at my pedigree," Heine noted, "he will wish he had never written it."[39] Heine sent his own book to Goethe with the inscription "I kiss the sacred hand that has shown me and the entire German people the way to heaven." On a walking tour of Thuringia he passed through Weimar and was invited to visit the great man in his stately home on the Frauenplatz ("Where a good man once sets foot / Remains forever consecrated."). He arrived in his stained travel clothes and in a cocky mood. After some small talk, Goethe asked politely, "What are you working on now?" "On a *Faust*." "Do you have other business in Weimar, Herr Heine?" "Having crossed Your Excellency's threshold, all my business in Weimar is done," Heine answered and took his leave.[40]

The critics hailed his poetry for its inimitable lyricism but condemned his political prose for "patriotic" reasons, snidely alluding to his Jewish origins. In the aftermath of the Napoleonic wars, German patriotism was strangely double-edged. It manifested itself both as a liberal campaign against the absolutism of the German monarchies and as a regressive rejection of the "anemic" rationalism of the Enlightenment, an appeal to tribal instincts, ethnic purity, and "blood." It spread xenophobic fears that Jewish emancipation might threaten the national integrity of the Christian state. In his prose, Heine himself spared neither Jew nor Gentile. In a series of articles, *Letters from Berlin,* published anonymously in a Rhineland newspaper, he decried the "faithful of both the Old and the New Testaments haggling at the Berlin stock exchange. . . . God, what faces! Such greed in every muscle!"[41] He also put to satiric use a comic and anticlimactic amorous adventure with a pretty baroness. Taking him for a Christian, she had casually dropped anti-Semitic remarks even as she made love to him in the Tiergarten. He alluded to the incident in a mordant poem, *Donna Clara,* in which a Spanish *señora* and a Marrano knight enact a similar farce. "It is a scene out of my own life," he confessed in a letter to a friend. "The baroness became a *señora* and I myself an Apollo or a knight of Saint George."[42]

Between semesters, Heine made an excursion to Poland as the guest of a fellow student, a Polish count named Breza. Alluding to the ferocity of the German intellectual debate, he noted with pleasure that the wolves that roamed Polish woods did not yet howl historical allusions at one another. Like many Western visitors before him and after, he was initially revolted by the sight of seedy, caftaned Polish Jews in the "pigsty-like holes" where they "live, whine, pray, haggle, and are miserable, . . . their spiritual world sunk in a morass of unedifying superstition, squeezed by crafty scholasticism into a thousand grotesque shapes." Revulsion, however, soon gave way to pity and admiration:

Despite the barbaric-looking fur cap on his head and the even more barbaric ideas within, I hold the Polish Jew in much higher regard than many a German Jew with a Bolivar hat on top of his head and Jean Paul inside it. In stark isolation, the character of the Polish Jew has evolved into an integral whole; by breathing the air of tolerance, this character has acquired the stamp of freedom. . . . As for me, I prefer the Polish Jew, with his grimy fur, his flea-bitten beard, his odor of garlic, and his wheeling and dealing to many others in all their savings-bond splendor.[43]

RAHEL Varnhagen's new salon was infused with liberal political sentiment of a kind that after the defeat of Napoleon was dangerously close to subversion. It was probably at her salon that Heine met Eduard Gans in the fall of 1821. Gans invited him to join the Society for the Culture and Science of the Jews. Heine readily accepted. For the first time in his life, perhaps, he met young Jews of his own generation who were as integrated into German culture and society as he was and yet intensely conscious (possibly because of the *Hep! Hep!* riots) of their identity. The emotional impact of Heine's encounters with Gans, Zunz, and Moser was profound. He sympathized with the aims of the society but mocked it for its ineffectiveness; he feared it was attempting "the rescue of a long-lost cause." Still, he attended the society's seminars faithfully and even volunteered to teach German literature twice a week to the Polish students who attended the society's Free School. He advised them "to emigrate to America, or at least to England. In those countries nobody asks, 'What do you and don't you believe?'"[44] He had no intention of emigrating himself. He was definitely, he said, a "German animal" and would always remain one; his breast, he insisted, not without a trace of self-irony, was a veritable "catalog of Germanic emotions."

In the summer of 1823, Heine returned to Göttingen, in the kingdom of Hanover, to prepare for his doctoral exams. He continued to maintain a lively correspondence with his friends at the society. His year of participation in its work had sobered him. "We no longer have the strength to grow a beard, to fast, to hate, and, through hate, to abide," he wrote to Immanuel Wohlwill, a society colleague who supported reform of synagogue worship.[45] Heine was dubious about fashionable modifications like German prayer books and organ music. They were merely imitative of Christianity and offered only a "new stage set and decor." The new rabbis (Heine called them *souffleurs*—prompters) wore a Protestant parson's "white band" in their collars. Reform Judaism was like mock turtle soup, he thought, "turtle soup without the turtle." Heine was an early precursor of the legendary Spanish anarchist who asked a Protestant missionary, "How can I believe in your religion when I don't even believe in mine, which is the only true one?"

The closer Heine came to receiving his doctorate the more he was forced to think about making a living afterward. He grew desperate. He could not hope to work as a lawyer since the bar associations remained closed to Jews. Lex Gans had also squashed any other chance of finding work in the public sector. "Forgive my bitterness," he wrote to Wohlwill. "You have not been hit by the blow of the abrogated edict [of emancipation]."[46] While writing his thesis, Heine moved to his parents' house in Lüneburg. He reported to Moser the dreariness of daily life in this small town. "The Jews here, as everywhere, are unbearable hagglers and stinkers. The Christian middle class is disagreeable and uncommonly mean to Jews. The higher classes ditto to a higher degree." Judaism, he wrote in a poem, was a "family disease, . . . a plague dragged from the Nile Valley, the unregenerate faith of ancient Egypt."[47] He was "indifferent" to all religions and his loyalty to Judaism, he informed another correspondent, was "rooted solely in a deep antipathy to Christianity."[48]

A few weeks later, to Moser: "As you might imagine, they are talking about baptism here. No one in my family is against it except me." Baptism would be a meaningless gesture for him anyway, Heine assured Moser, unless perhaps it enabled him to be more effective in the defense of his "unfortunate clansmen." Nevertheless, he wrote, "I consider it beneath my dignity and honor to convert to Protestantism in order to get a job in Prussia! In dear old Prussia! I might spite them, become a Catholic, and then hang myself. . . . These are sad times we live in. Scoundrels have become the best we've got, and the best we've got have all turned into scoundrels."[49] An uncle in Düsseldorf wrote to say that in the Rhineland Heine was now as despised for his interest in Jews as he had once been loved for writing marvelous German poems.

The poem "To Edom" grew out of these somber reflections, a comment on the painful imbalance of tolerance. (Edom is a name traditionally given by Jews to their enemies.) As soon as it was finished Heine sent it to Moser in Berlin. For more than a millennium, Heine wrote, Jews and non-Jews had been tolerating or suffering one another in "brotherly" fashion. The terms of this one-sided compromise were simple:

> *You endure the fact I breathe,*
> *While your rages I must suffer.*
> . . . .
> *Day by day our friendship deepens,*
> *Day by day I'm more like you*
> *Now we've grown so close together,*
> *That I've started raging too.*

Heine's despair was compounded by family quarrels, money problems, and the drudgery of preparing for his final exams. He passed them successfully and formally became a doctor of law. Gustav Hugo, dean of the Göttingen law faculty, who delivered the *laudatio* in Latin, hailed the rare union in Heine of the "dissimilar"—literature and jurisprudence. Speaking of Heine's poetry, he declared, *"Ut ne Goethium quidem eorum poenetire debere"*—Goethe himself would not have been ashamed of such poems.[50]

Despite Heine's repeated assertions to his friends that he would never convert, "To Edom" was the first indication that he, too, would soon have to "howl with the wolves," as he put it. He began to prepare for conversion with the help of Gottlieb Grimm, a country parson sympathetic to his plight, who promised to oversee it with a minimum of fuss. On June 28, 1825, in a mixed mood of cynicism and passive, unheroic fortitude, he traveled in a rainstorm across the nearby Hanover-Prussian border to Heiligenstadt, where nobody except the parson knew who he was. (At the border he was asked the usual "What do you have to declare?" and answered, "Nothing but thoughts and debts!") In Heiligenstadt, a small Prussian parish, Grimm baptized him "in utter secrecy."[51]

"Shortly before ten the bell rang," an eyewitness remembered. The parsonage maid opened the door and announced "the pale Göttingen student who has recently been here." Heine and Grimm closeted themselves upstairs in the parson's study. After a brief interrogation Grimm called a witness and pronounced Heine "a Christian . . . out of urgent inner need and deep conviction." The party then repaired to the parson's living quarters, where a festive family lunch was served to celebrate Heine's baptism and that of the parson's newborn daughter, which the parson had also performed that morning. During lunch Heine hardly spoke. Soon afterward, he excused himself and departed. One witness insisted there was a wet shimmer in his eye; another remarked on his pallor.

Heine's conversion was, like so many others', purely pragmatic. No trace of conviction was involved in the act. He went through the ceremony thoroughly disgusted with himself. Other concerns upset him even more. Would conversion enable him to find a legal or teaching position in Hamburg, Munich, or elsewhere? Would he obtain a measure of financial independence from his family? He hated himself for having to grovel before his rich uncle, the banker Salomon Heine, who had paid his tuition.

Heine was soon deeply sorry for having converted. "I would never have converted if it were permitted to steal silver spoons," he told Moser. "I deeply regret it. I don't see that my situation has improved as a result of it," he added a few months later. "On the contrary, I have had nothing but misfortune!"[52] News of his conversion must have spread for he was now defamed by both Christians and Jews, he complained. Still, his irony did not fail him. From Hamburg, where his rich uncle lived, he wrote Moser: "I am becoming a proper Christian. I sponge off rich Jews."

Six months after Heine's conversion, Eduard Gans also broke down. "If the state is so stupid as to demand that I profess something that the responsible minister knows well that I do not believe, well then—it shall have its way."[53] Gans converted to Christianity and was promptly rewarded with an associate professorship of law at the University of Berlin. Heine exploded with rage: Gans had been the society's captain; he should not have abandoned ship and broken his vow. Moser, Zunz, and other members of the society regarded the defection of their president as an unforgivable act of treason.

The society could not survive this blow and disbanded soon after, ceasing publication of its magazine as well. Heine never really forgave either Gans or himself. If Gans converted "out of conviction, he is a fool, if out of hypocrisy, he is a knave," he wrote Moser. "I will, however, not stop loving him. I confess that I would rather have received news that Gans had been caught stealing silver spoons."[54] In his poem "To an Apostate" he vented his anger at Gans (and at himself) for having "crawled to the cross," the very cross they had so despised:

> See what comes from all that reading
> Schlegel, Haller, Burke and all:
> Yesterday you were a hero
> Look how low the mighty fall.

Heine never published the poem, nor did Gans ever see it. The poem was found in Heine's papers after his death. "I think so often about Gans because I do not want to think about myself," he wrote Moser. "I get up at night and curse myself in front of the mirror."[55]

IN later years, Heine often joked about his conversion, saying "Berlin is well worth a sermon."* He said he had changed his religion only as a courtesy, much as the Russian czar put on the uniform of a Prussian hussar during a state visit to Berlin. Another time he insisted he would never have converted had Napoleon not been defeated

Eduard Gans, upon conversion, was finally given a professorship at the University of Berlin. Earlier, he had commented on the pitfalls of assimilation: "I belong to that unhappy class of men who are hated for having no education and are persecuted for trying to obtain one." *Courtesy Leo Baeck Institute, Jerusalem*

---

*The allusion is to "Paris is well worth a mass," a remark attributed to Henry IV, who converted to Catholicism in order to become king of France.

at Waterloo; his conversion was the fault of Napoleon's geography teacher, who failed to tell him that Moscow winters are very cold. "I was baptized but I did not convert," he told Balzac and other French friends. "All religions are the same; some skin their clients from the top down; others from the bottom up."[56]

The truth was, of course, that Heine had been only marginally Jewish before his baptism and did not become Christian after. As a convert, he identified more with his fellow Jews than ever before. They all belonged to a common community of fate. In the poem "Break Out in Loud Lament," which he wrote shortly after "To Edom," he evoked the "thousand-year-old-pain" to the point of sentimentality:

> And all the tears run southward,
> In silent streams of woe,
> Into the river Jordan:
> One great, unbroken flow.

The poem served as prologue to *The Rabbi of Bacharach*, a historical novel in the manner of Sir Walter Scott, which Heine was writing at the time of his baptism. Only a fragment of the work survives, but it throws an interesting light on Heine's disposition. The novel was the first fictional attempt by a leading German writer to convey the pathos of the German Jewish condition. In it, Heine excoriates a medieval pogrom, celebrates the simple wisdom of an intended victim, a pious rabbi, and hails the beauty of the rabbi's wife while strongly identifying with the assimilationist tendencies of the novel's other protagonist, a witty Jewish freethinker. Like Heine, he loves Jewish cooking but dismisses Jewish religious strictures as superstition. "See how poorly protected Israel is," this character laments by the walls of the Frankfurt ghetto. "On the outside, her gates are guarded by false friends, while inside they are maintained by fear and folly."[57] In *The Rabbi of Bacharach*, biblical imagery meshes with Romantic metaphor, Jewish liturgy with Teutonic fairy tales, the Taunus Mountains with Mount Sinai, the murmur of the Rhine with that of the Jordan.

For all Heine's ambivalence about conversion, his goals were clear: to win an academic or legal position and secure a steady monthly income. He failed in both. A first attempt in Hamburg, where his uncle was an influential citizen, came to nothing. His former religious affiliation should not have been an impediment, as his friend Eduard Gans's professorship in Berlin had just proved, and Felix Mendelssohn-Bartholdy was about to take up the position of concert master at the royal court. Nor should his literary bent have been an obstacle. Nearly all other German writers of note found jobs in the public sector: Novalis, Ludwig Tieck, Goethe, and Joseph von Eichendorff were government officials; Ludwig Uhland, Schlegel, Schiller, Friedrich Rückert, and the brothers Grimm university professors or librarians; Adalbert von Chamisso was a botanist, Eduard Mörike a parson, Kleist a clerk, Karl Immermann a judge. The main reason for Heine's failure must have been his liberal political views.

Instead of a legal or academic job, Heine found an enterprising Hamburg publisher, Julius Campe, willing to bring out a new collection of his poetry. Heine's *Book of Songs*, published in 1827, proved to be the turning point in his career. It made Heine the best-known, best-loved German poet after Goethe. He succeeded in what was urgently needed in the post-Goethe era: "the radical liberation of German poetry from the pathetic, . . . from the hymnlike, the 'dark,' and the 'sublime,'"[58] according to one critic. The poems resonated with what was widely considered the deepest, most authentic, innermost voice of the German "soul."

Some readers refused to believe that a Jew could have such a perfect German ear. Others held against him the fact that his poetry lent itself more easily than other German poetry to translation into foreign languages. Indeed, he would be charged with debasing the German language: "He loosened the bodice of the German language to the point where every petty clerk felt entitled to fondle her breasts," remarked Karl Kraus. On the assumption, common among certain academics, that what is murky and dark is "deep," Heine's enemies criticized his work as shallow; his clarity and lightness were proof of his mediocrity.

This was not how readers felt. Throughout the nineteenth century and for much of the twentieth, generations of readers in Germany and elsewhere in Central Europe recognized some of their most intimate feelings in Heine's poems. The appeal was widespread and profound. Schumann, Schubert, Liszt, and Brahms set them to music. There

à Mᵉ Henri Heine.

LES DEUX GRENADIERS
[Die beiden Grenadiere]
Mélodie de
RICHARD WAGNER

The French translation of one of Heine's most famous poems, celebrating two French grenadiers, was set to music by Richard Wagner. *Courtesy Leo Baeck Institute, Jerusalem*

were more than four thousand musical settings of Heine's poems, twice as many as of Goethe's. His work influenced Richard Wagner's *Tannhäuser* and *The Flying Dutchman,* and Wagner wrote the music for the French translation of Heine's "The Grenadiers."*

Despite the success Heine enjoyed, he remained financially dependent on his uncle. In 1826, when yet another prospective position, as a professor of literature at the University of Munich, failed to materialize—even though the Bavarian minister of education, Eduard von Schenk, recommended him as a "true genius"—Heine fell

*For this composition Wagner was made a chevalier of the French Legion of Honor and awarded an annual pension of twenty thousand francs out of Louis-Philippe's private purse.

into depression. "I feel an overwhelming urge to say good-bye to the German fatherland," he wrote to Moser. "Not so much for the joy of roaming about the world as out of the torment of my personal condition: the Jew in me that can never be washed off is driving me away."[59]

His letters from this time sound tortured. Misery only sharpened his self-irony. "All apostates should feel as wretched as I do," he said.[60] Despairing of his future in Germany, he began to travel, producing a series of remarkable travel pieces about Italy and England. His prose remained as brilliant as his poetry; his innovative style—worldly, urbane, full of esprit and charm—established a new genre, the short essay known as the feuilleton. Heine's travel essays were barbed, sly, and topical—they essentially expanded the range of political literature. Traveling through Italy, at the high point of Austrian repression under Metternich, Heine turned lighthearted feuilletons into discourses on the worldwide struggle between liberty and repression. Napoleon remained his great hero, the son of the French Revolution who had spread the gospel of human rights throughout Europe. Driving past the battlefield of Marengo, where Napoleon had scored a great victory over Austria in 1800, Heine's heart "leaped with joy":

> What is the great task of our time? It is emancipation. Not just of the Irish, the Greeks, the Frankfurt Jews, the West Indian blacks, and other oppressed people. It is the emancipation of the entire world, of Europe in particular. It has come of age and now tears itself loose from the iron reins of the privileged and the aristocracy.[61]

Banned in Austria and the Rhineland, his pieces were all the more widely read.

More than any German writer before him or after, Heine made righteousness *readable*. In his prose, he moved smoothly from the political and serious to the lyrical and dreamy, from the soberly realistic to the ironic and sarcastic. He could be mean and venomously vindictive about people he disliked, including those who published anti-Semitic slurs about him—there were several—and he wasted his energies in futile, furious quarrels, but he was nearly always witty and amusing.

For his humor, Heine was often compared to Aristophanes; it was a gift of the heart rather than the head. His irony was an outgrowth of his pain, a weapon against life's vicissitudes. Some of Heine's critics dismissed his irony as "Jew humor." Moritz Gottlieb Saphir, a fellow writer living in Paris, answered this charge: it was not the Jew in Heine that was funny, he said, but the human condition. "The tragic fate of his people was the source of its humor, the mother-of-vinegar for its wit. Centuries of pain have coated the walls of their brains with thick residues of sarcastic tartar."[62]

Heine's irony was nearly always double-edged. Even as he hailed Jews as an "ethical people," he noted facetiously that in this they resembled Germans. The composer Robert Schumann met Heine in Munich in 1828 and was struck by his warmth. Yet "on Heine's lips there was a bitter ironic smile."[63]

STOPPING in Frankfurt, on his way to Italy in 1827, Heine met the journalist Ludwig Börne. He had admired him for years. The two men had much in common. Both were baptized but remained Jews "psychologically." Both were liberal polemicists, their recurrent theme liberty. In Marcel Reich-Ranicki's memorable phrase, both were "born provocateurs, . . . eternal *Ruhestörer*"—arousers, intellectual troublemakers.[64] Both were at home first and foremost in the language. Their rootlessness provided a kind of Archimedian vantage point from which they assessed the world with greater freedom, wit, and acuity than others could. With Heine and Börne, a new kind of engaged liberal intellect— soon decried as typically "Jewish"—entered German life. Contemporaries found its challenges very appealing, albeit often frightening or uncanny. In the words of Heinrich von Treitschke, a leading mid-nineteenth-century German historian, "With Börne and Heine the eruption of the Jews into German literary history began, an ugly and infertile interlude."

Soon to be the major literary spokesmen of German liberal reform, Heine and Börne had a great deal to talk about. "We were inseparable up to the moment he saw me to the post chaise," Heine reported to August Varnhagen. They talked about Germans, Jews, literature, theater, and religion and quarreled about Napoleon, whom Börne decried for betraying the revolution but whom Heine worshiped as Europe's liberator. They agreed on Goethe's inexcusable aloofness from politics; his indifference to the burning issues of the day was outrageous. Goethe was now a "tame, toothless genius," sheepishly servile to a ridiculous little prince to whom he had been chained like a lapdog for more than half a century.

When he was not spending time with Börne, Heine sat for Moritz Oppenheim, known as "the first German Jewish painter." Heine liked Oppenheim's work. Even more, he liked Frau Oppenheim's cholent and other traditional Sabbath dishes and often spoke of them. Oppenheim's Biedermeier-style portraits of German Jewish life merge the ideals of German patriotism, Jewish piety, and cultural assimilation so common at the time: his *Return of the Jewish Volunteer from the Wars of Liberation,* for example, depicts a wounded soldier (bareheaded) returning to his traditionally observant family (his father wears a skull-cap). Among Oppenheim's patrons were the Rothschilds and Goethe, who as a minister in the duke of Weimar's government procured Oppenheim an honorary title. "Titles and medals can save you from being jostled in a crowd," Goethe assured him.[65]

The painter had studied in Rome with the Nazarenes, a school of Christian genre painters led by, among others, Moses Mendelssohn's grandsons Johannes and Philipp Veit, both staunch Catholics. Oppenheim asked Heine if it was true that he, too, had converted. Heine brushed the question aside. It was vastly more painful nowadays to have a tooth pulled than to convert, he quipped.

Oppenheim also painted a formal portrait of Börne. In their portraits both men display pale, determined, long faces; passionate, flashing eyes; firm, sensuous lips; strong, well-shaped noses. Börne looks up sharply with an air of curious expectancy, as though awaiting the answer to a terribly serious question; he wears a bright scarf under a fur-lined yellow coat. Heine, delicate as a porcelain figurine, wears soft velvet and a white open collar. He clenches his right fist.

Börne was the elder by eleven years. Unlike Heine, who grew up a free man, he was born in the Frankfurt ghetto at a time when Jews were still locked into the cavernous Judengasse at sunset and on Sundays and Christian holidays. In his youth, Börne and his tutor had been ordered off the paved sidewalk outside the ghetto; Jews were supposed to use only the muddy carriageway. He had to doff his hat to any urchin who met him in the street crying *"Jud, mach Mores!"*—Jew, show your manners. Long after his conversion, Börne wrote:

> As I was born a slave, I love freedom more than you. As I grew up a slave, I understand freedom better than you. As I had no fatherland to call my own, I long for it more passionately than you. And as the country of my birth was no bigger than the Judengasse, where beyond its gates lay the wide, uncharted world, so it takes more than a city to satisfy my yearning, more than a county, more than a province—it takes the whole great fatherland, as far as its language is spoken.[66]

Börne led Heine through what remained of the dark, prisonlike Judengasse. The bleak, dilapidated houses in the old ghetto evoked "sad stories one would rather forget."[67] The gates had been torn down but the high wall was still standing. "Look at this street," Börne sighed, daring Heine "to praise the Middle Ages," as so many Romantic German poets and fashionable historians were doing just then. Only the poorest Jews were still living in the Judengasse. The one exception was Meyer Amschel Rothschild's widow, who refused to vacate the old family home.

Börne came from a family of former court Jews. Like Heine, he was alienated from his family's commercial roots. He had little sympathy for people who spoke admiringly of Rothschild's riches as "an art lover speaks of Raphael's paintings." He had been one of a half dozen lucky ghetto boys sent to be educated in the new Free Schools in Halle and Berlin. As a teenager, Börne had attended Henriette Herz's famous salon. His adoption of Christianity in 1813 may have been more sincere than Heine's; he had not been in search of an academic or legal job. Like Heine, he soon regretted his conversion. The clergyman had charged three gold pieces for his services—three gold pieces for a tiny corner of the German nuthouse, as Börne put it. It had been a waste of money: "It's a miracle! I've gone through it a thousand times but each time I experience it as something new. Some reproach me for being a Jew; others forgive me for being one; there are even those who commend me for the same—but there's no one able to put this fact out of his mind. They all seem bound by the spell of this magic Jewish circle, from which none are able to escape."[68]

The abrogation of the emancipation edict and the *Hep! Hep!* riots—in Frankfurt they were among the worst—had shocked Börne badly. He bemoaned the "monstrous *Judenschmerz*" (he seems to have coined the expression), "the immense pain that was the Jews', handed on from one generation to the next . . . the dark, inexplicable horror that fills the Jewish people, haunting Christendom from the cradle like a sneering specter or the ghost of a murdered mother."[69] He now claimed it was his good fortune to be a Jew; his birth made him a citizen of the world. Moreover, he did not need to feel shame at being a German, because he was a Jew. He could enjoy the virtues of the Germans without sharing the flaws.

In 1808, when Börne was twenty-two and legally stateless, his native city, where his ancestors had lived since the sixteenth century, issued him a passport. Like Nazi passports 118 years later, it declared its bearer a Jew. He was determined to get even with the malicious authorities, vowing that one day he would be the one issuing passports for *them*. In a way, he made good on his vow, becoming a virtuosic polemicist with a cutting tongue. Heine claimed that while he himself was an "ordinary guillotine," Börne was a "steam-powered" one. One of the best-known and most-feared liberal journalists of his era, he was not an ideologue and had no fixed doctrine. Without being a socialist, he was among Europe's most challenging and humane social critics. In the heyday of Hegelian worship of the state, he argued in favor of as little state power as possible.

Nations, he believed, must be subjected to the same moral strictures as individuals. He was among the first of many German Jews who spent their lives in a ceaseless effort to civilize German patriotism. Jews had a special role to play in the task of taming the nationalist monster, he maintained: "They are the teachers of cosmopolitanism. The whole world is their school. For this reason they are also teachers of liberty."

Nothing was more dangerous to liberty than excessive patriotism, a "deceitful virtue that in its fervor surpassed all other known human vices." Börne was also the first to insist that Jewish emancipation and the emancipation of all humanity were inseparable. In this he anticipated Marx, Ferdinand Lassalle, Eduard Bernstein, Rosa Luxemburg, Léon Blum, and many other social reformers.

While Börne's literary output was vast, he never wrote a book, only essays and short journalistic comments. Despite frequent exaggerations, occasional factual errors, and unfounded assertions, his writings mirrored the finest liberal sensibilities of the time and remain readable and of interest to this day. His *Collected Works* in eight volumes came out in 1829 and was an instant classic, banned and then reprinted again and again (most recently in 1992). Determined to cure the ills of his "poor, sick fatherland," Börne was the archetype of the liberal Jewish man of letters. He brought the spirit of "the eighteenth century into nineteenth-century Germany; the century of the French Revolution into the century that mounted the Great War," Ludwig Marcuse, one of his biographers, wrote in 1929.[70]

Börne was fearless, undeterred by censorship, fines, and threats of arrest. In 1818, he founded a magazine, *Die Wage* (meaning "scales" but also suggesting "audacity" or "daring"), as a vehicle for his views. Like most radical liberals of his time he had a naïve faith in the power of public opinion and in the essential goodness of man. In the magazine's inaugural editorial, he wrote hopefully: "No one will deny what public opinion calls for, if the demand be in earnest. Petitions not granted are ones indifferently pursued."[71] Like the trumpets that toppled the walls of Jericho, public opinion would bring down despotism and tyranny. *Die Wage* elicited interest far beyond Frankfurt. Metternich's secretary, Friedrich von Gentz, told Rahel Varnhagen that Börne wrote the finest German prose since Lessing. He was less pleased, of course, with Börne's politics. Metternich himself—architect of the post-Napoleonic repression of liberalism on the European continent—tried in vain to shut Börne up with offers of title, rank, and the income of an imperial counselor, ostensibly without any reciprocal commitment on Börne's part, if he would live in Vienna. Like Heine, Börne was one of Rahel

Varnhagen's favorites. Indeed, she worshiped him. In one letter, she offered to be his flag bearer, his drummer and trumpeter, his field chaplain, as well as his laundress and canteen woman.[72]

HE "is a much better man than I, a greater man, but not as grandiose," Heine wrote Rahel and August Varnhagen in April 1828. Heine was radicalized by the encounter, though not as much as Börne would have liked, and the two men soon quarreled bitterly. Their quarrel was one of the most celebrated in nineteenth-century German letters.[73] Heine was not single-minded enough for Börne; too much the Romantic poet, too playful, he was talented but lacking in character. He only dabbled in politics; poetry was more important to him. For his part, Heine did not share Börne's optimism and simple faith in the power of public opinion. And he was embarrassed to be regarded, along with Börne, as a leading spirit of so-called Young Germany, the collective name given to several radical writers whose works were declared subversive. He was no less radical than they were. But he wanted to be his own man.

Heine spent the next three years living and writing in Munich, Hamburg, and Berlin and on the North Sea coast. In the summer of 1830, during a stormy affair with a young soprano with the Hamburg opera, he found himself on the little island of Helgoland, a British naval base at the mouth of the river Elbe. Once again he was waiting for a response to an application for public appointment. In a fit of depression over the futility of his political journalism, he wrote a friend:

> For my part, I'm tired of this guerilla war and need to rest. It's strange that I, of all people, was rousted from my tranquil life just to find myself rushing around, at odds with the censors and the police. . . . And what good has it done me . . . to shake your average German from his thousand-year hibernation? He merely opens his eyes for a moment, blinks, and shuts them once again; his yawns only make his snoring louder. . . . Where can I find someplace to rest? I should get hold of a German nightcap myself and pull it all the way down over my ears. . . . In Germany it's impossible; at any moment a constable might come along and shake me—just to see if I was really asleep.[74]

"This is how I looked this morning, April 16, 1829." *Courtesy Leo Baeck Institute, Jerusalem*

He spent the morning dozing in the sun on the dunes and the rest of the day with his lover and his books in a room he had rented from a local fisherman. He had brought along the Old Testament, Homer's *Iliad* and *Odyssey*, a history of the Longobards, and several texts on witch trials in medieval Germany. They were intended to transport him to another time and place and supply ideas for literary projects. The Old Testament seized his fancy: "Sweet, sunny Holy Land! How pleasantly one reposes beneath thy tents."

The report of a sudden upheaval in France shook him out of his sun-drenched lethargy and gave a new direction to his life. Mail arrived on Helgoland only once a week. Heine had been reading about the war between the Heruleans and the Longobards when a thick package of newspapers reached him from the mainland. "Sunbeams wrapped in newsprint," he exclaimed. A revolution had broken out in France. Charles X, the senile Bourbon despot who had tried to dismiss parliament and abolish freedom of the press, had been forced to abdicate. Heine was exuberant. "The Gallic cock has crowed for the second time." It seemed at first like a dream—the tricolor flying over Paris once again, the crowd singing the "Marseillaise" outside the National Assembly. As a small child, he had been told about all this by his mother. What had for so long been a fairy tale was becoming true. Lafayette himself was commanding the Paris national guard.

A few days later, he noted grandiloquently: "Gone is my longing for peace and quiet. Once again I know what I want, what I ought, what I must do. . . . I am a son of the revolution and will take up arms." An old fisherman, he reported, told him, "The poor have finally scored a victory." Then again he wondered if he was going mad. One of those "sunbeams wrapped in newsprint" had struck his brain, and his thoughts were "in a white glow." He left Helgoland, and presumably his lover, taking the next boat and rushing back to Hamburg. The revolution, meanwhile, was spreading to Belgium, Spain, Greece, Parma, Modena, the Papal States, and Poland. Would that it would break out in Germany too.

Two hundred miles away, in Soden, a small health resort in the Taunus Mountains, another vacationer was as thrilled and agitated as Heine. Ludwig Börne was recuperating from a bad attack of gout but braved his pain to walk on the country road each morning to meet the postman halfway and get the latest news half an hour earlier. Hopelessly optimistic at first, Börne expected royal heads to roll all over Europe; a dozen eggs would soon be worth more than a dozen princes. He abandoned his cure and rushed back to Frankfurt, but his restlessness soon drove him on to Paris. A man of independent means, he could afford to live and travel anywhere he pleased. As he crossed the Rhine at Strasbourg, he was thrilled to see the first revolutionary rosette affixed to a French peasant's cap. In Börne's eyes, the rosette was like a tricolored rainbow after the deluge. He noted with disgust that while France and Italy were in an uproar and the Poles were rising against the Russians and the Greeks against the Turks, the Germans remained servile and obedient to their thirty-six despotic rulers. The only uproar in Germany had come in the form of more *Hep! Hep!* riots in Hamburg, Breslau, Mannheim, Munich, and Karlsruhe.

Soon Paris also disappointed Börne. The July Revolution resulted in a few bankers and industrialists making more money than before and appointing a new king more to their liking. The French bourgeoisie repelled him: "no sooner have they emerged victorious—even before they've managed to wipe the sweat from their brows—than they set about establishing a new aristocracy, one that is governed by money." Börne's *Letters from Paris,* published over the next three years in three volumes, are a colorful record of the aftermath of the capsized revolution, a personal, argumentative, outraged record. The *Letters* were, in fact, excerpted from private missives he sent weekly to the woman he loved, a lady in Frankfurt named Jeanette Wohl, who extracted the strongest parts for serial publication. They were probably the best writing Börne ever produced. In some places they were banned as soon as they came out, but it was not difficult to obtain copies. Books outlawed in one German state were freely printed in another, and the borders between states were not sealed. Censorship was still a rather benign affair: prior review was mandatory only for publications of less than 280 pages, on the assumption, apparently, that only oddballs or harmless scholars would read fatter books than that.

WHILE Börne was writing the first of his letters, Heine found his own thoughts were losing their "white glow." He lingered in Hamburg agonizing over his money problems. At the age of thirty-three, he was still financially dependent on his family; the royalties from his books were not enough to live on. In September he witnessed the *Hep! Hep!* riots in Hamburg, during which the mob smashed the windows of his uncle's town house. His application for the position of legal officer in the Hamburg senate was still pending. Börne, learning of Heine's application from a Hamburg newspaper, was appalled. He could see why, in such volatile times, a government would want a genius like Heine tied down in "an administrative position or a professorship," he wrote Jeanette Wohl. But he could not understand Heine's motive: "only a fool would allow himself to be trapped."

In February 1831, the Hamburg senate rejected Heine's application. Börne proposed that Heine join him in publishing a new magazine, which they would print in Switzerland to evade censorship. Börne had another brainstorm as well: he and Heine should exchange weekly letters on politics and art and publish them in book form every three or four months. Nothing came of this plan either, possibly for the best. The two men might have inspired and excited each other but probably they would have quarreled even more.

"Every night, I dream that I am packing my suitcase for Paris, to breathe fresh air," Heine wrote August Varnhagen early in April 1831. A week later he finally left. The liberal newspaper *Augsburger Allgemeine Zeitung* had made Heine an offer he could not refuse: to be its correspondent in Paris. He was in no hurry, though, to get there. He traveled slowly, stopping over in Frankfurt, Heidelberg, Karlsruhe, and Strasbourg. Everywhere he went he was celebrated by young people for his poems and by liberals for his politics. In mid-July, Heine finally arrived in France. He claimed later that he had actually crossed the French border on May Day. This claim gave birth to the legend that the first of May was chosen as the international workers' day to commemorate Heine's escape to freedom.

HEINE's stay in Paris was meant to be temporary. As it turned out, he remained there until his death in 1856, returning to Germany only briefly on two occasions to visit his elderly mother. "I had to choose between laying down my arms completely or fighting my whole life," he wrote to Varnhagen, "and I chose the latter." He had no choice in taking up arms; the path of struggle had been forced on him in the cradle by "other people's scorn," he explained to Varnhagen, whose sister Maria visited him in Paris in 1835 and wrote her brother: "He is extremely happy and, understandably, not at all homesick for Germany."[75]

From Heine's first days in Paris, he was kept under surveillance by Prussian and Austrian agents, who reported rumors about his love affairs, politics, witticisms, anti-Prussian remarks, and reputed quarrels with other German exiles, who, according to one agent, were "a mishmash of political refugees, would-be poets, failed businessmen, loafers, buffoons, and adventurers of all kinds, mostly Jews."[76] One Austrian

spy suggested to his superiors that offering Heine a bribe might blunt
his sharp pen. In the margin of this report, someone in Vienna noted
that the danger Heine posed was "disproportionate to the financial sacrifice needed to win him over and keep him."[77] The Prussians took his
barbs more seriously. The Paris embassy was instructed to approach the
foreign ministry and demand Heine's expulsion. The French rejected
the Prussian overture.

Heine very quickly won the admiration of France's leading writers—
Victor Hugo, Honoré de Balzac, George Sand, Alexandre Dumas,
Alphonse de Lamartine, and Alfred de Musset. His poetry came out in
French though, according to Heine, the translations were more like
"moonlight stuffed with straw."[78] The French called him Monsieur
Aynn. George Sand considered him her "cousin." Théophile Gautier
described him as "a German Apollo" for his striking good looks and
shock of blond hair, "a charming god" with none of the affectations of
the other Romantic German exiles "but malicious as a devil."[79] Dumas
said, "If Germany rejects Heine we will willingly adopt him. Unfortunately, Heine loves Germany more than it deserves."[80] He became intimate with Baron James de Rothschild (like Börne, a native of the
Frankfurt ghetto) and often visited him in his office, where "not only
the chosen people but all other people bow and pay obeisance." Rothschild treated Heine quite "famillionairish." At dinner one night at the
baron's new palace on the rue Laffitte, conversation turned to the increasing pollution of the Seine. Rothschild had recently visited the river's
source and remarked that its waters were crystal clear there. "*Monsieur
le baron*, your late father is also said to have been a very honest man,"
Heine quipped. Rothschild, apparently, did not catch the barb. The
other guests bit their tongues.

Heine loved Paris. He felt "like a fish in water" or like "Tannhäuser
imprisoned in the Venusberg." His French was near perfect, though
inflected with a heavy German accent. He was expert at "handling the
French, with their self-importance and hollow arrogance," a Prussian
agent reported.[81] Interviews with Heine continued to appear in the
German press. His interviewers wondered endlessly whether he was
"homesick"; the idea that so important a German poet preferred to live
in France mystified and disturbed them.

Despite his predilection for France, Heine never became a French citizen. He did, however, marry a young French woman, whom he loved passionately. Mathilde Heine was a devout Catholic, ignorant of both her husband's poetry and his Jewishness. She disliked Germans, considering them priggish, arrogant, self-righteous, ill-mannered, and generally unbearable. Heine's German friends were annoyed by her simplemindedness but Heine only laughed when they complained. One of Heine's German acquaintances, the poet Alfred Meissner, a Christian, took Mathilde to task for her prejudice. Years later, Kafka imagined the scene that followed:

> "But you don't know the Germans at all," [Meissner] told her. "After all, the only people Heinrich sees are journalists, and here in Paris all of them are Jewish." "Oh," said Mathilde, "you're exaggerating, there might be a Jew among them here and there, for instance Seiffert—" "No," said Meissner, "he's the only one who isn't Jewish." "What?" said Mathilde, "you mean that Jeitteles (a large, strong, blond man) is Jewish?" "Absolutely," said Meissner. "But what about Bamberger?" "Bamberger too." "But Arnstein?" "The same." . . . Finally Mathilde got annoyed and said: "You're just pulling my leg, in the end you'll claim that Kohn is a Jewish name too, but Kohn is one of Heinrich's nephews and Heinrich is Lutheran."[82]

Börne, of course, showed no such naïveté. He recalled a church wedding in Paris a few months after Heine's arrival where both he and Heine signed as witnesses. "The ways of fate," he remarked. "Here a baptized Jew from Frankfurt is marrying a Christian woman from England—God only knows what her origins are. The wedding's in Paris and of the four witnesses, one is a Christian, one is a Jew, and two are converts who happen to be leading German writers and the pride of the German federation."

By 1835, the works of both Heine and Börne—"evil, anti-Christian, blasphemous, willfully defying all virtue, humility, and honor"—headed the lists of banned books in several German states. Metternich considered Heine "the best mind among the conspirators," referring to Young Germany. Although Heine and Börne were the only Jews among more than a dozen banned writers associated with Young Germany, it was often derided as Young Palestine. While Gentz confessed that he regularly immersed himself in "the melancholy sweet waters" of Heine's marvelous poetry, he decried the politics of this "infamous adventurer," now sitting in Paris defaming aristocrats and clergymen as well as respectable property owners and businessmen. "Who does he think ought to govern?" Gentz wondered. Frederick William IV of Prussia had Heine in mind when he snarled at the "despicable clique of Jews who in their speech, writing, and example daily strike at the root of what is German."[83] His police issued a warrant for Heine's arrest. Heine's name and description ("markedly Jewish type") appeared on wanted lists posted at Prussian border crossings.[84] The warrant remained in effect for years. To evade the Prussian police, Heine traveled by steamship from Le Havre to Hamburg in 1844 to visit his mother one last time.

In France, Heine became the classic German poet of homesickness, an affliction that during the first half of the next century would become widespread among German Jews. He would now write his most beautiful poetry and his sharpest critiques and satires of German politics and manners. Germans claimed that they believed in "ideas" that would conquer the world and yet, as Heine saw it, they cowered before every petty despot. He voiced the first, most acute prophecies about German nationalism and militarism. His darkest forebodings reveal a stunning, uncanny prescience. He warned his German readers that they were their own worst enemies. And he warned his French readers that Germans were not necessarily the idealistic thinkers and poets and unworldly philosophers described by the gullible Madame de Staël in her famous panegyric *On Germany*. He expressed his forebodings, remarkably, long before the establishment of a powerful united Reich when Germany was still fractured into thirty-six sovereignties and petty principalities. As early as 1834, he saw the demons lurking under the surface of German life and warned the French:

Watch out! I mean well with you and therefore I tell you the bitter truth. You have more to fear from a liberated Germany than from the entire Holy Alliance along with all Croats and Cossacks.

A drama will be enacted in Germany compared to which the French Revolution will seem like a harmless idyll. Christianity restrained the martial ardor of the Germans for a time but it did not destroy it; once the restraining talisman is shattered, savagery will rise again, . . . the mad fury of the berserk, of which Nordic poets sing and speak. . . . The old stony gods will rise from the rubble and rub the thousand-year-old dust from their eyes. Thor with the giant hammer will come forth and smash the gothic domes.

The German thunder . . . rolls slowly at first but it will come. And when you hear it roar, as it has never roared before in the history of the world, know that the German thunder has reached its target.[85]

Heine's intuitions about Communism, an obscure political movement during his lifetime, and about future dictatorships and wars were equally remarkable. In 1842, he wrote:

Though Communism is at present little talked about, vegetating in forgotten attics on miserable straw pallets, it is nevertheless the dismal hero destined to play a great, if transitory, role in the modern tragedy. . . . [It will be] the old absolutist tradition . . . but in different clothes and with new slogans and catch-phrases. . . . There will then be only *one* shepherd with an iron crook and *one* identically shorn, identically bleating human herd. . . . Somber times loom ahead. . . . I advise our grandchildren to be born with very thick skin.[86]

That same year, he wrote one of the most extraordinary pieces of political poetry in European literature. *Germany: A Winter's Tale*, an epic travelogue in verse, begins with Heine crossing into Germany at the Belgian border and ends two months later in Hamburg.* Its hallmark is irony and tough-mindedness. Wherever he turned on this

---

*It has been suggested that Heine wrote *A Winter's Tale* under the influence of a young exile he had just met, Karl Marx, but the evidence is not convincing and Heine's comments on Communism make it unlikely. His reaction to Communism conveys only fear and foreboding. The ideal world he postulates in *A Winter's Tale* is a poetic, decidedly un-Marxist one, free of political, social, and religious prejudice.

poetic journey he was distressed to discover how little things had changed since he had left: the same wooden, pedantic people, the same Romantic cult of the Middle Ages, the same fusion of reactionary politics and Christianity, the same religious prejudice. Writing about Cologne and its great, still unfinished cathedral (he was chairman of the Paris fund-raising committee for its construction), he observed:

> *Malice and stupidity*
> *Like street dogs here ran loose*
> *Their breed can still be recognized*
> *By their hatred of Jews.*

The liberal French writer François Wille read these lines in draft. "What business do you still have with the Jews?" he asked Heine. "You sympathize with neither their religion nor their nationality. You ridicule one nationalism. Why should you suddenly show a weakness for another?" Heine saw the force of this argument and changed the text:

> *Malice and stupidity*
> *Like street dogs used to mate*
> *Their breed can still be recognized*
> *In their sectarian hate.*[87]

He was not indifferent, however, to the lot of oppressed Jews, whether in Germany or in Damascus, and he continued to write warmly about them and their culture. He resented Felix Mendelssohn-Bartholdy's preoccupation with Christian music and wrote Ferdinand Lassalle in 1846: "I cannot forgive this man of independent means that he sees fit to serve the Christian pietists with his great and enormous talent. The more I admire his greatness, the more angry I am to see it so iniquitously misused. If I had the good fortune to be Moses Mendelssohn's grandson, I would not use my talents to set the piss of the Lamb to music."* Heine roared with laughter upon hearing the

---

*After a long struggle, Mendelssohn-Bartholdy had successfully revived Bach's nearly forgotten *Passion of St. Matthew*. He could not help exclaiming that it took a Jew to revive this most sacred Christian music.

sheepish reaction of another Mendelssohn grandson, the pious Catholic painter Philipp Veit, when told that his grandfather had firmly refused Lavater's attempt to baptize him. Veit said, "Who knows how he must now atone!"[88]

There always remained in Heine something of the hunted animal, restless, perpetually on guard. His friend Heinrich Laube, another exponent of Young Germany, reminded him of his eminent position in German letters and his European fame. Was he not being a little paranoid? Could he not relax a bit? Heine retorted: "How can I, in this skin of mine, which originally came from Palestine and which the Christians have been tanning for eighteen hundred years? And the holy baptismal water hasn't helped a bit."[89]

A Winter's Tale unleashed widespread criticism. Heine was accused of being insolent, "un-German from the bottom up."[90] The antisemitic historian Heinrich Treitschke credited Heine with possession of a dubious gift shared by Frenchmen and Jews alike, "the graceful vice of making the mean and loathsome attractive for a moment." Yet his fame continued to spread inside Germany as well as abroad, where he was swiftly becoming one of the great heroes of European culture.

Heine's "The Silesian Weavers," another powerful political poem, protested the exploitation of workers in the sweatshops of Silesia. It attracted as wide an audience as *A Winter's Tale*. Occasioned by a rebellion of famished linen weavers in two small Silesian villages that was brutally put down by government troops, the poem stands as one of the strongest indictments of early capitalism ever written. The weavers are depicted at their looms:

> *In gloomy eyes there wells no tear,*
> *Grinding their teeth, they are sitting here:*
> *"Germany, your shroud's on our loom,*
> *And in it we weave the threefold doom.*
> *We weave, we weave."*

The "threefold doom" is a curse on the God who was deaf to their prayers, a curse on the "the rich man's king" who was not moved by their suffering, a curse on their false fatherland, where nothing thrives but shame and disgrace. "We weave, we weave."

HEINE's last seven years were spent in the throes and excruciating pain of a viral disease that paralyzed half his body and severely affected his vision. Bedridden for the rest of his life, a seventy-pound skeleton, half blind and often unable to speak, he lay buried in what he called his mattress tomb. Yet he retained his creative powers to the end. He wrote almost to his last day. When he could not write, he dictated breathtakingly beautiful poetry and brilliant literary and political prose.

Upon seeing his emaciated face distorted by pain and paralysis, visitors spoke of a "head like Christ and the smile of a devil." ("Why not!" Heine retorted. "Christ, too, was a Jew.") As his isolation and restrictions grew, the geographic range of his prose and poetry became broader and

On his deathbed, Heine told his weeping wife, Mathilde: "God will forgive me; that's his job." Portrait by Ernst Benedict Kietz (1851). *Courtesy Leo Baeck Institute, Jerusalem*

the themes more universal, from slavery in the United States to feudalism in Russia. Increasingly incapacitated, the erstwhile pagan drew closer to what he called God, but in his own way, self-mocking and ironic. "Now that I must think hourly of my death I conduct serious conversations at night with Yehovah," he said. "I have come back to God . . . after tending the pigs for so long among the Hegelians."[91] Attempts to explain—or exploit—this denouement continue to this day. Opinions are still divided.

Heine certainly did not return to organized religion. He considered himself the great Spinoza's *Unglaubensgenosse*—his brother in disbelief—a term Freud would later apply to himself. He continued to despise the "rotten clergical scum" of all faiths: rabbis, pastors, mullahs, and priests. He wanted no Mass sung and no Kaddish said at his grave. On his tombstone he wished to be identified only as a German poet. "If I could walk with crutches I'd go to church, and if I could walk without I'd go to the whorehouse," he told a visitor.[92] He was still his own man, neither Jew nor Christian. His wife, whom he had married in a Catholic ceremony only to please her, wept at his deathbed. "Don't be afraid, my dear," he said. "God will forgive me; that's his job."

5

Spring of Nations

ON February 25, 1848, word of yet another French revolution reached the university town of Heidelberg. The young Ludwig Bamberger heard the news as he was sitting quietly at home, reading. He was a twenty-five-year-old law and philosophy student who had recently received a doctorate from the university. Since, as a Jew, he was still barred from practicing law, his future, as he put it, was "cast in deepest darkness."[1] He was wondering what he might do next. At midday, he was startled to hear someone under his window calling his name.

Two friends were outside shouting "Bamberger! A revolution in Paris! Bamberger! The king is gone!" He threw on his coat and rushed downstairs. His friends knew only that there had been an uprising in France and the people had deposed Louis-Philippe. The news put Bamberger and his friends in a state of high excitement. As a dedicated reader of radical French newspapers, Bamberger had half expected this to happen. He fondly recalled the moment in the memoirs he wrote more than half a century later, at the end of a long public career as a revolutionary, an exile, and, eventually, a prominent Reichstag deputy. He foresaw a "new world being born in one stroke."[2]

In France only, however. Nobody expected a revolution in Germany, where everything was still "so tightly swaddled in the diapers of sleepy, petty police states that one could not entertain even vague hopes for change." Nearly everybody Bamberger knew was of the same opinion. Within the next few days, they would be proven wrong. Sixteen months later, Bamberger would be a political refugee in Switzerland, sentenced to death in absentia for high treason and rebellion.

Bamberger was a native of Mainz, whose small Jewish community had been in existence for hundreds of years. Strong French influences had persisted in Mainz long after the end of Napoleonic rule. Indeed, it was one of the few cities in southwestern Germany where French reforms were informally retained and the social condition of Jews did not deteriorate. The gates of the Jewish ghetto had been ceremoniously lifted off their hinges by troops of the French Revolution as early as 1791, and the event was still celebrated annually with fireworks. Young townsmen of all faiths had fought in Napoléon's grand army. After his fall, popular sentiment in favor of constitutional parliamentary rule continued to run high in the city.

Bamberger was born in this relatively hospitable place in 1823. He came from a family of cosmopolitan bankers with far-reaching European interests and connections. On his mother's side (and later through his wife) he was related to August Belmont, the New York financier and sportsman, and to the Bischoffsheims, a French-German banking family. Bamberger's early years, much like Heine's in Düsseldorf, were pleasant. In the Catholic lycée he attended there was no friction between Christians and Jews. His best friend was a Catholic boy. "I often helped my Catholic fellow students make up their lists of sins for confession. The more sins a boy listed the prouder he was. I can still hear them say, 'Hey, Bamberger, have you got another good sin for me?'"[3] The abbés, Bamberger recalled, were relaxed and open-minded. French books and Börne's outlawed *Letters from Paris* passed from hand to hand. When he won a school prize, he was awarded a bound copy of a well-known radical book, François-Auguste Mignet's *History of the*

French Revolution. Bamberger was also an avid reader of Mignet's fiercely anti-Restoration *Courrier Français* and other republican magazines, such as *Charivari* and *Le National.*

At Heidelberg, Bamberger was well-liked and integrated into the social life of the university. Like many other young intellectuals of Jewish origin, he was a freethinker by conviction, a republican, and a follower of the early French utopian socialists Saint-Simon, Jean-Baptiste-Joseph Fourier, Louis Blanc, and Pierre-Joseph Proudhon. His tolerant indifference to all religions led some to say of him that he was a son not of the synagogue but of the emancipation. The degree of his social acceptance by his peers reflected the great strides German Jews of a certain class had made since the days of Moses Mendelssohn.

The possibility of revolution in Germany seeming to Bamberger remote, he convinced his friends to board the next train to the nearest French town and join the revolution there. Late that same night the three young men arrived in Strasbourg. Despite the late hour the city was in a festive mood. The walls were draped in revolutionary flags. The town hall was brightly lit. The streets were crowded with celebrating students, who invited Bamberger and his friends to attend the republican ceremonies the next day at the town hall. The following morning, Bamberger discovered that they had been promoted overnight to the "official delegation" from the German universities to republican Strasbourg. Wherever they went, the young Germans were cheered, given seats of honor, and asked to make speeches. Bamberger gloried in this role. His two friends, "who were less possessed by political demons than I," were more circumspect.[4] They grew nervous. Unlike Bamberger, who already had his doctorate, they still had to take their final exams. They feared that the newspapers might carry news of their doings back to Heidelberg and cause trouble with the authorities, even get them expelled from the university.

On their way back to Heidelberg, they had to change trains at Karlsruhe, capital of the Grand Duchy of Baden. The Karlsruhe station was in a complete uproar. To their utter astonishment, the young men heard that revolution was rumbling in the city and the nearby countryside. Petitions were circulating calling for the establishment of "a people's militia, education, and freedom for all." The grand duke of Baden was reportedly sequestered in a castle behind moats and high walls. Thousands were streaming into Karlsruhe for a mass demonstration to declare a republic, and more were said to be gathering in the countryside, preparing an armed uprising. The station was crowded with arriving militants and awash with rumors. The authorities were said to have made a futile attempt to block access to the city but trains from Heidelberg and Mannheim kept rolling in. Bamberger sent his friends on alone and remained in Karlsruhe for the planned demonstration.

To nearly everyone's surprise, the unrest spread far beyond Karlsruhe and Mannheim. It had started in Paris and Vienna and from there it was now leaping with remarkable speed to the main German cities. Across Europe, the declared aim of the rebels was to put an end to despotism and to inequalities under the law. In Poland, people were calling for liberation from Russian, Prussian, and Austrian rule. In Karlsruhe, as almost everywhere else in the German lands, the rebels were demanding universal suffrage, freedom of the press, and general elections to an all-German democratic parliament. Newspapers defied censorship. Citizens' militias were formed to ensure the success of the uprising.

In Vienna, the emperor panicked. He dismissed the hated chancellor Metternich, in hopes of saving his throne, allegedly with the words "Had I known how much they despised Metternich, I would have given him away long ago." The rebels were not content with this measure; they demanded much more. Unrest spread to Berlin, where the Prussian king was negotiating with the revolutionaries, and within a week it reached Mainz, where Bamberger, recently returned, was widely known as "red Ludwig," a fiery public speaker and columnist for a local daily. Among many other places, uprisings also occurred in Konstanz, Breslau, Frankfurt, Leipzig, Hamburg, Dresden, Düsseldorf, and Munich, where the people rose up against the king and his mistress, Lola Montez, an Irish woman who claimed to be an exotic Spanish dancer.

Jews had only recently begun to emerge into the light after centuries of injustice; nearly everywhere, they were naturally among the rebels and, in some cities, among the leaders. Ludwig Börne, who had died in exile eleven years earlier, was on many people's minds. "Oh, if only you could rise now to witness all this, Ludovico Börne!" the seventeen-year-old student Leopold Sonnemann (later the publisher of the liberal *Frankfurter Zeitung*) wrote ecstatically in his diary on February 29.[5] In Leipzig, a Viennese student named Hermann Jellinek, one of the leaders of the local uprising, evoked the same name ("Börne, the prophet of German liberation"). Jellinek's brother Adolf, later chief rabbi of Vienna, urged all young Jews to join the revolution. Many heeded his call. Every Jew is born a soldier of freedom, Jellinek proclaimed in *Der Orient*, a widely read Jewish literary magazine. "His religion teaches him to be free, to pursue equal rights, and to defend the oppressed."[6]

The leading Jewish family magazine, the *Allgemeine Zeitung des Judentums*, on March 11 called upon its readers to join this "timely movement sincerely and with all your hearts." The editors of the religiously traditional, politically conservative magazine *Der Treue Zionswächter*, normally eager to please the authorities, found the courage to announce that their fondest dreams were coming true. *Der Orient* printed news of the uprisings under the hopeful headline "United States of Germany."

In the euphoria of the first days, a German poet declared hopefully that "monarchy is dead, though the monarchs still live." For two or three weeks it appeared that the monarchies might indeed be dead. The demise of the French monarchy under the guillotine was still fresh in the minds of German despots. Faced with street demonstrations they were unable or reluctant to crush, kings and princelings scrambled to offer concessions and compromises. Their concessions, as one revolutionary freely conceded, were due more to "French corpses" than to the efforts of their German subjects. The rebels were remarkably reluctant to press their cause, and, awed by their despotic rulers, they were almost everywhere ready to meet them more than halfway. Except in Berlin—and later in Vienna—there were relatively few casualties. In most cases the demonstrators were orderly, heeding their leaders' warnings that anyone caught smashing a public lantern would pay a heavy fine.

But for a few glorious weeks the upheavals of the spring and early summer of 1848 promised to inaugurate a new era in public life. To placate the rebels, German rulers rushed to appoint prominent liberals, as ministers in the governments of Prussia, Bavaria, Saxony, Württemberg, Hesse, Hanover, and elsewhere. On April 1, a "pre-parliament" met in Frankfurt to plan general elections to an all-German National Assembly. The delegates included five prominent German Jews: Gabriel Riesser, a Hamburg jurist; Johann Jacoby, a doctor from Königsberg; the popular novelist Berthold Auerbach from Heidelberg; Julius Fürst and Ignaz Kuranda, journalists from Vienna and Berlin. In addition, four recently converted Jews—the jurists Heinrich Simon, Karl Rudolf Friedenthal (a future Prussian minister of agriculture), Maximilian Reinganum, and Moritz Heckscher—also participated in the sessions. Such appointments would have been inconceivable only a few weeks earlier, as would the citizens' militias that now sprouted everywhere, armed with guns seized from princely arsenals. Before the uprisings, most reigning despots had refused to allow a constitution to come, as they put it, "between them and their peoples." Liberal constitutions were now solemnly promised in most German states and in some cases granted, at least temporarily, with a semblance of goodwill.

Since Frederick William IV of Prussia had only a short time before seriously considered reviving the medieval estates, his assent to a constitution seemed a significant about-face. More than ten thousand Berliners had surrounded his palace, mounted barricades, and successfully defended them against foot soldiers, cavalry, and artillery. In March 1848, the king responded, acceding to all the rebels' demands, including a general amnesty for political offenses and violations of censorship. The insurgents voluntarily dismantled the barricades but insisted the king pay homage to the rebels killed by his troops. The king readily agreed. In the panic of the first few days, he even hailed the "glorious" revolution in a letter to the Russian czar, who must have been greatly disturbed by it. The corpses were laid out in the forecourt of his palace, and the king saluted them. At his side, the queen lamented: "The only thing missing now is the guillotine." Later, the king rode through the mourning crowd, a study in humility, wearing the black, red, and gold sash of the insurgents, followed by his court.

For a short time there was talk, even among conservatives, that the zeitgeist had changed course irreversibly. The king of Württemberg told a Russian minister, "One does not fight ideas on horseback." In France, the deposed Louis-Philippe confessed he had succumbed to an *insurrection morale*.

No sign of change was more dramatic than the shift in the situation of Jews. The tiny principality of Hesse-Homburg was the first to grant them full equality, only six days after the first mass demonstration in Karlsruhe. Other German principalities and free cities quickly followed. In Baden, early in April, a hurriedly established parliamentary commission unanimously approved a motion granting Jews full civic rights. The motion was passed on to the full plenum for approval without further clarifications. Words of elucidation would be superfluous, a "waste of time," since the "mighty spirit of our age" had already removed "in one blow" all impediments to the proposed law.[7]

THE uprisings of 1848, A. J. P. Taylor has written, marked the first time a revolution spread via train and telegraph; the leaders and their supporters were able to move quickly from one uprising to the next. After spending six thousand gold francs of his late father's estate on arms for Brussels workers, Karl Marx, scion of a long line of Jewish rabbis, took off for the revolution in Paris; from there he continued to Düsseldorf and Cologne, cities that had officially banished him. The *Communist Manifesto* had been published only a few weeks earlier. Marx presented copies to his friends in Paris and Cologne. In a critique of Hegel's philosophy of law published four years earlier, Marx had condemned religion as "the sigh of the oppressed, the heart of a heartless world, . . . the opium of the people." The nineteenth-century French historian Joseph-Ernest Renan said one should never believe a German who says that he is an atheist, and indeed Marx would soon found a new world religion—with disastrous consequences. While his political and philosophical treatises were the most influential of his writings, the force and ruthlessness that moved him and the glow and tenacity of his passion were more evident in the poetry he wrote during the past decade. His *Wild Songs*, a collection marked by a fascination with violence and death and the horrors of an imminent doomsday, ring with elemental fury: "We are the apes of a cold God . . . chained, shattered, empty, frightened"; "I shall howl gigantic curses on mankind."[8] The ferocity of this poetry, which he presented as a love gift to his wife, surfaced as well in the anti-Semitism of his polemics: "Let us consider the real Jew, not the Sabbath Jew. . . . What is the worldly cult of the Jew? Huckstering. . . . Money is the jealous God of Israel beside which no other God may exist. . . . The emancipation of the Jews is the emancipation of mankind from Judaism."[9]

Marx was otherwise a serious thinker and social theorist, and his most sweeping epigrams should perhaps not be taken literally. Marx proposed a new philosophy of history and revolutionary social, political, and economic reforms: state ownership of industry, centralization of credit, a heavy progressive income tax, abolition of the right of inheritance and of the difference between town and country. He hated nationalism with the rancor of a man whose ancestors had been outcasts for generations.

Marx arrived in Cologne in a mixed mood of hope and utter disgust. The uprising he was witnessing was hardly the class war he had predicted. Nearly everywhere in Germany, "bourgeoisie" and "proletariat" were in close alliance. In Cologne, Marx was able to pursue his revolutionary path by resuming publication of the *Rheinische Zeitung*, which he had edited before the Prussian government had suppressed it a few years earlier.

Stefan Born, the son of a Jewish surgeon in Posen, read every issue he could lay his hands on. A future labor leader, he, too, was in Brussels when the revolution broke out and left immediately for Paris. From there he was able to reach Hanover, where he continued by coach to Berlin. He arrived in time to mount the barricades outside the royal palace. He was one of the first to note with dismay the peculiar unwavering loyalty the insurgents displayed toward their despotic rulers even as they rose up against them. He missed the revolutionary fervor he had just witnessed in Brussels and Paris. In Berlin, Born observed, the rebels still removed their hats and bowed as the king rode by. They never stepped on the carefully manicured royal lawns. Born distrusted the king's conciliatory tone and feared that his "humility might soon turn to defiance."[10]

In Berlin, as in other cities, the rebels were mostly students, young workers, and small shopkeepers. All were swept up in a wave of unjustified optimism; all craved more freedom. Among the students, many felt sure they were translating the spirit of Beethoven's Ninth Symphony and Börne's prose into real life. A disproportionately high number were young Jews. The prospect of equality under the law, separation of church and state, universal suffrage, and freedom from arbitrary rule generated unbridled enthusiasm and support among young men only a generation or two out of the ghetto. The economic situation of German Jews had changed substantially over the past four decades as the eighteenth-century pattern of mass destitution on the one hand and a privileged few rich court factors on the other dissolved into the greater diversities of a rapidly growing middle class. (In Berlin, for example, 7 percent of the university students were Jews, more than twice their representation in the city population.) The ideal of *Bildung* had moved many to absorb and internalize German *Kultur* long before they gained full access to it socially. In Frankfurt and Breslau, according to *Der Orient*, Jews were "leaders of the freedom movements or among those who had organized them."[11] The most prominent were Ludwig Bamberger in Mainz, Ferdinand Lassalle in Düsseldorf, Gabriel Riesser in Hamburg, Johann Jacoby in Königsberg, Aron Bernstein in Berlin, Hermann Jellinek in Vienna, Moritz Hartmann in Prague, and Sigismund Asch in Breslau.

In some of the rural areas, the uprisings were trailed by another wave of anti-Semitic riots, staged, for the most part, by landless or impoverished peasants. A succession of bad harvests and near famine had helped trigger them. In the larger German cities, most attempts to incite the mob failed. But in Baden, Alsace, and more than a hundred rural localities in southern Germany, Jewish homes, pawnshops, peddlers' carts, and market stands were looted and synagogues were burned, along with manor houses, feudal rent offices, and church rectories. Some of the riots coincided with Christian holidays. In Heidelberg, Bamberger ran into one of the relatively rare urban riots. "The spirit of freedom generated by the news from Paris," he noted, "has moved members of the very honorable tailors' guild of Heidelberg to

During the liberal revolutions of 1848, German Jews were among the rebels. A figure believed to be Johann Jacoby addresses the Republican Club in Berlin. Newspaper illustration. *Courtesy Leo Baeck Institute, Jerusalem*

sack the shop of a Jewish clothier who angered the 'legitimate' trade with his ready-to-wear merchandise."[12]

But unlike during the earlier *Hep! Hep!* riots, now Germans joined Jews in some places to repel the mob. In Prague—at the time a predominantly German city—students joined Jews to hold back Czech rioters who assaulted the Jewish quarter. The students called for "Jews, Czechs, and Germans to join hands. We want to be free men, not slaves."[13] In Dresden and Mannheim, flyers were posted decrying the riots: *"Pfui*, shame on you! Down with Jew hatred!"[14] Richard Wagner, the Royal Saxonian *Kappelmeister* and notorious anti-Semite—as yet in a relatively liberal period of his life—"behaved one moment like a revolutionary and the next like a prince," joining hands on the barricades with the Russian anarchist Mikhail Bakunin and a Jewish musician named Haimberger, who had exchanged his violin for a gun "but winced at every shot fired in the distance."[15]

Although some Jews dismissed the riots as "marginal," one Jewish magazine described them as the "blood consecration of Germany's new freedom." The "German giant" was finally rising and breaking his chains; if some of the loose links were striking Jews, that was no reason to panic. For on the barricades, the alliance between Jews and Christians was being "sealed in blood," wrote *Der Treue Zionswächter*. In the euphoria of the rebellion's first few days, Berthold Auerbach, the Jewish novelist and author of sentimental German peasant tales, saw fit to belittle the riots and assured his father-in-law, who took part in the uprising, that "occasional stupidities committed by the proverbial German common man must be looked at from a broader perspective. . . . The upheaval as a whole is exalted and exalting."[16] The real cause of the widespread rioting, Auerbach felt, was the stubbornness and blindness of the hereditary despots who refused to loosen the chains until it was too late. There were dissenting opinions. The caption of one cartoon reflected the gallows humor so cherished by Jews: "Not too much emancipation, please, or there will be another riot."[17]

In Berlin, Leopold Zunz, founder of the Society for the Culture and Science of the Jews, assured his closest friend that the riots, "like all other nonsense, will pass without leaving a trace" but that "freedom will survive."[18] The friend agreed. "Isolated excesses, even against Jews, do not worry me," he wrote back. "They are being amply compensated. Germany has shown that it has learned something. *If Börne could only have lived to see it!*"[19] Ludwig Philippson, a rabbi in Magdeburg and the editor of the *Allgemeine Zeitung des Judentums*, wrote grandly in defense of German-Jewish brotherhood:

> No longer will we consider ours to be a special case; it is one with the cause of the fatherland: together the two shall conquer; together they shall fail. We are and only wish to be Germans! We have and only wish to have a German fatherland! We are no longer Israelites in anything but our beliefs—in every other aspect we very much belong to the state in which we live.[20]

A good half of the Jewish population still practiced the traditional rituals of Judaism; politically, they tended to be conservative. The other half had become increasingly urban and secularized in recent years, increasingly "German."* By 1848, large numbers of this other half considered themselves liberals or leftist liberals. Among Jewish public figures, the political dividing lines were often generational. According to one estimate, the average age of conservative Jewish public figures was 57.6—nearly twice the average age of Jewish democratic militants, 31.9.[21]

For the first time in German history, the traditional passivity of Jews was giving way to active political involvement and street action. It is no longer possible to determine the number of Jewish insurgents or the identities of most of them, since after the 1848 revolutions were crushed (a process that took seven to fourteen months), many made strenuous efforts to conceal their roles. Still, we can assume that hundreds, perhaps thousands—mostly students and manual workers—participated in the clashes. Roughly 80 percent of all Jewish journalists, doctors, and other professionals are thought to have supported the revolution in one way or another. The myth quickly spread, in any case, that "Jews and other foreign riffraff" had started it in the first place. Frederick William IV subscribed to this view, claiming that the revolution was masterminded by "budding South German Robespierres and Jews."[22] In his memoirs, General Karl von Prittwitz, the officer commanding the Prussian garrison in Berlin, laid the principal blame for the uprising on Jews, rascals, and vagabonds.[23] According to the nationalist historian Heinrich Treitschke, the Jews had been the revolution's "Oriental cheerleaders." The *Neue Preussische Zeitung* of January 28, 1849, offered to pay a million gulden to anyone who produced a "Jewish

---

*The spreading acculturation of even rabbis and the resultant mix of Jewish and German figures of speech can be seen in a message of congratulations and encouragement sent in July 1845 to a rabbinical conference in Frankfurt by the board and sixteen members of the Jewish congregation of Edenkoben in the Palatinate: "German men in Israel who are gathered in the name of the Lord! Permit a small group of loyal believers to approach you reverently and welcome you with a handshake of true German rectitude and a ringing cry of Barukh Haba from a true Israelite heart" (quoted in J. J. Petuchowski, "On the Validity of German-Jewish Self Definitions," Leo Baeck Memorial Lecture 29, New York, 1985, p. 3).

reactionary." At year's end, even the *London Standard* claimed that "all the mischief now brooding on the continent is done by Jews."[24]

Of course, not all Jews who participated in the uprising or who gave it passive support were intellectuals or even radical. A certain Isaac Moses Hersch published a series of revolutionary newsletters in a mixture of Yiddish and Berlin dialect for the benefit of those who stood on the barricades. The printer was "our fellow citizen Löwenherz, a man unafraid to print what is written for the just cause of liberty even if ten thousand lord mayors sue him for it."[25] And in Cologne, Abraham Oppenheim, head of the Jewish banking firm Sal. Oppenheim Jr. & Co., epitomized a type of conservative yearning for reform, but only if graciously granted by the Prussian king: "reform from above." His faith in the king had not been shattered by the failure of a pathetic appeal he had addressed to him in 1841 to ameliorate the civic condition of Jews ("We have not sinned but are punished").[26] In 1848, Oppenheim sympathized—up to a point—with the prevailing democratic sentiments. When the insurgents approached him with their political demands, he angrily withdrew his support: "What you ask for goes too far. You want a republic!"[27]

But on the whole, the Jewish activists, though drawn from a variety of milieus, united in their militant commitment. Among the more flamboyant and charismatic personalities was Ferdinand Lassalle, the twenty-three-year-old son of a Silesian Jewish stockbroker. Heine had been very much taken with Lassalle when he met him in Paris a few years earlier. He wrote August Varnhagen in 1846: "It turns out that Herr Lassalle is truly a man of these new times who refuses to countenance the tactics we resorted to in our time—the more or less hypocritical renunciation and modesty we employed as we blundered and blathered ahead. This new generation wants to enjoy life; they want to make themselves felt in the visible world— while those of our generation paid homage to the world of the unseen." As an adolescent Lassalle had dreamed of freeing the Jews by force of arms. As a grown man, he wrote: "The best balm for a man's wound is feverish, frantic, frantic, feverish activity."[28] His own activities resulted in one of the best-organized, best-disciplined uprisings, which took place in Düsseldorf. In and out of jail for much of 1848, Lassalle continued to correspond

Ludwig Bamberger, a son not of the synagogue but of the emancipation. In his old age, he contemplated escaping Bismarck's crude nationalism and emigrating to a more democratic land. *By permission of the Landesarchiv, Landesbildstelle, Berlin*

with his wealthy father in Breslau about buying and selling shares in such trying times. Sigismund Asch, son of a Jewish peddler, was a popular young doctor in Breslau, active in the local labor movement. Every morning between five and seven he offered free treatment to the poor in his infirmary. Asch emerged as one of the militants of the uprising in Silesia. Early in April, some ten thousand people attended one of his mass rallies. Asch gave a rousing speech. Citing Heine's famous poem "The Silesian Weavers," he reminded the insurgents not to be content with civic equality alone and exhorted them not to forget the nearby "weavers, wailing from hunger."[29] After this, a chorus sang the rebels' new hymn, *"Ich bin ein Deutscher"*—I am a German—written by another young Jewish insurgent, Julius Lasker. For this speech, Asch was later charged with lèse majesté and incitement to rebellion and sentenced to a year in prison. Lassalle and Asch, as well as Ludwig Bamberger and others, were under the spell of the French social utopians. All three were united in the view that, as Börne had put it, it was bliss to confront the accursed, execrable system on the battlefield.

In Mainz, meanwhile, Ludwig Bamberger had risen through the ranks to become one of the founders of the new Democratic party. On March 6, 1848, it was announced that the grand duke (Mainz was part of the duchy of Hesse) had granted the rebels all their demands: freedom of assembly and petition, freedom of the press, abolition of various oppressive police regulations, including the prohibition against smoking a pipe in the street. Standing in the throng, Bamberger, more outspoken in his republicanism than most other militants, was suspicious of what he heard.

An older generation of Jewish militants found a role as well. In Berlin, Leopold Zunz mounted the barricades together with the students. In his eyes, the Europe-wide revolution assumed near-messianic dimensions. Zunz believed that it augured a new age of peace and social justice: heaven on earth seemed imminent. "Absolutism is besieged on all sides; at long last it is being crushed underfoot, and with it the old priesthood. . . . The tyrants will finally be punished," he wrote to his friend Philipp Ehrenberg.[30] At a demonstration in the Königstrasse in Berlin, Zunz publicly called on the crowd to storm the royal arsenal to provide the insurgents with more guns and ammunition. The revolution needed "weapons and a national guard, twenty thousand strong." He was answered with a thunderous "Yes!" and the arsenal was stormed. Zunz remained hopeful throughout. He felt that "the bloody Day of Judgment is at hand for the oppressors of so many nations. . . . Plutocrats and bureaucrats, the black-robed papist police, the diplomats of Metternich—all are in the throes of fever, for the day of the Lord draws nigh. Perhaps by Purim, Amalek will be beaten."[31]

The feast of Purim, celebrating the Jews' victory over their enemy Haman, fell a few days later. Zunz filled his letters with oblique references to Amalek* and Haman (that is, Frederick William IV). On Purim itself, cannon fire in Berlin continued through the night until four in the morning. Zunz was on the barricades, ridiculing the king's proclamation (addressed "To my dear Berliners"), in which he assured the insurgents that his own tears were mixed with theirs and that he would gladly "grant" them everything if only they returned to "obedience."

The revolution was finally blasting open the gates of the ghettos, Zunz rejoiced. He acted on his optimism by proposing the establishment

---

*March 18, 1848, was the Sabbath of Remembrance, the day that Deuteronomy 25:17 is read with its solemn commandment to "remember what Amalek did unto thee."

of a chair in Jewish studies at the University of Berlin. The head of the faculty of philosophy replied that since Jews were no longer a separate nation there was no need now for such a chair.

Zunz's eschatological vision was not an isolated case. All over the country, rabbis in their sermons greeted the revolution as a truly messianic event. The draft constitution discussed by the insurgents stipulated separation of church and state. "The savior for whom we have prayed has appeared. The fatherland has given him to us. The messiah is freedom" raved the Jewish magazine *Der Orient*: "Our history is concluded. It has merged with the universal. Autonomous Judaism now lives only in the synagogue and in science." The magazine praised "the heroic Maccabean battle of our brethren on the barricades of Berlin. We have fought as true Prussians and true Germans." After one such battle, Christians on the scene had intoned "a *Hoch* [hail] to the Jews," according to *Der Orient*.[32] Several such claims can be found in Jewish newspapers of the time though practically nowhere else in the general press.

Some 230 Berliners were shot by Prussian troops during the uprising. Twenty-one were said to be Jews, proportionately almost three times their percentage of the city population. The Jews were buried in a common grave with the other rebels and eulogized at a joint ceremony by a Catholic priest, a Protestant minister, and a Jewish rabbi. The *Vossische Zeitung*, Berlin's leading newspaper, described the occasion as an unparalleled historic moment. In his eulogy, the rabbi had drawn a line marking the end of hundreds of years of discrimination, according to the newpaper. *Der Orient* saluted a "philosopher" named Weiss, "a heroic leader who died on the barricades with the German flag in one hand and a sword in the other. Victory is ours."[33] The new civil militia of Berlin, at a celebration for its commanding officer, intoned a new song. Its refrain was:

> *Hail to you, whether Christian or Jew,*
> *You are part of mankind, we are hailing you!*[34]

The young Moritz Steinschneider, in later years a well-known Orientalist and bibliophile, had eagerly helped carry stones to build the barricades. He wrote his fiancée in Prague: "There is no longer talk here of 'Jew' or 'Christian' and thank God for that. . . . The Jews of Prussia must be formally emancipated for the *people* have emancipated them already. Who can think of *himself* now? The Berlin rabble has made enormous cultural progress during these days."[35]

Levin Goldschmidt, a future prominent jurist, was equally optimistic, writing to his parents in March that "blood has not been shed in vain; it will bear rich fruit." The king was now "a mere puppet, a straw that any storm might sweep away." Several months later, long after the barricades had been dismantled, Goldschmidt still claimed that much of what he had longed for had been achieved: now the Jew, too, could choose his path according to his inclination and talent; he no longer needed to purchase his happiness by "surrendering his religion."[36]

THE uprising forced the king to permit elections for a new all-German National Assembly, to be conveyed in Frankfurt, and for a new Prussian parliament. Among the civic representatives negotiating with him were two Jewish booksellers. In the ensuing elections, two others were elected deputies from Berlin, Moritz Veit and Friedrich Wilhelm Levysohn. At least one observer thought the role of Jewish booksellers noteworthy. The number of Jewish-owned bookshops in Prussian cities had increased markedly in recent years. As early as 1821, complaints were heard that too many Jews were in the publishing and bookselling business; they might someday aim to "seize full control of the world of ideas."[37] The ubiquity of Jewish booksellers in some cities was, of course, related to the fact that other professions remained closed to Jewish graduates. They could not practice law or teach in universities or in most secondary schools. Jewish parochial schools also often hesitated to employ them; the conservative rabbis who ran parochial schools regarded university graduates as either too secular or, worse, dangerously close to the burgeoning reform movement. Since selling books was an occupation that required a fairly wide education, it was one of the few offering a measure of intellectual satisfaction to doctors of philosophy, philology, law, or classical studies.

In 1848, publishing was more than simply a way to make a living. Publishers of all faiths played important public roles. Their common, most immediate task was the abolition of censorship. Levysohn himself, a publisher as well as a bookseller, was sentenced to a year in prison for publishing a poem deemed critical of the king. The sentence was not carried out, because Levysohn's status as a deputy conferred immunity. In rural areas, the much-maligned Jewish *Dorfgeher*, or village peddler, was often the only source of political news and sometimes the sole purveyor of popular German books. In his memoirs, the philosopher Moritz Lazarus remembered a *Dorfgeher* in Pomerania who peddled his wares during the day and spent the night in a peasant's barn. Villagers would gather there in the evening to exchange gossip and hear the latest news but also to "listen to folk tales read by the peddler from books written in the German-Yiddish vernacular." There existed a "considerable body of German family literature printed in Hebrew letters that appealed mostly to women and girls but also to men of the lower classes."[38]

BERTHOLD Auerbach, perhaps the most widely read German novelist of his time, was an early activist in the revolution of 1848. The experience made him feel more German, he said, and at the same time more proud of his Jewish origins: "I am a German and cannot be anything else. I am a Swabian and I don't want to be anything else. I am a Jew. Together all this produces the right mixture."[39] Born in 1812 in Nordstetten, a remote hamlet in the Black Forest inhabited by some two hundred Catholic and thirty Jewish families, Auerbach has been all but forgotten today, except perhaps by historians of the aborted Jewish-German "dialogue." In his time, Auerbach was famous throughout Europe; Turgenev compared him to Dickens. Intending to become a rabbi, he studied theology in Tübingen on a government scholarship. He was a politically engaged student, and the two months he spent in jail for some alleged "treasonable" activity cost him his scholarship. The Jewish socialist Moses Hess, later known as the "communist rabbi," wrote to invite him to Cologne to meet Karl Marx, "a personality bound to attract the attention of all Germany. . . . Think of Rousseau, Voltaire, Lessing, Heine, and Hegel, not just thrown together but truly united in one person."[40] Auerbach did not respond. Instead, he quit his studies and became a freelance writer, turning out a number of unsuccessful novels about Jewish topics and several fictionalized biographies. In his late twenties, he returned to Nordstetten for literary inspiration and quickly became a German national hero. The first volume of his *Village Tales from the Black Forest* came out in 1843. Five more volumes followed in quick succession. The tales idealize simple peasant life in Nordstetten, a peaceful place where Jews (mostly peddlers) and Catholics coexist harmoniously side by side.

With his *Village Tales* Auerbach invented a new genre—the peasant tale—within the genre of *Heimat,* or homeland, literature. It became his trademark. He was beloved and often admired not only by middle-brow readers but by highbrows and intellectuals as well. German Jews were proud that one of their own had become a popular figure, the cherished articulator of themes as folksy as those of the brothers Grimm. Richard Wagner put aside his anti-Semitism, hailing Auerbach as a man truly "rooted" in German life; his tales portrayed the "innermost features of the German national soul."[41] Jakob Grimm thanked Auerbach for "curing him of prejudice." He "would not have thought a Jew capable of penetrating the German soul so deeply."[42]

Auerbach's country folk were cartoonish and often downright corny. Not all were fine and exceptional men and women—a few were mean or criminal—but most of them, with their high-minded sense of patriotism and civic duty, were remarkably bourgeois in their ethos. It was this elevated view coupled with Auerbach's unaffected style and descriptive talent that accounted for his great success. He wrote about his peasants lovingly but cautioned himself against personal illusions: "I knew that were I to walk among the peasants, my heart full of goodwill, the mention of one word—'Jew!'—would surely chase them away from me forever."[43]

Heine hated Auerbach's sentimentalism. During a brief illness in 1847, he wrote his friend Heinrich Laube: "My brain is as watery as if I were the author of Auerbach's *Village Tales,* and my stomach is as wretchedly sentimental, pious, and insipid as one of those tales. Nevertheless, I wish to come and visit you today at around 11. Your sick friend, H.H." But Ferdinand Freiligrath, the patriotic "poet of the 1848 revolution," celebrated the first volume of Auerbach's *Tales* in a long poem gushing with praise.

Auerbach was one of the first modern Jewish novelists who managed to become well integrated in German society without concealing his origins. He was admired by the general public, liked by intellectuals, and courted by aristocrats and members of princely families (especially the ladies). He remained close to his pious family in Nordstetten. His elderly mother basked in his success, and his royalties helped pay for his sisters' dowries. When his young nephew was subjected to an anti-Semitic comment by a classmate, Auerbach felt personally affronted. "You can't know," he told Freiligrath, "what a Jewish child must suffer in this world. . . . I do!"[44]

Auerbach himself seemed to enjoy a curious immunity from anti-Semitic slurs. Criticized as a writer yet never attacked as a Jew, he was conscious of his exceptional status. In a rare occurrence, a condescending Christian once said to him, "If only all Jews were like you!" Auerbach shot back: "Yes, and if only all Christians were also like me!"[45] Other prominent men and women of Jewish descent were routinely reminded of their background by their enemies and critics: Heine and Börne in literature, Mendelssohn, Offenbach, and Meyerbeer in music; Hess, Marx, and Lassalle in politics. But even those who disliked Auerbach's books or his politics never brought up his origins. Laube attributed his immunity to his deliberate retreat, in both his writings and his life, into the "chaste solitude" of country life.

In the winter of 1847–48, Auerbach was at work on another volume of village tales. He had recently married and was deliriously happy with his young wife, Auguste. At thirty-five, he was about to settle down for the first time in a cozy house of his own in Heidelberg, overlooking the romantic castle, the green hills, and the river Neckar. The revolution caught him there just as his wife entered the last weeks of pregnancy. The news of the liberal uprising thrilled him as much as the prospect of becoming a father. His wife's father was among the insurgents in Breslau. Auerbach himself was invited to join the revolutionary pre-parliament in Frankfurt.

In March 1848, however, Auguste gave birth prematurely, a result possibly of the traumatic shock of witnessing an anti-Semitic incident on a Heidelberg street, the same sacking of a Jewish shop described by Bamberger. There seemed little reason, at first, for concern. Mother and child were well. "A son! A son!" Auerbach rejoiced in a letter to his father-in-law. He added cheerfully: "The good fellow seems to have heard about the French revolution and of the great uprising in Germany; he wanted to participate and so came a few days early."[46]

Auguste's condition suddenly worsened. Intermittently unconscious, she hemorrhaged and ran a high fever and had difficulty breathing. Auerbach did not leave her side, missing the opening sessions of the Frankfurt pre-parliament. Auguste fought for her life. For much of the time, Auerbach "heard and saw as though through a thick veil."[47] On April 3, Auguste was somewhat better and Auerbach felt free to attend the pre-parliament for a few hours. He returned home in the early evening. The following day Auguste died.

They had been married for less than ten months. Auerbach was inconsolable. He poured out his grief in long letters to a cousin and to Auguste's father. Later in April he agreed to run as a candidate for the new National Assembly in elections scheduled by the pre-parliament for mid-May. Cowed by the continuing popular rebellion, the kings and ruling princes of the German states feigned readiness to cooperate with the proposed assembly. For Auerbach, the magnitude of political events was the only thing to lift him above his "endless pain,"[48] he wrote. Nothing came of his candidacy, however. Auerbach's biographer, Anton Bettelheim, assumes he withdrew because in the rural region where he planned to run his Jewishness—or the occasionally cruel realism of his village tales—might have been too great an impediment.

Three weeks after Auguste's death, Auerbach liquidated his household, taking his infant son to Auguste's parents in Breslau and staying there until early September. Together with Sigismund Asch, the popular young doctor, he addressed liberal mass meetings. He also corresponded with his friends in the National Assembly. He opposed the growing desire among its deputies to impose a hereditary emperor on the proposed new united Reich. It was their "old habitual submissiveness" to despotic princes.[49]

In September 1848, Auerbach traveled to Vienna, where the revolution was still in full swing and the insurgents were in control of the city. The minister of war had just been hung from a lamppost. The emperor had run for his life, but his troops were gathering to lay siege to the rebellious capital. A flyer handed out in the streets read:

An Israelite's Cry of Fear
by Bernhard Mauthner
Member of the National Guard

An ancient specter is creeping in the midst of this joyful tumult, . . . the ghost of the humiliated and disparaged Jew. . . . If we do not now attain complete deliverance, thousands will leave their fatherland, and thousands will convert without genuine conviction.[50]

Auerbach's *Vienna Diary,* published a few months later, portrays the somber atmosphere in the besieged city and the decline and eventual defeat of the Austrian democrats. The imperial army, manned largely by Croatian conscripts, moved artillery into place and bombarded the city. Auerbach shouldered a rifle and took up position on the walls. Still in pain over the loss of his wife, he wished only to die, he wrote. If it had not been for his child, "I would surely have sought death on the barricades." As the imperial army gained ground, Auerbach's radical friends slowly went into hiding. The revolutionary tricolor, at first ubiquitous, gradually disappeared from their lapels. In November, Auerbach watched the emperor's forces march back into the vanquished city. The soldiers were chanting slogans but among the spectators, too, many cried *"Vivat! Vivat!* Long live the emperor," to Auerbach's dismay. He hoped they were showing their support of the emperor only out of fear. The first execution was that of Robert Blum, a German liberal from Cologne and a member of the Frankfurt National Assembly who had come to support the Viennese insurgents. He was shot by a firing squad for his alleged role in the uprising. Blum's last words, as Auerbach recorded them, were: "Every drop of my blood will produce another martyr for human freedom." Where would it all end, Auerbach wondered. "What terrible horrors still await us?"[51]

Hermann Jellinek, the young Viennese Jew who some eight months earlier had honored Börne's memory, was executed a few days later. Before the uprising, Jellinek had been a student in Leipzig; he "had returned to Vienna imbued with the love of Germany," the *Leipziger Tageblatt* commented on the anniversary of his death a year later. Jellinek's last words were more resigned than Blum's: "My spirit is calm. I hope that my body will not play tricks with me. My cause is vanquished.

Hence it is in order that I fall."[52] Eulogizing Jellinek, *Der Orient* voiced the hope that his blood might be the "cement that will bind the various German religious tribes."[53] In Frankfurt and Leipzig, thousands mourned Blum's and Jellinek's deaths. Karl Marx's *Rheinische Zeitung*, however, called Jellinek a fraud; the siege of Vienna had enabled Jewish hucksters like him to amass fortunes. What the Croat soldiers had looted, the Jews immediately bought up from them for a "pittance."

BETWEEN May 1848 and June 1849, the newly elected National Assembly—a phantom parliament of a still nonexistent all-German state—was in continuous session. Its venue was St. Paul's Church in Frankfurt. A church had been chosen only because other halls in Frankfurt were not big enough to hold the more than five hundred deputies and their attendants. The proposed united states of Germany were to remain strictly separate from any church. Not since the Federal Constitutional Convention of 1787 in Philadelphia had so many learned and idealistic minds come together in an elected national parliament. More than three hundred of the delegates were professors, doctors, jurists, scientists, judges, poets, and historians. Among them were seven German and two Austrian Jews. (At this stage, the German-speaking parts of the Austrian empire were expected to join the all-German state.) The two most prominent were Gabriel Riesser, founder of the magazine *Der Jude* and a prominent Hamburg lawyer (still unable, he told the assembly, to practice his profession), and Johann Jacoby, a radical-leaning doctor from Königsberg. There were also seven baptized Jews with distinctly Jewish names, such as Simon, Simson, and Heckscher.

Of the Jewish participants, Riesser was the most relentless, Jacoby the most brilliant. According to one contemporary writer, "Jacoby's blue eyes gazed, calm and serious, but from time to time they lit up with the fire of burning yet cold passion."[54] Jacoby had made a name for himself a few years earlier as the courageous author of a banned pamphlet with the innocuous title *Four Questions Answered by an East Prussian*. It was a powerful and unprecedented plea for democracy. Although the pamphlet was published anonymously, the author's identity was soon widely known. Jacoby himself boldly, if recklessly, sent the king a signed copy. Infuriated by the "insolent Jew," Frederick William IV ordered Jacoby's prosecution. A lower court, finding him guilty of "sedition, impudence and lèse majesté," sentenced him to two and half years in jail and revoked his citizenship. A long legal battle ensued, at the end of which Jacoby was acquitted by an appellate court in Berlin. The judge promptly lost his post by order of the king. Jacoby soon became famous—or infamous—all over Germany. Like Riesser, he was a restless militant for Jewish rights. "Since I am at once a Jew and a German," he wrote in a letter, "I cannot become free as a German without also becoming free as a Jew. I cannot separate the two. . . . we all languish together in one great prison."[55]

Jacoby had been elected in Königsberg by an unusually large margin. The elections themselves had been an act of defiance, their authorization only grudgingly granted by the king. German Jews had gone to the polls in masses. In Prussia, voting had been open to all adult males, regardless of religion or economic status. As such, the election was more democratic than any in Europe or America at that time.

Once elected, the Frankfurt assembly made a heroic attempt to fill the political vacuum created by the March uprisings. In the absence of formal unification, the laws it enacted were not yet binding in the different states. Undeterred, in early July the assembly began to consider a bill of rights. The learned deputies on its benches were so engrossed in the legal details of this task, they paid too little heed to what was happening elsewhere. In Berlin, Vienna, and most other important cities, the old despots, having regained their composure, were preparing a counterattack. The Russian czar was mounting an expeditionary force to come to their aid. By September, what Karl Marx had called the "halfhearted revolution" of March was met by a massive counterrevolution. Austrian and Russian troops were about to smash the last remnants of the uprisings in Budapest and Vienna. In Berlin, it will be remembered, the insurgents had put their trust in the king's promises; they dismantled the barricades themselves. A few months later Frederick William ordered the army to reoccupy the city; he dismissed the liberal ministers he had named in a panic, sent troops to take control of the streets, imposed a state of siege, and appointed a new, ultrareactionary cabinet.

In the interim, Johann Jacoby had also won a seat in the Prussian

Landtag, the state parliament, to which in the past only conservatives handpicked by the government had been elected. On November 3, 1848, Jacoby was one of twenty-one deputies who went to the palace to plead with Frederick William and warn him of the consequences of his recent regressive measures. The meeting began and ended in farce. The king made no effort to hide his distaste at the deputies' very presence. He turned his back on them as they spoke and made to leave the room. Jacoby cried after him: "This is the tragedy of kings, that they refuse to hear the truth!" Jacoby had overestimated his colleagues, who rushed to apologize for his "inexcusable" audacity, assuring the king's courtiers that he had spoken only for himself. The delegation withdrew but the news of Jacoby's act quickly spread. His supporters honored him with a torchlight procession on Unter den Linden while the conservative press assaulted him for "insulting the king in his own house." Once again criminal charges were brought against him. But now, thanks to the reforms of recent months, Jacoby was tried by a jury that acquitted him, eight votes to four. Soon after, Prussian troops forced the first freely elected Prussian state parliament to disband.

Jacoby predicted early on that any revolution that allowed the well-organized old powers to continue functioning would be defeated. His warnings fell on deaf ears. In most German states, the March insurgents were content with cosmetic changes. After the appointment of a few liberal ministers, they had gone home to "sleep and snore," as Heine wrote. Few were committed republicans. Most remained sentimentally attached to their sovereigns. "Much carrying on, little willpower," lamented the young Theodor Fontane, who fought on the Berlin barricades. Bismarck, briefly a delegate to the Prussian Landtag, cynically remarked that only kings made revolutions in Germany. Fifteen years later, as premier, he would return to this theme with the oft-quoted pronouncement, "The great questions of the time are decided not by speeches and majority decisions—that was the error of 1848 and 1849—but by iron and blood." Nearly everywhere, the bourgeoisie, panicked by the disorders and riots of March and April, helped prevent various attempts to declare republics. Its first priority was the restoration of "law and order."

The Frankfurt National Assembly reflected these fears. When the

Johann Jacoby, at the height of the struggle between the revolutionary Prussian state parliament and the king: "This is the tragedy of kings, that they refuse to hear the truth." The king, aghast at the insolence of the Jew, leaves the room. Contemporary drawing from the *Leipziger Illustrierte Zeitung*. *Courtesy Leo Baeck Institute, Jerusalem*

Prussian king grew displeased with the assembly and ordered "his" deputies home, most of them sheepishly obeyed. By December 1848, the widely heralded assembly was little more than a ghostly remnant of what it had been in May, the heyday of what came to be called the "spring of nations." It had become slightly ridiculous. The speechmaking went on as before. The remaining deputies, fewer and fewer in number, playacted their way through constitutional, cabinet, and other crises, appointing and dismissing war ministers without an army, justice ministers without courts of law, and ministers of foreign affairs whose ambassadors were not recognized.

The deputies' task was difficult, to say the least. The French Revolution of 1789 had reformed an existing, highly centralized state. The Frankfurt deputies had yet to create one. Thirty-six absolute sovereigns, with their armies and treasuries intact, were in no mood to unite under their aegis and become constitutional figureheads. The sovereigns had briefly panicked in March, bowing to what seemed for a while overwhelming popular pressure. By October they were no longer ready to recognize that there was a *Volk*—a people; in their eyes there were only *Untertanen*—subjects.

There were more mundane difficulties as well. Only a fraction of the deputies drew salaries from their state governments while the others covered their own expenses. Few had the means—or the time—to remain in Frankfurt for months on end; many absented themselves for long periods. The deliberations dragged on for almost a year, with no fixed agenda. Obsessed with legal formalities, the deputies quarreled endlessly over minor differences. They desired far-reaching reforms but most deputies tied them to the consent of the hereditary princes. They favored a loose federation of kingdoms and principalities under one monarch, a hereditary kaiser. Even though, in the fall of 1848, Prussian, Austrian, Saxon, and Russian troops were already on the march against the remaining hard-line insurgents, the assembly spent weeks discussing this new German kaiser and whether he should be the king of Prussia or the emperor of Austria.

Heading the assembly in December were two deputies of Jewish origin: the timid Eduard Simson, a Königsberg lawyer, was president of the assembly, and Gabriel Riesser of Hamburg was one of the vice presidents. Riesser was strongly in favor of a federated Reich. Like most other German Jews, he hoped that within a federation united by law and a common language and culture, Jews would no longer stand out; they would simply be one among many ethnic groups and warring historical tribes—Saxons, Bavarians, Prussians, Hessians, Silesians, and others. If he had to choose between Jewish emancipation and German unification, Riesser said, he would "unhesitatingly opt for the latter" since it would undoubtedly "guarantee" the former.[56] At Riesser's urging, the assembly finally opted for Prussia and voted to offer the imperial crown to Frederick William IV. It says something about the mood of the time and place that on this most patriotic German occasion, under the presidency of a prominent Jew, another Jew should urge the crown of the new German Reich on the king of Prussia. Riesser's "kaiser speech" was described as one of the finest delivered at the assembly. It was "met by a storm of applause. Many deputies had hot tears in their eyes," wrote one witness, Heine's friend Heinrich Laube.[57]

Simson and Riesser led a delegation of deputies to Berlin to offer Frederick William the imperial crown. The king repulsed them with barely disguised disdain. In his view, an upstart parliament was trading in something it did not own by "right." Only his peers, the other kings and princes of the German lands, were entitled to make such an offer. In private he later remarked that he would not accept a "shit crown" from the hands of a parliament of "bakers and butchers." Soldiers, he said, were the only remedy against democrats.

The deputation withdrew in a mood of bleak disappointment. Later in the day, Simson met with the king's brother, William. "No one will be able to rule Germany who has not been anointed with a drop of democratic oil," Simson told the prince. "Yes," he replied. "That is my opinion too. A drop. But what you've got here is a full bottle!" The king refused to be a constitutional monarch. That same evening he is said to have told Riesser, within earshot of Simson: "Herr Doktor, I am sure you realize I could not have accepted your constitution uncircumcised."[58]

On June 6, 1849, the assembly, or what was left of it, sought refuge in Stuttgart; twelve days later it was ruthlessly shut down by Prussian troops. Had it continued functioning, its draft constitution would have been by far the most liberal and progressive of all legal instruments of its kind in mid-century Europe.* The draft stipulated a federation of self-governing democratic states. The proposed bill of rights promised "full freedom of faith and conscience." It established civil marriage and stipulated that religion must neither condition nor limit the enjoyment of civil and political rights. The debate on this paragraph was Riesser's second great moment at the assembly. Moritz Mohl, a leftist deputy from Stuttgart, proposed an amendment stipulating that, in view of the Jews' "national" character, their civil rights be legislated separately. Until that moment, Riesser had worn the mantle of an all-German politician. He now rose to speak as "an oppressed Jew," riveting the assembly with his passionate rhetoric. "I myself have lived under con-

---

*A full century later, in 1949, guilt-ridden and contrite, West German parliamentarians incorporated key sections of this draft, including its bill of rights, in the new federal constitution.

ditions of serious distress in my own paternal city of Hamburg. Until very recently, I would not have qualified for the job of night watchman," he told the hushed assembly.

> We are not immigrants—we were born here—and so we cannot claim any other home: either we are Germans or we have no homeland. Whoever disputes my claim to this my German fatherland disputes my right to my own thoughts, my feelings, my language—the very air I breathe. Therefore I must defend myself against him as I would against a murderer.[59]

Riesser's speech was met with thunderous applause. Mohr's amendment was rejected.

As these events were taking place, Heinrich Heine was already half paralyzed and all but totally bedridden in Paris. The ministrations of doctors did not amelio-rate his pain. The leeches and the cauterizations of his spine with opium only added to his torment. Friedrich Engels visited him and reported to Marx that Heine was close to death.[60] The news from Germany exasperated him terribly. Nearly blind, he depended on his secre-tary to read him the newspapers. "You can't imagine what it means to experience such a revolu-tion in my condition," he told a visitor. "I should have been either healthy or dead."[61]

In truth, Heine was

Gabriel Riesser, vice president of the revolutionary National Assembly, told his fellow deputies: "We are not immigrants—we were born here." Along with most other Jews, he hoped that in a united Germany they would become another German tribe, like Sax-ons and Bavarians. *Courtesy Leo Baeck Institute, Jeru-salem*

dubious about the revolution almost from start, suspecting that it would quickly come to grief. The events of 1848 seemed to him and others little more than a parody of those of 1789. The exiled Russian liberal Alexander Herzen said he had known a few German "Robespierres" personally: "they always wore clean shirts, washed their hands, and cleaned their nails."[62] Equally sardonic, Alexis de Tocqueville, a minister in the short-lived French Second Republic, claimed he had the feeling not so much of continuing the French Revolution as of watching a play about it. Heine felt the same about Germany. He decried the timidity of some of the liberal leaders and mocked the deputies elected to the new National Assembly for their sentimental attachment to the old despots. He believed that only a handful were uncompromisingly democratic:

> *The English and French, it has been determined*
> *Have shallower souls than your average German,*
> *Who is slow, and slow he'll stay*
> *Even when it's time to slay.*
> *The German will forever be*
> *Respectful of Authority.*

The belligerent nationalism of a few of the assembly's deputies also frightened Heine. He was shocked by their swaggering militarism, by their urging the recovery of "German territory" through war with the Danes and with the Poles. Their arrogance was as ridiculous as it was brutal, he noted. From his sickbed he warned the French journalist Jean-Jacques Dubochet to take their rhetoric seriously. War was what they wanted, and in this they were of one mind with the German princes. Even as the assembly was drafting the new democratic constitution, these deputies were calling for expanding the borders of the proposed unified German Reich southward into Italy and as far east as the Black Sea. Might was right. The Polish majority in Posen—land coveted by the nationalists—must be "mercilessly Germanized." If they only *willed* it enough, the thinking went, there was nothing that forty million Germans, united in one powerful Reich, could not accomplish.

HAD the revolution not collapsed, the ratification of the proposed constitution would have meant the end of the long battle for Jewish emancipation. The attempt failed. Nonetheless, the revolutionary year of 1848–49 was a crucial turning point for German Jews. It considerably strengthened their sense of finally becoming Germans. Never before had their representatives been so outspoken, insistent, and conscious of their rights. Liberals of all faiths drew closer to one another than ever before. Three or four decades after almost the entire Jewish intellectual elite had disappeared in the first wave of conversions, a new generation of vocal leaders had emerged. Hardly a single overt anti-Semitic remark either from the rostrum of the National Assembly or in the endless debates in the revolutionary state parliaments was reported.

The "year of folly" *(das tolle Jahr)*, as it came to be called, fostered a new intimacy between liberals of all faiths. In the assembly, Riesser and others forged strong bonds between the Jewish and other liberals, which held firm for the next three or four decades. The revolution brought more Jews into the orbit of the new liberal parties. In some of the smaller German states, where relatively few Jews lived, the new legislatures remained in existence and granted them a semblance of civic rights. The great exception was Prussia; it had promised equality but in reality never implemented it. One important right Jews—although wealthy ones only—finally won in 1848 was the right to vote and to hold political office. Universal male suffrage, however, was short-lived. In Prussia it was quickly replaced by a three-tiered voting system that restricted suffrage to the aristocracy, the landed gentry, and the urban rich.

In 1850 the king allowed a new Prussian constitution. It solemnly reinstated the doctrine of a "Christian state" that the National Assembly had hoped to overcome. Jews would continue to be barred from high positions in government, the judiciary, universities, and state schools. With few exceptions, these restrictions were reinstated elsewhere in Germany too, at least until 1868, when the state of Baden appointed Moritz Ellstätter minister of finance, a position he would hold without interruption for twenty-five years. Ellstätter was the first and, until 1918, the only unconverted Jew appointed a cabinet minister anywhere in Germany.

It is indicative of the growing role of Jews in German life that the three leading political ideologues of the moment were of Jewish origin—Jacoby for the liberals, Marx for the socialists, and Professor Friedrich Julius Stahl for the conservatives. Born Joel Golson in 1802, the son of an observant Jewish cattle dealer in Bavaria, Stahl was the chief German ideologue of the Christian state in the post-1848 era. At seventeen, Stahl had converted to Protestantism and changed his name to Stahl (steel). Unless he had already planned his move to Prussia at this early stage, his conversion to Protestantism in deeply Catholic Bavaria may well have been undertaken out of true belief. In 1828, he moved to Berlin, where he eventually succeeded Eduard Gans (Heine's erstwhile friend and later nemesis) at the Berlin faculty of jurisprudence. His public lectures at the university were social events attended by distinguished audiences, including members of the royal family. Stahl articulated the rules and needs of the authoritarian Christian state. In his opinion, it went against the divine order to allow Jews any influence; they were entitled to full civil but not political rights—these were a nation's dearest treasure. To enjoy them, Jews had first to adopt the state religion. During the 1848 uprising in Berlin, Stahl fled the democracy-infested city; the events of 1848 were, in his eyes, pure wickedness and crime. Political decisiveness required authoritarian, not majority, rule.

In the aftermath of the "year of folly," Stahl became leader of the conservatives in the upper house of the new Prussian state parliament. In the largest German state, where two-thirds of the Jewish population lived, he enunciated the "philosophical" basis for continuing discrimination against his former coreligionists. He was not a great thinker but an able propagandist, persuasively articulating the conservative demand for "authority" and the sacred union of church and throne. He preached the virtue of tradition, the infallibility of Christian doctrine, and the right of the monarch to be sole ruler. Christianity was the only antidote to revolution. The crime of the Enlightenment had been to upset the divine order of church and throne.

Bismarck called him "our beloved Stahl."[63] Though he may not have agreed with all of Stahl's theories, he shared Stahl's strictures against the admission of Jews to public office. He told the Prussian Landtag in 1847:

> I am no enemy of the Jews. . . . You might even say that I love them. I approve of their being granted all rights except that of holding high office in a Christian state. . . . I confess that I am full of the prejudices that I was nursed on. . . . This sentiment is one I share with the mass of common people, and I am not ashamed of their company.[64]

THE collapse of the revolution of 1848 has haunted and obsessed liberal Germans ever since. What went wrong? What real chance did it have? Was failure inevitable? Why were the insurgents so incapable of following up their early successes? Was it the efficacy of Prussian troops? The timidity of the insurgents? The notorious submissiveness of the German *Untertan*—the obedient subject—or the limited, hesitant response of the population? The answers to such questions have seldom been unequivocal. But there is little dispute that the failure of 1848 marked a decisive moment in German history.

The English historian Lewis Namier and others traced an unbroken line from the abortion of liberty in 1848 to World War I. In the jingoist enthusiasm of those Frankfurt Assembly deputies who called for a great Reich stretching from Hamburg to the Black Sea, Namier saw adumbrations of the expansionist goals of National Socialism. Heine, without benefit of such hindsight, nevertheless extrapolated from such jingoism his darkest fears for the future of Europe. He was convinced that the revolution had been defeated by the ingrained subservience of the German middle class, the widespread cult of military virtues, the tradition of chest out, belly in, and trap shut. After the collapse of the revolution, he wrote:

> *The wind's asleep that howled so wild*
> *At home it's quiet as can be.*
> *Germany, the great big child,*
> *Plays happily around its Christmas tree.*[65]

A few years later, Heine reached for a violent metaphor to describe the reluctance of the German middle class to free itself. Alluding to the treatment decreed in the Old Testament for liberated slaves who refuse to go free, he declaimed: "Oh, Moses, our teacher! *Moshe rabbenu!* Exalted fighter against slavery! Hand me hammer and nails so that I may take our complacent slaves in their red, white, and gold livery and nail them by their ears to the Brandenburg Gate." The National Assembly, Heine told a visitor, was full of "fossils! old trash! And the leaders!? Oh, the leaders!"[66]

Heine claimed all too accurately that the liberal leadership had been diffuse, contradictory, and uninspiring. Instead of arousing their fellow Germans, the professors of the assembly had mainly bored them. There was nothing "inevitable" about this. Other leaders might well have been more effective. The democratic revolution failed, too, through lack of popular support, especially in rural areas. Most of the radical militants had been city dwellers. They traveled by train, at unprecedented speeds, from one revolutionary hearth to another, overlooking the immobile, ultraconservative majority in the countryside. They did not foresee what Alexis de Tocqueville grasped so clearly, that the peasants, freed from their feudal overlords and given the vote, would become the most conservative of all classes. After World War II, the first president of West Germany, Theodor Heuss, openly lamented the "historical *Leid*"—the flaw—of the Germans: they had tried but never fully achieved democracy through their own efforts. Instead they waited for the Western Allies to impose it on them in 1949.[67]

THE political collapse of the revolution led to several final spasms of violence. New street battles flared up in Dresden. An armed uprising broke out in the Rhineland and in parts of Baden. In the Pfalz, a provisional revolutionary government was formed. After the breakup of the National Assembly by Prussian and Württembergian troops, some of the hardiest rebels formed an armed force in the Palatinate to continue the fight. Ludwig Bamberger, frustrated and discouraged by a brief term as an alternate deputy in the assembly, also decided to take matters into his own hands. Early in June 1849, he quit his position on the *Mainzer Zeitung* and took to the hills. "The time for editorials is over," he decided.[68] A week later, he was heading a contingent of republican rebels fighting government troops in the Baden countryside. "Will all of Germany rise up?" he wondered hopefully.[69] Less than a fortnight later, he knew that it would not.

The insurrection was short, futile, and tragic. Although some of the government troops went over to the rebels, they scored only a few local victories. At the outset, Bamberger could still take time off in the evening, after the fighting, to ride over to an isolated mill nearby for a rendezvous with his fiancée. Then the rebels' situation worsened. A promised legion of armed German exiles living in France never arrived. There was a shortage of officers, food, money, and arms. Bamberger, like most of the other commanders, lacked military experience. The peasants ("dull and narrow-minded," according to Bamberger) betrayed them. Morale among the men declined, and they were quickly over-powered by the Prussian army. Every tenth man who surrendered was ordered shot by the Prussian commanding general. Hundreds would spend years in jail. Bamberger and a last remnant of fighting men with-drew toward Karlsruhe and disbanded.

On June 22, 1849, Bamberger crossed into Switzerland. He would not see Mainz again for almost twenty years. He was tried in absentia, together with three hundred others, on charges of armed insurrection, insult to authority, and high treason. He was sentenced to death by hanging in the public square of Zweibrücken and fined "costs" amount-ing to two thousand thalers. It was difficult to obtain visas to France, even for transit to England, where Bamberger was assured refuge. The French consulate in Zurich issued passes for travel only to Besançon, the nearest French prefecture. There the prefect would decide whether to send Bamberger back to Switzerland or allow him to proceed to En-gland. When Bamberger arrived, the prefect had before him a police report describing Bamberger as "head of the bands who flooded the Palatinate in blood." He examined the slender young man with a dubi-ous eye ("I looked possibly even less Herculean than I do now," Bam-berger noted in a memoir he wrote shortly after the event) and asked: "So it was you who toppled several governments?" "Yes, *Monsieur le préfet*," Bamberger answered, "unfortunately not well enough!"[70]

6

Hopes and Anxieties

BAMBERGER spent the first years of his long exile in London. His maternal uncle, the Parisian banker Louis Bischoffsheim, disapproved of his nephew's politics, which he felt brought only misfortune to Bamberger and his family.[1] Still, Bischoffsheim made him an apprentice at the bank's branch office in London. Bamberger had only to shave his full beard, a distinguishing mark of the "forty-eighters" (as of the Cuban revolutionaries a century later); it was a red beard and he had not trimmed it since his student days. He did not entirely give up the bold rhetoric of his retort to the Besançon prefect but trimmed it to fit his new career as an investment banker. After two years at the London branch, he was promoted to clerk at the Amsterdam office. His fiancée, Anna Belmont, joined him and they married; he had last seen her as an insurgent in the hills of the Palatinate. They did not have a religious wedding: Bamberger informed his young fiancée that if he ever returned to God it would be "over the devil's bridge." Anna's cousin, the New York financier August Belmont, had just arrived in The Hague as the American chargé d'affaires. This relation widened the budding young banker's range of business opportunities.

In 1856, he moved to Paris as a director of Bischoffsheim's newly formed Banque de Paris et des Pays-Bas. He prospered. The couple made their home on the elegant Place Vendôme. In his early thirties, Bamberger was slim, tall, slightly haggard, an elegant young man with a penchant for the fine arts and an uncanny ability to invest in the volatile stock market of the day and nearly double his capital every year. In the reactionary regime of Napoleon III, Bamberger was at first regarded as potentially subversive. Men may change, but their police files never do. The secret police kept Bamberger under surveillance, although fortunately, the director of Paris security was "not disinclined," as Bamberger put it, "to maintain good relations with financiers."[2] (He was later indicted for stock fraud.)

Bamberger was happier in Paris than he had been in Holland. In Amsterdam most of his friends had been German exiles like himself. The Bambergers frequented some of the best salons. They made friends with Ernest Renan, Émile Zola, the brothers Goncourt, Heine, and Ivan Turgenev. Although in Holland there had been no overt hatred of Jews, of the sort that, when he wrote his memoirs in the late 1880s, he remembered only too well from Germany. Dutch Jews practiced a kind of voluntary self-segregation. It was only in Paris that Bamberger finally "breathed freely." Religious differences were ignored. "It was possible for families to socialize with one another for years without asking or being asked about their religion. The word *anti-Semitism* had not yet been invented in Germany, from where it later spread all over the world.[3] One of the first anti-Semitic attacks on Bamberger came, in fact, not from French or German conservatives but from the exiled German communist Karl Marx, who decried Bamberger for his role in the Paris "stock-exchange synagogue."[4]

In Paris, Bamberger began to write again, publishing articles in the French press. Nevertheless, he remained obsessed with German affairs. "I never thought of settling permanently abroad," he later wrote. "However pleasant or stimulating my life in Paris was, it never dimmed my desire to return to Germany and play a part in its politics."[5] He devoured the German press and published his own literary and political

"Paris German Yearbook." He was an officer of the Turnverein, a fraternity of liberal and republican German exiles in France, and sang in its male choir, which rendered "thundering" versions of "Deutschland, Deutschland über alles" at the group's annual gatherings. Thirty years later, an embittered man, a lonely old Jew feeling isolated among allegedly genuine Germans, Bamberger would look back on these rituals on foreign soil in a mood of wistful self-irony.[6] The patriotic hymn now seemed to him little more than an "anti-Semitic 'Marseillaise.'"[7]

In the mid-1850s, though, he had no such doubts or qualms. Along with other liberal exiles, he put his trust in the inevitable march of progress. He was sure he would one day play a role in the politics of a united, democratic Germany; it was bound to happen, Bamberger assured his mother in Mainz. He followed Bismarck's rise to power—and his ruthless determination to unify Germany—with passionate interest. All the while, he maintained a lively correspondence with other exiled veterans of 1848 and like-minded intellectuals and politicians (many of them Jews) both in Germany and elsewhere in Europe and America. For all the ease of his life in Paris, he felt himself an alien on French soil. "I try to justify my presence here by all kinds of pointless historical research," he wrote Eduard Lasker, another Jewish veteran of 1848, now one of the few liberal deputies in the new Prussian state parliament.[8]

Early in 1862 and without Bamberger's knowledge, his aged mother submitted a humbly worded plea to the chief minister of Hesse-Darmstadt asking for his compassion in allowing her son, whom she had not seen for many years, the privilege of a brief visit to Mainz. The request was granted on condition that he refrain from political activity. The family in Mainz expected Bamberger to be overjoyed. Instead, he was furious that they had not consulted him before the plea was made. He would never accept the clemency of a minister he considered one of the most reactionary in all Germany. He also suspected a trap designed to compromise him in the eyes of his friends. Although he did not wish to cause his family trouble, he wrote, he "felt the urgent need to do something that would constitute a protest against what had happened."[9]

An opportunity to demonstrate his continued distance from any post-1848 German regime soon presented itself. Heinrich Simon, one of the most outstanding liberal members of the dissolved Frankfurt National Assembly, drowned while swimming in Switzerland, where he had found refuge. The son of converted parents in Breslau and a former professor of constitutional law, he was the coauthor of a well-known book decrying the pitiful legal status of Jews in all parts of Prussia.[10] A Prussian arrest mandate and a sentence of life imprisonment had been issued in his absence.

The small Swiss town of Murg where Simon had lived since 1849 had made him an honorary citizen. Intent on proving that the spirit of 1848 was not dead, exiles and liberals from Germany were planning to attend the unveiling of a public monument in his honor on a hilltop overlooking the lake where he had drowned. The Prussian government intervened diplomatically to prevent the public ceremony, but the little township would not budge. Bamberger had not been sure at first whether he could attend; the embarrassing invitation from Mainz convinced him that he must. His presence would be reported to the German authorities. It would be a "good way of showing" that he "accepted no favors from them."[11]

In the event, more than three hundred veterans of 1848 attended the memorial. Many had been deputies in the National Assembly. Most arrived from Germany and Austria; others came from France, England, Italy, and even New York. Perhaps a fifth were Jews. From Königsberg came Simon's closest intimate, the indomitable Johann Jacoby, aged nestor of German radicals, still tirelessly battling for his views, as he had throughout his entire life, undeterred by frequent arrests. In Bamberger's eyes, Jacoby was "a saint of pure faith."[12] Moritz Hartmann, a veteran of the abortive Vienna uprising, came from that city; Fritz Kapp, one of the leaders of the armed uprising of 1848, from New York; the son of Robert Blum, who was executed for high treason in 1848, from Milan; Bamberger from Paris. "Steadfast in our shared conviction, we formed an amicable association whose ideals could, for the time being, find fulfillment only in exile," Bamberger wrote.[13] The scene in Murg was a "humanly moving and politically ghostly moment" of the kind that political émigrés would experience again and again over the next century.[14] Thirteen years after the demise of a great cause launched with so much hope, its vanquished veterans, dispersed all over the world, were meeting once more. Bamberger, Jacoby, and Hartmann eulogized their dead friend. Bamberger lamented their loneliness and their pain: the course of their lives "had been broken in half." But they would return, he swore, unbowed and victorious. Last to speak was one of Simon's Swiss admirers, a colonel in the army named Bernold. He simply could not fathom, he exclaimed, how a people as advanced in science and art and in civilized humanity as the Germans could at the same time be so hopelessly backward and politically helpless. It's a riddle, he cried. "I am at my wit's end."[15]

In the early 1860s, the first amnesty laws for the veterans of 1848–49 were enacted. The spectrum of repression now ran from the relatively liberal smaller principalities to the more rigid Prussia and Bavaria; veterans still wanted for high treason in one German state might now be the recipients of medals in another. It was only a question of time until Bamberger, too, would be able to return to his hometown. He waited anxiously. In 1863, he and his wife vacationed in Baden, where an amnesty law had been passed and liberal Prussian writers were given asylum. Knowledgeable people assured Bamberger that if he remained discreet and shunned all publicity he would not be at risk in Saxony or Prussia either. The likelihood of arrest and extradition to Bavaria (where his death sentence was still pending) or to Mainz was minimal. Bamberger visited old friends in Dresden, Leipzig, and Berlin. He had last seen them in the fall of 1848, when Prussian troops had just dissolved the first freely elected state parliament and the streets were deserted. In the fall of 1863, the mood among his friends in Berlin was still "grim," he noted. Prussia was in the grip of a parliamentary crisis provoked by Bismarck. In 1861, William I had succeeded his father, Frederick William IV, to the throne and appointed his staunch ally, Bismarck, prime minister. Bismarck sought to expand his realm of power and commit Prussia to war with Austria—perceived as a rival to his and William's imperial ambitions. Bamberger, in Berlin during this moment of political and constitutional conflict, was impressed by his friends' "powerful spirit of opposition" to Bismarck's authoritarian designs.[16]

Bamberger was also heartened by the growth of a new middle class of enlightened bureaucrats, liberal scholars, and independent entrepreneurs. He returned to Paris hoping that the foundations of the old German world of authoritarianism and repression were cracking. "It was a time of becoming, which is often more beautiful than the hour of fulfillment," he noted in his memoirs, recollecting his naïve optimism before he had had a chance to encounter the Prussian Junkers. "Everything I saw encouraged me to return." He would have condemned as "crack-brained" anyone who had accurately predicted the degree of devastation Bismarck's system would ultimately wreak on the lawmaking process and the overall spirit of the country. Nor could he have foreseen the day when he would be accused of conflicting loyalties and subjected to anti-Semitic slurs.[17]

Italian reunification and the results of the American Civil War reconfirmed Bamberger in his view that freedom and equality could be achieved only in a unified Germany under a democratically elected national government. The desire to quit Paris and move back to Germany became stronger. The Prussian victory over Austria in the war of 1866 was a turning point. It established Prussia's hegemony in Central Europe and led to a Prussian-orchestrated confederation of the North German states. This in turn—just as Bamberger had expected—led to the formal emancipation of Jews. Like other Jews, he hoped that the formal act would lead to genuine equality.

Bamberger grew convinced that sooner or later the new North German Confederation would encompass the South German states too. Prussia was the key to German unification. It appeared to him almost a law of nature that Prussia's political "force of gravity" must attract all smaller political masses in Germany. In the past, Prussia had evoked in Bamberger "neither trust nor love nor hope."[18] But a Prussia freed of the "vices of feudalism" and transformed into a modern constitutional monarchy might be another matter. Bamberger convinced himself that Prussia was Germany's best hope for a better future. Other homesick forty-eighters had reached the same conclusion. The example of Italy, for one, was fresh in their minds. Just as the crude power politics of Piedmont—rather than Garibaldi's bravura or Mazzini's noble rhetoric—had recently brought about the unification of Italy, so too Prussia might finally unite all Germans in a new, enlightened Reich. "If you want to be free," many said, "let us help make Prussia free. All else is wasted effort."

Bismarck's mainstay in the new North German Reichstag was the National Liberal Party, headed by Eduard Lasker, the son of an observant Jewish family in Posen who as a law student had fought on the barricades in Breslau and Vienna. He was not the only former revolutionary who pinned his hopes on Bismarck. Bamberger himself had even written a little book in French (*Monsieur de Bismarck*) hailing as a potential revolutionary the man who would soon be known as the Iron Chancellor. Indeed, few things are as curious in nineteenth-century German history as Bismarck's success in enlisting the services of the insurgents of 1848.

Bamberger had not forgotten the vow he had made in Murg to return and continue to fight. But the former Proudhon socialist was now a confirmed believer in the free-market economy known at the time as Manchesterism. A successful career in banking had made him rich by the relatively young age of forty; he could, if he so chose, live off his investments. When Hesse-Darmstadt, too, amnestied the veterans of 1848–49 and became part of Bismarck's North German Confederation, Bamberger resigned his position at the bank, moved back to Mainz, and immediately threw himself into local politics. His rise in Lasker's National Liberal Party was quick and seemingly effortless. Over the next fifteen years, Lasker's and Bamberger's flourishing political careers mirrored the growing integration of Jews in German politics.

In the parliamentary register Bamberger refrained from declaring his religion. His true religion was probably politics. As the historian Jacob Toury observes, Bamberger was publicly a German but privately a Jew. He continued to speak of both Jews and Germans in ethnic terms: Jews were *unsereiner*, people "like *us*"; Germans were people "like *them*." Germans baffled and sometimes frightened him. He could not understand their "lyrical servility, . . . a specifically German" quality. "They bathe in spittle and lick it like ambrosia."[19] If he was sharply critical of things "typically German" (servility, alcoholism), he was equally tough on "typically Jewish" flaws (greed, pushiness, bad manners). Theodor Mommsen, a leading contemporaneous German historian, regarded Bamberger as "the *most* German of men."[20] But although Bamberger served Bismarck, when he later criticized him, Bismarck darkly insinuated that Bamberger was a *"sujet mixte,"* by implication someone torn in his loyalties.[21]

In August 1870, war broke out between France and Germany. Bismarck had deliberately provoked it through shrewd international intrigues and calculated leaks to the press. Among other provocations seen by the French as unbearable was the nomination of a Hohenzollern prince to the vacant throne of Spain, an act that threatened to alter the European balance of power to the detriment of France. The French army was ill-prepared for war and badly led. Prussia's troops, well trained and led by Count Helmuth Moltke, a brilliant military strategist, quickly advanced to the outskirts of Paris. Napoléon III capitulated at Sedan but the French—and the people of Paris—fought on. Bamberger joined Bismarck's personal staff as an expert on French affairs and as a liaison with the National Liberal Party. Bismarck had been well pleased with Bamberger's adulatory pamphlet. For his part, Bamberger was eager to be close to "the genius personality . . . of the great chancellor," yet, judging from his diaries, he remained ambivalent about the war and the man who had unleashed it.[22]

In the autumn, Bamberger followed Bismarck to his field headquarters at the palace of Versailles, where, as the saying went, Germany's greatness would be reborn "at the pleasure seat of Louis XVI." The Prussian generals' privations were lavishly relieved with champagne, victuals, and cigars of exquisite quality supplied daily from Strasbourg and Brussels by Gerson Bleichröder, Bismarck's Jewish banker. Bamberger spent several weeks in Bismarck's entourage, frequently in his company. His reputation as a former insurgent was much commented on; according to Moritz Busch, Bismarck's press secretary, he was dubbed "the red Jew."[23] In the intimacy of small candlelit dinner parties, Bamberger grew to know Bismarck better and to like him less. His pleas to cease the merciless siege and bombardment of Paris were not heeded. Bismarck insisted that both be continued until Paris capitulated. "In that case," Bamberger warned, "they'll send their [famished] women and children across the lines to confront us." Bismarck replied: "Then we'll have to shoot them." One of the officers present remarked that Prussian soldiers might refuse to obey such an order; they were already reluctant to fire on hungry Frenchmen scavenging for potatoes in the fields. "In that case," Bismarck answered, "we'll have to shoot the soldiers too."[24]

On another occasion, enjoying a fat cigar after dinner, Bismarck remarked that he was now smoking much more than before the war. To Bamberger's comment that "war either kills you or makes you stronger," Bismarck retorted, "War is the natural state of mankind."[25]

Bamberger was not the only Jew at Bismarck's headquarters. As soon as it became clear that France was defeated, Bleichröder was summoned to Versailles. There was talk of imposing an enormous war indemnity, and Bleichröder was supposed to contact Rothschild in Paris to arrange terms of payment. Like Bamberger, Bleichröder was the son of a Jewish banker. Here the similarities ended. Bleichröder served power, never trying to change it. He was the last of the great German court Jews, "Bismarck's *Privatjude*," as he was known at Versailles. Said to be the richest man in Berlin ("a Bismarck in his field"), he could have been a character in a novel by Balzac. Bismarck systematically exploited his hunger for honors and decorations and his craving for social prominence. At Bleichröder's sumptuous parties, to which he never invited relatives, the guests—noblemen and ministers—mocked their host's appearance and ostentation.

Bleichröder had been in Bismarck's personal service since 1859, for which he was routinely rewarded with valuable political intelligence that enriched both him and his master. Bismarck was especially grateful to Bleichröder for having financed the Austro-Prussian War of 1866, a moment when, as Bismarck confessed, "I was almost as close to the gallows as to the throne."[26] Now Bleichröder's Berlin office was permitted to use military telegraph lines to transmit the daily stock market quotations to him in Versailles.

Bleichröder managed the ample slush fund Bismarck had designated for bribing the kings of Württemberg and Bavaria and other South German paladins who still hesitated to join Bismarck's North German Confederation in an all-German Reich. Bamberger and Lasker were also active in promoting this plan. According to Fritz Stern, Bleichröder's

biographer, Bismarck depended on his banker and on the Jewish parliamentarians for their liberal credentials, their connections, and their
financial acumen, yet when they came to Versailles he denigrated them.
According to Stern, "There was an insistent, harsh anti-Semitic tone at
Versailles: at no other time in his life did Bismarck speak so often, so
freely, so scathingly of the rootlessness of Jews, of their hustling, of
their omnipresence."[27]

Bismarck was moody and suspicious and saw Jewish "power" and
influence everywhere. Judging from their "physiognomy," he convinced
himself that most or all the members of the new French provisional
government with whom, after the abdication of Napoleon III, he was
negotiating an armistice were Jews. Here, too, says Stern, prejudice
hardened into policy.[28] We do not know if Bamberger personally experienced any of these slights; it is difficult to imagine he did not. In his
diary there is, however, not a single word about such matters.

The negotiations over the war indemnity dragged on. Vast sums of
six to eight billion gold francs were mentioned. When one of the
French emissaries said that if someone had started counting six billion
francs in Jesus' time he would still be at it, Bismarck replied that he had
"provided for that" by bringing Bleichröder the Jew, who had started
counting at the Creation.

Bamberger advised against imposing too crippling a burden on the
defeated French. In the interest of future reconciliation, he urged Bismarck not to give in to the demands of public opinion, which had in any
case been manufactured. His advice was not heeded. Bleichröder's
obsequious counterargument was that France would "benefit from a
crippling blow because it would reconcile her to a peaceful role and to
disarmament."[29]

The Francophile Bamberger was repelled by the prevailing arrogance. He experienced moments of serious doubt. How would Prussia
exploit its new military dominance in Germany and on the rest of the
Continent? He feared that even the recent legislation allowing the Jews
equal rights might be abrogated, as it had been in 1815. From Versailles,
during the siege of Paris, Bamberger wrote to a National Liberal colleague in Berlin: "Do see in good time that pressure is brought to bear
from above, within the broadest political circles, to ensure that the vic-

tories on the battlefield translate into something that benefits the German people."[30]

BERTHOLD Auerbach, the author of the famous *Village Tales from the Black Forest,* suffered no such doubts. He approved of the war wholeheartedly. He was flattered by the attentions of generals and elderly duchesses—the latter were among his most devoted fans. His *German Evenings,* a cloyingly sentimental collection, was dedicated to "Her Imperial Highness Grand Duchess Helena of Russia."

Like most other Germans, Auerbach regarded the war against France as a "national necessity" in which "justice, honor, and virtue" were entirely on their side. He even wrote a jingoistic pamphlet defending the righteousness of the German cause, *What the German Wants and What the Frenchman Wants,* and went on a reading tour with it through southwest Germany. The staunch burghers of Cannstatt serenaded him under his hotel window. Elsewhere he wrote: "I am a Swabian but anno 1870 I became a Prussian soldier. As a soldier I am ready to be mere cannon fodder. For this even a Jew like myself is good enough."[31]

In August, Auerbach accompanied his patron, the grand duke of Baden, to field headquarters at Lampertheim. In such august company he was able to watch the battle for Strasbourg from a safe vantage point. He saw a bit more than he bargained for. In a letter written in thick Swabian dialect he commented on what it was like to be "just a little Jew in the middle of all those mighty officers, and only yesterday . . . I rode out there with the grand duke and they carried a dead man right under my nose and that's something I can't abide."[32] But after attending the Prussian victory parade through the Brandenburg Gate in Berlin, Auerbach was once again aflame; he told his cousin that all "messianic hopes"—nothing less—had been fulfilled. Future generations would consider them fortunate to have lived in such glorious times. "It feels good to at last be in step with the great mass of your own people. . . . When they marched past carrying the eighty-one captured French tricolors and the golden eagles, I shuddered with emotion: it's over. The confounded demon, the bloodthirsty French *Gloire,* is vanquished, let us hope once and for all."[33]

.   .   .

WITH the crushing defeat of Napoléon III's army at Sedan, Bismarck's political glory reached its zenith. The dominant mood in the German press was triumphant. Wagner composed a rattling military march celebrating the entry of German troops into Paris, a city that had welcomed him and long been his spiritual home. Some said the victory was divinely ordained, others that it proved the superiority of German culture. The novelist Gustav Freytag was overcome by the "poetry of the historical process."[34] God was rewarding the manly, honest, upright Germans and punishing the decadent and predatory French.

Johann Jacoby, ever skeptical, was considerably more circumspect. He anticipated Nietzsche's warning in 1873 that a great military victory could be more dangerous to a people than a defeat, especially if misconstrued as evidence of the superiority of one culture over another. Jacoby had long feared Bismarck's scheme to unify Germany through war rather than through reform of the old social and power hierarchies; foreign wars only served to divert attention from domestic injustices. For these reasons, Jacoby had also opposed Prussia's attack on Denmark in 1864 and on Austria two years later and had landed in prison for his views. Bismarck's third war and its aftermath troubled him even more: the new Reich was an unholy union of "throne, altar, and money." Jacoby was fiercely attacked for such statements. If it were up to Jacoby and his friends, said one critic, "the French would now be in Berlin, not the Germans in Paris."[35] The historian Heinrich von Treitschke, an ardent supporter of the war, wrote ironically that in his inflexibility Jacoby was "more East Prussian than Jew."[36]

Ludwig Philippson, editor of the *Allgemeine Zeitung des Judentums*, also decried the rampant xenophobia generated by the war. He feared it might lead to a new wave of hatred toward Jews.* But the most critical and incisive antiwar voice in all Germany was that of Leopold Sonnemann, the Jewish publisher of the *Frankfurter Zeitung*, the leading

---

*The reaction of Philippson's son Martin was more in line with the common consensus. In a letter to his parents from Berlin he wrote: "Who would not be overjoyed at this moment knowing of the incomparable virtue that our gallant *Volk* has just proven on the battlefield. . . . Tears of joy and emotion fill my eyes (Toury, *Die politischen Orientierungen*, pp. 333–34).

liberal newspaper in Germany. Sonnemann detested Prussian militarism and authoritarianism and predicted that the new unity achieved through war would come at the expense of freedom. His readers were, in the main, concentrated in southern Germany; they included professionals, businessmen, academics, and independent-minded people whom Bismarck ridiculed as "pillars of public stupidity."[37]

The immediate consequence of Bismarck's victory was the fulfillment of the great goal that gave so much satisfaction to many liberals: the unification of all the German states. After Sedan, the southern states capitulated and joined the North German Confederation in a new German Reich. Sonnemann himself ran for election to the new all-German Reichstag, defeating another Frankfurt Jew, the conservative baron Karl von Rothschild. Sonnemann remained convinced that Prussia's military and diplomatic dominance in the new Reich threatened not only Germany's moral and political balance but also Europe's balance of power. His attitude echoed that of Georg Herwegh, the poet of 1848, who in his "Epilogue to War" now wrote:

> *A single flag: black, white, and red!*
> *United under one regime,*
> *Now German might commands esteem*
> *And glorified bloodshed reigns supreme.*
> *Germania, you fill my heart with dread.*[38]

In his distrust of Prussia, Sonnemann was the antithesis of the prewar Bamberger, whom he criticized as a turncoat and ridiculed as a half-baked Machiavellian. Sonnemann was an economist, a practical man rather than an ideologist or political philosopher. At a time when educated, politically involved German men were enamored of Bismarck's realpolitik, this eminently sober journalist offered a different version of patriotism and a warning that would prove tragically correct. An early advocate of a United States of Europe, he was one of very few who foresaw that the new empire would give birth to a dangerously militarized society. German unification had originally been the aspiration of the liberal middle class. But this new Reich was strictly a creation of the Prussian army. Sonnemann predicted that it would enshrine the wrong civic values—rigidity, chauvinism, prejudice, and blind obedience—and would lead to a Bismarck dictatorship. Neither the Prussian state parliament nor the new all-German Reichstag would be able to challenge his will or unseat him.

Bismarck did all he could to obstruct Sonnemann and his editors by legal and other means, including summary arrests, house searches, deportations, and heavy fines. Issues of the *Frankfurter Zeitung* were repeatedly confiscated during the war for spreading "defeatist news" or for citing foreign press reports of alleged French military successes and outrages committed by Prussian troops. "Outside of Russia," Sonnemann charged in a Reichstag speech, "I know of no other state where the press is as unfree as in Prussia."[39] For his active membership in Victor Hugo's pacifist International League for Peace and Freedom, he was accused of being a traitor.

Sonnemann was aghast at the arrogant way in which the new Reich was proclaimed—even as the cannons roared—in the Hall of Mirrors at Versailles, a deeply humiliating affront to French sensibilities. Present at the proclamation were mostly dukes, generals, and their minions, nearly all wearing military uniforms and battle helmets, including Bismarck and William I. It was the worst possible solution to the so-called problem of German disunity: a federation of absolute rulers presided over by the Prussian king now addressed as Germany's "kaiser." The black, red, and gold flag of 1848 was replaced by the black, red, and white colors of the house of Hohenzollern. There were no representatives of the people in the hall. Eduard Simson, president of the preunification North German Reichstag, had to wait in the wings until every German duke and landgrave had consented to unification (some only after receiving handsome bribes) before he, too, was allowed to petition the new kaiser to accept the imperial crown. The new Reichstag was a crippled parliament. It had a democratic franchise but little democratic function. The chancellor and his cabinet of ministers were appointed by the kaiser without parliamentary approval. The Reichstag could not dismiss them. War, too, was exclusively the kaiser's prerogative. The new Reichstag's powers were limited even in matters concerning the national budget. Defense spending and foreign policy were not within its purview: defense budgets were submitted for approval only once in seven years.

It was the second time that Simson, a converted Jew in a country where even converts were still not considered full Germans, was offering an imperial crown to a German king. He must have been aware of the changed circumstances: in 1849, as the representative of the democratically elected Frankfurt National Assembly, he had been a main figure; twenty-one years later, he was a mere rubber stamp, a sideshow, subordinate to the assembled dukes and generals, with their clanking spurs and medals. Bismarck and the new kaiser made clear how little they appreciated the participation of the parliamentarians at this historic event. Nevertheless, Simson was grateful for his friendly reception at Versailles, according to his biographer.

Sonnemann grasped more clearly than most other Germans the changing nature of German nationalism. Before the establishment of the new Reich, it had centered on unification and had been the cornerstone of a liberal ideology opposed to social and religious prejudice; with the establishment of the Reich, it became conservative, xenophobic, conformist, and worshipful of the militarists who had brought it about.

ON no subject were Sonnemann's warnings more clear-sighted than on the forcible annexation of Alsace and parts of Lorraine. Bismarck claimed these provinces in the name of "historical rights," for "reasons of state" and "national security"; no doubt their well-developed industries and rich deposits of iron ore and potash had something to do with the decision, too. While the nationalists sanctified the "right of conquest" as divinely ordained, Sonnemann argued that despite what "Bismarck and his Mameluks" wished to make people believe, the annexation was simply robbery.[40] Sonnemann thought little of the notion of historical rights. It was true that in the sixteenth century the territory had been under German rule, but the population was now largely French. "We cannot support the forcible annexation of 1.2 million souls against their will," Sonnemann told a jeering Reichstag.[41] "Reasons of state" would best be served by a reconciliation with France. The annexation of Alsace-Lorraine would inevitably lead to another war (as indeed it did forty-four years later). Any peace, he warned, would be "little more than an armistice."[42]

In the intoxicating atmosphere of postwar hubris, Sonnemann stood apart. To remain aloof and dispassionate, as he did, was a rare mark of character. Among other prominent political figures perhaps only the aged Johann Jacoby, the socialist August Bebel, and the writer and future diplomat Julius von Eckardt joined him in publicly opposing annexation. For his protest Jacoby was arrested by the military commander of the Königsberg area and led away in chains. Given Jacoby's reputation and age, even Bismarck recognized the folly of his arrest and quickly ordered his release.*

Bleichröder's response typified the general mood. He flooded Bismarck with letters of fulsome adoration. Even in terms of the rhetoric of the moment, his jingoism and obsequiousness reflected the price he was willing to pay for the title Bismarck conferred on him for his services soon after the war. He was the first Prussian Jew permitted to add the coveted "von" to his name without first converting to Christianity.[†] His palatial town house in the Behrendstrasse, which stunned even Disraeli with its ostentatiousness, became the site of "Lucullan feasts" celebrating Prussia's victory, the annexation of Alsace and Lorraine, and Bleichröder's elevation to the nobility.[43] To further demonstrate his patriotism, Bleichröder imported two thousand stones and rocks from the battlefield of Sedan where the Prussians had defeated the French. He directed his masons to assemble them in the park at his country estate as a monument to Prussian militarism.

Berthold Auerbach's reaction was more muted: he wrote a poem

---

*August Bebel and Wilhelm Liebknecht (also a socialist) were less lucky. They were arrested under martial law and transported to East Prussia, where they were to stand trial for high treason. The civilian courts, however, were unwilling to try them and they were eventually released. They sued the general who had arrested them and won, although the general was compensated by the kaiser from the privy purse.

† In England, it would take thirteen more years before Queen Victoria, in 1885, would confer a similar hereditary honor on an unconverted Jew.

hailing the annexation.* But he also recorded the words of a worried Alsatian Jew who told him woefully that until now he and his coreligionists had been Frenchmen: "But now we must become German Jews!"[44]† On the whole, German liberals were either swayed by the prevailing jingoism or cowed into silence by the increasing execration of all dissenters as unpatriotic. Sonnemann, however, rejected accusations of disloyalty, insisting that no loyalty could exist "at the expense of truth." In the Reichstag, he called for a referendum in the occupied provinces, a proposal scornfully rejected by the vast majority. In the voting, Sonnemann was joined by only two others in favor of a referendum: August Bebel and a lone Danish deputy from Schleswig-Hollstein, a province annexed by Bismarck in 1864. The majority booed them for their disregard of sacred national values. In another Reichstag speech, Sonnemann castigated the "dictatorial" administration of the annexed territories, the rigorous application of conscription laws, and the forced "Germanization" of the school curriculum. Despite promises that half the curriculum would remain French, "in the most important subjects, it is now entirely German," Sonnemann said. In the plenum there were cries of "Very good! They *are* Germans!" to which Sonnemann responded: "Yes, gentlemen, you say very good! You think you can force the entire population to be German!" Again, "But they are Germans!" and again, "You'll

---

*There's merely a river to divide
  My brother on the Alsatian side
  from me, who lives so very near.
  And yet it floods my heart with tears
  when I think that my very own brother
  has forgotten we have a single mother.
    (Bettelheim, *Berthold Auerbach*, p. 330)

†Thousands of other Jews of Alsace and Lorraine felt the same reluctance. The German-language *Strassburger Tageblatt* compared their flight from the annexed provinces to the exodus from Egypt. Opting for French citizenship after the annexation, 12.7 percent of them moved their domiciles to France. Two of the three chief rabbis turned down Prussian offers to remain at their posts at double salary.

Bismarck's Jewish banker, Gerson Bleichröder. *Courtesy Leo Baeck Institute, Jerusalem*

never be able to make them Germans by force."[45] The *Augsberger Zeitung* articulated the prevailing mood by demanding that the reeducation of the Alsatians "begin with the rod. The alienated children must feel our fist. Love will follow the disciplining, and it will make them German again."[46]

The attacks on Sonnemann would continue for almost a decade. He remained as isolated and committed as he had always been. "I did it in the interest of Germany," he said in a speech in 1876, "in the interest of the fatherland, of German honor, German justice. I would do it again today."[47]

Sonnemann's pleas, ironically, were rebutted even by Bamberger, whose own speeches reflected the baseness of the counterattack. He snidely referred to what he called Sonnemann's admiration for all things French. He even insinuated that Sonnemann might be receiving his orders from Paris. Bismarck said openly what Bamberger had implied. He called Sonnemann "a paid French agent."[48] History would soon show that even in "reasons of state," Sonnemann, not Bismarck, was the better patriot.

By and large, German Jews were glad to go along with the widely accepted cause of the war: French aggression. "My heart is full of rage and hatred against France, which wantonly started this war," wrote Jakob Grunwald, son of an old rabbinical family in Warburg, who had volunteered for military service.[49] The war was an opportunity for Jews to demonstrate their Germanness. Writing from outside the besieged French fortress of Metz, Grunwald happily informed his bride that all differences between Jews and non-Jews had disappeared. A few days later, after meeting a few other Jewish soldiers in the trenches, he added that Jews and Germans were really one big *Volk*; they needed no war to unite them. Ludwig Philippson of the *Allgemeine Zeitung des Judentums* undertook the remarkable task of collecting and publishing the names of all the Jewish frontline soldiers. Although Philippson had been personally critical of the war, he saw compiling the list as a "sacred duty." Defiance and abject apologetics were rarely so tightly entwined; nothing showed more clearly the continuing unease of many German Jews and the pressures weighing on them despite their recent formal emancipation. The list was prepared, Philippson wrote, "for educational reasons, for the Jews themselves, and to combat false accusations."[50] He included some 4,700 Jewish combat soldiers by name and hometown, among them 140 officers, 483 casualties, and 373 recipients of the Iron Cross. According to other counts, between 7,000 and 12,000 Jewish combatants took part.

"It was as though the Jews had resolved to put an end to their old image as reluctant and incompetent soldiers," wrote the novelist Theodor Fontane.[51] A report in the Berlin weekly *Allgemeine Israelitische Wochenschrift* described a scene at the Breslau station where a number of young Jewish conscripts boarded a train to the front: "Proud and brave they took leave of their families."[52]

Pride, or at least the public display of pride, was reflected in a printed cloth panel, copies of which soon appeared on walls in countless Jewish homes (and continue to be displayed in Jewish museums to this day). The scene depicted commemorates a Yom Kippur service held by Jewish combat soldiers on October 8, 1870, inside a ruined house in St. Barbe next to the Sixth Army Corps' field headquarters. An eyewitness account in the *Allgemeine Zeitung des Judentums* spoke of some sixty Jewish soldiers of the First Prussian Army Corps, mostly noncommissioned officers, who gathered for prayer in a small house with broken-down doors, shattered windows, and walls riddled with shells.[53] The panoramic image portrayed on the panel is drastically different. It shows a broad valley outside Metz filled with "1,200 fasting German warriors" engaged in fervent prayer, according to the rhymed inscription:

Allegorical representation of a Yom Kippur service outside Metz during the Franco-Prussian War. "Have we not all one father?" *Courtesy Tefen Museum, Israel*

At Metz the sun was setting.
And in the last soft light of day
Twelve hundred German warriors
Closed ranks and bravely marched away.

With cheerful heart advancing
Into the lovely vale below.
With solemn purpose marching
And as they marched their spirits rose.

They followed one sole leader
Eager and happy to comply
For he received his orders
From Him who reigns on high.

The soldiers' uniforms, swords, and spiked Prussian helmets are covered by traditional Jewish prayer shawls. A giant ark of the law is set up on a low hill. On the surrounding cliffs, Christian soldiers stand guard in a long line, protecting their Jewish comrades in arms from enemy attack. In the distance, beneath ominous clouds, the besieged city of Metz undergoes a barrage of cannon fire. The inscription asks: "Have we not all one father? Hath not one God created us?" (Malachi 2:10).

WITH the approval, in 1871, of a new emancipation law valid for the entire Reich, German Jews seemed to have achieved, at least in theory, the object of their long struggle. The new Reichstag abolished all restrictions on civil and political rights derived from "religious difference," with none of the implied reservations of the short-lived 1812 decree. Legally, Jews were finally recognized as equals; they were elated and reassured. Among those who left a record of their thoughts, no one suspected that some of the old restrictions would continue to prevail.

The new sense of security was legitimized by the greatest authority in the field. Heinrich Graetz ended the eleventh and final volume of his monumental *History of the Jews* (1871) on a note of supreme, almost triumphant confidence:

> Happier than any of my predecessors, I may conclude my history in the
> joyous feeling that in the civilized world the Jewish tribe has found at
> last not only justice and freedom but also recognition. It now finally has
> unlimited freedom to develop its talents, not due to [Gentile] mercy but
> as a right acquired through thousandfold suffering.

Graetz's history was a grand epic of persecution and little else besides. Except in its optimistic postscript, it breathed a gloomy, lachrymose spirit of almost unmitigated fatalism. In the wake of Prussia's "glorious victories" of 1870, however, Graetz, too, declared himself a German patriot and rhapsodized about Bismarck's "genius leadership." In a letter to the historian Heinrich von Treitschke he even promised that in the forthcoming English translation of his *History*, he would revise some of his earlier harsh judgments about Germany, which, as he put it, "had become untrue" in the light of recent events.[54]

So content was the philosopher of language Fritz Mauthner, a liberal militant until 1871, that after the establishment of the "glorious" new Reich, he withdrew from all political activity. It seemed sheer joy to be alive "while Bismarck governed the world."[55] The "great Junker" was now more likable in Mauthner's eyes than any progressive or social-democratic leader.

Heinrich Bernhard Oppenheim, one of Bamberger's fellow rebels in 1848 who, like Bamberger, had spent years in exile, reminisced with satisfaction that, despite the sporadic riots of 1819 and 1848, there had been no major outbreak of anti-Jewish feeling in Germany for more than a century. Oppenheim, a native of Frankfurt and a secular Jew, stated that with the German Reich no one less than the messiah had arrived.[56] In this conviction, apparently, Oppenheim was elected to the Reichstag in 1874 in a rural constituency with few if any Jewish voters. Between 1871 and 1878, thirty-six Jews, among them twelve converts, were elected to the Reichstag, a body of more than six hundred deputies. If in some eyes they were still outsiders, they were nonetheless outsiders at the very center of public life.

Even such skeptics as Jacoby and Sonnemann, who saw through the feigned constitutionalism of Bismarck's militarized monarchy, shared the optimism of assimilated and assimilating Jewry. With all its flaws, the new Reich seemed to afford better protection to Jews than France, Austria, and even England. And compared with the czarist and Ottoman empires, it was a veritable paradise.

This sense of well-being was buttressed by the community's material advances. At the beginning of the century, most German Jews had been paupers. In Prussia, where the majority lived, 70 percent had led "marginal, insecure" lives; many were wandering peddlers and beggars. By 1870, that figure had dropped to 5 percent. According to taxation figures that probably understated the real state of affairs, over 60 percent of all Prussian Jews were now of "secure middle-class status."[57] Theirs was perhaps the fastest and greatest leap any minority has experienced in modern European history. Jews had become the most upwardly mobile social group in Germany.

The majority were now city dwellers. Urbanization among Jews proceeded at a pace two or three times that of other Germans. Acculturation was equally rapid. According to the ethnologist Moritz Lazarus, by 1841 there were no longer any fourteen-year-old Jewish children unable to read and write German.[58] By 1867, 14.8 percent of high school students in Berlin were Jews, three or four times the total percentage of Jews in the city's population. Thousands of sons of shopkeepers, innkeepers, cattle dealers, and peddlers attended universities and entered professions. The rhythms of their lives, especially in Berlin, no longer followed the Jewish calendar; they followed the German. For Christmas, according to Oppenheim, "nearly all Jewish families have fragrant wax candles glimmering on richly adorned fir trees. They consider Christmas a historical and national holiday; they commit this petty heresy to avoid excluding their children from the general festivities or alienating them from their Christian friends."[59] Some of the leading Jewish families were becoming members of the minor European aristocracy. The Heine family was a case in point. The poet had two brothers, one of whom, a doctor in St. Petersburg, was made a nobleman and married into the Russian aristocracy; the other, a newspaper editor in Vienna, was made an Austrian baron. Heine sister's son was knighted and became the baron von Embden. One of his two daughters became Princess Murat through marriage while the other married the reigning prince of Monaco.[60]

Three generations after Moses Mendelssohn, Jews were Germans in language, dress, and national sentiment. In name, too. Siegfried and Sigismund were such common names among Jews that non-Jews began to shy away from them. One Jewish tomb from 1879 in the Schönhauser Allee cemetery in Berlin says much about the sensibilities of the time: "Here lies our beloved child, Alfred Deutschland," reads the inscription.[61] Itziks changed their name to Hitzig, Cohens to Kahn, Levis to Lau. On the other hand, a Dr. Theodor Cohn rose high in the Catholic hierarchy without changing his name. At the end of a long ecclesiastical career he became the reigning prince-archbishop of Olmütz, the most distinguished Catholic diocese in Austria.* At midcentury, only

---

*His appointment had to be confirmed by the emperor, Franz Joseph, who is said to have inquired of his adjutant: "Are you sure he is baptized?"

four of Moses Mendelssohn's fifty-six descendants were still Jews. When the last died, many of the Mendelssohns attending the funeral witnessed a Jewish rite for the first time in their lives.[62] Nevertheless, the converted "von Mendelssohns" continued to flaunt the name of their illustrious forefather.

Among pious Jews, fears ripened of the imminent death of the old faith. Bamberger, Oppenheimer, Jacoby, and many others refused to convert as a matter of principle but believed that any remaining differences between Jews and Germans were bound to disappear, at least among men of culture and education. Lazarus claimed that Judaism was as "German" a religion as Christianity. In *The Religion of Reason Out of the Sources of Judaism,* Hermann Cohen reaffirmed Mendelssohn's central idea a century after his death. Cohen was perhaps the most prominent Jewish theologian of his time; he went far beyond anything Mendelssohn had stood for in believing that Judaism and Christianity would eventually merge in one all-encompassing faith. The "connubium," as he put it, between Judaism and Christianity would be easier in Germany ("Immanuel Kant's nation") than anywhere else in Europe.[63]

The key to social integration lay in assimilation through *Bildung* and religious reform. The movement for reform was growing by leaps and bounds. Reformed Jews no longer worshiped in Hebrew. They affirmed their Jewishness through revised prayer books and their Germanness by discarding the traditional prayer for the coming of the messiah "in our days." They no longer desired to be led back to the Promised Land. Germany was their beloved home. Their thoughts now ripened better under fir trees than under palms, Lazarus mused. To serve Germany, Hermann Cohen announced, was sacred, "like service of the divine." One must not love one's country only when it is "lovely," as Burke claimed, but "because it is our fatherland."[64]

Inevitably, some families split. Jacob Bernays (1824–81) was a distinguished classical philologist, the author of important studies of Spinoza and Heraclitus. When, because of his Jewish origins, he was refused a professorship at the University of Bonn, he became pious and helped found the Jewish Theological Seminary of Breslau, where for the rest of his life he taught Jewish philosophy, Hebrew poetry, and Jewish literature. By contrast, his younger brother, Michael Bernays, converted and became a prominent professor of German literature in Munich. (With Michael Bernays and Ludwig Geiger, Goethe studies began in earnest in 1866. Geiger, the son of a rabbi, founded the central organ of international Goethe research, the Goethe Yearbook.) A third Bernays brother remained in the family business in Hamburg and was the father of Martha Bernays, Sigmund Freud's wife.

Berthold Auerbach euphorically claimed that integration was now an established fact. This was a half-truth, at best, but in some of the larger cities, especially in Berlin, it was far from being a pious lie. That the possibility of integration was a widely held belief was confirmed by the sharp decline in the number of conversions.* An 1874 law permitted mixed civil marriages for the first time. Auerbach's hope that within a generation or two the "problem" would be forgotten or, at least, inconsequential did not seem far-fetched. An English observer in Berlin during the Franco-Prussian War was impressed by the degree of social integration among middle-class Jews and Christians. "The Berlin Christian is a far more tolerant being than his English coreligionist," he wrote.[65] The social limits of integration varied, of course, from place to place. A report in the *Breslauer Morgenzeitung* in 1876 on the annual ball held by the local chamber of commerce made this clear: "Our Christian and Jewish merchants have marketed, discounted, dined, and supped together. They've even intermarried, but they never dance with one another. Is this not highly remarkable?"[66]

A measure of social integration seems to have taken place among the working class. Eduard Bernstein, the future founder of revisionist socialism, who successfully challenged some of the basic assumptions of Marxist doctrine, came from a blue-collar background. His father, a plumber by training, drove a locomotive on the new Berlin-Anhalt railway line. The family lived in a working-class district of Berlin. They attended a so-called Reform temple but, like so many other Berlin Jews, celebrated Christmas as a German folk custom. "I did not pray to

---

*It was difficult for a Jew to be converted, the joke went, for how could he bring himself to believe in the divinity of . . . another Jew?

Jesus," Bernstein recalls in his memoirs, "but I never doubted that he actually lived and suffered. I felt the deepest sympathy for him." He tells the story of his older brother, who walking in the street one day was called a Jew. He yelled back: "Jew yourself!" At home, the perplexed boy learned from his mother that he really was Jewish. "We who were born later," Bernstein writes, "grew up in this knowledge. For this reason we took it more philosophically." Only from street urchins did Bernstein ever hear a nasty word about Jews, and even that was rare. The Bernsteins' day of rest was Sunday. They did not observe the Jewish dietary laws, and they shared meals with their neighbors. It was this, above all, that brought the family "emotionally closer to the neighbors. What we believed . . . did not bother them." The Bernsteins' "national identity" was deduced in these circles from the kind of sausages they ate and with whom. The family's own consciousness of who they were was little affected by religious observance. In this respect, they were no different from other blue-collar families or from the agnostic Bambergers or Sonnemanns. "Ach, you Bernsteins are not really Jews," a neighbor once remarked. The comment was well-meant, Bernstein remembered, but "it depressed rather than elated me."[67]

NONETHELESS, the repertoire of anti-Semitism was scarcely affected by these changes. The term itself would be coined only in 1879, by one Wilhelm Marr, the obscure author of the diatribe *The Victory of Judaism over Germanicism*. Marr's point of view was purely secular, that is to say, racial. French savants had spearheaded the new racism long before it was taken up by Marr and other German "experts." The French count Joseph-Arthur de Gobineau seems to have been the first. His *Inequality of Human Races* (1853) hailed "Aryan" virtues and decried Semitic (and Latin) degeneracy. It became a notorious success. Nor did the Germans invent the opposition of "Aryan" and "Semite." Here, too, credit goes to a Frenchman, the historian and philologist Joseph-Ernest Renan, who identified and distinguished between "superior" Indo-European and "inferior" Semitic races. Renan's influential *Life of Jesus*, which believers and secularists read with equal fascination, portrayed Christ as a humanist immune to the "defects" of his race. In Germany, before the mid-1870s, only a handful of crackpots and marginal journalists preached this particular form of Jew hatred in the face of near-general public indifference.

In October 1873, a stock market crash changed this state of affairs in one blow. The economy had heated to the boiling point, a result of billions in French war reparation payments. The crash affected the entire Continent and came in the wake of feverish speculation in several European countries by reckless promoters with close political connections. Although the various governments had been warned of these machinations, they had done little to restrain them. The bubble burst first in Austria. From there the panic spread to Germany and the rest of Europe. In Germany alone, tens of thousands of middle-class and aristocratic families lost everything. The crash provoked a wave of anti-Semitic agitation unlike anything Germany—or France—had seen since the Crusades or the Black Death. Jews were said to be "inferior" and "immoral"; their successes over the preceding two or three decades were due entirely to devious, even criminal manipulations. It was not an accident that so many stockbrokers happened to be Jews. At whose expense had they been enriching themselves?

Nine months earlier, in a sensational speech in the Reichstag, the Jewish liberal Eduard Lasker had sounded a first dire warning.[68] Lasker exposed the ruthless activities of Bethel Henry Strousberg, a Prussian railroad tycoon and converted Jew, revealing Strousberg's notorious system, of winning government concessions by lining the pockets of parliamentarians and high officials. Strousberg had played a major role in the German economy for years. "That fellow will one day soon be emperor of Germany," Engels had written Marx in September 1869. "Wherever you go, everybody speaks only of Strousberg."[69] His enormous industrial and railroad holdings collapsed even before the general crash. For the sake of his aristocratic partners—who included the Silesian dukes of Ujest and Ratibor, the Prussian count Lehndorff-Steinort, and a Prince Wilhelm zu Putbus (soon dubbed Kaputbus)—Bismarck, with Bleichröder's assistance, made a last-minute effort to stave off their bankruptcy with state funds. In his characteristic style, Bismarck told the French ambassador:

2 dukes, 1 general, half a dozen ladies in waiting, twice that many chamberlains, 100 owners of coffeehouses and all the cabmen of Berlin found themselves totally ruined. The emperor took pity on the dukes, the aide de camp, the ladies in waiting and charged me with pulling them out of trouble. I appealed to Bleichröder, who on condition of getting a title of nobility, which as a Jew he very much valued, agreed to rescue the duke of Ujest and General Count Lehndorff. Two dukes & an aide de camp saved—frankly this is worth the "von" we bestowed on the good Bleichröder.[70]

In the event, they were not really "saved." Beyond the monetary losses, several Reichstag deputies and dignitaries of the royal court were seriously compromised by Lasker's revelations. As for Lasker himself, his disclosures of the swindles and corruption catapulted him overnight into the first rank of public figures. The *Allgemeine Zeitung des Judentums* wrote that the name of Eduard Lasker should be added to that of Moses Mendelssohn and other great Jews in history.[71] But little was done to put an end to the corruption Lasker exposed. His warning of an impending general crisis went unheeded, leading only to the appointment of a commission of inquiry into Strousberg's alleged system. It did not lead to concrete monetary and legal reform. In the absence of a clear political will it could not. The Reichstag had no power to subpoena generals, noblemen, and high government officials, who would not in any case have been held accountable by a commission of mere middle-class parliamentarians. A feverish rush for scapegoats ensued.

The main instigators of the new racism were failed aristocrats hit by the inevitable crash, conservative rabble-rousers, and demagogic clergymen; the chorus, in Engels's words, was the howling mob of the petite bourgeoisie. Prominent members of the landed aristocracy, hurt also by a drastic decline in agricultural prices due to cheaper imports from America, were mesmerized by the new wealth of the urban commercial middle class. The main object of their scorn and envy was the notorious "Jewish parvenu." They convinced themselves that their sudden poverty was the fault of the newly rich Jews who were buying up their ancestral country estates and their palatial town houses in the historic center of Berlin. There was no dearth of hypocrisy here: no subject except sex was so laden with hypocrisy as that of money. When enjoyed by Jews, the same luxuries the aristocracy could no longer afford were decried as "vices." The ostentation of someone like Bleichröder gave this prejudice an appearance of principle and idealism.

Disdain for new wealth was common everywhere; in Germany, where feudal sentiments were stronger than in France or England, it was especially virulent. Aristocrats were, of course, as greedy as anyone else. Bismarck's undoubtedly corrupt alliance with Bleichröder had made both men very rich indeed. In the prevailing myth, however, aristocrats remained great statesmen, valiant soldiers, and devoted public servants. In the aftermath of the crash, popular fury was directed not at them and the government they dominated but at the Jews.

The crash ushered in the German economy's longest recession of the nineteenth century. Like the world economic crisis of 1929, it was all the harder to remedy because it was part of a wider slump. The slump revealed the internal fragility of Bismarck's new empire despite its muscle flexing and trappings of power. One is struck by the sharp contrast between the optimism of the relatively easygoing years before 1873 and the gloom that prevailed afterward; an abyss opened between Germans and Jews. The sudden outbreak of Judeophobia in 1873 was the "gravest and most durable" result of the financial crisis, its "sordid afterbirth," according to Volker Ullrich, a current historian of Bismarck's empire. Judeophobia would follow the new empire to its last day in 1918, a "major component of its political culture."[72]

At its root was a myth of Jewish "deviousness" and "power" reinterpreted in secular terms. Jews were held responsible not only for the crisis but for capitalism itself: Judaism was "capitalism in the extreme." No less than 90 percent of all "capitalist promoters" in Germany were said to be Jews. Under their auspices, capitalism was generating a materialist society that consumed the hard-earned life savings of good Christians. Strousberg and Bleichröder were archvillains who incarnated Jewish money power in the popular mind. In a bizarre reversal, Lasker, too, was blamed: by exposing a single corrupt manipulator (Strousberg), he was accused of covering up for all the other swindlers and crooks, most of them Jews. The attacks extended to Bamberger and

Oppenheim, spokesmen for liberalism, the free market, and democracy. The mass-circulation family magazine *Gartenlaube* and the conservative *Kreuzzeitung*, Bismarck's mouthpiece, led the way with a series of vicious anti-Semitic diatribes. Published as books soon after, these became best-sellers. Newspapers all over Germany followed suit: "The Jews form a single chain, from the baptized cabinet minister to the Polish *schnorrer* . . . a physically and psychologically degenerate race . . . governing the entire universe through fraud and usury."[73] The attacks fell on eager ears. Spreading unemployment did the rest. August Bebel argued in vain that anti-Semitism was the socialism of fools.

The new anti-Semitism was indirectly facilitated by Bismarck himself. As incriminations against Jews mounted, he maintained an icy silence. He had his reasons. He was not a Jew hater or racist. (He believed that "German stallions should be paired off with Jewish mares," rich ones, presumably.) He was a cynic, a misanthrope, a man of fathomless cunning. His silence was politically convenient. Clearly, he saw it as a means to deflect popular disaffection and weaken the liberal block—once his mainstay but now at odds with his authoritarianism and protectionist economic policies. Two of its leading figures, Bamberger and Lasker—whom Bismarck had come to loathe—were, after all, Jews; so were many liberal voters. Privately, Bismarck referred to his own minister of agriculture, Rudolph von Friedenthal, a converted Jew, as his "Semitic pants shitter."[74] Bamberger had fallen out with Bismarck not only because of such slurs and Bismarck's economic policies; he was equally irritated by the crude nationalism Bismarck generated in the aftermath of the war. Though he and Lasker convinced themselves that the animus against Jews was a passing fad, Bamberger was soon forced to acknowledge that "the cult of nationality" easily degenerates. "From hatred for others across the frontier it is only a small step to the hatred of others within one's *Heimat*."[75]*

---

*It was under Bismarck, according to Volker Ullrich, that "the thunderbolt of excommunication first hit Catholics, later Social Democrats, and, increasingly, minorities and citizens of Jewish extraction or faith, who were denied membership in the German *Volksnation*" (*Die nervöse Grossmacht*, p. 90).

BERTHOLD Auerbach had been living in Berlin since 1860, a frequent guest at court and the recipient of many medals. His books continued to be widely read. He enjoyed being recognized on the street as a famous and beloved author. But his optimism was gone. "I am baffled by the newly awakened *furor teutonicus*," he wrote to his cousin in 1876. "I wish I knew its origin. Could it be a feeling of self-confidence, of knowing their own worth, that Germans now have?"[76]

Others were not at all baffled. Nietzsche regarded Christian anti-Semitism with scorn. Paul Vasili, author of *La société de Berlin* (1884), was perhaps overly smug when, comparing Berlin with Paris, he claimed that prejudices that had long disappeared in France thrived in Berlin: "There is no city in the entire world where the children of Israel are more repulsed by society or where that society makes greater use of them."[77] But he was, of course, right in his assessment of the growing intolerance in Germany. In its sudden intensity it seemed far greater than anywhere else in Western Europe. In 1886, the Jewish population of Berlin numbered more than fifty thousand, 5 percent of the total. A fifth of all high school students were said to be Jewish. The modern world of commerce, industry, and democracy threatened many established privileges. The perceived dangers of modernity spawned inchoate fears. Jews had been disliked in the past and at times despised; now, for the first time, they were also feared.

New phrases came into usage (German is a great language for suggestive portmanteau words): *Judenjahrhundert* (century of the Jews), *Judendreistigkeit* (Jewish impudence), *Judenparasitenökonomie* (Jewish parasitic economy), and *Judenweltherrschaft* (Jewish world domination). The word *Demokratie* was said by some to be a translation of a French Jewish word "alien" to the German language. The idea of democracy itself was allegedly advocated only by the *Judenpresseungeziefer* (the vermin writing for the Jewish-owned press).

In a process analogous to Freud's narcissism of minor difference, the more Jews came to resemble other Germans the more, it seemed, Germans resented them. In parts of the emerging German middle class and the intelligentsia, anti-Semitism became a cultural code, shorthand for a complete worldview. Student fraternities were increasingly infested with it. As the Marxist philosopher Georg Lukács would later claim, the German bourgeoisie had not yet overcome feudalism when the proletariat drove it into the arms of conservatives. Anti-Semitism was becoming a convenient mainstay of the militarized Prussian monarchy.

IN 1879, Adolf Stöcker, a prominent Protestant clergyman in Berlin and the official chaplain of the imperial court, joined the anti-Semitic pack, endowing it with an elevated social and spiritual aura. Thousands attended his sermons, at which he insisted: "If we wish to recover, if we wish to hold fast to our German national character, we must get rid of the poisonous Jewish drop in our blood."[78] As Stöcker saw it, Christians were on the defensive. He disingenuously pleaded with the Jews for "a little more tolerance" toward Christians and "please, a little more equality," too.[79] The emperor did not approve of Stöcker but was said to consider his conduct "useful in order to make the Jews somewhat more modest."[80] And Bismarck was pleased with Stöcker's parallel attempt to form a conservative Christian labor party. The recession was in its sixth year; Stöcker's efforts to lure the unemployed away from the growing socialist movement were useful indeed.

The editors of the *Allgemeine Zeitung des Judentums* remained convinced that the best tactic was to ignore Stöcker. In the long run, the educated middle class would not take its cue from a religious fanatic. Bleichröder went out of his way to reassure his business partners, Nathaniel Rothschild in London and Moritz von Goldschmidt in Vienna, that the agitation was a passing phenomenon. Goldschmidt wrote back to say that he disagreed. Rothschild, for his part, rushed to tell Disraeli that Bleichröder himself was one of the causes of Jewish persecution: "He has been employed so often by the German government that he has become arrogant and forgets that he is very often merely a 'trial balloon.' . . . I hear also that Madame von Bleichröder is most disagreeable and haughty."[81] As Bleichröder's biographer, Fritz Stern, comments: "A wretched picture of Bleichröder—and of the Rothschilds."[82] At the end of October 1879, the *Allgemeine Zeitung des Judentums* still noted optimistically that the hostility seemed to have "passed its zenith and was on the decline."[83]

Two weeks later, all such complacency disappeared. Stöcker's virulence was suddenly legitimized by a powerful and distinguished academic voice. In an essay published in the influential *Preussische Jahrbücher*, Heinrich von Treitschke, Prussia's leading historian, brought the wisdom of the beer cellars, in Graetz's words, to the rostrum of a great university. His unmatched prestige lent seriousness and respectability to Stöcker's cause. Treitschke inveighed against the "dominance" of Jews in German life and the corruption of Germanic and Christian ideals by the most "pushy" among them. The threat was deadly serious, he warned, but Germans were finally awakening to the menace, he announced. He welcomed the "amazing, powerful excitement" that was finally moving "the deep recesses of our national life. . . . It is as though the nation were recovering its sense of self. It is pitilessly sitting in judgment on itself." Even among men of the highest culture inclined to reject national arrogance or religious intolerance, "the cry is everywhere the same: the Jews are our misfortune!"

> Year after year, the inexhaustible Polish cradle spawns hordes of ambitious young men who come pushing across our border to peddle their trousers and whose children and grandchildren are supposed to one day dominate the German stock market and German newspapers. . . . In thousands of German villages there is a Jew practicing usury and driving his neighbors to ruin and buying them up. . . . But the most dangerous of all is the unfair dominance that the Jews exert in the daily press.[84]

Treitschke's essay threw the Jewish community into shock. Over the next twelve months, the number of conversions rose to double the average over the preceding five years.[85] A grand controversy ensued. With only one prominent exception, Treitschke's critics were Jews, among them rabbis, politicians—Bamberger, Lasker, Oppenheim—and the historian Graetz, whom Treitschke had attacked personally for his derogatory comments on medieval Christianity. (Bamberger joined Treitschke on this score, calling Graetz "the Stöcker of the synagogue.") The others included Paul Cassel, a convert who served as a Christian clergyman in Berlin, and Hermann Cohen, who agreed with Treitschke's main thesis on the necessary unity of state and religion but argued that

Judaism and Christianity would soon merge within the framework of a common "religion of reason."* He went so far as to ask Treitschke to be more patient: the acculturation process was advancing quickly. He even predicted that Jews would eventually be as blond and blue-eyed as their fellow Germans: they wished nothing more ardently than to look "like the Germans, whose appearance we currently mimic only in superficial ways."[86]

The sole prominent Christian who spoke out publicly was Treitschke's fellow historian at the University of Berlin, Theodor Mommsen. Calling the new anti-Semitism "mass insanity," he sharply criticized its "true prophet, Herr von Treitschke."[87] Providence understood far better than Stöcker and Treitschke that German metal improved considerably when alloyed with a "small measure" of Israel. He did, however, qualify his support: "No Moses will lead them back to the Promised Land; they may sell trousers or write books but they must . . . shed their peculiarity."[88] He did not specify what this peculiarity was. The extensive discussion filled the daily press and the learned journals for months. Treitschke responded to his critics with growing impatience, and they answered, trying to make their case.

AUERBACH followed the debate in a mood of growing hopelessness. His letters bear ample evidence of his gloom. Treitschke had been one of his close friends. Auerbach decided never to speak to him again. "It is enough to drive you to despair," he noted on March 19, 1880. "Arrogance and aversion are lurking inside even the most open-minded liberals, just waiting for a chance to spring. What exactly do they mean when they say that the Jews first must prove their worth? Isn't that a kind of Inquisition?"

A full year passed before seventy-five Berlin university professors finally signed a petition protesting the foul wave of racism and calling on all Christians to defend "Lessing's heritage." The signatories included the university rector and some of Treitschke's most distin-

*Cohen's idea of religion was Platonic. Asked how one could possibly love an "idea," he answered: "One always loves an idea and nothing but an idea. Even in sensual love one loves only the 'idea' of a person."

guished colleagues. The petition improved Auerbach's mood temporarily: "One is able to breathe again!" But only a week later, hundreds of students gave Treitschke a hero's welcome. The following day, Auerbach spent an evening with his old friend Fritz Kapp, a veteran of 1848, now a liberal Reichstag deputy. "Of the thousands I know, he is one of the few who, if some conflict erupted, wouldn't say: 'There goes the Jew.'" Kapp tried to reassure him: within two months everything would be over. Auerbach replied: "I don't believe it. The fire's caught and will go on burning. It's to the point where you have to be grateful to almost every single person who declares himself free of prejudice."

Kaiserin Augusta Victoria and the grand duke and duchess of Baden invited Auerbach for tea. They bemoaned the recent assassination of Czar Alexander II by an anarchist's bomb. Auerbach replied that "the ongoing orchestration of the campaign against the Jews is just another way of throwing bombs." The empress assured him that the mood would not prevail. Auerbach, who rarely challenged royalty, disagreed.

"It's no trifling matter having to be told that one does not belong with the Germans, that one has no fatherland," he pointed out. "Believe me," the duchess responded, "these ugly things are only happening here in Berlin." There was little or none of it in Karlsruhe, where she came from. The empress added that even in Berlin it was temporary. "I had to disagree," Auerbach informed his cousin.[89] The government itself, he said, was succumbing to the agitation by continuing to exclude Jews from the officers corps and from key positions in the administration. Germans simply refused to be a modern nation like the Dutch or the French. They wanted to remain a tribe, held together by their tribal idols. Such arguments were wasted on his present company.

Auerbach was leaving a Berlin restaurant one evening when someone yelled *"Hep! Hep!"* after him. He wept as he told his friend Eduard Lasker what had happened. Lasker consoled him. "Would you scold a sick man for having cholera? Anti-Semitism is an epidemic afflicting these people!"[90]

Shortly after, Lasker and Bamberger left the National Liberal Party and joined the Progressives, a new party to the left of the National Liberals. Bamberger was soon more repelled by the equanimity of "three-quarters of his Progressive colleagues" than by the rabble-rousers, and he broke with that party too.[91] Two decades after his return from exile, he contemplated emigration. He was certain, he wrote, that the attacks on the Jews were part of the Prussian Junkers' campaign against liberalism, and it was "loathsome." In 1879, the slogan *Wählet keine Juden!*—Don't vote for Jews!—figured prominently for the first time in an election to the Prussian state parliament. Over the next six years, the number of deputies of Jewish extraction elected to local parliaments in Germany dropped from sixty-six to thirty-eight, of whom thirteen were baptized.

Theodor Fontane, perhaps the most sophisticated German writer after Heine and especially beloved by Jewish readers, publicly criticized Stöcker. Privately, he expressed fervid anti-Semitism. He wrote his friend Mathilde von Rohr that he was thoroughly "convinced" of the Jews' guilt. Their main fault was their "boundless impertinence." Fontane not only predicted they would suffer "a serious defeat" but heartily "wished them one."[92]

Auerbach grew more and more disconsolate. Almost overnight he visibly aged, becoming "a sick, tired, broken old man, his skin yellow and dry, his eyes lusterless," according to one account.[93] On November 22, 1880, enraged and disgusted, he spent the entire afternoon and evening in the visitors' gallery of the Prussian state parliament, where, amid anti-Semitic catcalls, a motion to disenfranchise the Jews was under discussion.

Auerbach returned home in a state of acute depression. The following day, he summed up the despair that two generations later would become the tragedy of all German Jews.[94] He noted: "I have lived and worked in vain."[95]

7

Years of Progress

THEN, the wave of rowdy anti-Semitism ebbed; things quieted down. The "years of anxiety," as the late 1870s came to be called, passed. The economic recession ended. Living standards rose once more. The new prosperity benefited the masses as well as the rich. Adolf Stöcker was finally denounced by the emperor as a "political pastor" and demoted from his post as court chaplain.

Stöcker had been the first German politician to accumulate political power by the deliberate dissemination of anti-Jewish slogans. But his Christian Social Party was short-lived. A series of corruption and forgery scandals tainted the party with the very infamy that it had attached to the Jews. Stöcker's alliance with the conservatives broke down. Other anti-Semitic splinter groups also tended to disintegrate. In the Reichstag elections of 1884, a Jewish candidate, Paul Singer—later cochairman of the Social Democratic Party—soundly defeated a well-known anti-Semite. A self-made manufacturer of women's coats with an acute social conscience, Singer had left his thriving business to agitate for workers' rights and social reform. This was a courageous step as Bismarck's antisocialist law of 1878—abrogated only after his political demise in 1890—rendered such activity illegal and sanctioned house searches, arrest, and expulsion for those who engaged in it. The law had helped prompt Singer to join the nascent party in the first place and to contribute to it generously. Said to be the most popular left-wing politician in Berlin, Singer kept his Reichstag seat for twenty-seven years. At his death in 1911, more than a million Berlin workers attended his funeral.

THE two and a half decades before the Great War of 1914–18 are often obscured by the disasters that came afterward. As the historian Gordon A. Craig points out, these years are generally explored today "only for the clues they yield to the catastrophe that was to follow." This produces an "unfortunate distortion, for seen in its own right the period between 1888 and 1914 was characterized by . . . institutional stability, technological progress, and economic prosperity."[1] New developments belied old fears. Germany was economically and militarily the most powerful nation on the European continent, although war was increasingly considered unlikely, if only because of its exorbitant cost. Bourgeois life was firmly grounded in the rule of law. In *The World of Yesterday*, written after Hitler's rise to power, Stefan Zweig looked back at the "Golden Age of Security" half a century earlier, when he grew up as the son of well-to-do Viennese Jewish parents. Everything "seemed based on permanency, and the state itself was the chief guarantor of this stability." Whoever built a house looked upon it as a secure domicile for his children, grandchildren, and great-grandchildren. In his chronicle of a turn-of-the-century Berlin childhood, Walter Benjamin evoked a similar sense of bourgeois solidity in the prosperous lakeside suburb of Grunewald where his family lived. He grew up, he said, among a species that, no matter how compliantly it bowed to the minor whims of fashion, was "wholly convinced of itself and its permanence." In his grandmother's "twelve-or-fourteen-room" home, with its upholstered window alcoves, walls lined with books, fine paintings, and precious objects, Benjamin noted "the almost immemorial feelings of bourgeois security that emanated from these rooms."[2]

The years of anxiety had not broken Jewish faith in German culture and its expected social and political ramifications; if anything, it had grown stronger. The process of acculturation continued. Three or four generations after *Bildung* struck roots among Jews, it was no longer "a recent acquisition" but a precious "heritage shared with other Germans."[3] What discrimination remained was deemed marginal and, in any case, unconstitutional—hence, a curable disease, bound to be short-lived.

Class privilege was still formidable and widely observed; indeed, it gave succor and protection to German Jews along with the rest of the bourgeoisie. "The well-dressed bourgeois, Jew or Christian, was a 'Herr' and had a right to be treated respectfully," the Zionist Richard Lichtheim remembered.[4] Lichtheim came from a family of Jewish doctors assimilated for five generations, descendants of the Königsberg radical democrat Johann Jacoby. Before 1914, Lichtheim claimed, he had never personally experienced anti-Semitism. Social exclusion was, if anything, partly self-imposed. Walter Benjamin recalled knowing no world other than the cloistered, privileged haven of his family, a "leased ghetto," a "gilded cage." Most middle-class Jews simply felt more comfortable in the company of other Jews.

They had to know their place, of course. Class-conscious, respectful conservatives like Zweig's father avoided dining at the Sacher, Vienna's most elegant hotel. He did so "not for reasons of economy—the difference in price from other hotels was insignificant—but because of a natural feeling of respect; it would have been distressing or unbecoming for him to sit at a table next to a Prince Schwarzenberg or Lobkowitz."[5] In the army, too, prejudice may have had less to do with religion than with social class. The regular officer corps was a fiefdom of the old landed aristocracy. In Prussia, there were relatively fewer nonaristocratic officers in the army in 1913 than in 1870. Jews were not given commissions, even in the Prussian reserves; in the Bavarian and Austrian reserves, however, they were. (The Bavarian army continued to exist after unification, though under the command of the kaiser.) The fact that prejudice was often applied inconsistently fueled hopes that it would soon be overcome.

Although not part of unified Germany, Vienna was nonetheless the most important center of German-language theater, literature, and music. According to Zweig, almost all the Viennese art and culture recognized and admired by the world was promoted, nourished, or created by Jews. Even after the election of the anti-Semitic rabble-rouser Karl Lueger as Vienna's burgomaster in 1895, Jews continued to live well there, Zweig maintained. Lueger's anti-Semitism was of a homespun, flexible variety—one might almost say gemütlich. Asked to explain the fact that many of his friends were Jews, Lueger famously replied, "I decide who is a Jew." Viennese Jews—at least Zweig's friends and acquaintances— were never personally affected. They were "free" from all "confinement and prejudice," Zweig insisted. "Neither in school nor in the university, nor in the world of literature" did Zweig experience the "slightest suppression or indignity as a Jew." Nowhere on the Continent was it easier to be a "European."[6]

The playwright Arthur Schnitzler was more circumspect. He testified to the existence of anti-Semitism, "an emotion rampant in numerous hearts," but insisted that it "did not play an important role politically or socially."[7] Schnitzler became the Viennese writer par excellence. One of his popular works of fiction, *The Road into the Open,* was so full of characters tormented by or for their Jewishness that it was later considered a proto-Zionist novel. In *My Youth in Vienna* (1912), Schnitzler commented that a Jew in public life "could not ignore the fact that he was a Jew; nobody else did, not the Gentiles and even less the Jews. You had the choice of being considered insensitive, obtrusive and fresh; or of being oversensitive, shy and suffering from feelings of persecution."[8]

Schnitzler's pessimism in many ways better reflected fin-de-siècle Austria, which, under the aged Franz Joseph I, was a disintegrating empire of warring nationalities. While Stefan Zweig recollected an idyll, Robert Musil in his novel *The Man without Qualities* called Austria "Kakania," a word that spoke its own derision. The satirist and playwright Karl Kraus said that Vienna was a *"Versuchsstation des Weltuntergangs,"* a proving ground for the apocalypse.

In Germany, there was no such morbid twilight atmosphere. It was, by and large, a more hopeful, more orderly, and more law-abiding society, and though still only a semiliberal, semifeudal authoritarian society, it was also a remarkably stable and uncommonly creative environment, culturally and scientifically. Unlike Schnitzler, German Jews saw only marginal evidence of the "Jewish problem." The leading quality newspapers—the *Berliner Tageblatt*, the *Vossische Zeitung*, and the *Frankfurter Zeitung*—rarely mentioned it. Fedor Mamroth, the Jewish literary editor of the *Frankfurter Zeitung*, stipulated in his will that his ashes be strewn in the sacred Rhine as a token of his abiding German fidelity and identity.

If the position of Germany's Jews was not perfect, it was certainly bearable—at least for the well-to-do—and even quite hopeful in the eyes of the intelligentsia. Intermarriage became common, increasing from 8.4 percent in 1901 to 29.86 percent in 1915.[9] Felix Theilhaber, a Zionist doctor in Munich, hysterically warned in 1911 that intermarriage and sinking birthrates—the result of modern women's uppityness, he lamented—would bring about the complete disappearance of German Jewry by 1950. According to Theilhaber, marriage among Jews had in the past been a "national-religious" institution, designed to "serve the preservation of the family and the nation"; now, however, it was increasingly "based purely on erotic attraction," as among Gentiles.[10] Theilhaber decried the recent decline of what he called "racial consciousness" among Jews. Philosophies could be abjured at will, he announced. "Blood" was more permanent.

Theilhaber traveled from one German Jewish community to another speaking out against "racial mixing" through intermarriage. Kafka attended a speech in which Theilhaber warned of the biological damage caused by racial mixing: children of mixed marriages were likely to be decadent or morally depraved, and they often ended up as the worst anti-Semites. However preposterous, Theilhaber's stereotypes must be read in historical context. The vocabulary of sociobiology and "race" was then an integral part of civilized public discourse. More remarkable was the lack of response to Theilhaber's tirades. Intermarriage continued to flourish. In Breslau, a less "multicultural" city than Berlin, intermarriage rose from 11 percent in 1890 to 52 percent during the First World War, suggesting that integration was even more advanced in the provinces than was commonly thought.

Mixed love affairs were often still charged with atavistic fears. Kafka's infatuation with Milena Jesenská caused him nightmares. He consoled himself that since Milena was exactly thirteen years younger, fate had given her to him as a bar mitzvah present. The problems affected Gentile and Jew alike, of course. Theilhaber complained that they were, in too many cases, all too easily overcome. The Social Democratic lawyer Philipp Löwenfeld, shortly after his engagement to his Gentile girlfriend, was coldly received by her parents. Her father left him standing and asked curtly:

"What can I do for you?"

"I've come to inform you that your daughter and I intend to marry."

"That's out of the question."

"In that case, I'm free to leave. I only came for the sake of custom and propriety. . . . As you know, since we are both of age, we do not require your consent."

That broke the ice. Switching to the intimate "Du," the father said softly: "Please take a seat."[11]

Money and sex were the base around which much of the mutual prejudice—and attraction—often turned. Myths of eroticism and attractiveness were at work on both sides. Hebrew and Yiddish works often evoked the erotic bliss allegedly awaiting puritanical Jewish men and women in the more vital, more passionate Gentile world. The historian and political scientist Hans Kohn wrote with regard to Martin Buber's marriage to Paula Winkler:

Ever since the age of Enlightenment, many of the best young Jews [have wed] non-Jewish women, whose beauty and free, self-assured spirit they considered to be the personification of a humanitarian ideal. . . . Since Heine, these "Hellenic" traits have represented for the Jews a lighter, brighter side of life they have had little access to, characterized by confidence and poise, free of inner doubt and therefore possessed of external grace and natural dignity—which young Jews have found embodied by women of a different stock.[12]

The Gentile world, in turn, considered Jews to be sexually hyperactive. Echoing the novelist and playwright Karl Gutzkow's verdict of 1835 that "we are bad lovers," a myth arose among Gentiles that Jews were better or, at least, more considerate sexual partners.

Ritual differences between Jews and Christians continued to wane. As in countless other Jewish homes, Rabbi Wilhelm Klemperer's little boys said the following prayer as they were put to bed in the evening:

> *I trust in God and His embrace*
> *In His mercy and good grace.*

The evening prayer of Protestant children was only slightly different:

> *I trust in God and His embrace*
> *In Christ's blood and His good grace.*[13]

During the holiday season, Father Christmas and Father Hanukkah brought children their gifts. Reform Jews celebrated the Sabbath on Sunday. (By 1870, Reform, or Liberal, Judaism was dominant in virtually all urban centers.) Far from proving, as some claimed, that Reform Jews were indifferent to their faith, this shift demonstrated a continuing effort to retain it even as they amalgamated with the majority by sharing its day of rest. The theologian Hermann Cohen declared that Jews must be masters of the Sabbath, not its slaves.

Georg Tietz, a department-store tycoon, remembered another manifestation of integration. As a schoolboy in turn-of-the-century Munich, every Saturday morning at nine he joined a "column of Jewish pupils" who were "marched from school to the nearby synagogue. . . . Most of the Catholic boys joined us there; in return, they invited us to a game of tag in the Frauenkirche on Sunday."[14] (Tietz's Latin teacher, however, was "loathsome." His name was Himmler; his son Heinrich later became chief of the Gestapo.)

The point of transition from traditional (that is, Orthodox) to Reform Judaism was noted by some as a moment of high drama. More than a half century after the fact, Victor Klemperer, a linguist and professor of Romance languages, still remembered it vividly. His father, Wilhelm, was the Orthodox rabbi of Landsberg an der Warthe, a small semirural community in West Prussia. The city register listed Dr. Klemperer as one of Landsberg's two "country preachers," the other being the Protestant pastor. Early in 1890, when Victor was nine years old, Dr. Klemperer applied for the position of "auxiliary preacher" at the new Reform temple in Berlin, where the congregants no longer observed the dietary laws, the prayers were recited in German, and the Sabbath was celebrated on Sunday to the accompaniment of organ music. He was summoned to Berlin for an interview. Victor never forgot the afternoon his father's telegram arrived announcing, "Everything went well, thank God."[15] His appointment had been confirmed. That afternoon, Victor's mother gave him a dramatic foretaste of the new life awaiting him. She took him shopping. It was already getting dark. Not without "first carefully looking around," the mother entered a nonkosher butcher shop. In an excited but controlled voice she requested "mixed cold cuts, a little of every kind." Then she quickly and proudly hurried out. At home, immediately upon unwrapping the package, she sampled a slice herself and gave Victor one too. It hardly tasted different than their customary sausage. His mother chewed it with a radiant expression on her face. "This is what the others eat," she said. "Now we may eat it too."[16]

"Deep down, she certainly sensed something grander at the time," Klemperer said of his mother. The act of eating a pork sausage was "a form of communion."[17] It made her feel truly German. Half a century later in Nazi Dresden, fearing his imminent deportation, Klemperer proudly recalled his mother's gesture as a voluntary act of reform, not one imposed from above as in Russia, where Peter the Great had ordered all men to shave their beards, or in Turkey, where Kemal Ataturk had outlawed the fez.

Countless other memoirs testify to the growing estrangement of Jews from traditional ritual and custom. Fewer and fewer Jews, especially the educated and rich, were observant. Many were *konfessionslos*, creedless. Walter Benjamin's friend Kurt Hiller claimed that his parents were freethinkers. They had neither circumcised nor confirmed him. They would not even dream of having him baptized. "Theirs was a model point of view based on reason: Let the boy decide for himself when he's grown up. And that's exactly what I did when I chose to remain without a faith and cast my lot with the agnostics."[18] The writer Emil Ludwig (born Cohn) remembered that his parents practiced neither Judaism nor Christianity but rather the cult of *Bildung*. For the

Cohns, the "practical" substitute for religion was moral education, while the "mystical" substitute was the worship of music.[19] Ludwig visited a synagogue for the first time, in Constantinople, only as an adult.

Walter Benjamin, who liked Easter eggs, felt only "mistrust" toward Jewish religious ceremonies. They "promised nothing but embarrassment."[20] The novelist Max Brod dismissed the religious instruction of his youth as "mere routine, boredom, something utterly exhausted and spent."[21] Franz Kafka "almost suffocated from the terrible boredom and pointlessness of the hours in the synagogue." They were, he said, "the rehearsals staged by hell for my later office life."[22] Kafka argued with his Jewishness throughout his life. The word *Jew* did not appear in any of his short stories or novels. The little religion he received at home he described as an "insignificant scrap" he was meant to cling to "for the sake of piety at least." But it was "a mere nothing, a joke—not even a joke." Four days a year his father went to synagogue, where he was, according to the son, "closer to the indifferent than to those who took it seriously."[23]

One's parents wished only "to drag one down to them, back to the old days from which one longs to free oneself and escape," he wrote his fiancée, Felice Bauer. "They do it out of love, of course, and that's what makes it so horrible."[24] The tired, dreary routine of the yeshiva, to say nothing of its "stench and heat," struck Kafka as the natural cradle of apostasy. "In the recent past, all the progressive writers, politicians, journalists, and scholars have come out of these schools." Elsewhere, Kafka wondered, "What have I in common with Jews? I have hardly anything in common with myself and should stand very quietly in a corner, content that I can breathe."[25]

Secularization was on the rise among adherents of all faiths. Religious observance declined among Protestants as among Jews. The philologist Fritz Mauthner hailed Jews for their more pronounced secularism. Their historical task once again was to lead the world, he said, this time as pioneers of modern "godlessness."[26]

Indifference to religion together with the hope of social improvement produced a new wave of conversion. The rate of baptisms among Jewish men jumped from 8.4 percent in 1901 to 21 percent in 1918. Converts came mostly from secularized families; as in previous waves of conversions, those who took the step were nominal Jews before and

nominal Christians after. Most converted to Protestantism. In a caricature in the satirical magazine *Simplicissimus*, a Jew is asked why he
insists on converting to Catholicism. "Well, you know," he answers,
"there are far too many Jews among the Protestants." An anti-Semitic
social register published in 1912, the *Semi-Gotha Almanach*, pretended
to "expose" 1,540 converted Jewish families within the German nobility.

In 1903, on the eve of Victor Klemperer's induction into the army,
his brothers and cousins—among them Otto Klemperer, later an
acclaimed conductor—pressed him to convert, if only to qualify for a
commission in the Bavarian army reserves. Klemperer refused. His
brother, a successful surgeon married to the daughter of a Prussian general, assured him that religion now had little more significance than
articles of clothing; you chose what to wear according to the customs of
the time and place. Klemperer cried: "But this is terrible." "Nonsense."
"But it means a change of faith, and I don't believe the Christian
dogma." "Do you mean to say you believe in Old Testament Jehovah!" "I
don't believe that either; I'd rather be considered a dissident than anything else." "Am I going to have to tell you the world's oldest dissident
joke? A sergeant asks a new recruit what denomination he is, and the
man says 'dissident.' 'What's that?' asks the sergeant: 'Protestant,
Catholic, or Israelite?' 'None of the above, Sergeant, I have no denomination.' 'It is now nine o'clock. I'm giving you three hours' leave. At
twelve o'clock sharp you are to report back with a proper denomination!'"[27]

Klemperer retorted angrily that conversion was hardly a joking matter. His brother protested: "But we want to be Germans! Don't we?"
That decided the issue. The converting pastor, sensing Klemperer's
unease, tried to reassure him that the moral law was the same in both
religions. The ceremony lasted only a few minutes. To become Protestant, all Klemperer had to do was to say yes, shake hands, and vow loyalty to the Church. In a businesslike tone, the pastor then presented a
bill for fourteen marks and seventy-five pfennig. Klemperer found the
entire matter "repugnant." In the end he was rejected by the army for
health reasons.

Others were less conformist. Heinrich Braun, a socialist writer, was
urged to convert to qualify for an academic post. He refused "despite

the fact, or perhaps rather because, I have no deep connection to Judaism." Baptism, he quipped, "was much too Jewish."[28] Arthur Scholem, the father of Gershom Scholem, the scholar of Jewish mysticism, was a sober, assimilated, well-to-do Berliner and a confirmed German patriot. He felt that conversion was an "unprincipled, servile act" and avoided those of his relatives who had left the ancestral faith. Nonetheless, Scholem was a so-called Christmas Jew, celebrating both Jewish and Christian holidays. In his eyes, Christmas was a German *Volksfest*. The Scholems enjoyed their Christmas tree "as Germans, not as Jews," and their children enjoyed their presents.

The majority of assimilated Jews made similar accommodations, refusing baptism not so much out of any remaining religious sentiment as out of reluctance to face accusations of cowardice or treachery. Hermann Cohen decried baptism as "religious perjury."[29] The Zionist Lichtheim, like many other assimilated young men, briefly considered conversion—most of his uncles and cousins had already been baptized—but decided against it when his best friend, the scion of a noble Prussian family, warned him that taking that step would make him downright "despicable." The medievalist Harry Bresslau complained to his mentor, the great historian Leopold von Ranke, that religion was blocking his appointment as a professor. Ranke asked, "Why don't you convert? After all, you too are a 'historical' Christian." Bresslau refused to confirm his status as a historical Christian, whatever that meant. In the end he obtained a professorship anyway. Richard Willstätter, an organic chemist, was similarly stymied; he, too, refused. He eventually won a Nobel Prize. By contrast, Fritz Haber, another future Nobel laureate, became a Christian and forced his young bride to do likewise, only to wait another twelve years before achieving the rank of full professor.

THE conflicting pressures on sensitive young men and women invariably caused much bitterness. Among some of the most privileged or gifted it produced a reaction later known as "Jewish self-hatred." Its roots were not simply professional or political but emotional. Ludwig Jacobowski's novel *Werther the Jew* tells the story of a man who dies of unrequited love for Germany. Reprinted seven times and translated into six languages the novel was hailed as a masterpiece by Georg Brandeis, the leading literary critic of the day. Sometimes the self-hatred was oedipal, or at least rooted in familial unhappiness, as it was for Walther Rathenau, the future German foreign minister. Rathenau was burdened as much by a domineering father as by his Jewish origins. The moody, eccentric, enormously gifted scion of an old Prussian Jewish family, he was the eldest son of the industrialist and entrepreneur Emil Rathenau, who after acquiring Thomas Edison's patents at the Paris Grand Exposition had become one of the founders of the German electric industry. A contemptuous courtier, referring to Walther's "Jewish-looking face," snidely inquired how long he had lived in Berlin. Rathenau's answer was "almost seven generations." At thirty, he headed one of his father's electrochemical factories in Bitterfeld. In his spare time he frequented the literary salons of Berlin, wrote melancholy political and philosophic tracts, moved in aristocratic circles, and became personally acquainted with the kaiser. He was romantically—and perhaps erotically—attracted to blond, blue-eyed Prussian nationalists. Under the transparent pseudonym W. Hartenau, he published a bizarre text in the leading political magazine of Berlin, *Die Zukunft*, entitled "Hear, O Israel!," a desperate plea to his coreligionists to accelerate their assimilation by consciously imitating Prussian manners. They needed also to work on their physical appearance, developing longer limbs and straighter noses: "Once you recognize the unshapely form of your bodies, the raised shoulders, the clumsy feet, the soft roundness of your forms, as signs of bodily decline, you will be able to start working for a couple of generations on your bodily rebirth."[30] The bitter tone was not a pose; Rathenau genuinely believed in his strictures. From the portentous opening sentence, "I wish to confess at the outset that I am a Jew," the text was shot through with suffering and rancor. It was "like the opening movement of a tragic symphony," and in retrospect it seems even ominous, for Rathenau was to die for his Jewishness.[31]

Rathenau was painfully aware that in "Hear, O Israel!" he was identifying with the anti-Semitic rabble-rousers whom he despised. (In a first draft he said so explicitly.) He insisted, however, that Jewish arrivistes were largely responsible for the resentments Jews aroused. If only they had longer limbs and blond hair! If only they didn't talk so loud! If only they were more discreet! Less clannish! Less ostentatious! Rathenau's portrait of the Jews he saw in the lobbies of theaters and in the fashionable upper-middle-class Tiergartenstrasse in Berlin on a Sunday morning was a "strange sight" indeed: "There, in the midst of Germanic life, is an isolated race of men. Loud and self-conscious in their dress, hot-blooded and restless in their manner. . . . An Asiatic horde on the sandy plains of Prussia, . . . not a living limb of the people but an alien organism in its body."* Rathenau asked German Jews to "look in the mirror," reeducate themselves, and leave the dank, sultry ghettos to breathe "German mountain and forest air." Inbreeding produced degener-

Walther Rathenau. The pose in this painting by Edvard Munch suggests pride, power, and hauteur. *By permission of the Maerkisches Museum, Berlin; Photo—Archiv für Kunst und Geschichte, Berlin*

acy; massive intermarriage was the only cure. In Rathenau's opinion, Jews would survive as Jews, paradoxically, through assimilation.

---

*A few years earlier, as though anticipating "Hear, O Israel!," the assimilationist project had been savagely caricatured by Oskar Panizza in a nightmarish satire, "The Operated Jew" (1893). It is the story of one Itzig Faitel, a morally corrupt, physically deformed Jew who submits to painful surgery in the hope of becoming thoroughly German in appearance and character. The intervention fails. Faitel's straight blond hair curls and turns black, his artificially lengthened limbs crumble, his flesh rots, exuding a terrible stench.

Rathenau's vocabulary reflected the fashionable terminology of social Darwinism. Jews were by nature a "people of fear," Germans a "people of courage," he claimed. And yet, Jews must beware of mere "mimicry"; they should truly become more like the German "species" in mind and body. Let them be not "sloppy" in appearance but "militarily robust" like the host people. And they must "consciously adopt the tribal qualities of the host country," the behavioral patterns of the racially superior "tough, militarily bred" Prussian aristocracy. The result, Rathenau promised, would be a "moral metamorphosis." Jews should also try to be less cosmopolitan, opined this most cosmopolitan of Jews; better if they had fewer international connections and fewer in-laws and cousins. "Despite their denials, [cosmopolitan German Jews] may be less at home in Paris, New York, or Budapest than in this country." He who loves his fatherland "should be a bit chauvinistic."[32] The host people might then be more likely to recognize Jews as just another German tribe.

"Hear, O Israel!" caused a sensation. Rathenau's father vainly tried to suppress it by buying up all the available copies. Many Jews were outraged. Rathenau himself soon wished that the text had never seen the light of day. He had written it, he later claimed, in a particularly depressing period of his life, in the dreary factory town of Bitterfeld. He left the essay out of his collected works. The fact that it was widely read and long remembered was due largely to the anti-Semites who continued to cite it approvingly. The Nazi historian Walter Frank lauded what he called Rathenau's striking formulations. The *völkisch* ideologue Wilhelm Schwaner was deeply impressed and became Rathenau's lifelong friend.

What seems to have particularly rankled Rathenau was his humiliation as a young recruit when, like other Jews, he was refused an officer's commission in the elite Prussian regiment in which he completed his military service. (Military service was mandatory in Prussia, although university graduates served only one year.) Rathenau was discharged with the rank of a lowly lance corporal. "For every German Jew," he wrote, "there is a painful moment that he remembers his entire life: the moment he is first made fully conscious [in the army?] that he was born a second-class citizen. No ability and no achievement can free him from this."[33] And indeed, his roles as industrialist, author, society figure, and artist could not compensate for his essential dissatisfaction. Besides

heading the executive boards of
almost eighty major enterprises
and corporations, Rathenau
painted, played the piano pass-
ably, wrote poetry and books on
political, philosophical, and economic subjects. His intellectual
ambitions grew over the years.
Together with Martin Buber,
Gustav Landauer, Gerhart Hauptmann, and other intellectual
luminaries, both Christian and
Jewish, in 1914 he founded an
international club named after
the Italian seaside resort of Forte
dei Marmi. Under the more
clement skies of Tuscany, Rathenau
and the other club members hoped
to achieve "spiritual communion"
and even come up with insights
that would affect the future of
European culture and politics.
The First World War intervened
and put an end to this under-
taking.

Walther Rathenau in the resplendent uniform of a Prussian army corporal. Both the
regular and reserve officer corps were closed
to Jews. *Courtesy Leo Baeck Institute, Jerusalem*

Rathenau intrigued his contemporaries. Some thought it slightly
comic that this hard-boiled millionaire preached the rebirth of the soul
and condemned luxury while building himself an ostentatious villa in
the fashionable neo-Germanic style. Count Harry Kessler, Rathenau's
close friend and biographer, wrote that "you would run into him in court
society where everyone knew everyone else. At first he was an outsider,
but once you noticed him, you could never forget the unique effect he had
on people. . . . He was interesting and somewhat mysterious."[34] The
facial features of this admirer of blond demigods were slightly Negroid.
Edvard Munch pictured him in a full-length portrait as a tall man, slim,
with piercing eyes, dressed in black Baudelairean elegance against a

field of light blue. He leans backward in a pose suggesting pride, power, and hauteur. In his left hand he holds a drink; his right foot is thrust forward defiantly. Robert Musil caricatured him as Paul Arnheim, the protagonist of *The Man without Qualities*.

If anything, Rathenau had too many contradictory qualities. Some of his comments about Jews anticipated the self-criticism of the Zionists, their desire to produce a new breed of "muscular Jews." Yet in political Zionism he saw nothing but atavism: "the best among the Jews," he insisted, "have lost all national feeling; they recognize only human beings."[35] Though Rathenau disdained baptism as dishonorable, he resigned from the Jewish community, but then wherever he went, he obsessively declared himself a Jew. This aroused curiosity and occasionally even opened doors to him that might otherwise have remained closed. He was considered one of the most brilliant men in Berlin, according to one Prussian society lady, "the most desirable dinner companion this side of the Rhine." He could be pompous and theatrical, provoking amusement or surprise. Bernhard von Bülow, William II's imperial chancellor from 1900 to 1909, recorded one such occasion in his memoirs. Bülow was considering Rathenau for a ministerial post. Rathenau came to see him, bowing ceremoniously before taking a seat. Then, putting his right hand on his heart, he solemnly exclaimed, "Your Highness, . . . before I am deigned worthy of an audience, I wish to make an announcement and a confession." He paused dramatically. "Your Highness, I am a Jew!" Bülow knew perfectly well who Rathenau was and replied curtly, but not entirely truthfully, that he had never given anyone cause to suspect him of harboring anti-Semitic prejudices. Rathenau, according to Bülow, made another ceremonious bow and said, "I expected this noble answer from Your Highness." Then, Bülow noted, "he stayed for a long time."[36]

In Vienna, the reaction of certain Jews to their situation was equally if not more bizarre. It must have shocked even thick-skinned Jewish visitors from Berlin. One of the most prominent Austrian anti-Semites was Otto Weininger, a brilliant young Jew. At twenty-three, he published a 608-page tome entitled *Sex and Character*, a double attack on women and Jews. Weininger was fully aware of the ramifications of his deed.

"What I have discovered here pains no one more than it pains me," he wrote. "This book constitutes a death sentence either for the book or for its author." The book was an instant best-seller. Weininger promptly killed himself in the very room in Vienna where Beethoven, his idol, had died seventy-six years earlier. His death elevated him to the rank of a full-fledged Romantic hero while his book inspired the typically Viennese adage that anti-Semitism did not really get serious until it was taken up by Jews.

Stefan Zweig, Weininger's fellow student at the university, recalled that he always looked as if he had just spent thirty hours on a luggage rack. August Strindberg claimed Weininger as a brother in spirit; both were born "guilt-ridden," he wrote, both worshiped Beethoven. Arthur Schnitzler recalled another self-hating Viennese Jew, Louis Friedmann, a strikingly handsome man, a successful industrialist, champion skier, and renowned alpinist who vowed to remain single, or at least childless, so that the hated blood flowing in his veins might not be passed on. In *The Road into the Open*, Schnitzler describes his main protagonist, Georg von Wergenthin, as meeting in Vienna "only Jews who were ashamed of being Jews, or such that were proud of it and afraid that someone might think they were ashamed."[37]

At the turn of the century, a young philosopher, a graduate of the University of Vienna equally at home in German letters and traditional Eastern European Jewish folk culture, suggested an alternative response to the "Jewish question," neither conversion nor traditional separatism but rather a conscious embrace of Jewish history as part of one's German culture. The young man, Martin Buber, postulated nothing less than a "renaissance" of Jewish secular and literary identity through folktale and myth. Buber introduced Hasidism—a counterculture of pietistic and ecstatic mysticism outside "official" Judaism, widespread since the eighteenth century in Poland, Hungary, and the Ukraine—to enlightened Jewish and non-Jewish Germans, popularizing it as no one in the West had done before. Hasidism resembled other Eastern European traditions of ecstasy and worship of charismatic, miracle-working saints. Although Hasidism's "wonder rabbis" were

The young Martin Buber, shown here in 1902, was interested in the mythic core at the heart of every culture. He postulated nothing less than a renaissance of Jewish culture. *Courtesy Leo Baeck Institute, Jerusalem*

often not learned Talmudic scholars, they were widely regarded to be men of great wisdom and experience, linked to the divine through mystic contemplation; some were also healers, working with magic formulas, amulets, and spells. Their concern for the poor and downtrodden attracted thousands to their "courts" to be cured or uplifted through communion, heartfelt prayer, song, and dance. At the beginning of the twentieth century, Hasidism was still alive in Eastern Europe but, like cabala, was overlooked or derogated in the West as mere superstition and primitive belief. A story was told of the great German Jewish bibliophile Moritz Steinschneider, the father of modern Jewish bibliography. One day as he was proudly showing a young scholar through his vast library, the visitor pointed to a room full of obscure Hebrew texts on Hasidism and remarked, awestruck: "And you, Herr Professor, have studied them all!" "Certainly not, young man," Steinschneider responded. "You don't expect me to read that nonsense."

It was just such emphatic insistence on dry rationalism that Buber opposed, hailing instead the creative "life-giving" force of Hasidism. Born in Vienna in 1878, Buber had grown up on his grandfather's estate in Galicia, a remote eastern province of the Habsburg empire, with a mixed population of Poles, Ukrainians, and observant Jews. Like many other Polish Jews, Buber's grandparents were Germanophiles. They imbued him with a love for both German poetry and Jewish folklore and tradition. After finishing his university studies, he married Paula Winkler, a brilliant Catholic writer from a Bavarian peasant family who was as interested in the mythic core of cultures as he was. Buber seems to have begun collecting Hasidic tales as a teenager in Galicia, and now he and his wife translated them rather freely from Yiddish and Hebrew into German. Buber's *Tales of Rabbi Nachman* (1906) and *Legend of the Baal-Shem* (1908) were critical and popular successes. At least one German poet, Börries von Münchhausen, a champion of the German *völkisch* revival, welcomed the *Tales* warmly. He assumed that Buber, through his emphasis on roots rather than ritual, might help make Jews into more authentic Germans:

> *Escape this scorn and spite, O outcast tribe!*
> *Regain the happy youth for which you yearn!*
> *Make one word both your compass and your guide*
> *And let that one word be: return!*

In trying to bridge the old gulf between German and East European Jews, Buber hoped to expand and enrich the possibilities of German Jewish identity. His vivid and colorful interpretations of Hasidic tales and homilies appealed all the more to young Germans—Jews and Gentiles alike—as it coincided with an upsurge in Germany of interest in spirituality and the "exotic" cultures of Asia and Africa. Buber called on secular young German Jews to seek, as he put it, a genuine *Erlebnis*— an "inner experience"—of the popular "soul" of Judaism, a Judaism beyond the restrictions and injunctions of Talmudic law, which most German Jews, including Buber, no longer observed. Though ridiculed by some as a pretentious neo-Romantic affectation, his message was taken up by a new generation.

Hasidism came to be hailed (especially by secular Jews) as a vital force, more genuine and robust than fossilized orthodoxy or secularized reform. After watching a troupe of Yiddish actors perform in Prague's Café Savoy, Kafka concluded that here was a genuine folk spirit, warmer and more humane than the stiffness and self-denial of Western Jews. Buber's *Tales of Rabbi Nachman* and *Legend of the Baal-Shem* prompted the philosopher Georg Simmel to use the pronoun "we" in a Jewish context, allegedly for the first time in his life. Simmel said to Buber: "We really are a very strange people."[38] Buber even moved Rathenau—so staunchly Germanic at heart—to resume the Hebrew lessons he had given up as a boy: Rathenau eventually published and annotated a number of Talmudic tales and financed the publication of Michah Berdichevsky's great anthology, *Mimekor Yisrael: Classical Jewish Folktales*. For some time, Rathenau also attended Buber's "Thursday Society" at Buber's villa in the Berlin garden suburb of Zehlendorf, where Jewish savants met with Protestant theologians and mystically inclined German poets to discuss the true Jewish *Geist*, so much more appealing than the rootless materialism of the average middle-class German Jew.

Buber identified himself as a Zionist, but in a cultural rather than a political sense, not so much a knee-jerk reaction to discrimination as a search for "roots." He railed against assimilationist half-truths and against what he called the "degeneration" (*Entartung*) of the Jewish "species." He appealed to the rebellious young, who had begun to suspect that their parents had paid too high a price for affluence and success. He sparked a cult of authenticity. In a series of influential lectures in Prague following the publication of the *Tales* and *Legend*, he called on young Jews to be above all true to themselves, an end they would not achieve through "devotion to God," he said, "for nowadays we have no God," but through fidelity to the "substance of their being." That substance was still "singular" as Jehovah had been "singular and unique" in the distant past.[39] With this slightly sacrilegious formulation (which he deleted in the printed edition of the lectures), Buber pressed for cultural nationalism.

In texts that astonish only in retrospect, he continued to draw upon the *völkisch*, occasionally even racist coinage of his day: it was not yet pernicious to speak about the importance of "blood." Like Theilhaber, Buber tended to equate "blood" with "Volk." He introduced such notions as "destiny," "organic folk community," and what he called the "ur-dream" of a people into Jewish parlance, terms that had long played a major role in nationalistic thought. He was soon criticized for the saccharine affectation of his Hasidic tales and his overemphasis on a kind of folk essence: "What we are and know is more than the dark urgings of our blood," complained one reader in the Zionist *Jüdische Rundschau*.[40] Unlike other *völkisch* thinkers, however, Buber never implied the domination or disqualification of other species.

Stefan Zweig also mystified blood. It was "earth's deepest force." Zweig heard his own blood "singing" in his veins. Hugo Salus, a Jew, perhaps the most prominent German Jewish poet in Bohemia, wrote:

> *But blood remains blood*
> *With a drop in you and a drop in me*
> *We know we are brothers for eternity,*
> *Brothers born of a single darkness.*

The poet and playwright Richard Beer-Hoffmann invoked the same spirit in a lullaby to his daughter Miriam:

> *Miriam, my child, are you asleep?*
> *We are but shores, and blood in us deep*
> *Flows from those past to those yet to come,*
> *Blood of our forefathers, proud, restless, and deep*
> *All are within us. Who feels alone?*
> *You are their life—their life is your own.*
> *Miriam, my life's well, my child, sleep!*[41]

The same Beer-Hoffmann, however, confessed shock when, on a cold winter day in Berlin, wrapped in a scarf that showed only his eyes, he was accosted in the street by a bearded, caftaned Polish Jew with earlocks who said, "My good Sir seems to be one of us. . . . Could he tell me how to get to the Nollendorfplatz!"[42]

UNDETERRED by such soul-searching, the assimilationists continued to put their trust in a better future, built not on such fragile elements as love and hope but on more sturdy political, cultural, and economic bases. They took heart from the failure of Stöcker's party and from their accelerated acculturation within the German middle class. The increased political influence of Jews—because of their wealth and their role in the arts, sciences, and press—contributed to the growing confidence, as did the rise of the Social Democrats, who militated openly for human rights. There was a new willingness on the part of Jewish organizations to engage in direct political action. In March 1893, German Jews united to establish a national lobby, the Centralverein (Central

Union of German Citizens of the Jewish Faith). It quickly became the largest representative Jewish body in the Reich. The name was carefully chosen to denote what the new Verein was and was not. "We are not German Jews," the Verein said in one of its first statements. "We are German citizens of the Jewish faith." A time-honored taboo had nevertheless been broken: after a century of advancement through accommodation and manipulations behind the scenes, Jews finally dared to mobilize politically in defense of their civil rights.

Moses Mendelssohn had preferred Gentiles like Lessing or Dohm to speak for him. Jewish notables and politicians were similarly reluctant to speak up, as some put it, "in their own cause." Riesser's rousing speech to the abortive Frankfurt National Assembly in 1848 was a rare exception. Jacoby, Bamberger, Sonnemann, and Lasker fought for Jewish rights as part of the larger struggle for democracy.

A few months before the birth of the new Verein, some of the more timid notables of the Berlin Jewish community had considered making another discreet and "humble" approach to the kaiser with earnest prayers and supplications for his "grace, protection, and support" against anti-Semitism. Nothing came of it. James Simon, the German Jewish "cotton king," advised them to desist. With the tired resignation of one who had tried and failed, Simon told his fellow notables: "Politically, there is no way to talk to him."

The new Verein ignored the conventional wisdom that stepchildren always be on their best behavior. It resolved to fight publicly, in the name of "pride," "manly courage," and "honor"—martial virtues highly regarded in the Germany of the kaisers. The mere launching of the new society unleashed the usual fears: it could amount to a public confession of the emancipation's failure. Jewish family magazines studiously ignored it at first. "One is almost tempted to say that initially the Verein met with more difficulties among coreligionists than among their enemies," according to its historian, Arnold Paucker.[43]

To counter these concerns, spokesmen for the Verein emphasized that it represented a religious rather than an ethnic minority. Since so many of its members were indifferent to religion, such insistence seemed somewhat beside the point. The truth was that the Verein represented a community not of faith but of fate. A widely shared family or clan culture continued to bind together believers and nonbelievers, linking the baptized with those who refused to convert.

The Verein's initiatives were apparent in a number of areas. The association published a glossy magazine named, suggestively, *Im Deutschen Reich*—In the German Empire. As is often the case with such magazines, it was more widely distributed than actually read. Proclaiming that Jews had no more in common with their coreligionists in France or England than Catholics and Protestants with their coreligionists abroad, the magazine preached German patriotism as staunchly as it denounced baptism as dishonorable and called for more Jewish self-respect. The magazine warned its readers that if they would not fight for their rights no one would. In calling for Jewish self-assertion and condemning baptism—a practice forced on Jews by hypocrites to confirm their prejudices—the Verein helped, paradoxically, to promote Buber's proto-Zionist "renaissance," a process of dissimilation among some of the most assimilated German Jews.

On the regional level, the new body advised and coordinated communities, student organizations, and other associated groups. Nationally, it acted as a parliamentary lobby, helped finance political campaigns, and joined non-Jewish efforts to promote tolerance and democracy. The Verein was a long-overdue act of political defiance. Its militancy was in contrast to the relative timidity of French Jews during the Dreyfus Affair. Had Germany truly been a constitutional monarchy, the Verein might have been more successful. In the circumstances, it was able to reach only the margins of power. Real power in Germany was centered not in the Reichstag but in the occult triangle of monarch, army, and bureaucracy.

Jewish university students were now often emboldened to challenge anti-Semites to duels, with occasionally fatal results. In fact, some grew so skilled at dueling that most elite student fraternities resolved that Jews no longer deserved chivalrous "satisfaction."

WILLY Ritter Liebermann von Wahlendorf was emblematic of the new, more demanding approach. Liebermann was Walther Rathenau's cousin. He and other members of the Jewish *jeunesse dorée* were impatient with the disadvantages they still experienced, specifically their exclusion from the officer corps of the army reserves. They had to be content with the rank of lance corporal, at best. The regular officer corps was closed—albeit unofficially—even to converted Jews. The grandsons of the converted composer Felix von Mendelssohn-Bartholdy attained the rank of lieutenants in the reserves, but when one of them asked to serve in the regular army his request was denied.[44]

In Liebermann's elegant social world of young aristocrats and sportsmen, anti-Semitism was peripheral, polite, ironic, and tinged with self-deprecation. As a young man he claimed that it existed "mostly in the exaggerated fantasy of Jews" and "in the lingering reluctance of indolent Christians to forgo a beloved old habit." There was enough room for hope. Years later, in his memoirs, he bitterly scolded himself for not having seen the difference between his elegant cocoon and the real world: "I failed to take into account our petite bourgeoisie, whose narrow-mindedness could spark a wildfire."[45]

Jewish students grew so skilled at dueling that most elite student fraternities refused to duel with Jews, claiming that Jews did not warrant chivalrous "satisfaction." *Courtesy Leo Baeck Institute, Jerusalem*

Liebermann was no ordinary dandy. He combined some of the finest qualities of both the assimilationists and the self-assertive Jews of Buber's renaissance. A renowned equestrian, marksman, member of elite clubs and dueling fraternities, art collector, and landowner, he was tall and good-looking and cut the figure of the archetypical Prussian nobleman. His grandfather Joseph had settled in Berlin around 1790 and established one of the largest and most modern textile factories on the Continent. At his death in 1856, he left each of his ten children half a million gold marks. He was a man of some consequence; Frederick William IV himself once called on him at home. During the visit, Joseph, speaking of his family, grandly remarked, "Your Majesty, we are the same Liebermanns who ousted the English from the Continent!"[46] The king, more accustomed to think in terms of battles than of bales of cotton, was confused by this remark and stared blankly. Joseph Liebermann had to explain that the Liebermanns had driven back not troops but English cotton imports. Joseph's son Adolf was a philanthropist and art patron who retired early to lead the life of a worldly bon vivant; after Bleichröder, he was the second unconverted Berlin Jew to be made a nobleman. The Liebermanns of the older generation conducted their social life mostly among Jews of their own class. They despised the "egotism" of the converts; in their eyes, converts were guilty of moral suicide.[47] With their cousins the Rathenaus and with the Gersons, the Reichenheims, and other wealthy Berliners, they observed the High Holidays dressed in tails and top hats, seated under the gilded dome in the front rows of the grand new synagogue on the Oranienburgerstrasse.

The family mansion in the Tiergarten section was surrounded by three acres of landscaped garden and attended by four liveried lackeys, a porter, a majordomo, two coachmen, two gardeners, a cook, and half a dozen maids. The house was known for its lavish art gallery that doubled as a ballroom occupying an entire wing fifteen meters high and lit naturally through a skylight. The gallery was hung with English and French masters—Whistlers, Corots, and Courbets—a fine Murillo, and the best of contemporary German art: Caspar David Friedrich, Adolph Menzel, Franz von Lenbach, and Willy's first cousin Max Liebermann, Germany's leading Impressionist painter and future president of the Prussian Academy of Arts.* The family balls were attended by the intellectual pride of Berlin and by officers serving in elite Prussian regiments. At the beginning of each season, newly arrived officers would leave their calling cards with the porter and come by later to pay their respects to the lady of the house. Crown Prince Frederick and his wife, Queen Victoria's eldest daughter, came to visit. Little Willy was instructed that if the crown prince inquired whether he would like to become a soldier, as was likely, he was to answer: "Jawohl, Your Imperial Highness, a soldier!" Instead, the crown prince said: "Well, my boy, does it please you to see all these pretty pictures every day?"[48]

Willy's burning ambition was indeed to become an officer, at the very least in the reserves. In 1887, he was about to conclude his mandatory one-year training course in an elite cavalry regiment. The other university graduates in his course—all Christians—were given commissions as reserve officers. Only he was discharged as a corporal. The commanding officer, a Major von Mackensen, made things worse by invoking the honor of the king's name and voicing what Liebermann later reported simply as a "condescending" remark. Liebermann fumed. He was far more concerned with the honor of his own "family and race," as he put it, than with the king's.[49] Within an hour, Liebermann sent his seconds to challenge his commanding officer to a duel with pistols at close range.

Liebermann was known as one of the best shots in his regiment. Mackensen lamely sent word that no "personal" insult had been meant; he had spoken and acted in his "official" capacity only. Liebermann retorted that he would suffer neither "personal" nor "official" insults and insisted on a duel. It took place three days later. Mackensen aimed at Liebermann's head and missed by a few millimeters; Liebermann aimed at Mackensen's lower leg but hit his thigh, rendering him an invalid for life.

Though widely practiced, especially by "men of honor," dueling was illegal. Liebermann was charged with a criminal offense. While the trial

---

*Max Liebermann was told by an admirer that there were only two great painters, he and Velázquez. "Why Velázquez?" Liebermann retorted.

was pending, an Anglophile uncle urged him to seek refuge in England, the one country in Europe, according to the uncle, where a man like Willy could lead a free and respectable life as a gentleman of independent means. Liebermann refused to run away. The trial was brief. The courts were customarily lenient to officers and gentlemen guilty of shooting each other over affairs of honor. Liebermann was sentenced to three years' confinement in the relative comfort of the citadel of Koblenz. There he was treated well, given rooms overlooking the Rhine. His meals were brought in from a nearby inn. Liebermann enjoyed frequent leaves to visit coffeehouses, barbershops, and girlfriends in town. Liebermann's aunt Julie, who was acquainted with Empress Auguste, successfully intervened on his behalf. Liebermann was pardoned and released after only eight months.

The case was a sensation throughout Germany. Where would things end if subalterns could challenge superior officers to duels? Some were scandalized by Liebermann's early release. Others thanked him for having acted in the interest of tolerance and fairness. Liebermann himself was transformed by the affair from a pampered young bon vivant to a sworn enemy of military arrogance. Before the duel he had wanted nothing more than to be an officer. Now he felt his "moral backbone" steeled, his "pride in Judaism and [his] Jewish roots" galvanized.[50] After the duel Liebermann refrained from attending court functions. He was always ready to fight for his convictions and his honor, with loaded pistols, if need be.

The many ups and downs of his life are described in a 1936 memoir, written in exile, after Hitler's rise to power. The manuscript was entitled *Mein Kampf: Memoirs of a German Jew, 1863–1936*. The words *Mein Kampf*, underlined three times, referred to his failed effort to prove his Anglophile uncle wrong. He confessed that his refusal to follow his uncle's advice had been the greatest blunder in a life "not lacking in stupidities and mistakes." Liebermann felt ashamed for having been, "so to speak, a fool." He had sacrificed his life to a supposed fatherland and an "exaggerated Germanic idea of 'honor.'" He had lived simultaneously in two worlds. The first was his own, the world of leading Jewish families ("to the end of my life, I could not have wished for better company"), where one met scholars and artists, foreign ambassadors, and, he added ironically, maybe even a (Christian) "officer of the royal cavalry guard."[51] Rank and wealth came paired with high-mindedness, learning, and good manners. The other world was that of his aristocratic fellow students, Christians who, like him, belonged to the exclusive fraternity Starkenburgia, devoted to pleasure and excess in their social and aesthetic pursuits. Each world had its attractions for him. Had he not been denied a commission in the army, he now reflected gratefully, he might have gone on living the life of a rich, privileged fop.

THE spectacle of intelligent young men fighting to become officers in the army reserves might seem ridiculous. In the context of the time and place it was a serious matter. Germany was a semimilitarized society. Martial imagery dominated the national fantasy; war monuments overlooked river valleys and public squares everywhere. Reserve officers enjoyed a special status. Schoolteachers, doctors, lawyers, professors, and businessmen listed their rank in the reserves on embossed calling cards. On Sedan Day, the anniversary of Bismarck's victory over France, Latin teachers appeared in their classrooms in full uniform with their medals and refought Caesar's battles on the blackboard in terms appropriated from Clausewitz and Moltke.[52] A commission in the army reserves was a sine qua non for senior careers in government. In May 1909, the *Frankfurter Zeitung* claimed that twenty-five to thirty thousand Jews, qualified by their educations to become officers, had served in the army since 1880. Not one had been promoted to officer, although some three hundred converts had.

The Verein spent a lot of time and money on this issue. At its instigation, Social Democratic deputies raised it annually in the Reichstag. But with no result. The ostensible official excuse was that candidates had to be accepted by the entire officer corps, a seemingly "democratic" feature. The alleged consensus among officers was that it was unthinkable for Jews to command Germans. The Reichstag had no say in the matter. The emperor shared the ingrained prejudice of the old officer class. Although he tried to secure a commission for the Jewish baron Albert Goldschmidt, he failed and did not press the matter. Goldschmidt had to be content with the post of attaché at the German embassy in London (the diplomatic corps was usually closed to Jews as well).

OWING mostly to declining birthrates, Jews were now a shrinking minority. Their representation in the population dropped by one-third, from 1.3 percent in 1880 to 0.9 percent thirty years later. To the majority of Germans they remained as visible as ever. They continued to believe in their ultimate integration. In retrospect, of course, they were wrong. At the time, though, as Peter Gay observes, they had good reason to believe they were right.[53]

What were the alternatives? In most other European countries, prejudice and discrimination seemed equally or more prevalent. With all its shortcomings, Germany stood out as a country where acculturation, social integration, and day-to-day tolerance seemed to have as good a chance as anywhere else in Western Europe. England in 1900 imposed strict limitations on Jewish immigration. In Italy, Jews were so few as to be almost invisible.

In Western Europe, anti-Semitism was generally thought to be most virulent in France. For nearly a century, French Jews had enjoyed the libertarian legacy of the 1789 revolution. In the mid-1890s, however, republican France was suddenly infected with the racial hatred generated by the trial of Captain Alfred Dreyfus, the only Jew on the general staff of the French army. Dreyfus, a wealthy Alsatian, was accused of spying on behalf of Germany and in 1894 was tried for treason. The eponymous affair institutionalized anti-Semitism in France in a manner thought unlikely in Germany. A cabal of soldiers, clericalists, aristocrats, politicians, frustrated monarchists, and pseudoscientific savants—disciples of Joseph-Arthur de Gobineau, Edouard-Adolphe Drumont, Alphonse de Toussenel, and other racist theorists—agitated against Dreyfus and the community to which he belonged. Outside the courtroom where he was tried, the mob growled, "Death to the Jews." In the courtyard of the Ecole Militaire, where he was publicly stripped of his rank before being incarcerated on Devil's Island in French Guiana, he continued to proclaim his innocence. Most French Jews were cowed and passive. Alarmed German Jewish tourists in Paris hurried back to Frankfurt and Berlin. Hans Levy-Dorfmann, a young student of medicine at the Sorbonne, wrote his bride in Mainz that at the end of the academic year he would try to move back to a "decent German university."

The Dreyfus Affair convulsed France for more than a decade. The growing evidence that Dreyfus had been convicted on trumped-up charges seemed to poison the atmosphere even more: Jews were accused of being a pro-German fifth column, responsible for France's defeat in the war of 1870. In the *Allgemeine Zeitung des Judentums,* a correspondent wondered whether Jews could continue to live in France. The passionate anti-Dreyfus camp included not only socialites and *salonnières* but also the editors of *Le Figaro,* the poet Paul Valéry, the painter Edgar Degas, the politician and writer Maurice Barrès, the ducs d'Uzès, de Brissac, de La Rochefoucauld, and de Luynes, and the comtesse de Martel (the model for Proust's Odette), and even the president of the republic. The Dreyfusards, who clamored for a retrial, were no less vocal—socialists, republicans, anticlericalists, artists, and writers joined the cause, convinced that French democracy was at stake. Public disorder reached such a pitch that for a while it looked as if the army would rise up against the government to prevent a retrial and put an end to the republic. The violent upheaval reconfirmed German Jews in their patriotic fervor. They considered themselves lucky to live in an orderly country under a relatively benign regime. Maximilian Harden (a convert, born Felix Ernst Witkowski), one of the most influential German political commentators prior to 1914, at first assumed that Dreyfus was guilty. As the affair grew in intensity and scope, Harden was shocked to see the alleged crime of one man ascribed to an entire community. He gave in to what for him was a rare show of pride in being a German—indeed gratitude for it—even under a government he hated and an emperor he despised. In Alsace-Lorraine, at the time of its annexation to Germany in 1871, thousands of Jews had chosen to leave for France "in order not to become Germans."[54] Many of those who had stayed now felt fortunate to be Germans.

In Eastern Europe, anti-Semitism was most savage in czarist Russia. At the turn of the century, five million Jews lived there as aliens among Russians, Byelorussians, Poles, Lithuanians, Letts, Estonians, Cossacks, Georgians, and Ukrainians, a multitude of diverse people, hostile to one another and especially to Jews. Most Russian Jews were confined by law to the so-called Pale of Settlement, a region permeated by poverty and hopelessness. The czar's chief adviser on Jewish affairs was Konstantin Pobedonostsev, a fanatical Slavophile. His formula for solving Russia's "Jewish problem" was simple: "one third must emigrate, one third convert, and one third must die."

Russia was the only European country that banned foreign Jews from entering it, at least in principle. Since it was also the only European country with a real border where foreigners were required to carry passports and were likely to be interrogated, German Jews were liable to be turned away at the frontier. Russia had also been notorious in recent years as the land of pogroms. The word *pogrom*—meaning "devastation" in Russian—was entering the international lexicon to describe violent outrages against a particular ethnic group. From the early 1880s, Russia's recurrent anti-Semitic pogroms were government-inspired diversions from the miseries of daily life. Nearly two million Jews fled Russia between 1880 and 1910; more than 100,000 crossed Germany every year on their way to North Sea ports and safer havens in North and South America. Relief funds for these emigrants and for those left behind were solicited among Jews all over Germany. The *Allgemeine Zeitung des Judentums* spoke of Russia as a land of hatred and iniquity, the great nineteenth-century Jewish "House of Bondage."

The novelist Arthur Landsberger (who committed suicide when the Nazis came to power) was convinced that even the United States was infested with "unparalleled anti-Semitism."[55] Eduard Lasker, on a visit to the United States shortly before his death, was shocked to discover a quota for Jews at Harvard University and a prohibition against Jewish guests at some of the best resort hotels. He concluded that though the United States might be more democratic than Germany in many ways, in terms of Jewish integration it lagged woefully behind. In 1891, Paul Dimidow cautioned in a pamphlet entitled *Where To? A Word of Warning to Western European Jews* that anti-Semitism had migrated to the United States together with the Russian Jews. And Ludwig Geiger, a Goethe scholar and quintessential *Bildungsbürger*, while protesting the lot of Eastern European Jews, noted that the situation elsewhere was worse. It was rare to find a Jewish professor in the United States and England. As late as 1911, the distinguished English historian Louis

Namier was denied an Oxford fellowship by the warden and fellows of All Souls College because of his "Polish-Jewish origin."[56]

The status of Jews in Austria-Hungary was also more worrisome than in Germany. The Austrian Social Democrat Karl Kautsky wrote that Austrian anti-Semitism was more dangerous than the German variant because of its pseudodemocratic cast, which appealed to workers and oppressed nationalities. Visiting Austria in 1910, the scholar Victor Klemperer claimed that whereas he felt "abroad" in Italy or France, in Austrian-ruled Bohemia he sensed he was in "enemy territory."[57] Anti-Semitism, unequaled elsewhere in the West, was said to be rampant there.[58] Though Jews were prominent in Viennese cultural life and in the national economy, their condition throughout the multinational Habsburg empire was becoming ever more precarious. In Bohemia, Czechs hated them for being Germans and Germans despised them for being Jews. As the only minority truly loyal to the shaky Habsburg crown, they felt all the more politically isolated and exposed. Nowhere in Central Europe was their material plight as desperate as in the Austrian province of Galicia, where population growth combined with economic crisis to produce recurrent famines. Five thousand Galician Jews were said to starve to death annually.

Klemperer was not alone in feeling the dark cloud hanging over the Austro-Hungarian empire. Wickham Steed of the London Times lived in Vienna from 1902 to 1913. He was so penetrated by a sense of doom, he said in his memoirs, that he left the Austrian capital with the relief of a man who escapes an impending disaster.

WE are lucky to be German, the economist Franz Oppenheimer wrote his wife after a visit to Galicia. Quite apart from the fact that most people do not easily leave their homes and language behind, German Jews understandably felt that, with all its shortcomings, Germany seemed more civilized and above all more orderly than most other states. The humanist ideal of Bildung, which for many Jews was their only religion, continued to evoke a promise that kept their love affair with Germany alive. When German Jews did emigrate, they took along their faith in the Old Country. Children born in the United States were given German names, often those of the heroes and heroines of

Schiller's and Goethe's plays. In England, men of the Rothschild family tended to marry German Jewish women for a full century after they settled there. Despite his mixed Iraqi-German-Jewish background, one major English literary figure was named Siegfried Sassoon. In the United States, a number of German Jewish immigrants sent their children to German schools, ordered newspapers and books in German, and sang in German choirs. The entrance to the most exclusive Jewish club in New York (it still exists under its German name, the Harmonie Club) was graced with a portrait of Kaiser William II, at least until 1914. German Jews remained attached to the Old Country far longer than other Jewish immigrants to America. A few tried to correct the flaws of their beloved homeland in the New World, even financing the purchase of a fountain depicting Heine's Lorelei for placement in New York's Central Park; originally designed as a monument to Heine in his hometown of Düsseldorf, the fountain had been vetoed by that city because the poet was Jewish.* In New York, it fared a little better. Rejected for Central Park by the city's art council, it found a place in a neighborhood of the Bronx where many of the immigrants lived.

Prominent German American Jews protested against America's joining England and France in the war against imperial Germany in 1914. Jacob H. Schiff, head of Kuhn, Loeb—at the time the largest private bank in the United States after J. P. Morgan—declared that he could no more disavow his loyalty to Germany than he could renounce his own parents. Schiff prayed for Germany's victory. In a statement to the *New York Times* on November 22, 1914, he charged the British and the French with attempting to destroy Germany for reasons of trade. Eastern European Jews in the United States, repelled by the anti-Semitism of czarist Russia, were equally pro-German.[59] In Russia itself, Jews of the Pale greeted German troops advancing into Poland, Byelorussia, and the Ukraine as liberators. In a sense, they were.

The British government took these developments very seriously. In a fit of paranoia, the British ambassador in Washington even suspected

---

*Heine's poem on the legendary Lorelei was so much part of the German canon that even the Nazis were unable to eradicate it. Books published under the Nazis described it as a "folk song" by an "unknown author."

the existence of a veritable German Jewish conspiracy in the United States directed at Britain. The 1917 Balfour Declaration, calling for the establishment of a Jewish national home in Palestine, was at least partly motivated by the British government's desire to win support among pro-German American Jews.

THE election system for the Prussian state parliament was based on rank and personal wealth, giving disproportional voting power to the nobility and the well-to-do middle class. Since most Jews were middle-class and more than half of them were self-employed in business or other entrepreneurial activities, the system enabled them to exert political influence beyond their numbers; most Jewish voters nevertheless continued to criticize this imbalance and to favor electoral and constitutional reform. By 1890, more than 60 percent of them supported the Social Democrats and similar opposition parties, voting against what Marxists would have called their class interests. By 1912, two years before the outbreak of war, 85 percent of the Jewish vote went to this largely pacifist left-of-center bloc.

Middle- and upper-middle-class Jewish voters were remarkably more liberal than other German middle-class voters. Wilhelm Liebknecht, the socialist leader and veteran of the 1848 revolution, found among them "a much greater sum of idealism than among non-Jews." August Bebel advised Engels in 1891 that "for decent company one must cultivate Jews." Engels was not sure this was a good thing but agreed that Jews had more brains than "others of the bourgeoisie."[60] As the National Liberal Party, for which most Jews had voted in the early 1870s, became increasingly conservative and chauvinist, middle-class Jews abandoned it and lent their support to the new left-of-center parties. By contrast, the non-Jewish German middle class had on the whole been liberal before 1871; in Bismarck's new Reich, however, much of its liberalism was eroded by relentless patriotic and martial propaganda. In his novel *Man of Straw*, Heinrich Mann portrayed with inspired bitterness the resultant servility, conformism, cowardice, and shallow religiosity of the post-1871 bourgeoisie.*

---

*Its original subtitle was *A History of the German Psyche under William II.*

Henry Adams, who fondly remembered the unique cult of *Bildung* and civic virtue he had encountered on a visit to Germany half a century earlier, was sickened on a return visit to Nürnberg by the dominant bourgeois preferences in politics and in art. It conveyed to him a sense of hopeless failure and doom.

German Jews did not take the reactionary turn of the German middle class.[61] The assertion, occasionally still heard, that the Jewish bourgeoisie was as conservative as the rest of Germans is false. Arnold Paucker, an authority on the subject, concluded in 1976 that "nothing is more misleading."[62] The corollary claim, voiced in 1991 by the noted German historian Nicolaus Sombart, that "without Jews the liberal tradition in Germany might have vanished completely after the establishment of the Reich" is nevertheless overstated.[63] But there is no doubt that their abiding liberalism fueled the German democratic project.

The Social Democrats appreciated the growing support from Jewish voters; they were less pleased by the reputation it gave them in some circles as the "Jews' party." They did not, however, soften their stand on the obstacles Jews continued to face. On the contrary, in the Reichstag they kept up their protests against discrimination in the army, the bureaucracy, the diplomatic service, and the universities. Not only Jewish intellectuals and professionals but also businessmen and even department-store tycoons supported them. It was the socialists' record on human rights and their unequivocal opposition to all forms of anti-Semitism that induced many Jewish capitalists to vote for them at a time when the party still advocated, at least in theory, the abolition of private property. Jewish middle-class support further increased after the party's rejection of doctrinaire Marxism. Ideologically, there seemed little difference between the Social Democratic leader Paul Singer, the kaiser's particular bête noire, and other prominent Berlin Jews, such as Oskar Tietz, Salman Schocken, and Walther Rathenau. Tietz and Rathenau shared Singer's mix of theoretical radicalism and sober, practical, liberal common sense. As a "class" in the Marxist sense of the word, the Jewish bourgeoisie remained an anomaly. They lived like bankers but voted like hard-pressed workers and leftist intellectuals.

The number of Social Democratic deputies in the Reichstag rose steadily after 1898. The party was the only one that, contrary to political wisdom, did not hesitate to present Jewish candidates. These candidates almost never converted; as a leading Jewish Social Democrat put it, one does not quit a persecuted minority. The Reichstag was not the only forum in which Jewish Social Democrats were quite visible. They were now also prominent among the advocates for disarmament, world peace, the abolition of royal prerogatives and of the death penalty, and other liberal reforms. Alfred Fried (winner of the 1911 Nobel Peace Prize) and Max Hirsch were among the founders of the German Peace Society. Its supporters included the Jewish publishing and advertising magnates Leopold Ullstein, Rudolf Mosse, and Leopold Sonnemann. Women's rights was yet another area of activity.

Relatively speaking, many more Jewish women were entering the labor market than non-Jewish women. Plagued by a double handicap, many had to be content with inferior jobs. Sadly, very little is known of Jewish women in nineteenth-century Germany; most available sources deal exclusively with men. A notable exception until recently was the feminist Bertha Pappenheim, known in the annals of psychoanalysis as Freud's "Anna O." She deserves a wider reputation less for her psychological recovery on Freud's couch than for her tireless battle against the thriving traffic in sex slaves. Many victims of the sex trade were Jewish girls from Eastern Europe sold, presumably by their impoverished families, to brothels in North and South America and even to a notorious bordello in the Orthodox Mea Shaarim quarter in Jerusalem. Pappenheim urged Jewish women in Eastern Europe to rebel. She infuriated religious conservatives by maintaining that Judaism viewed women solely as "biological crea-

The Expressionist poet Else Lasker-Schüler as a young woman in 1905. *Courtesy Leo Baeck Institute, Jerusalem*

tures." Another exceptionally gifted woman, well known in her prime, was the Expressionist poet Else Lasker-Schüler. The daughter of an Eberfeld banker, she was a small, slender woman with large, gleaming eyes who dressed in fantastic robes and counted among her lovers and friends Oskar Kokoschka, George Grosz, Adolf Loos, and Gottfried Benn. Always poor, she sometimes slept on park benches and lived for weeks on nuts and fruits. Appreciative critics celebrated her as the "black swan of Israel" and the "psalmist of the avant-garde." According to the cultural historian Claudia Schmölders, she was "love-crazed, fantastically communicative, multicultural before that term had been invented, dividing herself between Eberfeld, Berlin, and Jerusalem."[64] A sweet, unstillable sadness pervades her work, which stands at the zenith of German Jewish poetry before 1933. Not since Heine had there been a poet so German and at the same time so hauntingly Jewish, so musical and alluring:

> *Adam built himself in Eden's sod*
> *A city raised of earth and leaf*
> *And practiced to converse with God.*

In perhaps her most celebrated poem, the sensuality of

> *Sweet Lama son upon a musk plant throne,*
> *How long will your lips likely kiss my own*
> *And cheek on cheek the brightly knotted times go on.*

elaborates in three musically interconnected lines "a metaphysical conceit worthy of John Donne," as Peter Gay observes.[65] Sense and sound, word and image are marvelously interwoven.

Asked whether she would like her poetry to be translated into Hebrew, Lasker-Schüler replied disarmingly that that was unnecessary since she had written it in Hebrew anyway.

8

Assimilation and Its Discontents

A T the turn of the century, middle-class German Jews prospered. A few
grew rich. Of the two hundred wealthiest Prussian families, forty were
said to be Jews. In Berlin they constituted 5 percent of the population
but paid more than 30 percent of the city's taxes.[1] The richest man in
Berlin was still the kaiser, for reasons perhaps of divine right, bribery,
petty theft, legacy hunting, and treasonable treaties, as Karl Marx put
it; the second-richest man was Fritz von Friedländer-Fuld, the converted son of a Silesian family of coal magnates.[2] An express bus commonly known as the "roaring Moses" ran every morning from Berlin's
elegant suburb in the Grunewald forest, where bankers and brokers
lived in large villas, to the new stock exchange building downtown. In
Hamburg, where the Christian bourgeoisie was said to be far less prejudiced than that in Berlin, half the Jewish population lived in the two
wealthiest quarters, Harvestehude and Rotherbaum. In Frankfurt, the
average tax paid by Jews was four times higher than that of Protestants
and eight times that of Catholics.

Grand synagogues rose in the main cities. Their gilded splendor—piety combined with swagger—was visible from afar and reflected the Jews' growing wealth and self-satisfaction. Neo-Romanesque or Gothic, some were hardly distinguishable from churches. The largest, most pompous synagogues were in garish pseudo-Moorish style, perhaps under the influence of Byron and the popular novels of Benjamin Disraeli, who had lent the proud Jews of medieval Spain an aura of marvelous nobility. The new synagogues recalled the golden age of tolerance in Moslem Spain and articulated the growing hope for a "symbiosis" similar to that between Jews and Moslems in thirteenth-century Cordoba and Seville. The Spanish decor also served to disassociate the rich Western Jews from their poor "primitive" coreligionists in Poland and Russia. Some families, including Theodor Herzl's, went so far as to invent a distant Sephardic genealogy. A few of the new synagogues were far too large for the needs of their increasingly secular middle- and upper-middle-class congregations, whose true house of worship was the opera house or the concert hall.

No other class in Germany (or the rest of Europe) carried love of art to as great lengths as did middle- and upper-middle-class Jews in turn-of-century Germany. The novelist Theodor Fontane (a self-confessed lover of the Prussian aristocracy) lauded German Jews for adorning their villas with music rooms rather than riding stables and for lining their walls with books instead of ancestral portraits. They were proud of their patronage of the arts. In 1881, a terrible fire swept through Vienna's Ringtheater, killing many in the audience. Reporting the disaster, the *Allgemeine Zeitung des Judentums* reveled in the "disproportionately" high number of Jews in theater audiences everywhere, compared with the very few who patronized beer halls.[3]

The hatemongers saw the phenomenon in a different light. Jewish art patrons were still inevitably ridiculed as parvenus. A contemporary caricature entitled "Friday Night," preserved at the Frankfurt Jewish Museum, shows ugly, hook-nosed, black-haired, corpulent men and bejeweled women—more like reptiles than human beings—occupying the first rows of a concert hall. Jewish nouveaux riches were the butt of countless jokes: A recently converted stockbroker shows a visitor through his refurbished mansion. The living room is "genuine eighteenth century," he explains; the study, "sixteenth-century German Renaissance." Then the host marches his visitor quickly through a sparsely furnished room. "What's this?" the visitor asks. "Oh, nothing—just my late parents' old furniture." "I see," the visitor says. "It's the pre-Christian era!"

Richard Wagner's 1850 anti-Semitic essay "The Jews in Music" did

The splendor of the new synagogues reflected the growing wealth and self-satisfaction of the Jewish upper and middle classes. Steel engraving by J. Kolb of a new synagogue in Berlin. *Courtesy Leo Baeck Institute, Jerusalem*

not deter Jews from flocking to his operas; they remained among his most devoted fans. In his memoirs, Wagner noted the preponderance of Jews in his audiences and at the supper parties held in his honor afterward. Prominent Munich Jews, among them the mathematician and art patron Alfred Pringsheim (Thomas Mann's father-in-law), financed the construction of Wagner's concert hall in Bayreuth. The idea that he might not be considered 100 percent German would have struck Pringsheim and his many friends as absolutely ridiculous, according to Golo Mann, Pringsheim's grandson. After the triumphant premiere of *Lohengrin* in Berlin, a Jewish admirer cabled Wagner his congratulations: "Tremendous success. All Jews reconciled."[4]

Their large presence in concert audiences was ridiculed by their detractors as proof of passivity, an inability to be "creative." (The first great Jewish soloists emerged only later.) Martin Buber—narcissistically obsessed with Jewish "uniqueness"—countered with an equally outlandish claim that Jews were inherently a people of the "ear" summoned by God and enjoined since time immemorial to "hear," as in "Hear, O Israel." The ancient Greeks, according to Buber, had been a people of the "eye" and visual form; to the Jews, God had appeared only as a voice—hence their predilection for music.

The more affluent art patrons among the Jewish haute bourgeoisie of Berlin and Frankfurt collected Flemish and Italian Renaissance masters and works by Goya, Manet, Pissarro, Renoir, and Degas. They were among the first to do so in Berlin. Emil Ludwig's panegyric to the Jewish art collectors in their baronial mansions on the lakes and in the forests west of Berlin announced nothing less than that the aesthetic soul of Florence was alive four hundred years later in Charlottenburg and Wannsee. In the early 1880s, Karl Bernstein, a rich law professor, and his wife, Felice, were the first to decorate their home with Sisleys and Monets. Many were later donated to the new public museums. Paul Cassirer's Berlin art gallery was a major center of modern art, introducing Cézanne and van Gogh in Germany. Among his clients was James Simon, the "cotton king," perhaps the most prominent Jewish collector and certainly one of the most generous in his gifts to the Berlin state museums on the new "museum island" across from the Imperial Palace. Thanks to Simon and other Jewish donors, Berlin

museums were the first in Europe to display the Impressionists, ener-
gizing the entire German art world. Simon, Eduard Arnhold, and
Robert von Mendelssohn presented the new National Gallery with its
first van Goghs, Courbets, Gauguins, Pissarros, and Cézannes.[5] At a
time when most non-Jewish art collectors preferred works of the Italian
and Dutch Renaissance, Jewish patrons were interested in contemporary German art and even commissioned works by leading Impressionists and Expressionists.* They were unusually receptive to innovation,
eager—sometimes perhaps too eager—to follow and sponsor every
passing fashion; more often, they seemed to be endowed with a rare
instinct for quality.

Hugo von Tschudi, head of the National Gallery, complimented his
Jewish donors on their "vitality," imagination, and good judgment and
thanked them for making the city a major European art metropolis.
Tschudi's support for modern and contemporary art brought him into
conflict with the kaiser, who regarded modernism as "decadent" French
"gutter" art. When the kaiser refused to allocate public funds for the
acquisition of paintings by Cézanne and other French and German
modernists, Simon, Arnhold, and Mendelssohn readily stepped in. Of
the National Gallery's thirty-one key benefactors prior to World War I,
one historian has identified twenty-eight Jewish donors. Simon's donations included works by Mantegna, Vermeer, and Frans Hals. Simon, in
particular, refused all recompense as well as offers of medals and a title.
"I simply wanted to give an example to all cultivated citizens," he later
wrote.[6] One curator who had greatly benefited from Simon's generosity
half-jokingly "complained" that it was a pity Jews had been prohibited
only graven images and not music, theater, and other arts; out of sheer
contrariness, they might also have excelled in those.

German Jews were equally enthusiastic about theater. The diarist
Hildegard von Spitzemberg, a leading Berlin socialite, was present at
the 1896 premiere of Gerhart Hauptmann's *The Sunken Bell,* an avant-

---

*The opposite was also true. The Jewish press tycoon Rudolf Mosse commissioned the
kaiser's favorite kitsch painter of grand "historical" subjects to portray him and his family as seventeenth-century Dutch burghers.

garde play considered scandalous for its unabashed naturalism. She noted in her diary: "The house was packed to the last seat with Jews and their cohorts, representatives of the press and literary establishment: Harden, Sudermann, Schmidt, Fontane, Pietsch . . . although these last two shook their heads apprehensively and refused to join the supporters in their frenzied applause [for Hauptmann]."[7] The last two were the only non-Jews on Spitzemberg's list. One of them, Theodor Fontane, also benefited from Jewish patronage. In the years before Thomas Mann's first novels were published, Fontane was perhaps the greatest living German novelist. His books celebrated the old-fashioned, straitlaced, frugal common decency of the Prussian rural gentry. German Jews were among Fontane's most faithful readers. They loved him for his wisdom, humor, urbanity, sophistication, and fairness. It is doubtful they knew how prejudiced he was. Fontane's dislike of Jews, almost physical, became known only much later with the publication of his private correspondence. He believed that Jews were "capable of being thinkers and idealists to the highest degree and at the same time cheats or even downright frauds." They might become fully integrated in Germany, but only "physically," never "spiritually."[8] In 1894, on his seventy-fifth birthday, he began to have second thoughts. The occasion was a bitter disappointment; his beloved "old Prussia" almost completely ignored the anniversary of its greatest novelist. Fontane received hundreds of letters of congratulation, but not from the von Bülows, Arnims, and Schliefens whom he had celebrated in so many novels, travelogues, poems, and war books. Rather, those who marked this day of rejoicing bore "very, very different names." But they, too, were men

Who could clearly trace their lines
To nearly prehistoric times:
"Bergs" and "Heims" came flooding in,
With droves of "Mayers" and their kin;
Then last but certainly not least
Pollacks and others from farther east.
Abraham, Isaac, patriarchs all,
Kindly harking to the call,
Kindly making me their leader,

> Each one having been my reader,
> Greeting me like long-lost brothers.
> With friends like these, who needs the others?
> They know my books, from far and wide—
> "Ach, Herr Cohn! Do step inside!"[9]

MANY Jews were now self-employed in commerce and related trades. Some were bankers. Almost half of all private banks were still said to be in Jewish hands but private banks were increasingly marginal, ceding ground to more powerful financial institutions. Much of the new national wealth was augmented by corporate and state institutions that provided the new industries with broader bases for expansion. The most important among those—the Reichsbank, the Deutsche Bank, the Dresdner and Darmstätter banks—had been founded, or were still run, by Jewish directors.

Apart from the banks, several of the new industries—medium- and large-sized chemical factories, metalworks, electrical, smelting, and printing plants, and mills—had been founded by enterprising Jews. They established the first German aircraft factory and department-store chains and were among the first to introduce American production methods. Albert Ballin was perhaps the leading Jewish entrepreneur. From modest beginnings in a small family-owned travel agency in Hamburg, he rose to become one of the world's major shipping magnates, head of the Hamburg-America Line. Other prominent business leaders were the Hamburg banker Max Warburg (Ballin's close friend), the coal magnate Eduard Arnhold, the cotton magnate and art patron James Simon. Emil Rathenau and his son Walther were in a class by themselves. The elder Rathenau, known as the "Bismarck of the German electric industry," introduced electric light and trams to most German cities.

The wealth, prominence, and intellectual acuity of these men brought them into personal contact with the kaiser. Some came to be known as the "kaiser's Jews" (*Kaiserjuden*)—a slightly derogatory term supposedly coined by the Zionist leader Chaim Weizmann. Unlike the court Jews of old, the *Kaiserjuden* did not administer the monarch's private investments; Gerson von Bleichröder had been the last of those. Ballin, Warburg, Arnhold, Rathenau, and the other *Kaiserjuden* were younger, more self-assured, better-educated, more fully assimilated and integrated into German life than Bleichröder and his ilk. The kaiser consulted them regularly on questions of financial and cultural policy, and they flattered him with large donations to his favorite charities. The kaiser was fascinated by self-made tycoons. Like his English cousin Edward VII, he actively sought the company of rich men, but unlike Edward he avoided becoming intimate with them. With few exceptions, the *Kaiserjuden* were not spared anxieties that came to embitter their assimilated coreligionists. They were envied for their influence and respected, but only up to a point. Warburg and Rathenau never felt that they "belonged" as, for example, the Krupps or Siemenses did, or as the Rothschilds, Sir Ernest Cassel, or Samuel Montagu (Baron Swaythling) did in England. The emperor treated the *Kaiserjuden* with exquisite civility, inviting them to private lunches and stag dinners in

The kaiser was fascinated by self-made tycoons. Here he is with Albert Ballin, the son of a modest Jewish travel agent but himself the head of the Hamburg-America Line, one of the world's largest shipping companies. *Courtesy Leo Baeck Institute, Jerusalem*

the palace or on his yacht. In theory, then, they were *hoffähig* (present-able at court); in practice they were not. Invitations to the palace were never extended to their wives. This rankled.

William II was a difficult man to deal with under any circumstances. Combining a strong personality with a weak character, he was unpredictable, pompous, and paranoid. "My subjects simply ought to do as I tell them," he once said, "but they want to think for themselves and this produces all the difficulties."[10] He was filled with dark prejudices against his English relatives and against Jews, whom he considered the "parasites" of his empire. As a young prince, he had admired Stöcker and at one point even regarded him as a "second Luther." Though he deserted many of his anti-Semitic friends when he inherited the throne, he soon came under the influence of a bizarre English racist, Houston Stewart Chamberlain, who preached a crusade against Jews, blacks, the Japanese, and other "vermin." Wagner's son-in-law, Chamberlain wrote his books in German and went to great lengths to prove that Jesus was not a Jew but a blond Aryan.[11] The kaiser tried to make Chamberlain's books required reading in all German schools. His recommendation was not taken up by the ministry of education but the queen, his children, and their entourages had to submit to nightly readings from them. Notorious for his bombastic public utterances, the kaiser inveighed against phantom enemies and the "yellow danger" threatening Europe's integrity. In a speech to a German army contingent on its way to put down the Boxer Rebellion in China, he declared: "Just as the Huns a thousand years ago, under the leadership of Attila, gained a reputation by virtue of which they still live in history, so may the German name become known in such a manner in China that no Chinese will ever again dare to look askance at a German."[12] There was little reason to take seriously all he said or wrote—his ministers did not—and he often forgot what he had said or changed his mind overnight. In a sense, it was fortunate that the man who to a great extent determined the fate of Europe rarely subscribed to one idea for very long. Surrounded by saber-rattling generals and fawning courtiers, the kaiser was a political adventurer who made one diplomatic gaffe after another. He was sentimental to boot: the horn of his automobile played a tune from Wagner's *Das Rheingold*. He designed his own uniforms, plumes, and helmets, favoring fantastic shapes and a wealth of colors rare among living creatures, other than parrots perhaps.

Such was the man whom the *Kaiserjuden* had to please in order to bridge, however imperfectly, the gulf that still separated Jews from the apex of German power. Chaim Weizmann nonetheless despised the *Kaiserjuden* for their "obsequiousness" and "assimilationism" and for being "more German than the Germans, . . . superpatriotic, eagerly anticipating the wishes and plans of the masters of Germany." Weizmann, who was himself often accused of obsequiousness—but only to the English aristocracy—may have been "carried away by his double prejudice against German Jews and Germans in general."[13]

Weizmann hailed from Motol in Byelorussia, a place he called "one of the darkest and most forlorn corners of the Pale of Settlement."[14] His dislike of German Jews began early, when he was still a university student in Germany supporting himself as an assistant teacher at a Jewish day school. He got into an argument with Dr. Barness, the headmaster, whom he described as a "fatuous German of the Mosaic persuasion, . . . an intellectual coward and a toady." According to Weizmann, Barness believed that anti-Semitism was the result of only a "slight misunderstanding." It would disappear as soon as Germans became more aware of the fine qualities of their Jews, a recognition bound to come in the near future. Weizmann told Barness, "If a man has a piece of mud in his eye he doesn't want to know whether it's a piece of mud or a piece of gold. He just wants to get it out."[15]

In Weizmann's view, Ballin, Simon, Warburg, and the other *Kaiserjuden* were "slaves in the midst of freedom," reactionaries too blind politically and morally to see their shackles. Their constant exposure, as he put it, to so much German power and efficiency had instilled in them a deep sense of inferiority, causing them to grovel and "deny themselves."

Weizmann's opinion to the contrary, the *Kaiserjuden* were actually a rather diverse group. Politically, most were liberals; one or two voted conservative but were far to the left of the kaiser's reactionary and xenophobic entourage. Then, too, Simon was anything but obsequious. Rathenau delighted in confronting the kaiser and other German potentates with unpleasant truths. As one historian observes, Rathenau,

Simon, Ballin, and Warburg were "cosmopolitan, . . . outward looking, and liberal."[16] Whereas other industrialists shared William's paranoid view of European leaders and kings—the cannon manufacturer Krupp, for example, confirmed William in his fear that England and France were ganging up on Germany in a malicious strategy of encirclement—Ballin, Warburg, Arnhold, and Simon warned him that such thinking was simple-minded and perhaps self-interested. They urged him to seek an understanding with England. Warburg and Ballin were Anglophiles, charter members of the Foundation for Anglo-German Friendship launched by the king of England. Rathenau preached a European economic union to consolidate a lasting peace. Open-minded, neither servile nor self-denying, these men formed part of an intellectual milieu that ran counter to the official culture. Right-wingers decried their allegedly "pacifist" influence on the kaiser. In a 1904 Reichstag speech one conservative criticized the "Ballinization" of the government: "Aliens from Palestine and America have access to the highest steps of the throne."[17] Throughout the early 1900s, as German-English relations worsened over rearmament and competing imperial claims, Warburg and Ballin, together with Sir Ernest Cassel, an influential English financier of German Jewish origin, initiated more than one attempt to reduce tensions and suspicions.

Ballin seems to have been the original *Kaiserjude*. He first met the kaiser in 1906 in pouring rain at the annual Elbe regatta. The kaiser was very much taken with him. The two men shared a love of the sea and a desire to see Germany become a maritime nation like England. Ballin was perhaps the only *Kaiserjude* whose friendship and intimacy the kaiser actively sought. Whenever the kaiser and his wife visited Hamburg they dined with the Ballins in their town house on the Feldbrunnenstrasse. Ballin's luxury passenger steamships were at the kaiser's disposal at all times and the court made frequent use of them. The kaiser offered Ballin a title. Ballin declined it, though he became part of court society in Berlin.

Another *Kaiserjude,* James Simon, was not only an important art patron but also a founder of the German Orient Gesellschaft—Orient Society—and a generous backer of archaeological excavations in Egypt and Palestine; the kaiser sought his advice on Near Eastern policy and on the administration of the new state museums. "You cannot be in Simon's company," the kaiser said, "without learning something from him."[18] Simon invited William to visit the new synagogue on the Fasanenstrasse in Berlin, where, according to contemporaries, the blond cantor was a "mixture of Joshua and Parsifal."[19] William arrived in his dress uniform and a spiked helmet. As Simon showed him around, the kaiser asked: "What will people say about my strong interest in Jewish things?" "Your Majesty," Simon replied, "the rabbis are likely to assume that you wish to become a Jew."[20]

The kaiser welcomed Simon's judgment in matters of finance and art, but when Simon tried to engage him in speaking out against racial and religious prejudice or in acting decisively to reduce the remaining discrimination against German Jews in the army, universities, and bureaucracy, he was less successful. William would not or could not fulfill Simon's wish.

GERMAN Jews were shocked but not entirely surprised by the ferocity of the Russian pogroms of 1881. A veritable flood of frightened, penniless Jewish refugees streamed across the eastern border in search of safety. German Jews did not welcome them but contributed generously to their upkeep and eventual integration. Despite the harsh measures adopted by the government against this influx, tens of thousands of Russian, Romanian, and Galician Jews still managed to settle in Germany over the next two or three decades. By 1900, 10 to 15 percent of the Jewish population was said to be foreign-born. The illegals were periodically expelled across the Russian and Galician frontiers. More managed to get in. Closing the eastern border was seen as a "German cultural imperative," but it could not be enforced. Nor was it legally feasible, because of trade and other agreements with Russia and Austria-Hungary.

The influx from the East had begun in Heine's day:

> There are two kinds of rat,
> One hungry and one fat.
> The fat ones stay content at home,
> The hungry ones go out and roam.

A flood of refugees from the Russian pogroms. *Courtesy Leo Baeck Institute, Jerusalem*

The refugees were often the poorest of the poor, crowding into slums in the main cities. Anti-Semitic agitators exploited their arrival to foment panic. They were said to spread counterfeit money, filth, and disease. The repulsion felt by native-born Jews at the sight of Easterners—the *Ostjuden*—reflected a lingering fear of being identified with them. The newcomers embarrassed the assimilated by reminding them of their forebears. Gustav Mahler wrote to his wife from Lvov (Lemberg) that Polish Jews "run about this place as dogs do elsewhere. . . . God almighty, and I am supposed to be related to them?"[21] Rathenau had already fulminated against this "Asiatic horde."[22] With their earlocks, unkempt beards, and seedy caftans, they conjured up the old ghetto. Many tried to make a living as peddlers, confirming Treitschke's notorious stereotype of "pant-selling Jew boys." The myth of Eastern Jews as primitive and unmannered spread for so many years by travelers and popular writers was taken for granted. Welfare workers at the border were actually surprised to find that many did not wear earlocks or caftans but were "handsome, clean, and intelligent."[23]

The almost Pavlovian reaction of the *Allgemeine Zeitung des Judentums* to the first pogroms in April 1881 was to call on the Jews of Russia to redouble their loyalty to the czarist regime. In a condescending editorial, "What Our Russian Brothers Must Do," the paper warned that they should under no circumstances join illegal opposition parties.[24] As evidence grew of the Russian government's complicity in the pogroms and as thousands of Jews streamed to safety across the German frontier, the paper's position became untenable.

The Prussian state was particularly affected by the influx. An initial attempt to seal the border completely to Russian Jews was foiled by the intervention of James Simon on behalf of the Hilfsverein—the main German Jewish charity tending to persecuted or impoverished Jewish communities abroad—and the North German shipping companies that had a financial interest in ferrying the refugees on to North and South America. French Jewish charities joined the Hilfsverein in this effort. The compassion wealthy German and French Jews felt for their Russian coreligionists was not feigned. They gave generously but at the same time acted to prevent the refugees from settling in Germany or France. In 1882 alone, Jewish charities spent nearly a million marks either to help move the emigrants through Germany in sealed trains or to finance their repatriation to Russia. Welfare workers met the refugees at the main border crossings to protect them from scoundrels and smugglers trying to rob them; the Hilfsverein negotiated special rates for their passage with the main railway companies and shipping lines.

More than a million Jews—some put the figure as high as two million—are said to have crossed Germany between 1882 and 1914 on their way to the United States, Latin America, and England. They came in several waves, first from Russia and Austrian-controlled Galicia, then, after a series of massacres by the Romanian police, from Transylvania and Bukovina as well and, after the aborted revolution of 1905, from Russia again. The Romanians were often called *Fusgeyer*, foot wanderers, because they walked hundreds of miles to reach the German frontier, where they were received by Simon's Hilfsverein people and put on trains to the ports of Hamburg or Bremen. The massive population transfer was handled with military efficiency; the telling slogan of the Hilfsverein was "German thoroughness and Jewish heart." Unfortunately, there was considerably more of the former than of the latter. Steven Aschheim, a historian of the encounter between Western and Eastern Jews on German soil, reports that the rough treatment of the refugees only exacerbated their ragged condition and confirmed the prevailing stereotype. The refugees were confined to trains for days on end and allowed out only to pass through delousing stations. In Hamburg and Bremen, they awaited embarkation in locked quarantine. An eyewitness wrote:

> We emigrants were herded at the stations, packed in the cars, and driven from place to place like cattle. . . . White-clad Germans shouted commands, always accompanied with "Quick! Quick!"—the confused passengers obeyed all orders like meek children, only questioning now and then what was going to be done with them.[25]

The great cholera epidemic of 1892 threatened to stop the flow of refugees to the West. The shipping companies, which stood to lose millions, intervened yet again to countermand a planned closure of the border for health reasons. Special cleansing procedures and disinfecting stations were installed on the border itself.

IN addition to its expanding economy and powerful army, Germany now also boasted an unrivaled educational system, excellent scientific and research facilities, and a rich cultural life. The combination of material strength with cultural wealth was unparalleled on the Continent.[26] It was apparent in every realm, in the sciences and in the arts.* By 1913, more books were published in Germany annually—31,051 new titles— than in any other country in the world. In scientific research, German

---

*In 1979, the French and American historians Raymond Aron and Fritz Stern were in Berlin to commemorate the centenary of the birth of Albert Einstein. Aron had been a student in Berlin before the rise of Nazism, and Stern, German-born, had been chased out by the Nazis. Both had seen German promise turn to nemesis. Walking past some World War II ruins in the once-proud imperial capital (now divided by the Berlin Wall), Aron stopped at the sight of a bombed-out square and some decrepit mansions. Musing on what "might have been," he turned to his companion: "It could have been Germany's century!" he said. Stern never forgot the moment. In the history of modern Europe, Stern wrote, one great country has often dominated the culture of its age—first Spain, then France, Holland, and Great Britain. During the first decade of the twentieth century, there was good reason to believe that it was now Germany's turn.

universities surpassed those of other European countries. The contribution of the Jews to this preeminence was enormous; in some fields, it was overwhelming. The reasons for such an outburst of creativity in so many different fields has long been a matter for speculation. They may have been social or psychological rather than religious since there was little if any religiously Jewish content in the works of Einstein, Freud, Mahler, Zweig, Werfel, Husserl, Hofmannsthal, Ehrlich, Willstätter, Mauthner, or even Kafka. Nor could the reasons have been "ethnic"— what is "Flemish" in Flemish art, what is "German" or "Jewish" in mathematics, physics, chemistry, music, or medicine? What, then, was behind this prodigious output? Was it self-conscious marginality? The stimulus of suffering and blows? The interplay between challenge and response? Tribal pressure? If "ease is inimical to civilization," as Arnold Toynbee has claimed, adversity was not without its rewards. Within a relatively short time, families once on the margins of established society, outside the general culture and language, produced a surprisingly high number of outstanding men and women in the arts and sciences. Some were the offspring of families comfortably well-to-do for generations; others were the sons and daughters of hardworking shopkeepers and peddlers—Treitschke's pant-selling Jew boys—who had done well in business during the preceding decades. They had grown rich, producing talented scientists and literati to a degree far exceeding their numbers. In a familiar second- or third-generation phenomenon, the descendants of successful businessmen turned their backs on business and gravitated toward the arts and natural sciences, seeking full integration in the general culture and in many cases achieving it. Commenting on the proverbial industry of Jewish students, Einstein said that it was almost as though they had spent the last two thousand years preparing for university entrance exams. "Doctor" was said to be a Jewish first name. Some claimed that their parents had prodded them mercilessly to achieve better and better grades in school. "Good" was never good enough. They had to be excellent. By itself, this proved nothing, of course. Stern fathers pushing their children were a common feature of middle-class European life during the Wilhelminian and Victorian era.

A number of successful individuals came from the same family clusters. Walter Benjamin, Karl Marx, and Heinrich Heine were distant cousins. The intellectual genealogy of one remarkable North German Jewish family descended from a matriarch named Jente Hameln (1603–95). Nothing is known about Jente Hameln herself except that two centuries later her descendants included Felix Mendelssohn-Bartholdy, Heine, the jurist Eduard Gans, two Nobel Prize winners—the writer Paul Heyse and the chemist Adolf von Baeyer—the historian Johann Gustav Droysen, as well as the writers Johann Hermann Detmold, Theodor Lessing, Carl Sternheim, and Karl Wolfskehl.

The cumulative effect, however, transcended the contributions of any one family. It was as though a dam had given way to release a flood of talent. More Jews than ever entered journalism. Others became publishers, playwrights, novelists, poets, drama critics, gallery owners, theater directors, actors and actresses, concert pianists, conductors, sculptors, and painters. By the early 1900s, some people came to believe that certain fields were actually "dominated" by Jews, so great was their presence.* In 1912, Moritz Goldstein, a young Jewish journalist, delighted anti-Semites by publishing an article in the conservative magazine *Der Kunstwart* claiming that Jews now largely controlled German culture. As he saw it, "We are administrating the spiritual property of a nation that denies our right and our ability to do so."[27] A heated debate ensued in the pages of *Der Kunstwart* and elsewhere. Goldstein wanted Jews to stop pretending they were Germans. Germans, after all, only paid attention to "the Asiatic in us." The terms *control* and *administrate* were, of course, gross exaggerations. It was possible to contribute to a culture—even in a major way—without controlling or administrating it. While Jews played an important part in the arts and the press, nearly all the country's leading literary and artistic figures were non-Jews: Thomas Mann, Gerhart Hauptmann, Stefan George, Rainer Maria Rilke, and Hermann Hesse in literature; Richard Strauss and Wagner

---

*The vast majority of German Jews were, of course, perfectly ordinary businessmen, shopkeepers, professionals—hardworking, but no more so than others. Peter Gay, in *Freud, Jews, and Other Germans*, eloquently pleads for a historical and sociological study of the "stupid Jew": "The material would be in abundance. The results would correct the widespread and untenable notion that Jews are by endowment more intelligent than other people."

in music; Erich Heckel, Ludwig Kirchner, Karl Schmidt-Rottluff, and Franz Marc in painting. On the other hand, Thomas Mann chose this moment to deny recurrent rumors that he was himself a Jew; his timing could not have been a mere accident. To prove his case, this scion of a North German patrician family (married to a woman of Jewish origin) asked: "What of *Buddenbrooks*, the book that made my name? What would it be if it had been written by a Jew? A snob's book!"[28]

One area in which Jews were especially prominent, though they were far from controlling it, was the sciences. The decades before the First World War saw tremendous progress in medicine, chemistry, electrochemistry, biology, mathematics, and physics, culminating in Einstein's general theory of relativity. A succession of remarkable breakthroughs was facilitated partly by the German government and partly by privately endowed research institutes. In the natural sciences there was talk of a new German "age of genius," second only to the era of Goethe, Schiller, Hegel, and Kant. A surprisingly large number of Jewish scientists—steeped also in humanistic culture to an extent that has since become quite rare—played a major role in this flowering. Students from all over the world flocked to their seminars and institutes. The historian Shulamit Volkov has identified thirty-nine leading German Jewish scientists born before 1880, ten of whom won Nobel Prizes.[29] Best-known among the ten are Albert Einstein and Paul Ehrlich. Both came from well-to-do merchant families. Both suffered setbacks because of their origins. Einstein, the "new Newton," radically changed our view of the universe; Ehrlich discovered chemotherapy, thus helping to save countless lives. Ehrlich's institute in Berlin rivaled Pasteur's in Paris and the Rockefeller Institute in New York. But for Ehrlich's early death, he would probably have won a second Nobel Prize for his contributions to immunology and for developing the first effective treatment for syphilis. The German pacifist Friedrich Foerster called Ehrlich the ideal German—"as God wanted Germans to be."[30]

Other Nobel laureates included Fritz Haber, the son of a prosperous die merchant and alderman of the city of Breslau, who was honored for producing ammonia synthetically, a discovery immensely important in the production of artificial fertilizers. Einstein and Haber were close friends, though they were radically different in character and in their politics. Einstein was a cosmopolitan bohemian, Haber a stiff and disciplined German patriot. Einstein was a conscious Jew; Haber converted to Christianity. Even so, they formed a tight partnership, sustaining each other as scientists and as Jews. At home and abroad, they were celebrated as Germans, though Einstein always maintained that if their theories proved right Germans would hail them as heroes and Frenchmen would say they were Jews but that if their theories were disproved Germans would damn them as Jews and Frenchmen as filthy Germans.

Both worked at the new Kaiser Wilhelm Institute in Berlin, the major center of advanced research known as "the emperor's academic guard regiment" and particularly noteworthy for the significant role of Jews both academically and philanthropically. The institute's four main units were headed by Jews. Jewish philanthropists contributed more than a third of the donations to establish the institute and keep it running. The arms manufacturer Gustav Krupp was the largest donor (1.4 million Reichsmark), followed by the retired Jewish banker Leopold Koppel (1 million) and the *Kaiserjuden* James Simon and Eduard Arnhold.

Thorstein Veblen and Sigmund Freud maintained that the success of Jewish scientists resulted from their "creative skepticism," an outgrowth of their difficulties in gaining acceptance. Einstein evaded these difficulties by working for years in Switzerland, where he was granted citizenship; Haber had to convert. Volkov claims that, at least initially, many Jewish scientists who had been denied professorships and were forced to the margins of academic life were driven by these circumstances to pioneer and develop entirely new disciplines. They achieved breakthroughs that might not have been possible had they been tenured, overworked professors. The glory of German intellectual life, the unpaid *Privatgelehrte,* or independent scholar, had to rely on an independent income; unable to get professorships, educated Jews often worked as independent scholars. Inherited income not only facilitated the adoption of liberal ideals but also enabled gifted young scientists to dedicate their lives to research and aspiring writers to be content with low or uncertain royalties. Scientific research was still possible without great financial outlay; this was true of serious work in the humanities as

Aby Warburg, the great art historian. He sold his younger brother, Max, his birthright as the eldest son of the prominent Hamburg banking family Warburg, in return for a solemn pledge that the bank would buy him all the books he might want throughout his life. *Courtesy Leo Baeck Institute, Jerusalem*

well. Aby Warburg was the eldest son of Moritz Warburg, owner of the Hamburg banking firm with branches in New York and London, patriarch of an illustrious family. In line to succeed his father as head of the venerable old bank, Aby was more interested in learned books than in financial ledgers; early on he decided to become a scholar. According to family legend, he offered his birthright to his brother Max, who became the well-known *Kaiserjude*—not for a mess of pottage but for a promise to keep him supplied with all the books he might ever want. Max agreed. "It was the most lighthearted agreement of my life," Max wrote in his memoirs. Not surprisingly, he "never regretted it."[31]*

Aby Warburg was a nervous, ailing young genius, an aesthete ever on the verge of mental breakdown. He professed that he was a Hamburger by birth but a Florentine at heart. Yet his German patriotism was deep and sincere. During the First World War he obsessively collected press clippings and other material to disprove British allegations of German atrocities in Belgium. After the war he divided his time between Florence and Hamburg. Living the rarefied life of a solitary scholar, he became a noted art historian, developing a radically new interpretation of

*The story, with its allusions to Jacob and Esau, suggests that the two boys were more familiar with the Old Testament than assimilated young German Jews were generally thought to have been.

the Renaissance. To document and illustrate his vision of art and civilization, he assembled a formidable scholarly library, which after his death became a public institution and was eventually moved to London. There was something almost Talmudic in Aby Warburg's relentless attempt at exegesis, in his bookishness, and in his unique library. If it makes any sense to call Jews the people of the book, Peter Gay has written, "the Warburg library is, almost by definition the most Jewish of creations, a maze of volumes in which one title led to another and the whole to a comprehensive vision of man defining himself in words, pictures, beliefs."[32]

THEODOR Herzl, the founder of modern Zionism, was deeply marked by the Jewish love affair with Germany. His hero when he was a young man had been Bismarck and his fondest dream to be a Prussian nobleman. As a prominent journalist in Vienna, however, he had come to believe that the resolution of the "Jewish question" lay in founding a Jewish state. He also believed that Germany, in its wisdom and generosity, would facilitate this. In October 1898, Herzl was shuttered in his room in the Hotel Einsiedler in Potsdam, directly facing the kaiser's palace, impatiently awaiting a summons to confer with the German foreign minister, Bernhard von Bülow. The summons to the palace was delayed. Herzl put on his best patent leather boots, so as not to lose time dressing when it finally arrived.

He was deep into an elaborate project in international diplomacy and intrigue. Over the previous few months, the project had matured in close consultation with the kaiser's uncle Frederick, the grand duke of Baden; the duke's English confessor, the Reverend William Hechler; and Prince Philipp von Eulenburg, the German ambassador in Vienna. The moment had come, or so Herzl hoped. Two years of assiduous diplomatic preparatory work was about to bear fruit: Eulenburg had just assured him that the kaiser was ready to establish a Jewish national home in Palestine as a German protectorate. William II was about to leave on a pilgrimage to the Holy Land; he would officially endorse the plan and, possibly, proclaim it publicly in Jerusalem.

The kaiser was, in fact, "fire and flame" for Herzl's project, according to von Bülow's memoirs.[33] There had been little need to coax him.

The kaiser's motives seemed a mixture of bigotry and self-interest: he was not averse to an early exodus of certain German Jews (troublesome socialists and arrogant intellectuals) whom he considered a menace, and he also wanted the Jewish world, whose power he overrated, to revere and appreciate him.

Prince Eulenburg had raised the issue with William in a casual way only a few days earlier during a brief stay at the kaiser's hunting lodge at Rominten in East Prussia. Between rounds of stag and pheasant hunting, Eulenburg and the kaiser discussed the Jews and the political and ideological ramifications of Herzl's idea. Eulenburg had pushed his case with persistence and charm. From Rominten, on September 29, 1898, the kaiser wrote to his uncle Frederick why he was inclined to endorse Herzl's project:

> My dear uncle,
> My stags have taken a moment's intermission from their amorous concerts and allowed me to devote a few lines to you. It would be a tremendous achievement for Germany if the world of the Hebrews looked up to me in gratitude. . . . Moreover, Zionism could harness the creative energies of the tribe of Sem to better purpose than bloodsucking; all the Semites currently pursuing socialism in the East could engage in useful occupations.
>
> Now, I realize that nine-tenths of all Germans will shrink from me in horror when they discover that I sympathize with the Zionists or that I would place them under my protection. But I would merely like to note that the good Lord knows better than we do that it was the Jews who killed the Savior, and He has punished them accordingly. But neither the anti-Semites nor all the Germans nor I myself am authorized by God to mistreat them as we will *ad majorem Dei gloriam!* I believe I may also state here: He that is without sin among you, let him first cast a stone.[34]

That same day, Eulenburg wrote Herzl that the kaiser was already "living the idea of the protectorate." Difficulties were expected with England or France but the kaiser was ready to ignore these: "The world . . . will just have to put up with it."[35] That Palestine was part of the Ottoman Empire seemed not to be an obstacle. The grand duke informed Herzl that the Turks had been sounded out and wished to please their German allies. The sultan depended on the kaiser's goodwill and would refuse him nothing. The kaiser, for his part, would receive Herzl in Constantinople and in Jerusalem.

"Wunderbar, wunderbar," Herzl rejoiced in his diary. "I see he's a Prussian through and through—that's the grand old forceful style. Straight out of the backwoods. That's how they've always gotten things done." Sitting in his hotel room, Herzl felt closer to achieving his aim than at any time since the publication of his

Theodor Herzl: "Through Zionism it will again be possible for Jews to love this Germany to which our hearts remained attached despite everything."
Courtesy Leo Baeck Institute, Jerusalem

seminal pamphlet *The Jewish State* in 1896. For two years he had courted Eulenburg, Bülow, and the grand duke. Frederick had simply been overwhelmed by Herzl's persuasive force.

Through the window of his hotel room Herzl watched the changing of the imperial guard and the stream of vigorous young cadets in the square below. He rejoiced at the colorful scene. Here they were, the future officers of this "inexhaustible Germany, which wishes to place us under its wings":

> Life under the protectorate of this powerful, great, moral, splendidly administered, firmly governed Germany can only have the most salutary effects on the Jewish national character. . . . Strange ways of destiny! Through Zionism it will again be possible for Jews to love this Germany to which our hearts remained attached despite everything.[36]

At the palace—Germany's Versailles—a few hours later, Herzl realized that he was further from his aim than he had thought. He was led into a small rococo salon, where Bülow waited for him at a small table. Bülow was not alone. A frail-looking old man was at his side; a dueling scar marred the left side of his chin. It was the imperial chancellor, Chlodwig von Hohenlohe, wearing a yellow sash across his blue court dress. The medals on their chests clanked as the two Germans rose. Hohenlohe's greeting came as a shock: "Do you really think that the Jews will abandon their stock exchange and follow you to Palestine?" It was the first nasty remark Herzl had heard in these exalted circles. Eulenburg and the kaiser's uncle had always professed respect for Jews.

"Your Highness," Herzl replied, "I don't know whether the Jews of Berlin West will come, but those who live in Berlin East and Berlin North—wherever it is that the poor Jews live—they will go with us."

Bülow said: "In any event, it would be the first eastbound Jewish migration. So far they have always moved west."

"Not at all," Herzl said lightly. "They have gone west . . . and have circled the globe."

The Germans smiled, but not for long. They grilled Herzl with tough questions. How many potential emigrants were there? How much territory, exactly, did the Zionists require? As far north as Beirut, or even beyond? Herzl said they would purchase all the land they needed from their present owners.

"Who are they?"

"Oh, the whole 'mixed multitude'* of the Orient," Herzl replied, "Arabs, Greeks."

"And *that's* where you want to establish a state?" Hohenlohe remarked caustically. What would Turkey say to this? More important, how much money did the Zionists have? Herzl mentioned various Jewish foundations, Rothschild's and that of Baron Hirsch, a Bavarian Jewish millionaire who had financed the settlement of Russian Jews in Argentina. The latter's foundation alone was worth ten million pounds sterling.

"That's a lot," Bülow exclaimed. He turned to Hohenlohe. "The

---

*English in the original.

money might do the trick!"[37] Hohenlohe said nothing. He and Bülow were suddenly pressed to leave for lunch. They agreed to meet with Herzl again in Constantinople en route to Jerusalem, where, at the head of a Zionist delegation, he would be received by the kaiser.

Herzl left the palace in an agitated state. Could Eulenburg have misled him? He had Eulenburg's assurances in writing. Only twenty-four hours earlier, the grand duke had also assured him of the kaiser's enthusiasm. Perhaps the grand duke was mistaken. A week later, in Constantinople, Herzl had a long private audience with the kaiser. Once again he was euphoric. The kaiser clearly stated in Bülow's presence that he favored Herzl's scheme of a Jewish national home in Palestine under German protection. The Ottoman sultan was in no position to say no. A Jewish national home would give Germany another political foothold in the Near East and at the same time, as the kaiser put it, rid Germany of usurers and other undesirables. Herzl, annoyed at William's identification of an entire people with a handful of dishonest men, promptly treated him to a short lesson on anti-Semitism. Jews were no better and no worse than others, but anti-Semitism stabbed the best of them in the heart. "We have been deeply hurt," he said. Bülow sourly repeated Hohenlohe's remark that rich Jews would never follow Herzl to the Holy Land; he would get only the paupers. But the kaiser said that rich Jews might also be willing to go to Palestine if they knew they were under his protection; they would not really be, so to speak, leaving Germany. "Let us hope they'll be grateful for that!" Bülow injected. The kaiser intimated that he might announce his support for the scheme at their forthcoming public meeting in Jerusalem.

In the end, nothing came of the scheme. Hohenlohe, Bülow, and the sultan all vetoed it. Herzl, who had been dazzled by the kaiser's graciousness, realized to his dismay that charm was part of a monarch's stock in trade, not necessarily an indication of character. The kaiser soon had other things on his mind. One enthusiasm quickly gave way to the next. Many factors had gone into the making of this denouement. Not the least had been Herzl's infatuation with Prussian "character" and the personality of the kaiser.

Herzl welcoming the kaiser outside Jerusalem. Nothing came of his plan to establish a Jewish state under a German protectorate. *Courtesy Leo Baeck Institute, Jerusalem*

HERZL'S solution to the Jewish problem, as he had outlined it in 1896 in *The Jewish State*, was in part inspired by the triumph of German unification in 1870. He believed he could galvanize the Jews as Bismarck had galvanized and united the Germans. A flag might be nothing more than a rag fixed to a wooden pole but "with a flag you lead men," Herzl wrote. "For a flag they live and die. In fact, it is the only thing for which they are ready to die in masses, if you train them for it." As in the creation of the German empire, "dreams, songs, fantasies" would go into the making of Herzl's scheme. "All Bismarck did was shake the tree planted by the dreamers."[38]

Herzl had grown up as a German in Budapest. He attended the Protestant *Gymnasium*, a high temple of German language and culture in the heart of a great Hungarian city. Luther was one of his youthful heroes. He wrote:

> By Martin Luther's power and might,
> The German spirit came to light,
> Awakened from the long dark night.
>
> They bask in newfound freedom
> And harken to this appeal:
> For us there's no Canossa, for we shall never kneel.[39]

Until his conversion to Zionism in 1895, Herzl had been not only a leading Viennese journalist but a moderately successful playwright. He stood outside the religious tradition and chose not to circumcise his son. The Viennese Burgtheater, where his plays were produced, meant far more to him than the faith of his ancestors. The chief rabbi of Vienna, visiting Herzl at home, was astonished to find him lighting Christmas tree candles for his children. Herzl first conceived the idea of a national state for Jews in Paris after witnessing the public degradation of Alfred Dreyfus and hearing the mob outside the iron gates of the Ecole Militaire shouting, "Death to the Jews." Herzl went away as in a trance and immediately set to work feverishly on the first draft of *The Jewish State: An Attempt at a Modern Solution of the Jewish Question.* His approach was practical and purely political:

> We are a people—one people. We have honestly endeavored every-
> where to merge ourselves in the social life of surrounding communities
> and to preserve the faith of our fathers. We are not permitted to do so.
> The majority may decide which are the strangers; for this, as indeed
> every point which arises in the relations between nations, is a question
> of might.[40]

During the writing of the pamphlet, the sole diversion Herzl permitted himself was to attend Wagner operas. Wagner's music, especially *Tannhäuser*, roused his spirit when it flagged. He noted that only on evenings when Wagner was not played at the Paris Opera did he have any doubts about the feasibility of his project.[41]

Herzl envisaged a modern Exodus organized on a "scientific" basis. He would go to the kaiser and say, "Let us depart! We are strangers here. We are not allowed to merge with the Germans, nor are we able to. Let my people go!"[42] The kaiser would understand him; he was trained to understand great things. The Jews would depart, taking the German language with them; it would flourish in the new land, wherever that would be. Herzl was neither sentimental nor nostalgic when it came to the choice of a suitable territory: the homeland could be Argentina or elsewhere, preferably far from the imperial rivalries of the European powers. The place would be chosen by a committee of rational, scientific geographers and economists; the mass of Jews, how-ever, would settle for whatever place they were offered. The new national home would not be "Jewish" but a multicultural, multilingual state like Switzerland, even though most citizens would probably continue to speak German. The *Berliner Tageblatt* and the Viennese *Neue Freie Presse* would print local editions in the new country.

As he worked on his draft, Herzl wrote a long letter to Bismarck ("he is great enough either to understand me or to cure me"). He told Bismarck that he had found the solution to the Jewish problem, not just any solution but "the" solution, the only one. He would like to offer his ideas to the German government. The emancipation failed, he told Bismarck, because it came before the Jews had assimilated. It should have come after the assimilation. "In any case, it is now too late for that."[43] He suggested that if Bismarck wished he could make inquiries in Vienna to verify that his correspondent was not a madman, and he asked to be granted an audience.

Bismarck never answered Herzl's letter. Herzl was not surprised. Napoleon had not understood the steamboat either, and he was younger than Bismarck, more accessible to new ideas. The reaction of most German and Austrian Jews to Herzl's plan was hardly more forthcoming. A Lovers of Zion movement of a few small, loosely organized proto-Zionist groups had existed, mostly in Russia and Romania, since the pogroms of 1882. In the West it counted no more than a dozen or so sympathizers in Cologne and a few romantically inclined Viennese Jews of Eastern European origin whose purpose was to help settle Russian and Romanian Jews as farmers in Palestine on a nonpolitical basis. The project was financially supported by Baron Edmund de Rothschild, who hoped to send destitute Jews to estates he was buying in Palestine. Rothschild's devotion to this cause was surpassed only by his munificence toward the Louvre. Nevertheless, in the fifteen years since its inception the project had attracted few candidates and was an economic failure.

There had been other antecedents as well. Five years before Herzl's pamphlet, the Cologne lawyer Max Bodenheimer had published *Whither the Russian Jews?* in which he proposed Syria as a place of refuge.[44] Bodenheimer's proposal was also largely ignored in Germany. Equally overlooked was a more radical publication, Leo Pinsker's *Auto-Emancipation: An Appeal to His People by a Russian Jew,* published in Berlin in 1882.

According to Pinsker, Jews were by nature "inassimilable": "For the living, the Jew is a dead man, for the natives an alien and a vagrant, for property holders a beggar, for the poor an exploiter and a millionaire, for patriots a man without a country—for all classes a hated rival."[45] Almost the entire first printing of Pinsker's tract was found unsold in the basement of a Berlin printer; it had no more than a dozen or so German readers. Another obscure publication of this kind was *Before the Storm: A Serious Word of Warning to the Jews of Germany,* which came out in Berlin in 1896. The author was a physician named Bernhard Cohn who minced no words advising German Jews to "expect the worst": another St. Bartholomew's Day was in the making, he said, referring to the sixteenth-century massacre of Huguenots in France. German anti-Semitism had "method" and was therefore "more dangerous" even than Russian anti-Semitism: "Between Jews and non-Jews in Germany there exists, in effect, a state of war. It is no longer a legal question. The demand is not for our defeat or submission—this they have already achieved—but for our destruction."[46] Cohn urged the immediate evacuation of all German Jews to America. He, too, was ignored. Not a single reference to his pamphlet can be found in the Jewish or general press of the time.

Herzl was unaware of these publications. His own pamphlet was widely noted and in most cases ridiculed or sharply attacked. He found a handful of sympathetic readers, mainly Russian Jews living in Germany and Austria. In Vienna, where Herzl was a bit of a celebrity, *The Jewish State* was briefly the talk of the literati and the cynics, who insinuated that the author must have lost his mind. Stefan Zweig noted the "general annoyance of the Jewish bourgeoisie" at the publication of "this obtuse text, this piece of nonsense."[47] Herzl's own newspaper, the Jewish-owned *Neue Freie Presse,* icily ignored it. When Herzl asked his friend Arthur Schnitzler whether he would come to strike roots in the new land, Schnitzler replied, "Trees have roots, men have legs. As a poet I have wings." His words were to become the recurrent slogan of Herzl's intellectual opponents for decades.

In Germany, too, the reaction to Herzl's tract veered, by and large, between the vehemently derogatory and the snide. A Munich newspaper attacked it as "an imbecile prospectus for a Jewish Switzerland on the installment plan." The *Berliner Tageblatt* hinted that Herzl was a British agent. Asked what he was ready to do for Herzl's cause, a well-known publisher replied: "If Herzl needs to be taken to a lunatic asylum, I shall happily put my carriage at his disposal." Edmund de Rothschild panicked at the political aspects of Herzl's project; unlike Rothschild, Herzl wanted a "state" established with the consent of the great powers, not a purely humanitarian effort for a few destitute refugees. Rothschild refused to have anything to do with Herzl. At their one brief and disastrous meeting, Rothschild told Herzl, "One should not have eyes bigger than one's stomach." The Orthodox German Rabbinical Union roundly condemned Herzl's project as a violation of religious law. But the sharpest attacks came from Reform rabbis. "As long as they wrote in Hebrew, the Zionists were not dangerous," warned an official statement. "Now that they write in German, they must be resisted."[48] Abraham Geiger, one of the founders of Reform Judaism, declared: "Jerusalem is a noble memory from the past and the cradle of our religion; but it holds no hope for the future. No new life can begin there. Let us not disturb its rest."[49] His son, Ludwig Geiger (the leading Goethe scholar in Germany), even objected to helping Russian Jews settle in Palestine. He felt no greater sympathy for them, he said, than for famished German day laborers.

Opposition to Herzl's Zionism seemed more vehement in Germany than elsewhere in Europe. It was certainly more shrill. His program seemed to threaten German Jews to their very core, and German Zionists remained few and isolated for many years. Herzl tried in vain to interest Walther Rathenau in his cause. "The Jews are no longer a nation and will never become one," Rathenau responded. German Jews were now a German tribe like Saxonians and Bavarians. "Zionist aspirations are atavistic."[50] In a letter to Maximilian Harden, he ridiculed Herzl's approach. "He has offered me a job as a guardian of Zion . . . on condition that on every Sabbath I curse the Savior in the *Neue Freie Presse*." For his part, Herzl derided Rathenau, the author of "Hear, O Israel," for advising Jews to develop longer limbs and straighter noses.[51]

Upon being told that Zionism would produce a "happy new breed of Jews," the philosopher Hermann Cohen, with the scorn of an old stoic, exclaimed: "Aha! So they want to be happy now, do they?" In Cohen's opinion, the Jews' task was "to go on living among the nations as the God-sent dew, to remain with them and be fruitful for them."[52] The *Allgemeine Zeitung des Judentums* reproached the Zionists for assuming that the Arabs of Palestine would welcome an influx of Jews—one of the earliest warnings against the widespread assumption that Palestine had, in effect, no politically conscious native population; as a land without people it was thought to be ideally suited for a people without a land. The opposition only grew more bitter over the years. Max Arendt, in the early 1900s chairman of the Königsberg city parliament (Hannah Arendt's grandfather), passed a motion denying members of the Zionist sports club Maccabi the right to use city facilities.

Of the 207 delegates who attended the first Zionist Congress in 1897, only sixteen came from Germany, and most of these were Russian or Polish Jews. Protests against holding the congress in Munich were so vehement Herzl was forced at the last moment to move it to Basel in Switzerland. Although the second Zionist Congress a year later opened to the sounds of the overture to Wagner's *Tannhäuser*, the movement had hardly made any progress in Germany. Local Zionist organizations were known as "ten-men clubs." In 1899, only some four hundred of the half million German Jews had registered as Zionists. The number rose to six thousand in 1904—1.2 percent of all German Jews. Most were said to be *Ostjuden*, recently arrived from Eastern Europe. In Hanover, where many Polish and Russian Jews had settled, the terms *Ostjude* and *Zionist* were considered interchangeable; both were "socially unacceptable."[53] With few exceptions, even those who were registered Zionists were "third-party Zionists," that is, one Jew soliciting funds from a second so that a third might be able to settle in Palestine. German Zionists continued to be ardent German patriots. Their love of the fatherland was only "enhanced," they proclaimed, by their love of the ancient Palestinian homeland: what they had lost there they had found again in Germany.[54] The noted economist Franz Oppenheimer joined the Zionists despite the fact that his emotional and intellectual makeup, as he put it, was "99% Kant and Goethe and 1% Old Testament via Spinoza and Luther's translation of the Bible."[55] In sum, few were touched personally by the cause, and even when they were, it was primarily as an activity "German Jews would lead and direct but in which the Jews of Eastern Europe must be the actors."[56]

The advent of a younger, more radical generation after 1909 changed the passive, halfhearted nature of German Zionism. There were still only ten thousand dues-paying Zionists. They were committed to wage war against assimilation—so committed, in fact, that during the 1912 elections to the Reichstag they urged all Jews to vote for anti-Semitic rather than baptized Jewish candidates.[57] Influenced by Buber and his cult of authenticity, the new radicals sought a "fully" Jewish way of being. They applauded Werner Sombart, a sociologist who in a recent book had called on Jews to have enough "tact" to not demand full equality and to refrain from occupying influential social and cultural positions.

The chief spokesmen of the new radicalism were Richard Lichtheim and Kurt Blumenfeld, who hailed from wealthy, well-integrated families. Assimilation had been in vain, they declared; emancipation had essentially failed. Every form of "cultural and political integration" had been tried and found wanting. In the absence of any material concerns, these men's sense of discrimination had been distilled and sharpened into an issue of "personal dignity, truth, and freedom."[58] Blumenfeld's father was a district judge in East Prussia. Even as a schoolboy the younger Blumenfeld had resisted assimilationist behavior. A teacher once asked him to name his hero in the Second Punic War. Unaware that his teacher was a right-wing nationalist, Blumenfeld replied: "Hannibal!" Why not Scipio, who vanquished the perfidious Carthaginians? demanded the teacher. Blumenfeld remained firm. "Homer also sympathized with Hector," he said. The teacher replied snidely, "So you always sympathize with the loser?" "Hannibal was a Jew!" Blumenfeld insisted. "You mean Semite!" the teacher corrected him. "Isn't that the same?" asked Blumenfeld. His father praised him for his correct reaction to "this pan-German" nationalist.

For Blumenfeld, Zionism was almost exclusively a question of "character." He was one of the few who even before the First World War saw past the splendid facades of the Wilhelminian empire. He sensed the coming of a great disaster, able to smell, as he put it, "rottenness" and "putrefaction" where others, "strangely enough, only experienced well-being."[59] The man who as a boy had sympathized with the loser claimed to have been converted to Zionism "by the grace of Goethe." He often quoted Goethe's hymn to authenticity:

> *Nations, rulers, slaves subjected,*
> *All on this one point agree:*
> *Joy of earthlings is perfected*
> *In the personality.*
>
> *Every life is worth the choosing*
> *If oneself one does not miss;*
> *Everything is worth the losing*
> *To continue as one is.*[60]

Goethe was to remain Blumenfeld's idol until his death in Israel in 1963.

Blumenfeld preached what he termed "postassimilationist" Zionism, rejecting the older philanthropic version and earlier assumptions of German-Jewish coexistence. Recognizing his generation's complete lack of "Jewish" substance, Blumenfeld saw Zionism as a catalyst for personal transformation and a quest to reacquire a primary Jewish self. It had more to do with German idealism than with Jewish tradition. According to his close friend Hannah Arendt, he even claimed that Zionism was "Germany's gift to its Jews."[61] The bankruptcy of emancipation, Blumenfeld said, was the "dirty little secret" suppressed by the German Jewish bourgeoisie, much

The Zionist leader Kurt Blumenfeld warned Zionists not to succumb to inauthentic religiosity. Rather, they should read Nietzsche. *Courtesy Leo Baeck Institute, Jerusalem*

like sweat and sex in Victorian England. Had the Jewish bourgeoisie not been so complacent, so insular, it would not have succumbed to the delusion that it was "rooted" in German society. "My parents had fewer non-Jewish acquaintances than my grandparents," he wrote, "and I have fewer still."[62]

On the strength of his harsh judgments, Blumenfeld was elected president of the German Zionist Federation in 1909. He was embraced primarily by young Jews rebelling against their bourgeois parents. On one occasion he tried to convert a well-known newspaper editor to the Zionist project. The man objected, "But you have to admit this cause has absolutely no prospect of success." According to Hannah Arendt, Blumenfeld replied disdainfully, "Who ever said I was interested in success!"[63] That he was nonetheless elected to head the Zionists could happen only in Germany, Arendt thought. Blumenfeld also warned Zionists against succumbing to inauthentic religiosity; better to read Fichte, Nietzsche, or Hölderlin—Nietzsche would turn them into "stronger Jews"—than adopt rituals in which they did not believe. He did not believe in them either.

In the same spirit, the future historian of nationalism Hans Kohn rationalized his adherence to the Zionist cause by reference to Fichte's seminal *Speeches to the German Nation* (1805). Transferring Fichte's teachings to "the context of our own situation," Kohn endorsed his appeal to put "all the power of the rationally and ethically mature individual at the service of his nation." Blumenfeld went further. In 1912, he successfully convinced the annual convention of German Zionists to affirm "the duty of all Zionists," especially those with independent economic means, to "include emigration to Palestine in their life program."[64] Not even the few Zionists in pogrom-ridden Russia had gone that far. For Franz Oppenheimer the resolution was too much: it annulled the ideal of integration upheld since the days of Mendelssohn. Oppenheimer and other Zionists of the older generation withdrew from active participation in the movement.

The discussion of Blumenfeld's resolution coincided with Sombart's book and followed soon after the 1912 general elections. The election results showed that most German voters disapproved of all racist politics. The anti-Semitic splinter parties effectively disappeared. The conservative right, which had campaigned against "Jew lovers," "Jewish money," and "Jewish-owned newspapers," suffered a serious setback. The Social Democrats, who had vigorously opposed anti-Semitic "Junkers and priests, knights and Christian saints," won an astounding 35 percent of the popular vote, doubling their strength and becoming the largest single party in the Reichstag. The number of Jewish deputies rose from eight to nineteen, of whom twelve were Social Democrats. The Social Democratic party was the envy of socialists throughout Europe. It had grown so fast it seemed almost irresistible and was widely expected to come into power soon, finally breaking, as it promised, the fetters of capitalism, militarism, feudalism, and anti-Semitic prejudice.

The brilliant young writer Kurt Tucholsky, eldest son of an affluent upper-middle-class Jewish family, rejoiced at the results. He had just published a highly successful novel, *Rheinsberg: A Picture Book for Lovers*, the story of an attractive young couple. The man, a student, is modeled on Tucholsky himself while his girlfriend is a witty, apparently non-Jewish Berliner. The lovers spend a blissful weekend in a remote country hotel in defiance of social and moral convention. The novel pictures a utopian idyll, celebrating the symbiotic link between two appealing, open-minded people. Many read it as a parable heralding the rise of a better world of political and erotic freedom.

Two years later, the First World War broke out. The liberal euphoria quickly proved to be misplaced. The 1912 elections notwithstanding, the ultrapatriotic voices in the Reichstag, in the military, in the popular press, and in the palace had their say. The Social Democrats agitated against the war, staging mass demonstrations in many cities. Their opposition collapsed at the last moment in the face of what seemed like overwhelming public support for war. The immediate cause of the war was the assassination of the Austrian crown prince in Sarajevo; the underlying cause was the rivalry of the great imperialist powers over the past two decades. In July 1914, it erupted in a continent-wide killing spree that embroiled Germany, France, England, Austria-Hungary, Serbia, Italy, and Russia. While decrying the orgy of "drunken" nationalism, Kurt Tucholsky immediately volunteered for war service. More than ten thousand other young German Jews did the same. One of them, Ludwig Frank, was a prominent Social Democratic Reichstag deputy. Only two days earlier, he, too, had attacked the cheap "coffee-house enthusiasm" of the warmongers.[65] Like all other Social Democrats, by August 4 he had changed his mind and joined the majority in voting for the war budget demanded by the government. That same afternoon he enlisted. "I march in line with all the others, joyful and sure of our victory," he wrote.[66] Three weeks later he was killed in action. What had moved Frank and so many others? Abiding faith in Germany? Political opportunism? A lurking death wish, as was later speculated? Even Freud forgot himself for a moment. For the first time in his life he felt something like pride in being an Austrian national.

The Great War would prove, as George Kennan has written, the seminal catastrophe of the twentieth century. At the time, few if any suspected the extent of its horror. Max Reinhardt, the director who had revolutionized German theater and was recognized as "one of the first Austrian Jews to conquer Berlin," certainly did not.[67] He happened to be in Paris on the eve of the war attending the first premiere of a German work at the Paris Opera in nearly half a century: Richard Strauss and Nijinsky's biblical ballet *The Legend of Joseph*, staged by Diaghilev in Venetian costume.

As Harry Kessler, the librettist, noted, all of Paris was there, intellectuals as well as people in government and the Faubourg Saint-Germain set. "The premiere was the last, most spectacular parade of prewar Europe at its most brilliant, even as the catastrophe was already under way," Kessler later wrote. He had "unconsciously" woven the tragic horror of the moment into his libretto.[68]

Kessler remembered the festive supper party everyone attended at 2:00 A.M. to celebrate the event. Reinhardt, Diaghilev, and Marcel Proust were present, along with Hugo von Hoffmannsthal, Jean Cocteau, Richard Strauss, and the star of the show, Nijinsky of the Ballets Russes. Everyone expected a few days of war. In the early morning hours, Reinhardt and the other Germans and Austrians took the last available trains to reach the border before it closed. By the time he arrived back in Berlin, Reinhardt announced that the war was necessary in defense of German culture.

Albert Einstein was one of the few who did not share this view. He loathed German militarism. He had recently moved back from Switzerland to Berlin to take up an appointment at the Kaiser Wilhelm Institute, only "to discover for the first time that [he] was a Jew."[69] He was aghast at the headlong plunge toward war and the widespread readiness of leading intellectuals to welcome it. At times such as this, he noted, one realized "to what sad species of animal one belongs."[70] The scarcity of people around him who shared his anguish deepened his depression.

Einstein's dismay was further exacerbated by the pain of an agonizing divorce. Only "love of science" lifted him out of his "vale of tears."[71] His two boys were about to join his estranged wife in Switzerland. On July 29, Austria had just declared war on Serbia when Einstein saw them off at the Berlin railway station. Fritz Haber was at his side. Einstein spent the rest of the evening grieving over his loss and, presumably, quarreling with his friend. Haber did not share Einstein's despair over the coming war. On the contrary, he had already registered as a volunteer. Haber believed that in times of peace scientists belonged to the world but in times of war to their country. Like most other Germans, Haber expected a quick and easy victory. Nobody anticipated that the war would be long and awful and inaugurate a half century of mass killing, revolution, and chaos: the collapse of civilization in Germany, the rise of Nazi, Fascist, and Communist totalitarianism, and more than a hundred million dead.

9

War Fever

KAFKA's diary entry for Sunday, August 2, 1914, is suggestive: "Germany has declared war on Russia—swimming in the afternoon." In a diary otherwise so lucid and opinionated, Kafka leaves no record of what he thinks of the war itself. If he was not overly disturbed, neither were millions of educated Germans of all faiths, Frenchmen, Russians, Austrians, and Britons.

Four days later, with the massed armies of Europe already writhing in mud and blood, Kafka witnessed a parade of German patriots on a street in Prague (at the time still under Austrian rule). "These parades are one of the most disgusting accompaniments of the war," he noted. That is all he had to say. Like most people, he must have been convinced that everything would be over in a couple of weeks. Austrian warmongers were insistent on punishing Serbia for the assassination in Sarajevo (by a Bosnian adolescent) of Archduke Franz Ferdinand, heir to the Austro-Hungarian throne. It would have been in Germany's power at that stage to defuse or localize the mounting crisis, but the kaiser supported Austria in the name of "Nibelung loyalty." In reckless disregard of Europe's interlocking alliances, he risked world war by giving the Austrians the equivalent of a blank check. A cabal of conservative politicians and powerful generals in Berlin was bent on breaking the peace for its own reasons—to humiliate France and extend German power in Europe and overseas. A furious arms race—the first in the history of Europe—had been going on for almost a decade; still, the conservative schemers expected a quick victory, as in 1870. Intoxicated by his own rhetoric, the kaiser assured the soldiers that they would be home "before the leaves fall from the trees."

Walther Rathenau was one of the few in the social and intellectual elite of Berlin who foresaw the disastrous consequences of a world war. Theodor Wolff, the Jewish editor of the *Berliner Tageblatt,* was another. Both followed the mounting crisis with growing concern. In more than forty years of peace, the peoples of Western Europe had reached an unprecedented level of comfort and civilization, and support was growing for a European economic union. The so-called Concert of Europe was anything but an empty phrase. It would be sheer madness to give in to the militants and risk all that had been achieved.

With remarkable foresight, Rathenau warned that the war would not be short but would likely go on for years, and at terrible human and material cost. In the prevailing atmosphere of widespread enthusiasm for war, Rathenau failed to convert others to his view. He was a man of astounding contradictions, who had always perplexed people. His moralizing rhetoric had earned him the sobriquet "Christ in a tuxedo." A multimillionaire tycoon who recited poetry while presiding over board meetings, he was fussy, emotionally insecure, and innerly torn, while seeming imperturbable and aloof. An occasional victim of anti-Semitic diatribes, Rathenau worshiped the blond "Nordic man," the prototype "Aryan." He controlled a vast industrial and financial empire, lived in grand luxury—it was said that he spent ten minutes each morning choosing from among his vast collection of ties—and at the same time published quasi-Communist essays.

Eight days before the declaration of war, Rathenau went to see Chancellor Theobald von Bethmann-Hollweg. He warned that Germany was getting trapped in a situation that did not serve its true interests:

"Your partners are bankrupt. Watch out that [the Austrians] do not surprise you!" The chancellor assured him that the German government was in full control of events. Rathenau was not convinced. In conversation with friends, he predicted disaster for Germany and all of Europe—politically, morally, and economically. In a world that still thought of war in preindustrial terms, he was one of the few who surmised the full meaning of *total* war. The prospect terrified him; on one occasion he broke into tears as he spoke of it. In an article published in the *Berliner Tageblatt* the day before Germany's declaration of war, he protested the government's readiness to follow Austria's lead blindly. Austria's excessive demands for reparations from Serbia for the act of one young fanatic were insufficient reason for a world war. A punitive military campaign against Serbia was sure to provoke a response from Russia, backed by France and its British ally. Rathenau feared that Austria, fortified by assurances of unconditional German support, was expecting its humiliating ultimatum to Serbia to be declined and thus lead to a war on three or four fronts; Russia was already mobilizing. Rathenau held to his view unwaveringly. He was desperate, "as though at the bed of a dying man."[1]

The shipping tycoon Albert Ballin felt much the same. He, too, pleaded with Bethmann-Hollweg to go slow. Why was he in such a hurry to drag Russia into a war? Bethmann-Hollweg replied that he needed to bring Russia into the war or lose the support of the Social Democrats. The chancellor knew that an attack on the czarist regime, the most repressive in Europe, was the fig leaf German Social Democrats and other liberals needed to march into battle as good patriots. More than war, which Social Democratic leaders had loudly decried in recent weeks, they feared public opinion and a split in their own ranks. Party chairman Hugo Haase and pacifists like Rosa Luxemburg, Eduard Bernstein, and Karl Liebknecht opposed war until the last minute—the first three were Jews, and Liebknecht was widely said to be one. In the end they were overruled and all but Luxemburg bowed to the majority. Haase was a weak party hack, a "melancholic whose lifelong role was to be outvoted and then to submit to the majority."[2] He even agreed to introduce the party's motion in the Reichstag in support of the war, saying, "We must not abandon the fatherland in its hour of need."

Bethmann-Hollweg foolishly believed that a quick strike on the Continent and a few mollifying gestures in England's direction would keep the British out of the war and allow Germany and Austria to retain their military gains. The kaiser had Napoleonic ambitions to redraw the map of Europe and finally make Germany a world power like England. He aspired to extend German hegemony over the entire continent and acquire new colonies in Asia and Africa, "a place in the sun." His generals plotted the annexation of Belgian and French coal and steel resources along with major seaports on the English Channel. At the same time, his foreign ministry proposed to dismantle Russia and establish a buffer state on Lithuanian, Byelorussian, and Ukrainian soil.

In view of the catastrophe that ensued, its instigators later spoke of the First World War as a natural disaster far beyond their scope and responsibility, much like an earthquake or the eruption of a volcano. "I did not want it," the Austro-Hungarian emperor Franz-Josef fatuously declared just before his death in 1916, a remark that was bitterly parodied. William II had some last-minute jitters. Former chancellor Bülow found him looking pallid, frightened, almost desperate. On July 30, the kaiser lamely asked his generals if the war could not be limited to the Balkans and was told that since war was bound to break out anyway within the next two years it was not in Germany's interest to delay it. Better to wage and win it now, they claimed, before Russia finished building its Baltic fleet and laying strategic railway lines through Poland.

Rosa Luxemburg, a rare voice of dissent: "If they expect us to murder our French brothers, let us tell them they are mistaken." Her letters from prison during World War I were circulated in an early form of samizdat. *By permission of the Landesarchiv, Landesbildstelle, Berlin*

In public, the kaiser showed

none of these misgivings. From the balcony of his palace in Berlin he addressed the crowd in grandiloquent terms, crying, "I raise the sword that has been forced into my hand." The crowd roared, having been told in the past—often by the kaiser himself—that Germany was being encircled by a ring of conspiring enemies. Rowdy mobs waving sticks, hats, and beer bottles gathered outside the chancellery on Wilhelmstrasse, shouting, "War, war," "Long live Austria," and "Serbians must die!" Bethmann-Hollweg, it seems, also had reservations. His secretary, Kurt Rietzler (the painter Max Liebermann's son-in-law), reported seeing him looking distraught. According to Rietzler, the demonstrators below his windows helped Bethmann-Hollweg overcome his concerns, especially when he was told that similar demonstrations were taking place all over Germany.[3] Bethmann-Hollweg and others later excused their appalling lack of judgment by invoking fate, the Almighty, and the bellicose public opinion they themselves had inflamed.

Theodor Wolff early on suspected a guiding hand behind the mobs calling for blood. On his way to the Foreign Ministry a few days before the war, Wolff ran into one such mob outside Bethmann-Hollweg's offices. The demonstrators seemed to have come straight from a beer hall and to have brought the bar girls with them.[4] Wolff voiced his suspicions to the foreign minister, Gottlieb von Jagow. Jagow seemed to agree with him, though perhaps mostly out of disdain for the unwashed masses. In an angry editorial in the *Berliner Tageblatt* the next morning, Wolff condemned "the fusion of foreign policy with street mobs." It only earned him a flood of hate mail.

The pressure of public opinion has frequently been cited as one of the reasons—along with the folly and negligence of statesmen and generals—that the great powers staggered and stumbled into war. And since many people believe that great events must have great impersonal causes, the war has often been blamed on such abstractions as monopoly capitalism, cultural discontent, imperialism, and even the death wish inherent in civilization. More banal factors have also been cited, such as the weather and the decline in old-fashioned marital virtue among the royalty. Had it rained during the last week in July, as it had the previous summer, there might have been no mob scenes to persuade jittery politicians and thus, perhaps, no war. Henry Kissinger has argued that had Archduke Franz Ferdinand not entered into marriage with a mere countess—a misalliance—the czar of Russia and the king of England might have attended the couple's funeral in Vienna; between them, the crowned heads of Europe, consulting in person, might have been able to avert the crisis. Yet another point of view holds that the tensions between the powers were so great they simply had to snap. But tensions had been far greater in the past and had not led to war. All such abstract, anecdotal, and grand theories merely obscure the real reason for war: the recklessness and lack of judgment of a few politicians. Rathenau famously claimed that two hundred elderly men who knew one another controlled the fate of Europe and the world. He should have added the old truism that in war millions of young men butcher millions of other young men who have done them no harm and whom they have never met—all on behalf of a few old men who know one another only too well.

THE patriotic hysteria at the outbreak of World War I has been described often. Germans of all classes and faiths apparently greeted the war with fervent enthusiasm. The protagonist of Thomas Mann's *Doctor Faustus* celebrates the "spirit of 1914" in glowing terms: "We . . . marched off enthusiastically—filled with the certainty that the hour of Germany's era had come, that history was holding its hand over us, that after Spain, France, and England it was now *our turn* to put our stamp upon the world and lead it."[5]

Blinded by slogans and lies, millions went off willingly to the trenches. Pacifists fell silent. As German troops passed through Belgium on the way to France, the Social Democratic deputy Ludwig Frank justified Germany's breach of Belgian neutrality as an act of self-defense. A few weeks later he died in action, firmly convinced that as a Jew and a socialist he was fighting for a just cause. Frank was certain that Germany would emerge from the war as a constitutional monarchy like England; new electoral laws would put an end to the rule of bankers, industrialists, militarists, and Junkers.

Contemporary photographs show excited men and remarkably few women welcoming the declaration of war in the larger German cities. One such picture is of special interest. Visible in the crowd on Munich's Odeonsplatz is the pale, waxy face of Adolf Hitler. At twenty-five, he was still without a steady job, without friends or women in his life. He looks slightly disheveled. His eyes shine wildly. In *Mein Kampf* he remembered the moment. The war had not been forced on the masses, he wrote:

> No, by the living God—it was desired by the whole people. . . . Even today I am not ashamed to say that, overpowered by stormy enthusiasm, I fell down on my knees and thanked Heaven from an overflowing heart for granting me the good fortune of being permitted to live at this time.[6]

The psychosis was contagious. Millions volunteered with pure joy. The war seemed like a magic holiday, an interruption of dreary routine as well as an opportunity to rise above it into heroic spheres. Conscripts and volunteers on their way to the front scribbled on their railway carriages: "More declarations of war accepted here." They were heard to cry in a rhymed chorus: *"Jeder Schuss ein Russ, jeder Stoss ein Franzos,*

Adolf Hitler celebrates the outbreak of war in 1914. *By permission of the Archiv für Kunst und Geschichte, Berlin*

und die Serben müssen sterben!"—every *Schuss* [shot] a Russ, every kick a Frenchman, and the Serbs must perish! Young girls showered them with flowers. Ernst Simon, of a long-assimilated Berlin Jewish family, volunteered for service on the front "intoxicated with joy" at finally being a "real man" able to "float in the great stream . . . with millions of others" in the service of the fatherland.[7]

Myths and delusions flourished in this atmosphere. In the ecstasy of the first few days in the trenches, Ernst Simon later confessed, the rattle of machine guns seemed as beautiful as the music of the spheres. At Ypres, according to an official German communiqué, the young soldiers of two regiments—singing *Deutschland über Alles* as they stormed the French lines—took two thousand prisoners. Hitler claimed in *Mein Kampf* that he had heard the soldiers singing with his own ears.[8] The entire story, it later turned out, had been fabricated by the military propaganda machine.

German writers and artists also welcomed the war. Thomas Mann, in an essay written early in 1915, saw it as an opportunity to transcend oneself, to cleanse one's soul and escape the "materialism" and "intellectual vermin" of a "horrible world of peace."[9] For Mann, the war was a struggle between German *Kultur* and the materialistic *Zivilisation* of England and France. He had long felt the compelling "moral and psychological need" for such a war, Mann wrote his Jewish publisher, Samuel Fischer, on August 26, 1914. There is no record of Fischer's reply. Elsewhere, he suggested that democracy was an "un-German" activity. In 1916, long after the bloody stalemate on the Western Front had begun, with millions of deaths every year, Mann still hailed the war as the harbinger of a mystic "synthesis of might and spirit," a "Third Reich," no less.[10] Many shared such feelings. Rainer Maria Rilke, the greatest living German poet, welcomed the resurrection "at long last" of a "God . . . the God of hosts." The poet Stefan George, a cult figure, especially among Jewish aesthetes, hailed war as a sacred, liberating spring:

> *tens of thousands must fall in sacred madness*
> *tens of thousands vanquished by the sacred pestilence*
> *tens of thousands—in the sacred war.*

Karl Wolfskehl, scion of an ancient Jewish family of doctors and scholars and one of George's most ardent fans, had this poem in mind when he sent an open letter to the French pacifist Romain Rolland. This war was a "sheer necessity," he wrote. "It had to break out for the sake of Germany and the world. . . . We did not want it, yet it is from God!"[11]

One of the very few voices publicly raised against these intellectual excesses was that of the Austrian satirist and media critic Karl Kraus, the son of a Jewish paper merchant in Bohemia. He had no equivalent in Germany, perhaps because censorship was more stringent there than in Austria. Protest was raised by Hermann Hesse as well, but from the safe haven of Switzerland, and his was directed more at the style of the literary warmongers ("Oh friends, not such tones!") than at war itself. Rosa Luxemburg was effectively silenced: in the winter of 1914–15 she began serving a prison sentence for having criticized the oncoming war.

An avalanche of prowar books and pamphlets appeared within months of the outbreak of hostilities. Karl Joel, a philosopher from a well-known family of rabbis, found proof of the war's purity and idealism in the fact that so many German soldiers went off to battle with copies of *Faust, Thus Spake Zarathustra,* and the Bible in their knapsacks. The sociologist Max Weber opined that "regardless of eventual success, this war is great and *wunderbar.*"[12] Pastors, priests, and rabbis preached that the German war was necessary and just. Reading the surviving sermons today, one would think there was nothing finer and more honorable in life than war. God was on the side of Germany, speaking to it "in cannon thunder." Leading pastors called for massive annexations in France, Belgium, and Russia. No clergyman of any faith seems publicly to have dissented. Leo Baeck, the leading German Reform rabbi, conceded that war as such was evil but excepted this particular one as a useful evil: "It allows us to sense how the life of the fatherland is ours and how its conscience resonates in our own."[13]

Jingoism was running "stark mad," Colonel House wrote to President Woodrow Wilson after touring the Continent. Whether it really was as widespread as interested politicians later claimed can no longer be determined with any degree of certainty. The English historian Niall Ferguson in *The Pity of War* (1999) has gone to the other extreme, declaring it a "myth."[14] There were no public opinion polls at the time, no radio and television. Up-to-date news was available only on the street, where special editions of the newspapers went on sale. The widely reported ecstasy may have erupted only in the larger cities, the enthusiasm emanating mainly from the urban bourgeoisie. Photographs of the crowds outside Berlin's imperial palace show mostly well-dressed men waving bowlers and boaters and boys in jackets and ties or well-pressed sailor suits, the uniform that distinguished middle-class children from their working-class peers. Some of the mob scenes outside Bethmann-Hollweg's chancellery, as Wolff suspected, were probably not spontaneous. None of this, however, contradicts the record of overwhelming war fervor among intellectuals.

THE first scene of Karl Kraus's monumental war drama, *The Last Days of Mankind*, takes place on the Ringstrasse, Vienna's elegant promenade. A Jewish couple is walking along.

Newsboy:	Extra! Extra! Heir to the throne assassinated! Killer arrested!
Man* (to his wife):	Thank God he's not a Jew!
His wife (pulls him away):	Let's go home!

When war actually broke out, five weeks after the assassination, middle- and upper-middle-class urban Jews did not "go home." They joined up. By volunteering for war service long before being called up they hoped they would finally overcome the remaining informal impediments to full integration in German society. *Im Deutschen Reich*, the official organ of the Centralverein, the largest and most representative German-Jewish organization, announced that Germany was only defending its *Kultur*; the paper condemned "Russian malice," "French thirst for revenge," "English deviousness," and "Serbian lust for murder." The

---

*In the original manuscript Kraus used the term *Börsenspekulant*, meaning a speculator on the stock exchange, or, in common usage, a Jew. In the published version he amended this.

Centralverein itself solemnly called on its members "to serve the fatherland beyond the call of duty. Hasten to volunteer for service! All you men and women must dedicate yourselves to the fatherland through every kind of service." Eugen Fuchs, the chairman of the Centralverein, proclaimed himself German "down to my bones." He assailed "murderous Russia" and her allies, "insidious England" and "bloodthirsty France," for "maliciously" attacking Germany from the rear. He also allowed himself a bit of racism: in their greedy "struggle against German *Kultur*," the Allies had even enlisted "the help of Japan's yellow highway robbers."[15]

A Jewish cavalry soldier, Ludwig Bornstein, is saluted by two friends as he rides down Unter den Linden on August 12, 1914. All three later immigrated to Israel. *Courtesy Leo Baeck Institute, Jerusalem*

All traces of Jewish "cosmopolitanism" seemed to have vanished overnight. Jewish publications abounded in self-conscious tribal pride; a stream of stories appeared testifying to Jewish heroics and patriotic devotion. The *Allgemeine Zeitung des Judentums* insisted that the youngest German volunteer was a fourteen-year-old Jewish boy from Allenstein in East Prussia. The same paper also celebrated a Jewish soldier named Fischer said to have captured the first French flag of the war. When this turned out to be an error, the paper corrected itself with a poem:

> *First in battle and first to win*
> *Was neither Jew nor Christian.*
> *No liberal, Junker, or democrat:*
> *The flag was caught by a German* Soldat!

The common experience of war was generally expected to cement firm new bonds among Germans of all faiths. The term used for that experience was *Erlebnis,* an emotionally charged word that refers more to a spiritual and even aesthetic phenomenon than to a physical and concrete one; a more accurate translation might be "rite of passage." A young Jewish volunteer, Julius Holz, invoked his *Erlebnis* on December 7, 1914, his twentieth birthday, in a letter to his father from the front. He vowed to "fight like a man, as a good German of true Jewish faith and for the greater honor of my family."*

Jews living in the more remote rural areas were probably more circumspect. The novelist Manes Sperber, who grew up in a small Galician town close to the Russian border, remembered his father telling a roomful of children and relatives, "For us the war is a terrible disaster."

"Why a disaster?" someone asked. "Our kaiser will be victorious and the czar will be defeated and will never oppress his subjects again."

"For us every war is a disaster," Sperber's father answered firmly. "No one in this room can be sure of his survival."[16]

In the main urban centers, liberal, leftist, and perhaps even some pacifist Jews were swayed by the prevailing emphasis on Russia. It was easier to endorse a war directed against the last despotic and openly anti-Semitic regime in Europe. At long last Russia would be punished for the pogroms of Kishinev, Homel, and Siberia, the philosopher Samuel Hugo Bergmann, a Zionist, noted in his diary.[17] He thanked the Lord that as an officer serving in the Austro-Hungarian army on the Russian front he would be able personally to avenge his people. A son of German-speaking Prague Jews, Bergmann saw himself as defending *Kultur* against the barbarians of the East. More than ever, he wrote, he felt part of German culture body and soul. "At least in war we are equal," another volunteer wrote home from the front line in France, shortly before he was killed.[18]

---

*Holz fell in battle in 1918. Twenty-four years later, on the eve of her deportation to an extermination camp, his eighty-one-year-old mother wrote the authorities asking to be spared in view of her son's death in action, as attested by attached documents. She received a one-line reply: "Your application to be released from 'labor service' is refused."

The hope for full integration was boosted considerably by the kaiser in a speech he gave from the throne on August 4 affirming his government's decision to go to war. The entire Reichstag and representatives of leading churches and synagogues were gathered in the White Hall of the imperial palace. The kaiser solemnly assured his audience by proclaiming that differences of religion, political affiliation, class, and ethnic origin no longer counted. He appealed to "all peoples and tribes of the German Reich . . . irrespective of party, kinship, and confession, to hold steadfastly with me through thick and thin, deprivation and death."[19] He added: "I no longer know any parties, I know only Germans," at which point the Reichstag broke into a "storm of bravos." No one, except perhaps Theodor Wolff of the *Berliner Tageblatt*, who witnessed the event, seems to have wondered whether the end of parties was actually a good thing in a democracy; over the next four years the country would, in fact, be governed by the military high command. Liberals commended the kaiser for his "noble" speech. Jews in particular were grateful. "The nation is like one family now," Paul Rieger of the Centralverein wrote. War had inaugurated a "divine peace" among all Germans; love of the fatherland had "torn down all dividing walls," he added happily.[20]

Several changes seemed at first to confirm the kaiser's promise. Some were cosmetic. Venom once directed at Jews was now diverted to "perfidious England," producing a solidarity that seemed to confirm Freud's dictum that it is easier to promote goodwill between two groups if there is a third they can both hate. The sociologist Werner Sombart, who only two years earlier had criticized Jews for their clannishness, now assaulted the English for their crass materialism, emphasizing the moral difference between German "heroes" and English "shopkeepers." Heine's bitter condemnation of England (Napoleon's "treacherous" jailers) brought him—six decades after his death—a brief spell of admiration even among anti-Semites. The leading "scientific" racist Houston Chamberlain lauded German Jews for doing their duty at the front and at home. Some such compliments were double-edged. On receiving his Iron Cross, the wounded Jewish poet Ernst Toller was told: "This should compensate for the stigma of your ancestry."[21]

Other changes were more significant. A few long-standing obstacles to the appointment of Jews to the higher ranks of the civil service and the judiciary were finally removed. Hundreds (later thousands) were given commissions in the army. Lieutenant Hugo Gutmann, a Jewish regimental adjutant, went to considerable lengths to secure Adolf Hitler an Iron Cross for bravery in the line of action. The divisional commander doubted that Hitler deserved it. Gutmann finally convinced him and personally affixed the medal to Hitler's chest.[22]

For several months after the outbreak of war, Jewish volunteers and conscripts felt little if any hostility in the ranks. In the name of the kaiser's "civic truce," the military authorities ordered the more radical anti-Semitic periodicals to refrain from anti-Jewish agitation.

THE Zionists were still a negligible minority among German Jews. At a conference just eight weeks before the war, they had reaffirmed their conviction that they were aliens in Germany. Once war was declared, though, they joined in with as much—and often more—enthusiasm than others, ready if necessary to shoot at French or Russian Zionists. The Danzig Zionist leader with the symbiotic name of Siegfried Moses (later a highly placed civil servant in Israel) called on his fellow Zionists to stand unhesitatingly behind "our kaiser" in his crusade for peace.

The Zionist *Jüdische Rundschau*, in its first issue after the outbreak of war, exhorted readers to volunteer unhesitatingly and en masse: "Russia has been able to assemble an aggressive coalition against our fatherland."[23] The appeal was headlined "Enemies Everywhere!" German Zionists already settled in Palestine hurried back to volunteer. Elias Auerbach, a doctor in Haifa, wrote in the same issue of the *Jüdische Rundschau*, "We came back joyfully. It was not only our duty, it was mostly love for the country of our birth." The German consul in Palestine reported that Jews of German origin were rushing to the colors "as fervently as the sons of Christian German colonists." Kurt Blumenfeld, president of the German Zionist Federation, warmly welcomed the "spirit of 1914" and even cited approvingly the jingoist slogan that German *Kultur* would yet cure the world of its ills.[24]

For some members of the Zionist youth movement Blau-Weiss—Blue-White—the struggle for Jewish nationalism became mystically interwoven with the "German war."* Zionism, in their eyes, would promote German political influence in Palestine and other countries in the Middle East. The death of one Blau-Weiss man in battle was eulogized as "a truly Maccabean end."[25] The Russian-born Nahum Goldmann, a future president of the World Zionist Organization, joined the German War Ministry as a propagandist. His booklet *The Spirit of Militarism* hailed Prussia's military ethos as a life-giving force: discipline and subordination enhanced the aristocratic form of government at its best. Even more grandiose: the Prussian "drill sergeant personifies Kant's categorical imperative."[26] Until the end of the war, Goldmann remained in Berlin in the odd position of having to report to the police twice weekly as an enemy alien, even as he was employed by the War Ministry's propaganda department and traveled in the occupied territories on a German diplomatic passport. "I had a natural feeling of gratitude for Germany," he later wrote.

In a series of memoranda to the German high command, the veteran Zionist leader Max Bodenheimer proclaimed Germany's imperial aims consonant with Jewish interests. Jews were the "pioneers of Germanness in Eastern Europe," Bodenheimer informed the generals. He and three other prominent Zionists founded the German Committee for the Liberation of Russian Jews. Generals and diplomats with little previous contact with Jews or Zionists responded positively to this initiative, drafting an appeal to Jews of the East to rise up in arms against their oppressors. Two weeks after the war began, the Foreign Ministry official in charge of Jewish affairs informed his superiors of a real coup: "The entire Zionist organization has been won over to our cause." In its strict discipline, he wrote, the Zionist movement was "comparable to the Jesuit order."[27]

Large parts of the Pale of Settlement in Russia soon came under German military rule. Nearly everywhere, Russian Jews welcomed

---

*Blau-Weiss was modeled on the German youth movement Wandervogel, which combined patriotism with love of nature.

the German troops as liberators.* Bodenheimer visited the two leading German generals, Erich Ludendorff (later Hitler's sidekick) and Paul von Hindenburg, at their field headquarters in the East, situated, as was common at the time, in a comfortable castle well behind the front lines. It had an excellent wine cellar. Hindenburg was said to enjoy war physically, indeed to regard it as like "taking the waters at a health resort."[28] Bodenheimer dined with the two generals and, in an effort to prove that Yiddish was but another German dialect, presented them with a Yiddish text transcribed in Latin letters. Jews, he explained, were in effect a German tribe displaced by the tempests of history to the remote East. Hindenburg and Ludendorff were impressed. Ludendorff asked whether it was true that much of the supply of food and fodder for the Russian army was in the hands of Jewish middlemen. If their sympathy could be won, it might be of strategic importance. Bodenheimer assured him that it could. He repeated his favorite argument to the effect that Jews had long been pioneers of German culture and commerce in the East. And while the mass of Russian Jews might well be primitive and lice-ridden, direct German rule would have a salutary effect on them. Quite possibly, Russian Jews would one day rise to the level of their German coreligionists.

In follow-up memoranda, Bodenheimer announced that Germany's best interests lay in promoting Jewish national self-determination in the East. He proposed that a German-controlled buffer state be established in the East in those areas where the largely pro-German Jewish minority would maintain the balance of power between other warring minorities—Lithuanians, Letts, Poles, and Byelorussians. Germany would thus be freed, once and for all, from the threat of Russian attack.

Bodenheimer's efforts aroused the assimilationists' ire. Theodor Wolff, Max Warburg, and Albert Ballin attacked Bodenheimer's scheme for its Zionist overtones: Russian Jews were no more a "nation" than the

---

*The memory of this first German occupation survived until 1941. In some of the more remote villages of Byelorussia and the Ukraine, Jews reportedly welcomed troops of the Nazi Waffen SS as liberators only to be forced, a few days later, to dig their own graves.

Jews of Germany, they announced. In the end, nothing came of Bodenheimer's proposals. The government preferred to cut a deal with the
more numerous Poles. But German army commanders in the newly
occupied territories addressed solemn appeals in Hebrew and Yiddish
to "My dear Jews," promising an end to discrimination: "Our banners
bring you justice and freedom, civil rights and freedom, freedom of
belief, freedom to work unhindered. . . . We come to you as friends.
The barbaric foreign government is gone. The same rights for all will be
established on firm foundations."[29] The Russian authorities responded
by deporting half a million Jews to the interior. The German army, for
its part, deported some 100,000 Polish and Lithuanian Jews to Germany
as forced laborers in the war industry. German Jewish objections to this
maltreatment were subdued and ineffective. German Jews were far
more concerned with demonstrating support for the war effort.

WALTHER Rathenau, who had been against war until the very last
moment, received word of its outbreak with great distress. "A frightful
pallor spread across his face," according to the playwright Gerhart
Hauptmann, who was with him. "This terrible disaster could have been
prevented," he muttered.[30] The war was likely to be so murderous and
costly, he felt, as to ruin the country for generations. That same day, in
a characteristic gesture of loyalty—or perhaps guilt—the forty-seven-
year-old tycoon rushed a fawning letter to the imperial chancellor himself offering his services to the state "in any activity whatsoever" for the
duration of the war.[31] He cited his command of "French, English, and
some Italian" and even his army service as a corporal almost thirty years
earlier.

Undeterred by Bethmann-Hollweg's failure to answer his letter,
Rathenau followed it up with a stream of memoranda on what Germany's war aims ought to be: annexation of key territories in the West
and, among other penalties, the imposition of huge indemnity payments on the vanquished enemies. France alone was to be presented
with a bill for forty million gold marks. In one memorandum he
proposed the postwar establishment of a common European market
under German hegemony comprising France, Belgium, Holland, and

possibly Austria-Hungary.[32] And in a letter to Wilhelm Schwaner, an ultranationalist crackpot, the author of a pagan Germanic Bible to whom, paradoxically, Rathenau was tied by mutual bonds of friendship, he waxed euphoric: "This war is something we deeply needed. Now everything that is outmoded and unbearable will give way to a new hope! . . . Our army deserves this victory."[33] Six weeks after the outbreak of hostilities, he suggested a strategy of massive air bombardment, presumably by zeppelins, in order to "systematically undermine the nerves of the [English] civilian population."[34] Later he had no scruples about recommending the deportation—in violation of international treaties—of up to 700,000 Belgian and Polish workers as forced laborers for the German war industry.

He was aghast at the failure of government planners to make adequate preparations for a long and difficult campaign. Rathenau seems to have been among the first to realize that the war would soon become a life-and-death struggle for raw materials and equipment. In a meeting at the War Ministry early on, he alerted the government to the shortages Germany was certain to face once it was cut off from world markets; even gunpowder and explosives requiring a steady supply of nitrates would soon run out. With England's entry into the war, Germany had become "a fortress under siege . . . cut off on land and sea, left to its own resources."[35] He was appalled by the prevailing belief that the neutral American merchant marine would continue to supply Germany with all its needs from overseas.

The War Ministry's initial response to Rathenau's warnings was condescending. A Colonel Weitz interrupted Rathenau after his first sentence: "But, dearest doctor, what can you be thinking? In four weeks we shall be in Paris. . . . There is no need to worry about the supply of raw materials."[36] Rathenau had more success a few days later in a meeting with General Erich von Falkenhayn, the war minister, who immediately grasped the seriousness of Rathenau's message and the potentially disastrous consequences of continuing to ignore it. On August 12, 1914, Falkenhayn appointed Rathenau head of a new department in his ministry with the temporary rank of general, charged with reorganizing the national economy as a whole. In his eight months in this post, Rathenau established the first truly planned modern economy in

Europe. It is no exaggeration to say that, but for Rathenau and the gifted scientists, economists, and managers he engaged, Germany might have succumbed within months; its adversaries had greater stocks of food, minerals, cannonballs, bullets, and open supply lines if stocks ran out. Without constant supplies of nitrates—imported from Latin America—Germany would have run out not only of fertilizers (and therefore bread) but of gunpowder. By November 1914, before Rathenau's urgent measures produced results, alarmed army commanders warned that they were forced to limit shooting on the Western Front, where success in trench warfare required superior firepower. Even Falkenhayn had started to doubt the certainty of a German victory. "There are certain unique men," Gerhart Hauptmann would later write of Rathenau's role during the war, "whose contribution to the well-being of nations is more significant than the combined effort of thousands. One of these men is Rathenau."[37]

To maximize the use of existing supplies Rathenau introduced tight controls on local industries. He oversaw the distribution of raw materials plundered by the army in occupied Belgium and Poland and found ways to temporarily replace imported nitrates and other vital chemicals with locally produced compounds. His friends claimed he was another Joseph the Provider. His enemies, on the other hand, charged that his department only helped make him and other prominent Jewish businessmen richer.

On the first day of the war, Fritz Haber, Einstein's associate at the Kaiser Wilhelm Institute, had placed himself at the disposal of the War Ministry and had been given the temporary rank of captain. The son of a superpatriotic family, he approved of the war with unqualified enthusiasm. His father, Siegfried, was one of the first Jews elected a town councillor in Breslau and had named his son after the legendary Old Fritz, a founder of the royal house of Hohenzollern. Haber was pleased to see that under Rathenau's auspices one of his own discoveries—the Haber-Bosch process for producing nitric acid—was applied to serve the war effort. With record speed, Rathenau's new department established several plants for that purpose. Local production soon ended the shortage of fertilizers and explosives. By 1916, 300 million tons would be produced annually.

Haber soon invested his energies in another project, the development of a new, hopefully ultimate weapon, poison gas.* The highest priority was assigned to this project: poison gas might yet break the stalemate of trench warfare. Haber was charged with all preparations. He and his staff worked on the gas project tirelessly, and in October 1914 they conducted the first field experiments. These were failures. Several other techniques of dispatching chlorine gas across battle lines were tested. The main challenge was to avoid the asphyxiation of one's own men in the event of the wind's turning. The use of poison gas violated international war conventions, but Haber had no pangs of conscience. Conventional military wisdom held that it was more merciful to gas a man than to blow him up; gas was even thought to perhaps be more humane since asphyxiation did not always lead to immediate death. The truth was, of course, that gas was used not instead of but in addition to bayonets, machine guns, and cannons. Death by chlorine and other lethal substances such as mustard gas (soon in common use) was prolonged and agonizing. Furthermore, gas victims who survived were often debilitated for life. Haber had helped make barbarism "scientific."

Einstein was not blind to his friend's character flaws. Before the war, he had already complained of the vanity and tastelessness to which "this otherwise so splendid man has succumbed." Such defects were not exclusive to Haber; Einstein found them widely diffused among many of his scientific colleagues in the Kaiser Wilhelm Institute:

> When these people are together with French or English people, what a difference! How raw and primitive they are. Vanity without authentic self-esteem. Civilization (nicely brushed teeth, elegant ties, dapper snout, perfect suit) but no personal culture (raw in speech, movement, voice, feeling).[38]

---

*Haber also experimented with pesticides and developed the deadly gas Zyklon B. "The horror of Haber's involvement with the gas that later murdered millions, including friends and distant relatives, beggars description," writes Fritz Stern (*Einstein's German World*, p. 135).

By December 1914, Haber (in a somewhat fantastic uniform of his own design) was spending most of his time on the Western Front. During one field experiment the wind suddenly turned and Haber was almost poisoned. Coughing but undeterred, he returned to his task a few hours later. Among Haber's eminent scientific assistants were the physicist James Franck and the chemists Richard Willstätter and Max Kerschbaum. All three were Jews. As one of Haber's main consultants in the poison-gas project, Willstätter worked mostly on developing effective gas masks. The history of gas warfare began on April 22, 1915, Willstätter later wrote, when Haber and his aides succeeded in blowing a chlorine cloud six kilometers long and six to nine hundred meters wide from steel cylinders onto the French trenches near Ypres. The experiment did not work entirely according to plan, but German troops, wearing Willstätter's gas masks, were able to move into the cloud, advancing the line by a few dozen meters. The scorched earth was littered with dead, wounded, and asphyxiated French Algerian conscripts, yellow mucus frothing from their mouths.

A week later, Haber returned to Berlin. During the night of May 1, after an argument, Haber's wife, Clara, shot herself with his army pistol.[39] According to rumors, Clara was appalled by the war and her husband's role in it and had killed herself in despair. The rumor was never confirmed. "No explanation of hers has survived, neither for the son who found his dying mother nor for her husband," Fritz Stern notes. Haber returned immediately to his duties on the front. He continued to drive himself ruthlessly until almost the last days of the war, when his name appeared on an Allied list of war criminals and he suffered a nervous breakdown.

HABER's case was extreme but not unusual. Innumerable texts produced in the first sixteen months of the conflict attest to the fact that it was a war of intellectuals. Caught in a web of conformism, writers, journalists, poets, scientists, painters, musicians joined in hailing the justness of Germany's cause. High school principals and university professors—often men of almost self-caricaturing pomposity—were especially diligent in fanning the jingoist fires. As state employees, professors were traditionally apolitical men (there were no female professors). They tended to respect and obey authority, or *Obrigkeit*: Luther had lent the term a quasi-religious aura. Golo Mann told of a patriotic professor who claimed he had nothing to do with politics. His field, he maintained, was philosophy. What if a house were on fire? Wouldn't he try to help? No, if a house were on fire he would call the fire department. Fighting fires was a skill that had to be learned and he had not learned it; he had learned only to philosophize. So by the same token, a political crisis had to be handled by experts, that is, by politicians. The philosopher's job, as he saw it, was to provide the state with moral, historical, and philosophic arguments.[40]

Jewish intellectuals, for once, were as conformist as others. It was perhaps their worst hour since the unification of Germany in 1870. Chaim Weizmann even told the last British ambassador in Berlin that on the eve of the war Jewish intellectuals were the most arrogant and belligerent of all Germans.[41] Weizmann's comment may have been tainted with prejudice, but he was not far from the truth. During the first week of war, even Freud succumbed to the general euphoria: he could not wait to see German troops march triumphantly into Paris. Auden's lament—and prayer—evoking Julien Benda's book *La trahison des clercs* (*The Treason of the Intellectuals*) comes to mind: "There is no end / To the vanity of our calling: make intercession / For the treason of all clerks."[42]

A humanist predilection to temper or civilize German patriotism, making patriots more tolerant of others, had over the years become almost second nature for German Jewish intellectuals. The war was perhaps the only occasion in half a century when many of them abandoned this disposition in the hope, no doubt, of finally completing integration with the majority. The philosopher Max Scheler published a bloodcurdling tract called *The Genius of War and the German War*. It was one of many such apologia that lent the war the approval of intellectuals.

Martin Buber, the thirty-six-year-old prophet of a Jewish cultural renaissance, celebrated the war as a liberating, quasi-redemptive communal experience; it conveyed a sense of belonging that he welcomed in convoluted, almost eschatological terms. "Not in faith but in devotion is the divine revealed," he wrote.[43] He mystified sacrifice: the coward who now "loveth his life shall lose it," he warned, quoting the Gospel of St. John (12:25). For Buber the war was a "sacred spring," a wonderful purification through violence. He basked in the sheer moral beauty of it. War was finally rousing Europe from its bourgeois lethargy, he claimed; the soul of man was no longer "stagnating" and "shriveling." Moreover, the war would finally unite Germans and Jews in a joint "world historical mission": to civilize the Near East.

Germany was only defending itself, Buber assured some of his shocked pacifist friends abroad. Breaching Belgian neutrality—causing England to join the war against Germany—had been an elemental necessity. Buber chided the Dutch pacifist Frederik van Eeden for his "childish vilification" of Germany. From his villa in Zehlendorf, on the outskirts of Berlin, he downplayed the massacre of two hundred Belgian civilians by drunken German soldiers in Louvain. "I know personally," he wrote van Eeden, "that Belgian women amused themselves by putting out the eyes of wounded German soldiers and forcing buttons ripped from their uniforms into the empty sockets."[44]

Buber would later change his mind radically. But caught up in the fervor of the first weeks of war, he wrote Hans Kohn:

> Never has the concept *Volk* become such a reality to me as during these weeks. Among Jews too. The prevailing feeling is one of solemn exaltation. Among the millions who volunteered were [the prominent German Jewish writers] Karl Wolfskehl and Friedrich Gundolf. I myself, unfortunately, have not the slightest prospect of being called up; but I am trying to help in my own way.

"Power and spirit are now going to become one. *Incipit vita nuova* [the new life begins]!"[45] Buber added triumphantly, alluding to Dante's remark upon first setting eyes on his beloved Beatrice. It is difficult to imagine a more odious comparison.

Stefan Zweig, an avowed pacifist who claimed he would never touch a gun, not even at a shooting range, was as thrilled as most other Austrian and German Jewish writers to be living at this wonderful moment.

He wrote his publisher, Kiepenberg, excitedly: "I do envy you that you're allowed to be an officer in this army, able to win in France—this France we must chastise because we love it so."[46] Zweig was grateful to find himself in the midst of ecstatic masses celebrating the war, sharing the "majestic, rapturous, even seductive" feeling of solidarity with his fellow Austrians. He felt "purified of all selfishness." He would not have wanted, he said, "to miss the memory of those first days." Zweig volunteered for active service—in the war archive, where his knowledge of foreign languages might be useful.

Hermann Cohen, author of *Religion of Reason Out of the Sources of Judaism*, believed his finest ideals would be realized in this patriotic war. The "God of justice and love" was sure to grant Germany a "heroic victory" over her wicked enemies. The aged philosopher even offered to travel to the United States to convince American Jews that Germany's motives were pure and its cause a model for the entire world.[47]

Felix Klemperer, a prominent neurosurgeon, was surprised and in the end delighted to find himself so moved by the "splendor" of a war even though such military glorification was not part of his "heritage" as a rabbi's son.[48] His younger brother, the linguist Victor, shared Felix's exaltation. "We, we Germans, are better than other nations," he exclaimed in his diary. "Freer in thought, purer in feeling, juster in action. We, we Germans, are a truly chosen people."[49] England, by contrast, was simply vile and despicable. Klemperer prayed that for every German soldier who fell in battle an English civilian would be killed by German zeppelins. "First Europe must be at our feet, then we'll settle our accounts with Asia."[50] Klemperer's Italian colleague the philosopher Benedetto Croce was taken aback by Klemperer's parochialism; in his "Marginal Remarks of a Philosopher on the World War," Croce wrote that Klemperer was a "German in the most arrogant, foolhardy sense of the word—incapable of understanding the psychology and spiritual makeup of other nations."[51]

The number of Jews among the intellectual war zealots was disproportionately high. Their general venom was directed at England for letting Germany down; France might be Germany's hereditary enemy but England had betrayed her. Long devoted to the cult of *Bildung*, they convinced themselves, like Klemperer, that the superiority of German *Kultur* justified the German cause; it would inevitably result in the victory of German arms. The romantic distortion of *Kultur* nourished a poetic idea of war as a "cleansing bath" of steel and fire. Ephraim Frisch, son of a pious Ukrainian family and editor of the prominent literary monthly *Der Neue Merkur,* celebrated the war as a rebirth. "A nation cannot achieve greatness without war," he proclaimed, "and long-lasting peace is accomplished by promoting mediocrity."

The influential polemicist Maximilian Harden and the biographer Emil Ludwig were two other cases in point. Overnight, Harden discarded his role of the past twenty years as a merciless critic of the kaiser and the militarist cabal. In his magazine, *Die Zukunft,* he published bloodthirsty poems and a long diatribe against Germany's enemies proudly entitled "We *Are* Barbarians." Shameless England was allied, he wrote, with "stinking [Japanese] yellow apes"; it rejoiced at the news that "German men are treacherously butchered and German women are violated by drunken Cossacks." Three weeks after the war began, he announced that Germany had a "right to extend its borders and the might to enforce this right against all foes." Two weeks later, he observed that "Germany has never been so beautiful." Might was right. Germany was entitled to "extend its sovereign territory according to need."[52] He would go on to be satirized as a mindless warmongering polemicist.

Emil Ludwig rushed into print with his diary of June 28 to August 15, 1914, entitled "These Great Times." Gushing with enthusiasm, he described the prowar mob scenes in Berlin:

AUGUST 1   *We would be wrong to label this "war fervor." It's more the outcry of a wounded animal. A nation has been set upon. But the people are so disciplined that they will suppress their cry until their trusted leaders have taken some decisive steps, unwavering and resolute.*

AUGUST 4   *During the past few days every individual formed part of the whole, every subject wore the German crown.*

AUGUST 15   *The German body politic is filled with a moral force that our adversaries cannot possibly possess today. Even if our soldiers weren't the best, we would still emerge victorious.*[53]

Less than a year later, he came to regret his belligerence. In his 1931 memoirs, he confessed his foolishness in believing that Germany had been the innocent victim of an unprovoked attack.[54]

The budding novelist Arnold Zweig, son of a Jewish saddler in Silesia, shelved his pacifism and defined himself as a German militarist on Nietzschean grounds. His collection of short stories *The Beast*, published in November 1914, teemed with upright, heroic Germans trying hopelessly to defend themselves against murderous Belgian civilians. In the title story, three innocent German soldiers seek refuge in a Belgian peasant's cellar. The peasant—the eponymous beast—butchers them in their sleep. He dons an apron "and proceeds to remove the entrails from the open abdomen, the lungs, the heart—grinning with clenched teeth at the surprise discovery that it all looked about the same as it did with pigs."

It was the war of the poets, too. Hugo von Hofmannsthal, Richard Dehmel, Ludwig Ganghofer, and others volunteered for service with full knowledge that precious lives such as theirs would of course not be placed at risk in the trenches. In August alone, German newspapers reputedly received some fifty thousand war poems daily. The lyrical battleground was aflame for several months. Rhyming *Not* (necessity) with *Tod* and *Krieg* with *Sieg*, war poems continued to arrive in great piles. Many found their way into print. One of the worst was published on page 1 of the Orthodox *Israelitisches Familienblatt* of Frankfurt:

> *Storm the Russians! Strike them for keeps*
> *Pile up their corpses in heaps and heaps!*[55]

Alfred Kerr, a poet and the drama critic for the *Berliner Tageblatt*, compared the sound of machine-gun fire to the music of the spheres.

The Jewish theater critic Julius Bab was a diligent anthologist and chronicler of these rhymed hymns to chauvinism and hatred, born, he claimed, of nothing but love. In his villa in the Grunewald section of Berlin, where he lived with his wife and his poodle, Bab placed himself entirely at the service of the national war. His anthologies, in festive bindings, entitled *The German War in German Poetry* appeared in installments every three months and occasionally included his own poetic effusions:

> *My fatherland in sore distress*
> *Shall hate its foes unto their death.*

And:

> *Do you love Germany? What a question!*
> *Can I love my own hair, my blood, my very self?*

Each installment was introduced by Bab's notes and short essays on such topics as "Bad people have no songs . . . robbers very few."* The fact that so many poems were being composed was proof enough in Bab's eyes that even in war Germans remained rooted in Kantian spirituality and Goethean humanism. When he was not anthologizing or writing poetry, Bab visited army barracks and toured the front, lecturing on Lessing and Goethe to the soldiers in the trenches. He expressed his credo in two brief lines: "With Germany I stand or fall / That's who I am."

Several of the best-known warrior poets anthologized by Bab were fellow Jews. From Alfred Kerr:

> *We must give our very last,*
> *A miracle must happen.*
> *Germany fights for its life,*
> *It will not go under.*[56]

From the early Expressionist Walter Hasenclever, famed for his antiauthoritarian 1914 drama *The Son:*

---

*Bab's was the leading anthology, but during the first year of the war there were an estimated four or five hundred such collections.

> *Keep awake the hatred,*
> *Keep alive the pain.*
> *Flames, burn on,*
> *The time cometh!*

And from the Austrian Hugo Zuckermann, whose popular "Cavalry Song" the Hitler Youth continued to sing until 1945:

> *Who knows where I will fall.*
> *Perhaps in Poland?*
> *It is of no account:*
> *Before they come to fetch my soul*
> *I shall die upon my mount.*
>
> *No reason to be sad:*
> *If I can only live to see*
> *Our banners over Belgrade.*

Victor Klemperer first read this poem in a Munich paper. He admired its patriotic flair and added with satisfaction that it proved "not all Austrian Jews are Zionists," as he had assumed.[57]

Cultural chauvinism was further exacerbated by Italy's entry into the war against Germany early in 1915. The prominent essayist Rudolf Borchardt, the scion of a long line of rabbis, was appalled that Dante had written the *Divine Comedy* in Italian rather than in German, as he should have. To make up for that failing, Borchardt translated the poem into medieval German himself, an accomplishment, according to George Steiner, of almost "pathological intensity."[58] But the most famous, fervent, and popular of the war poets was Ernst Lissauer with his "Hymn of Hate against England":

> *We shall hate you with a long-lasting hate,*
> *A hate that endures and will never abate.*
> *Hatred by sea and hatred by land,*
> *From those who wear crowns or who work by their hand,*
> *Seventy millions all as one man,*
> *United in love and united in woe,*

United in hatred of one single foe:
England!

James W. Gerard, the American ambassador in Berlin, reported in his memoirs that German Jews were proud that the author of this song was an avowed, if secular, Jew. The "Hymn" made hatred of England proverbial in Germany. Victor Klemperer approved of it "passionately": It echoed his "deepest feelings" and those of the people he knew.[59] Bab hailed it for its "powerful rhetoric" and "near-religious feeling for the *Volk*." In truth, Lissauer's song did not need Bab's warm endorsement and inclusion in his third anthology to become the best known of all the war poems. Its success was immediate, exploding "like a bomb in an ammunition depot," Stefan Zweig wrote.[60] Recited and reprinted more often than even "Watch on the Rhine," it was set to music and sung in schools and army barracks, adapted for chorus, and performed in theaters and opera houses. Officers read it to their assembled men. Banks and commercial houses had it translated into foreign languages and appended it to their correspondence with customers in neutral countries. Crown Prince Rupprecht of Bavaria ordered it printed on leaflets and distributed to every soldier in the army. "We now have the good fortune to confront English soldiers," he told his troops. "Take your revenge on them, they are our main enemy."[61] The kaiser decorated Lissauer with the Order of the Red Eagle.

Lissauer, too, would soon regret writing the poem. The anti-Semites were quick to turn it against Lissauer himself. "Only Jews are capable of such hatred!" they said. "Jews pray for Germany not because they love it but because they hate England." After the war Lissauer claimed lamely that poetry cannot be "willed"; the poem had swelled in his heart and forced its way out.[62] It continued to stick to him, however, like a burning "shirt of Nessus" until his death in 1937 in exile from Nazi Germany.

The abdication of the intellectuals was at its most shameful in October 1914 with the "Manifesto of the Ninety-three," one of the first public appeals of its kind. The manifesto originated in the War Ministry, which sought to enlist the international prestige of German scientists, academics, and artists in the service of the propaganda machine. At the ministry's instigation, Ludwig Fulda, a playwright and son of an old Jewish family in Frankfurt, solicited the support of prominent figures in the arts and sciences for an appeal to the international world of culture proclaiming Germany's innocence in precipitating the war. The document, drafted by Fulda in consultation with the imperial navy's press officer, denounced all criticism of Germany as poisonous lies. It celebrated German militarism—"without [it] our culture would have long been purged from the face of the earth"—and defended the breach of Belgian neutrality as necessary "to repel the threatened assault." The appeal firmly denied press reports that Germany was committing war crimes in Belgium. The incident in Louvain in which civilians had been massacred by drunken soldiers had been an act of self-defense committed by Germans "with aching hearts."

The appeal revealed an astounding insensitivity to public opinion abroad, which was precisely what it was designed to sway. Translated into fourteen languages, it completely misfired. In the West, according to Fritz Stern, it was perceived as "a second, a moral declaration of war, . . . an example of autistic arrogance."[63] Bertrand Russell in England and Henri Bergson in France found it simply shameful. Romain Rolland saw his worst fear confirmed: the militarization of the German intellectual elite. Indeed, ninety-three prominent German intellectuals signed the appeal. Many did so without even reading it, on the strength of Fulda's cabled invitation: "Your signature urgently required for protest against foreign press lies. Haste imperative. Please do not ask for the text." Among the prominent Jewish scientists and artists who readily signed were the chemists Fritz Haber, Richard Willstätter, Paul Ehrlich, and Adolf von Baeyer, the theater director Max Reinhardt, the painter Max Liebermann, and the playwright Herbert Eulenberg.* Einstein refused to sign.

The appeal provoked ridicule at home and anger abroad. In the

---

*There were chauvinists as well in England and France, where authors, artists, and professors signed similar manifestos. But unlike in Germany, there were notable antiwar voices, including those of Bertrand Russell, George Bernard Shaw, Henri Bergson, and Henri Barbusse.

Berliner Tageblatt, Theodor Wolff found it "incomprehensible that Germany's top 'thinkers' . . . were personally ready to guarantee that German soldiers were incapable of performing shameful acts . . . and that in war everything is always done in a just and orderly manner."[64] A few of the listed luminaries, among them Paul Ehrlich, repudiated their signatures. Romain Rolland issued a counterappeal to intellectuals of all countries to be more critical of their respective governments; war was a product of "weakness and stupidity," he announced. In an open letter published in a Swiss newspaper, he implored German intellectuals to join him in a protest against the bestiality of nationalism. None would—or could—respond.

THERE were, of course, a few—very few—independent voices protesting the all-out embrace of war. A lamentably small number of German writers kept their distance from the warmongers, among them Hermann Hesse, the satirist Karl Kraus, and the playwright Arthur Schnitzler. Schnitzler's publishers, editors, and directors—even his own wife—urged him to write a patriotic play; they despaired at his stubborn refusal, which hurt his popularity while prowar authors were making a lot of money. Schnitzler remained firm. On August 5, 1914, Schnitzler wrote in his diary, "World War = World Ruin."

Freud's early enthusiasm for the war was short-lived. After two or three weeks it gave way to anger and despair. He wondered at the astonishing ease with which men discovered passions more important than life. Some primal force must be at work, he surmised, a hatred of life or a lack of talent for living. "Never," he commented, "has an event destroyed so much that was precious in the common property of mankind, confused so many of the most lucid minds, so thoroughly debased the elevated."[65] Freud and his future biographer Ernest Jones exchanged letters on Armageddon and warned each other that deceit was rampant everywhere. Karl Popper, another Viennese of Jewish origin, who would go on to write *The Open Society and Its Enemies,* was a conscientious objector.[66]

It was difficult, even dangerous, to oppose the war. Antiwar writings were banned by the military censor. The leading prewar German pacifist, Ludwig Quidde, was ordered by the authorities to stop "proselytizing" or risk a prison sentence. A production of *1913,* an antiwar drama by Carl Sternheim, son of a Leipzig Jewish banker, was canceled by order of the military authorities. Rosa Luxemburg's letters from prison were circulated by her friends in an early form of samizdat. The poet Erich Mühsam, son of a Jewish pharmacist in Berlin, went to jail for decrying the "staging of this mass warmongering, the monstrous system by which people are injected with bacteria that have been cultivated over the years to produce a psychosis of hatred and zeal."[67] At about the same time Karl Liebknecht finally dared speak up in the Reichstag and vote against the war budget; his speech was struck from the official record. He himself was drafted into an army work battalion.

In the winter of 1914, a Berlin cardiologist, Georg Friedrich Nicolai (né Lewinstein), tried to launch another appeal countering Fulda's manifesto. Only two men were prepared to sign it—he and Albert Einstein. For want of signatures it was not made public in Germany. It would not in any case have passed the censors. Six of nine "prominent pacifists" on a list submitted by army headquarters to the Berlin police were Jews, including Einstein and the socialist Eduard Bernstein; the police were requested to keep an eye on their activities and deny them exit visas.

Einstein was too prominent a member of the Prussian Academy of Sciences to be treated harshly or prevented from traveling abroad. He was also a Swiss national. But he had to be careful and expressed his views only privately. He was shocked, as he later told Freud, that intellectuals proved to be the most likely to yield to the collective psychosis of hate: perhaps this was so, he speculated, because they had no contact with life in the raw but only with life on the printed page.

Without doubt, the most vocal and consistent protest of any German-language intellectual—and for almost a year the only one—came from Karl Kraus. Kraus was a brilliant Viennese polemicist, linguist, poet, and media critic (his views anticipated those of Marshall McLuhan half a century later). He was the founder of and often sole writer for the aggressively satirical magazine *Die Fackel,* which he published until his death in 1936. His bitter critique of the war resounded to some acclaim in Austria, which practiced a form of repressive tolerance and was less systematic (or more slovenly) in the application of censorship. To retain his public pulpit, Kraus veiled his attack as essentially an attack on the intellectual warmongers. His message was not lost on his growing audience. His fans crowded into the public readings he gave in Viennese concert halls.

Kraus had foreseen the war long before the fighting began. He had been publishing his dark premonitions in *Die Fackel* for several years. Civilization itself was about to collapse, he warned. His critical analysis of the Viennese press's sentimental reports on the Balkan wars—which he contrasted with the more realistic and truthful accounts in the *Times* of London—left him with no illusions about war correspondents and their readers. His particular target was a correspondent named Paul Goldmann, who sent the *Neue Freie Presse,* Vienna's prestigious newspaper, flowery feuilletons on the picturesque Balkan landscape as seen, mostly, through the window of a general's armored train. Covering the same war, the *Times* correspondent concentrated instead on its horrors—the casualties and destruction and famished orphans in rags wandering through the desolate countryside. To illustrate his case, Kraus published the two versions side by side.

As Kraus saw it, the war was brought about by frivolous politicians, stupid generals, and corrupt journalists. The reasons for their shortsightedness were cultural and political: a disastrous "failure of the imagination" and an almost deliberate refusal to envisage the inevitable consequences of words and acts. Man had invented the airplane but his political imagination was still dragging through the mud like mail coaches before the age of railways. The brainwashing was made possible, above all, by the corruption of language in politics and in some of the major newspapers. The newpapers ignored the horrors. They found words only for the courage of young men at war and none for the madness of those who sent them there. Kraus warned of the world's impending downfall through the "black magic" of newsprint. Wartime clichés stood firmly on two feet; the humans who did the fighting were often left with one foot only.

On November 19, 1914, at a lecture in Vienna, Kraus made a barely disguised attack on the war. The acid irony of his talk, entitled "In These Great Times," was obvious to everyone. The text was reprinted three weeks later in *Die Fackel*. It was the first of a series of such lectures, each more vitriolic than the last. Kraus's sharpest words were directed against the intellectual and poetic war zealots. There was nothing heroic about this war, as they were claiming in print and on the stage. Clichés and abstractions had dulled public sensibilities to what was actually happening. Kitsch was death in disguise: it replaced ethics with aesthetics.

Kraus spoke to a packed audience. The impact of his lecture was all the more dramatic against the background of the recent battle on the Marne, where the spectacular German advance had finally been brought to a stop. It had become clear that this would be not a short war of quick outcomes but a war of deadlock and prolonged battering. How was it possible, Kraus asked, that even as, on a single day, fifty thousand human beings lay dying, caught in barbed wire, poets still found words to laud the carnage? The war was at a stalemate, yet the bloodbath continued—indeed, it seemed as if it might go on forever.

Kraus remained adamant in his principled position throughout the war. By 1915, he was already at work on his great play *The Last Days of Mankind*, five acts of bitter sarcasm and sheer horror, a work of wild fiction in which every word is true. Its "most improbable" scenes and dialogue, Kraus warned in his introduction, had actually happened; the most blatant inventions were "mere quotes."

Perhaps the earliest antiwar poem to slip through German censorship was Lion Feuchtwanger's "Song of the Dead Soldiers." The son of an Orthodox family in Munich, Feuchtwanger later became an internationally successful novelist, author of *Power* (*Jud Süss*), the trilogy *Josephus*, and *The Devil in France*. Feuchtwanger's "Song of the Dead Soldiers" appeared on February 15, 1915, in the literary magazine *Die Schaubühne* (The Stage). Mysteriously, it even found its way into one of Julius Bab's patriotic anthologies. On a cursory reading the poem may have seemed one more patriotic hymn (and for that reason probably passed the military censors). Closer reading reveals a passionate call for rebellion, more threatening with every stanza. The recurrent question "Why?" evokes the sheer madness of war; the repeated phrase "We're waiting" echoes Heine's "Silesian Weavers":

Song of the Dead Soldiers

The skin has shriveled from our faces
Worms gnaw their way through our brains
Our flesh reverts to fertile land
Our mouths are stuffed with dirt and sand.
  We're waiting.

The flesh decays, the bones lie bare,
One question seeks an answer fair,
One question nevermore shall die
And is not still. Why? Why?
  We're waiting.

Our mouths are stuffed with dust and sand
And our question bursts the ground,
And bursts the clods that cover us,
And rests not till the answer's found.
  We're waiting.

We're waiting, yet we are but seeds
The answer comes, the answer speeds,
It damns the guilty, lauds the just
The answer tarries, come it must.[68]

THE conflicting sensibilities of young German Jews clashed on occasion within a single family. Arthur Scholem, the owner of a large printing plant, found himself at odds with his sons, Reinhold, Werner, and Gerhard (Gershom). There had been tensions in the family prior to the war. Arthur was assimilated but despised relatives who had converted. Reinhold wished him to be more "German"; Gerhard, the youngest, wished him to be more "Jewish." As Gerhard put it, Arthur had left Jehovah's great army but insisted on the right to wear His uniform. He was known to light his after-dinner cigar from the flame of Frau Scholem's Sabbath candles, intoning a parody of the Hebrew prayer "Blessed be He who created the tobacco plant."[69] Gerhard, a sensitive adolescent in search of "roots" and "Jewish authenticity," resented, even despised his father's lightheartedness. When he first told his father, "I think I want to be a Jew!" Arthur Scholem's reply was that of many assimilationists: "Jews are good only for the synagogue. . . . Do you want to return to the ghetto?" Gerhard insisted, "*You* are in a ghetto! I've never met a Christian in your house except on formal occasions, like your fiftieth birthday!"[70]

There were other points of conflict. Reinhard, the eldest son, had declared himself a right-wing German nationalist. His ultraconservative views drove his father to distraction.* The middle son, Werner, was a Communist whose bitter opposition to the war shocked his father. (Later a Reichstag deputy, Werner would be killed by the Nazis in the Buchenwald concentration camp.) As a conscript, he was wounded in action and sent home to convalesce. Still limping and still in army uniform, he led one of the first antiwar demonstrations in a public square. He was arrested and charged with treason.

Arthur was beside himself with shame and anger. The charge was later reduced to "offending the kaiser's uniform and honor." As if all this were not enough, seventeen-year-old Gerhard also got into trouble. Emotionally and intellectually, he was close to his brother Werner and chose to oppose the war. "You are just a coward," his father told him. In an underground publication, Gerhard ridiculed Martin Buber's war enthusiasm, calling it a form of "Buberty." He also helped his brother distribute antiwar leaflets printed clandestinely on one of their father's presses. The final blow came when he sent an angry letter to the *Jüdische Rundschau* protesting one of their many prowar articles. The letter was not printed but a copy fell into the wrong hands. A few months before graduation, Gerhard was thrown out of high school.

For Scholem senior, the prospect of Werner's court-martial had been bad enough; Gerhard's expulsion was altogether too much. His reaction was merciless. The scene at the family breakfast table was a high moment of bourgeois tragicomedy. The maid brought in a registered

---

*Half a century later, in his Australian exile, Reinhard held to his nationalist creed. He told his brother, "I will not let Hitler dictate my political views."

letter that had just arrived and handed it to Gerhard. It was couched in formal terms:

February 15, 1917

Gerhard:

I have resolved to cease paying your support and consequently would like to inform you of the following: You must leave my apartment by the first of March and from then on will no longer be allowed to enter it without my express permission. So as not to leave you without any means of support I will transfer 100 marks to your name. You should not count on further payments from me. You would thus do well to present yourself to the civil service authority to be assigned a salaried position in keeping with your abilities. Whether I shall make further funds available after the war so that you might continue your studies will depend on your subsequent behavior.

Your father,
Arthur Scholem[71]

The pacifying efforts of Frau Scholem were of no avail. Neither were those of relatives and family friends. Gerhard moved out of the house. He successfully evaded military service on a fake claim of dementia and was admitted to a university even though he had not finished high school. At his interview for the university, the examiner casually asked why he had dropped out of high school. Gerhard looked confused and stammered; the examiner patted him reassuringly on his shoulder and said with a knowing smile, "Ah, an affair with a girl!" Getting a girl pregnant was a gentleman's dereliction; opposing the war was an act of treason.

EARLY in 1916, little was left of the war ecstasy except in the rhetoric of conservative politicians and the poems that continued to appear in Bab's anthologies. Short wars may produce unanimity but long, seemingly endless wars lead to bitter dissension. The great indecisive battles in the West had been a turning point. At the battle of the Somme alone, there had been nearly half a million German casualties. (The British and French lost 620,000.)[72]

Kurt Tucholsky, who in the patriotic enthusiasm of the first few days had volunteered for service, came to regard the war as a "worldwide latrine filled with blood, barbed wire, and hate songs." He tried every trick to get out of fighting. After the war he claimed that he was "only sorry that unlike the great Karl Liebknecht I did not have the guts to say no and refuse service; of this I am ashamed. . . . I did everything I could not to shoot and not to get shot."[73]

The Social Democrats' party discipline crumbled. Several deputies emulated Liebknecht's early example and voted against the war budgets. Party chairman Hugo Haase was finally prepared to speak out. A grand debate now dominated the little that was left of public life, given the general servility and impotence of the parliament. Those who were ready to sue for a *Verhandlungsfrieden*, a negotiated peace without annexations and indemnities, battled those militating for a *Siegfrieden*, the enemy's unconditional surrender with annexations and reparation payments, as after the Franco-Prussian War of 1870.

The liberal press, largely Jewish-owned, and a growing number of Reichstag deputies were in favor of a negotiated peace. They had little influence, however, on the military establishment, which was in effect the country's real government. Chancellor Bethmann-Hollweg, too, came to support a negotiated peace, but the military forced his resignation and had no trouble ignoring even the Reichstag, where in 1917 the majority voted for a negotiated peace without annexations. The military was supported by an extraparliamentary coalition of conservatives, generals, university professors, industrialists, and war profiteers who continued to insist on a *Siegfrieden*. Their demands ranged from dismembering only Russia to the dismantlement also of France, Belgium, and the British Empire. The leading warlord, Quartermaster-General Erich Ludendorff, surpassed the others with his annexationist demands, anticipating nearly all that Hitler hoped to realize in 1940.

Despite their miscalculations, the generals still enjoyed considerable support among intellectuals. Even so civilized a man as Harry Kessler, who as a pacifist would later be known in Berlin as the Red Count, favored the annexation of Belgium because "without it, England will finally destroy us." He also felt Germany needed to secure a vast bridge of land through the African continent, down almost as far as Cape Town.[74] Bethmann-Hollweg's successor authorized indiscriminate

U-boat attacks on neutral freighters in the Atlantic. The moderates rightly foresaw that unlimited U-boat warfare would bring the United States into the war. By now, the Western Allies were militating for a *Siegfrieden* of their own. The argument became even more heated once America entered the war. The liberal metropolitan newspapers, the *Berliner Tageblatt* and the *Frankfurter Zeitung* (and, to a lesser extent, the Berlin *Vossische Zeitung*), led the plea for moderation. They opposed submarine and gas warfare as inhuman and argued vociferously for a negotiated peace. The war party damned what it called the *Judenpresse*. The *Frankfurter Zeitung* was frequently closed down for its editorials and other violations of censorship.

There is unanimity among scholars that had a poll been taken at the time the majority of German Jews would have supported the moderates. In 1916, Eduard Bernstein announced that a Jew's patriotism must be cosmopolitan; he appealed to Jews everywhere in Europe to exert pressure on their governments to make peace. Georg Friedrich Nicolai published the text of his counterappeal in Switzerland in 1917 as part of his book *The Biology of War*. For this he was dismissed from his position at the University of Berlin. By the end of 1916, most of the best-known Jews among the zealots had changed their minds, including Maximilian Harden, Emil Ludwig, and Martin Buber. Having realized early that the war could not be won on the militarists' terms, Harden was among the first whose passions cooled. His magazine, *Die Zukunft*, was repeatedly confiscated for allegedly undermining the war effort. In May 1915, he came out publicly in favor of a negotiated peace. By December, the Berlin military command ordered *Die Zukunft* closed for the duration of the war. Harden was also forbidden to speak publicly without first clearing his text with the military; the ban was later lifted. According to Harden's biographer, he was forbidden to tell his readers the reasons either for the ban or for its lifting.[75] Harden only became more critical. In 1917, the magazine was again shut down, this time for five months.

Walther Rathenau, while still serving as head of the War Ministry's supply department, reverted to his original opposition to the war. In March 1915, he met Colonel House, President Wilson's special peace envoy to Europe. House was struck by Rathenau's pessimism and gloom, bordering on despair. With great emotion, Rathenau urged

House to persevere in his efforts to make peace. House asked how many people shared his views. Rathenau replied that as far as he knew no one did. Indeed, he was beginning to wonder if it was he who was insane or everyone else.[76] House was slightly taken aback by Rathenau's histrionics. Shortly after the meeting, Rathenau resigned from the War Ministry. He received no thanks for his efforts. "For rendering the state a service as a private citizen and a Jew," he wrote to Emil Ludwig in 1916, "none of the concerned parties is able to forgive me."[77]

Albert Ballin shared Rathenau's gloom. As the war went on, he too grew desperate. He rarely met the kaiser now. On the few occasions when they did meet, the kaiser's entourage made sure they were not left alone; Ballin grew somewhat paranoid over this slight. Bernard Guttmann, a journalist for the *Frankfurter Zeitung*, visited Ballin in 1916 at his grand headquarters on the Alster. The Hamburg-America shipping line, Germany's largest, was paralyzed. The offices were deserted. "No other man I spoke to during the war was in such despair over the tragedy of Germany," Guttmann wrote.[78]

The annexationist drive gathered steam in 1916 when a number of key business and industry figures, led by Krupp von Bohlen, drew up a memorandum calling for a *Siegfrieden* more or less along the lines of Ludendorff's plan. The memorandum was endorsed by some 1,300 notables (including 352 university professors and 252 artists, writers, and publishers). Theodor Wolff of the *Berliner Tageblatt*, August Stein of the *Frankfurter Zeitung*, the historian Hans Delbrück, and others tried to stem the tide by submitting a memorandum in favor of peace. They gathered only 140 signatures. The more militant warriors on the right condemned any negotiated peace as a "Jew peace." Delbrück later summed up the debate and the role of liberal Jews and radical Social Democrats in it:

> During the war, the very classes that had been oppressed in the past (Social Democrats and Jews) proved to have better political instincts. . . . Not, of course, because they were endowed by nature with more political wisdom but because of the internationalist trend of their thinking. It saved them from the nationalist insanity that clouded the minds of others.[79]

DISILLUSION was slow to sink in. Max Rothmann, a neurologist and professor in Berlin, had been one of the privileged few invited to attend the kaiser's August 4, 1914, speech in the White Hall of the imperial palace. He was there as a representative of the Berlin Reform synagogue community. Rothmann had been delighted to hear the kaiser say that all Germans were now equal in his eyes, irrespective of faith and ethnic origin. His family had long prided itself on its military tradition, and his elder son was already on his way to the Western Front. Rothmann himself was a twice-decorated royal *Oberarzt*—chief doctor—in the Prussian army reserve. His father and grandfather had been decorated in the wars of 1815 and 1870, respectively.

Rothmann had another son, a fifteen-year-old. Soon after the kaiser's speech, Rothmann sought to enroll the boy in the Prussian cadet academy, believing like most other German Jews that the kaiser's words heralded a new era. A rude shock awaited him: his application was rejected. The excuse given was that the boy had taken Latin rather than English in the fourth grade. Rothmann supplied proof that other boys with similar records in his son's class had been accepted by the academy. He asked for an appointment with the principal. His request was refused without explanation.

Two months later, in October 1914, Rothmann's elder son fell in action. Rothmann turned to the army chief of staff, Helmuth von Moltke, informing him of his loss, and to the kaiser himself, renewing his request. The kaiser did not reply. The deputy war minister, Gustav von Wandel, wrote to Rothmann that cadet schools were Christian institutions: "Since your son adheres to the Jewish faith, the War Ministry regrets that it must reject your application." The chief of staff also wrote—to express "congratulations upon the heroic death" of his son, "who sealed his oath of loyalty to the fatherland with his heart's blood."[80]

Rothmann's bitter disappointment was not an isolated event. Far from uniting Germans and Jews, the war seemed only to deepen the gulf between them. As soon as the war turned sour, chauvinism turned inward. Rathenau saw it coming. "The more Jews die in this conflict," he wrote on August 4, 1916, "the more persistent will be their opponents'

complaints that the Jews did nothing but sit behind the front lines prof-
iteering from the war. The hatred will double and triple."[81] Ferdinand
Avenarius, the publisher of the high-brow *Kunstwart* magazine, warned
a Jewish friend that Jews did not even begin to surmise the rage that
was "boiling deep within the people." Such feelings were exacerbated
by the sudden influx of impoverished Jews from occupied Poland and
Russia, many brought against their will, to work in industry and agriculture. Living in abject conditions on the edges of the larger cities,
they elicited revulsion.

The strategy of wearing down the enemy through sustained attrition
proved self-defeating. It wore down the spirit of the army and demoralized the home front. A search for scapegoats ensued. The war was now
said to drag on only because Jews like Rathenau and Ballin had not yet
amassed enough money. The War Ministry was flooded with complaints about Jewish draft dodgers. Ludwig III, the king of Bavaria, held
back his approval of Richard Willstätter, Haber's collaborator on the gas
project, for a professorship at the University of Munich. On September
4, 1916, after repeated proddings by his minister of education, the king
finally gave in, although not before warning the minister: "This is the
last time I agree to the appointment of a Jew." It was indeed the last,
Willstätter noted in his memoirs.[82]

In October 1916, when almost three thousand Jews had already died
on the battlefield and more than seven thousand had been decorated,
War Minister Wild von Hohenborn saw fit to sanction the growing prejudices. He ordered a "Jew census" in the army to determine the actual
number of Jews on the front lines as opposed to those serving in the
rear. Ignoring protests in the Reichstag and the press, he proceeded
with his head count. The results were not made public, ostensibly to
"spare Jewish feelings." The truth was that the census disproved the
accusations: 80 percent served on the front lines.[83]

The Jew census had a devastating effect on German Jews, generating an unprecedented moral crisis among those on the front line. An
artillery captain named Georg Meyer, in civilian life an accountant with
Siemens in Berlin, felt as though he had been given a terrible slap in
the face. "Now," he wrote, "I must endure it."[84] Two months later

Meyer fell outside Verdun, one of twelve thousand Jews who gave their lives for Germany during the war.

Ernst Simon's reaction was even stronger. In 1914, Simon had fully shared the "intoxicating joy" of going to war. The Jew census turned this "de-Judaized aesthete," as he described himself, into a confirmed Zionist. The census was a "betrayal"; its popularity within the army horrified Simon. The dream of community was gone. In one horrendous blow, the census reopened the deep chasm that "could not be bridged by common language, work, civilization, and custom."[85]

Simon's reaction was particularly emphatic, and his conversion to Zionism was a relatively isolated event. Most Jewish soldiers, like Julius Marx, a young frontline volunteer, felt anger and frustration but did not sever their ties with their native country as Simon did after the war. In his diary, though, Marx recorded an infuriating exchange with his company commander:

A while back I was summoned to see the company commander. A questionnaire was lying on the table.

"Reporting!"

"I have to take down your particulars," he said.

"Might I ask, Lieutenant, what for?"

"Yes, well . . . the Ministry of War . . . someone suggested to the minister . . . they want to know how many Jews are serving on the front . . ."

"And how many are behind the lines!? What kind of nonsense is this! What do they want to do? Demote us to second-class soldiers and make us look ridiculous in the eyes of the entire army? They subject us to all kinds of harassment, refuse to promote us, and then wax indignant if they catch someone watching the war from the rear."

"You're absolutely right, but there's nothing I can do about it. So, what's your date of birth?"

"Damn it to hell! So that's why we're risking our necks for this country?"[86]

The banker Max Warburg failed to convince the War Ministry to make the results of the census public. Instead, the ministry leaked some of its findings to a well-known anti-Semitic rabble-rouser, who then published two distorted papers on it. When, in the aftermath of the census, the Federation of Jews in France accused the German government of anti-Semitism, the government asked the kaiser's "friend" James Simon to counter the charge. Simon refused. He wrote Secretary of State Arthur Zimmermann that visible steps to end the prevailing discrimination would be more effective than denials.[87] The early warmonger Arnold Zweig decided after the census that he would rather be a prisoner of war than a German soldier. He published a macabre short story in *Die Schaubühne* called "Census at Verdun," in which the ghosts of the dead are summoned from their graves to complete the War Ministry's questionnaire.

The census also produced an avalanche of Jewish apologetics. Rabbis and other spokesmen fell over one another to proclaim that they were as patriotic as—or more than—the next German. In this spectacle of offended innocence, the speech of Jewish Reichstag deputy Ludwig Haas was refreshingly candid. Conceding that Jews might have been less than eager to serve in the war, he argued that their reluctance was the fault of generations of non-Jews who had oppressed them for centuries. Haas cited Franz Grillparzer: "We cripple them and complain that they limp."[88]

Only two years earlier, Nahum Goldmann had hailed the glories of Prussian militarists and their wonderful war. Now he wrote (under a pseudonym) in Buber's new pro-Zionist magazine, *Der Jude,* that Jews had nothing to do with this war; its origins, its aims, its content were totally alien to them. It was taking place outside their sphere.

By September 1918, even Ludendorff and other war enthusiasts felt that Germany's defeat was inevitable. The country, impoverished and exhausted, was on the verge of collapse. The inevitable result of four years of misery and bloodshed—five million Germans dead, two million orphans, one million invalids, one million widows—was the revolution of 1918. It began as a revolution from above. The popular Prince Max von Baden was hastily appointed chancellor. He instituted drastic constitutional reforms designed to save the monarchy. Germany was to became a constitutional monarchy like England, at least in theory. It was too late. A revolution from below was mounting everywhere. Dramatic upheavals followed in quick succession: soldiers deserted their units or mutinied; workers went on strike, marching through the streets, waving red flags, crying for peace; embittered soldiers and striking workers formed independent councils to promote direct democracy. Bertolt Brecht said that if indeed the soldiers had gone to war carrying Goethe's *Faust,* the book was gone from the knapsacks of those who came back.

The uprisings defied Lenin's adage that German revolutionaries would never occupy a railway station without first buying tickets. They were entirely spontaneous. Other than in Munich, the revolution had no leaders and no organization. On November 5, the navy mutinied in Kiel, refusing orders to attack British warships. The mutiny quickly spread. On November 7, it hit Bremen, Hamburg, Wilhelmshaven, and Hanover. On the eighth, it reached Berlin, Frankfurt, Cologne, Munich, and Leipzig. It met with no resistance. Nearly everywhere, striking workers and war veterans, in and out of uniform, joined the demonstrations. They called for peace and direct democracy. The Social Democratic leaders were taken completely by surprise. They quickly moved to "adopt" the revolution, the better to be able, as it turned out, to crush it later on in collaboration with the military establishment.

Before its total demise, the old regime nominated the Social Democratic leader Friedrich Ebert as chancellor. The regime and the party were working in tandem to prevent the thing both feared most: a Communist takeover, as in Russia. Ebert was well suited to his task. He worshiped order and authority and detested public disturbances, famously declaring, "I hate social revolution like sin." But the monarchy that had nominated him for his position could no longer be saved, not even by the socialists. Max von Baden urged the kaiser to abdicate in favor of his son. The kaiser refused to step down for the sake, as he put it, "of a few hundred Jews and a thousand workers."[89] He was not the only one obsessed with alleged Jewish plots: the British army, he felt sure, would come to his rescue to crush the danger of Bolshevism in Germany. When it didn't, the kaiser fled Berlin, where he no longer felt safe. He

In five days, the revolution spread throughout Germany.

spent a few idle days and nights in his sleeping car on a railway siding outside the supreme army headquarters at Spa, a small Belgian town. The generals confronted him with a bitter choice: either abdicate or go to the front as a regimental commander and meet an "honorable end" with his troops. He would hear of neither. When the army declined to guarantee him the safety that, as Maximilian Harden observed, "millions had lived without for four years," he escaped to Holland on November 10.[90] There he formally announced his abdication. Ludendorff, using a false name, fled to Sweden.

The great edifice of the old Reich collapsed almost by itself. Without the firing of a single shot, more than two dozen ancient dynasties—including the Hohenzollern—disappeared overnight, to be replaced by hastily assembled republican governments. German Jews figured prominently in the new federal and regional governments, running the affairs of state at the highest positions of authority. They "sat at Bismarck's desk," having been appointed and then elected prime ministers of Prussia, Saxony, and Bavaria. Ebert headed a provisional federal government of six ministers—three Social Democrats and three former Social Democrats who had split from the party in protest over its war policy. Two were Jews, Hugo Haase and Otto Landsberg, a conservative Social Democrat of whom it was said that the only red thing about him was his beard.

The kaiser's friend Albert Ballin was shattered by the downfall of his benefactor. On the day the kaiser fled Germany, Ballin died from an overdose of sleeping pills, a suicide, according to Theodor Wolff and others. The kaiser now claimed that he should have appointed Ballin chancellor instead of Bethmann-Hollweg, that Ballin would have avoided the conflict with England and prevented the war.[91] Another *Kaiserjude*, the coal magnate Eduard Arnhold, offered the exiled kaiser financial aid and placed his villa on the Wannsee at the disposal of the former crown prince, whose residence on Unter den Linden had been seized by the republican government.

Ludendorff, Hindenburg, and other high-ranking officers wished above all to save the army. At their urging, the republican government accepted the terms of a humiliating armistice. The republicans should have compelled the generals to assume responsibility for this step; instead, they readily took it upon themselves—with disastrous political consequences later on. Rathenau, meanwhile, performed another volte-face. He was so upset by the Allied armistice terms, issued on a take-it-or-leave-it basis, he briefly rejoined the war party. He recommended a last-minute *"levée en masse,"* as he put it, an uprising by armed civilian militias to oppose the Allied forces. Not even the army high command believed that this was feasible.

In Berlin, the kaiser's portraits came down from the walls. The palace was ransacked by mutinous marines. Harry Kessler walked through the hideous clutter of tasteless *objets* in the empress's private rooms, past armoires larger than any calculation of use could have required, stuffed with kitschy plates, trinkets, souvenirs, and other knickknacks. Kessler felt no anger at the looters; he was merely astonished at the mediocrity of the august personalities who had favored this trash. "Out of this atmosphere was born the World War," he noted in his diary the next day. "I feel no sympathy, only aversion and complicity when I reflect that this world was not done away with long ago, but on the contrary still continues to exist, in somewhat different forms, elsewhere.[92]

Theodor Wolff, too, sensed a need to point an accusing finger at those responsible for the general disaster—not just Kaiser William but the social structures that had benefited from the old regime. The republic was declared from a window of the Reichstag on November 9, 1918. Wolff's editorial in the *Berliner Tageblatt* ended with the following sentences:

> William II was not the sole author of an insanely shortsighted policy that misinterpreted all the forces and ideas prevalent in foreign countries; he was the symbol of an era and of a social spirit that in its arrogance and thirst for power brought about the disaster. He would have had to abdicate even if the rebellions all over the country had not been so fervent and indomitable, as none had expected. Those who hailed him in 1914 when he promised them "wonderful times" and a most brilliant victory must reproach themselves.

Wolff was a liberal conservative, not a revolutionary. Yet he welcomed the upheaval as perhaps "the greatest of all revolutions," claiming that "no other Bastille so solidly built has ever been overthrown in a single blow." Wolff wished the uprising to emulate the English revolution, the "model" of all true upheavals, which had abolished old idols without brutally smashing them and had respected individual rights.[93] A mature and sensible people should now do likewise. Wolff's hyperbole came as a surprise to readers accustomed to his usually cool and careful reasoning. It contained a large component of wishful thinking. Like many others, Wolff failed to see that the revolution had been one more in form than in substance. Too much remained the same: the old bureaucracy continued in place; the army elite remained intact; old attitudes and authoritarian frames of mind prevailed among captains of industry, lawyers, and professors. The new Social Democratic regime had irreparably discredited itself in these groups' eyes by meeting the victors' harsh and humiliating peace terms.

Even Einstein was deluded for a while by what he considered the enormity of the upheaval. "Something great has truly been attained," he enthused in December 1918. "The religion of militarism has disappeared."[94] He felt certain that soon Germans would again be proud of their country, this time with good reason. The physicist Franz Ollendorff, at the time a young student (and later a professor in Israel), remembered a moving scene in January 1919 in a cavernous, unheated Berlin university lecture hall. Einstein, enjoying the reputation of an unblemished pacifist, was at the rostrum facing a room full of pale, excited students in overcoats and ragged gray field uniforms. "None of us felt cold or hunger: was this not the dawn of a new era that had inscribed 'Never Again War' on its banner? And had not this powerful, wonderful breakthrough started right here in Berlin?" Leo Szilard, who later played a leading role in developing the American atom bomb, whispered excitedly in Ollendorff's ear: "One feels that the whole world is changing."[95]

Einstein warned his audience against revolutionary excesses. During the first few weeks of the republic, such excesses were remarkably few. Some angry war veterans ripped off the rank insignias of officers, but that was the worst of it. There were no lynchings and no arrests; political prisoners were freed. The insurgents were wonderfully self-disciplined. According to Theodor Wolff, the revolution was "good-natured," fomented by a "decent and naïve class of men . . . completely devoid of cruel instincts, . . . the revolution of schlemiels." Their motto, he said, could have been "Love your enemies more than yourselves."[96] Violence came almost exclusively from right-wing counterrevolutionaries. Panicked at the prospect of a Bolshevik coup, the new republican regime attempted to end the influence of the soldiers' and workers' councils that had sprung up spontaneously all over Germany. Ebert reassigned German army units to quelling radical resistance to the authority of his provisional government. Shortly after being released from prison by the new republican regime, Rosa Luxemburg, who had played no role in the revolution, was brutally assassinated by fanatical army officers and her body dumped in a canal. Luxemburg had little interest in Jewish problems. In a letter from prison on February 16, 1917, she wrote her friend Mathilde Wurm: "What do you want with these special Jewish pains? I feel as close to the wretched victims of the rubber plantations in Putumayo and the blacks of Africa with whose bodies the Europeans play ball. . . . I have no special corner in my heart for the ghetto: I am at home in the entire world, where there are clouds and birds and human tears." In the eyes of her murderers she embodied the mythical threat of what was called "Jewish Bolshevism." As a woman, a socialist, and a Polish Jew, she was a triple outsider. For this reason, historians have claimed that her murder was a foretaste of the horrors to come.

The soldiers' councils, mostly composed of common soldiers, featured a disproportionate number of Jews. The reason was simple: there were relatively few Jewish army officers and, among the lower ranks, Jews were generally better educated than others. They naturally attracted attention as public speakers. Their predominance in the councils and the quick appointment of a number of Jewish liberals and Social Democrats as ministers and state secretaries provided grist for the mills of conservatives and anti-Semites. The visibility of Jews on the soldiers' councils gave rise not only to the legend that the revolution was part of a worldwide Jewish conspiracy but also to the assertion that Germany had lost the war only because the Jews had "stabbed it in the back." Ludendorff, the reckless general whose miscalculations were directly responsible for the defeat, invented the "stab in the back" legend, though for the moment he only mooted the idea in private circles. The first prominent German to allude to it publicly was in fact Friedrich Ebert. On November 11, 1918, the day the armistice went into effect, Ebert had greeted the returning troops at the Brandenburg Gate. "We are pleased to welcome you to the homeland," he said. "No enemy has been able to vanquish you." Wittingly or not, Ebert lent credence to the "stab in the back" legend. As the historian Saul Friedländer has pointed out, that day "the seed for the Second World War was sown."[97]

NOWHERE were Jewish revolutionaries so visible and prominent as they were in Bavaria. Their number included a few ruthless fanatics and many politically inexperienced dreamers, abstract philosophers, good-natured anarchists, and unworldly poets—and some very able, humane politicians. Foremost among the latter was Kurt Eisner. A genuine leader, perhaps the only one the revolution produced, he was appointed prime minister of a new Republic of Bavaria and dominated the local scene until his assassination in February 1919. Other prominent Jews were the Expressionist poets Ernst Toller and Erich Mühsam; the literary critic and philosopher Gustav Landauer, author of a major work on Shakespeare; the Communists Erich and Rosa Levine, Touvia Axelrod, and Frida Friedjung. "My Germanness and my Jewishness . . . are like two brothers equally loved by the same mother," Mühsam wrote. "I delight in their intimate closeness."[98] After the Second World War, some of these men and women were worshiped in Germany as heroes and fighters for freedom and social justice; in their time, they caused widespread panic among the settled bourgeoisie. Conservatives saw them as so many Dantons and Robespierres. Anti-Semites reviled them as "Jew pigs" and Russian agents.

The fire had spread to Bavaria early. Hours after the November 5 mutiny in Kiel, Eisner went into action. Thousands of factory workers were ready to follow his call. Unlike in the rest of Germany, in Bavaria many peasants, disgruntled by government requisitioning of farm produce, joined in as well. A Berlin-born minor theater critic and journalist before the war, Eisner had resigned from the Social Democratic Party in 1916 in protest against its prowar policy. Early in 1918, he had organized a strike in several machine-gun factories in Munich, for which he was imprisoned without trial. Released from prison three weeks before the Kiel mutiny, he roused fifty thousand workers to strike in Munich on November 9, 1918, to protest the war. That afternoon they attended a rally on the Theresienwiese (site of the traditional October *Bierfest*). There were no red flags in evidence, except among a small group of mutinying soldiers. The main speaker was Kurt Eisner. He called for immediate peace and the abolition of the monarchy. Stormy applause greeted his speech. Together with the veteran Bavarian peasant leader Ludwig Gangdorfer, Eisner then led a procession to the army barracks in the northern outskirts of Munich, where thousands of soldiers disobeyed their officers and joined the march to the city center. By evening all government buildings, the Bavarian royal palace, and most army barracks were in the hands of the insurgents. Armed soldiers patrolled the streets of the inner city on the insurgents' behalf. The Bavarian king fled; not a single shot had been fired. That night Eisner consolidated his leadership by convoking a "revolutionary parliament." It met in one of the large beer halls and included soldiers, workers, and peasants. A Bavarian republic was declared, and Eisner was appointed prime minister of a provisional government. Until that point, the Bavarian Social Democrats had been careful to keep a certain distance; now they jumped on Eisner's bandwagon, joining his cabinet. Eisner's republican coup, which he seems to have prepared for days or even weeks, electrified the rest of Germany. He had been the first to oust a German monarch.

In Munich, the new republic was celebrated at the National Theater. Bruno Walter conducted the *Leonore* Overture, after which Eisner spoke, drawing parallels between recent events and the movements of Beethoven's music. Eisner was cheered as he walked through the narrow streets of the inner city. In a workers' district, Lion Feuchtwanger witnessed an elderly man urging his fellow metalworkers to pray for "our Eisner." Eisner was an unlikely local hero: not only was he not Bavarian, he was a Jew, or, as his enemies would soon say, a Jew pig from Galicia in the pay of the Russian government. A short, slim man in his early forties who let his hair grow long behind a bald, professorial forehead and dressed in baggy pants and crumpled jackets, he was the picture of an intellectual. His rimless pince-nez rode precariously on his nose, apt at any moment to fall and interrupt his speeches. "We are the dreamers, the idealists, the poets," he said on one occasion, "while the others are calculating and clever. . . . But for four and a half years, we idealists and dreamers were not mistaken, while the others, the sober judges of fact, now admit that they spent four and a half years deceiving themselves."[99]

This was not entirely true. In August 1914, Eisner had also believed in Germany's innocence; he had hailed the "kaiser of peace" and supported the Social Democrats' vote in the Reichstag in favor of war. But he soon realized his mistake. By 1915, he blamed Germany for the war, pointing to the kaiser's hectoring style of diplomacy and observing that anyone who seriously followed German policy over the past decade knew that the current conflagration was strictly a "German-made world war."[100]

Eisner's measures to establish a democratic socialist regime ("neither Bolshevik nor bourgeois") seemed at first to be welcomed by many both in Munich and in the conservative, Catholic countryside. The old government apparatus cooperated with his regime. The welcome was a fleeting response and would not last. Eisner's principled federalism, his desire to retain Bavarian state rights vis-à-vis the centralist Social Democrats of Berlin—even to the point of seceding from the Reich—met with considerable support. Unlike Ebert, Eisner believed that a clean break with the past was essential. By acknowledging German guilt, Eisner may have hoped to extract better terms for Bavaria in the forthcoming reparations negotiations, but he genuinely believed that there needed to be a similar confession from other German states as well. The new Germany had to distance itself from the iniquities of the vanquished old, he felt. Eisner called on the Western powers to put their faith in the German people, who, he said, were seriously determined to live in a new spirit: "The people are innocent of the crimes of the past. Their only guilt is to have allowed lies to lead them astray. Today we are free, and because we are free we can speak the truth. For this reason we can also demand to be treated humanely."[101]

When Eisner's aides found incriminating documents in the Bavarian state archive that shed light on Germany's role in provoking the war—proof that it had actively encouraged Austrian intransigence—he promptly made these findings public. The revelations infuriated the new central government in Berlin. Ebert considered them inconvenient; conservatives and anti-Semites saw them as treasonous. Eisner dismissed Berlin's fears. The Bavarian representative in Berlin wrote Eisner that Ebert was unimaginative and narrow-minded.[102] At one point, Eisner even broke off "diplomatic relations" with the capital.

The propaganda assaults on Eisner's Bavarian "Jewish republic" grew steadily. Victor Klemperer, who never met Eisner, was nevertheless taken aback by his more utopian collaborators. After attending several mass meetings in Munich, he decided they were "schmucks, lit-terateurs, windbags, swindlers, cowards! What on earth do they mean when they say that people must give up their money, collaborate, sub-mit?"[103] The wealthier among the Munich Jewish bourgeoisie com-plained that Eisner was discrediting the entire community. A local Jewish notable, Josef Mayer, wrote Eisner to demand that he resign for tactical reasons. Eisner wrote back, a little too caustically perhaps, deploring Mayer's request:

> I didn't become prime minister of Bavaria for the pleasure of it. I will bless the day I no longer hold that office. But I am the creator and rep-resentative of this movement, this most wonderful movement of libera-tion, and therefore it is my duty to persevere as a living symbol. I have greater concerns than would permit me to waste so much as a minute brooding about questions of tact from a bygone era.[104]

Eisner remained consistent in his view that Germany had played a cen-tral role in provoking the war. In a talk he gave at an international socialist congress in Switzerland, he spoke of Germany's obligation to help rebuild the ruined war zones in northern France, infuriating his enemies even more. From this point on, he was accompanied by a bodyguard wherever he went.

The hate campaign against Eisner was bound to end in violence. In February, fighting broke out in the countryside over Bavaria's resistance to federal hegemony. On February 21, 1919, as Eisner walked to the newly elected Bavarian diet to announce his resignation, he was shot and killed. The gunman, who had come up from behind, was a young ultranationalist aristocrat by the name of Anton Arco-Valley who had recently been thrown out of a proto-Nazi organization for having con-cealed the fact that his mother was Jewish. The young count was said to have wanted to prove that "even a half Jew was capable of a heroic act."[105] Arco-Valley was tried for murder and sentenced to death. Less than twenty-four hours later, the sentence was commuted to ten years in prison. The state prosecutor himself recognized the murderer's motive as "true, deeply rooted love of the fatherland." If only more young men were animated by such love, he said, "we would be able to view our future more hopefully." In the end, Arco-Valley spent only five years in the comfortable confinement furnished especially for him, as a gentleman delinquent, at a former citadel.

The assassination caused widespread shock. Mourners in the tens of thousands attended Eisner's funeral. City people, peasants, and rough-looking mountain folk in green striped coats and leather pants joined to grieve for the murdered Berlin Jew who they felt had understood them so well.[106] Then anarchy broke out. Armed men roamed the streets, shooting, looting, beating, and attacking innocent bystanders. Strikes and counterstrikes erupted all over Bavaria. Wild rumors flourished. As soon as he heard of the murder, Alois Lindner, a young butcher's apprentice and member of a marginal Marxist organization, assumed that Eisner had been killed by the Social Democrats. He rushed to the parliament building and shot Eisner's Social Democratic minister of the interior, Erhard Auer, just as he was about to eulogize the dead prime minister. Panic ensued. Bavaria was without a government. Of the two central figures in the outgoing government, Eisner was dead and Auer was seriously wounded. Of the remaining six ministers, four were in hiding or had fled the city and could not be reached.

Eisner's coalition government had successfully maintained public order. After his death, order was never properly restored. The power vacuum was filled by an assortment of more or less chaotic left-wing figures, many of whom Eisner had distrusted. All invoked Eisner's name, hailing him as the great martyr of the revolution. After weeks of negotiations a new Social Democratic government was formed, but it lasted only very briefly. Next the First Soviet Bavarian Republic was declared. Gustav Landauer, "minister of public enlightenment" in this government, and Erich Mühsam drafted its manifesto, promising a new era of peace and humane concern. At Landauer's suggestion, the Soviet Republic was inaugurated by church bells pealing all over Bavaria. Mühsam seemed even more unworldly than Landauer: "I am a pilgrim without a destination / I sense the smoke but see no conflagration," he wrote.[107] It is difficult to conceive of two more saintly, unpolitical, and inept men who combined naïveté and personal integrity to such a remarkable degree. A religious anarchist opposed to all violence at a time when violence increased incrementally every day, Landauer preached an ethical and religiously inspired socialism, postulating "an ideal community without capitalism and without coercion." Asked whether he was a German Jew or a Jewish German, he answered with a slightly pained smile that he was, and would always remain, both.[108]

The Social Democrats were not alone in opposing the new Soviet Republic. The Communists disdained it as the creation of Anarchists. It lasted less than a week, long enough for Landauer to be marked for death by rightists and anti-Semites. Mühsam was arrested by the Social Democratic countergovernment set up in nearby Bamberg. On April 14, amid more turmoil and more casualties, the Russian-born Communist Eugen Levine declared the Second Soviet Bavarian Republic. Under Levine, the first "antirevolutionaries" were arrested; ten were shot. The end came in early May. Right-wing paramilitary White Guards sanctioned by the central government arrived on the scene, joining forces with federal troops sent by the Berlin government.* A terrible bloodbath ensued. Jews fought on both sides. The poet Ernst Toller, having helped to depose Levine, commanded the Bavarian "Red Army" confronting the White Guards outside Dachau. Among those who served in the White Guards and were wounded in action was the future Berkeley and Princeton historian Ernst H. Kantorowicz.† Landauer was arrested by government troops and beaten to death in a prison courtyard. (There had, however, to be *Ordnung*: one of the killers was tried

---

*By tolerating and even sponsoring the paramilitary White Guards, the Social Democratic central government in Berlin inadvertently prepared the ground for the destruction of democracy and of the Social Democratic party itself.

†The son of a Jewish professional, Kantorowicz fought alongside future Nazi hoodlums who, thirteen years later, would seize power and expel him and his family. (Later a prominent medievalist, he would write a celebrated biography of the Holy Roman emporer Frederick II, which Hermann Göring would proudly present to Mussolini as a model of German historiography.) During the McCarthy hearings, Kantorowicz would assure his inquisitors that he was not a Communist. To prove it, he would add: "I have twice volunteered to fight actively, with rifle and gun, the left-wing radicals in Germany; but I know also that by joining the white battalions I have prepared, if indirectly and against my intention, the road leading to National Socialism and its rise to power."

in disciplinary court and punished for pocketing Landauer's cigarette lighter.) Levine was executed. Toller (who later committed suicide) and Mühsam (later killed in a Nazi concentration camp) received prison sentences. In jail, the warden asked Mühsam his religion. "None of your business," Mühsam replied. The warden turned to his clerk: "In that case, write 'Jewish.'"

THE war had materially impoverished and morally confounded millions. The existential panic it left behind corrupted ethical standards, eroded manners, convulsed culture, and polarized society. The liberals were weak and, except for the first months of the republic, dispirited. The bureaucracy remained pro-monarchist and authoritarian at heart. The conservatives despised the new republican regime. The Communists strove to overthrow it. The Social Democrats were disoriented; their leaders, for the most part, were mediocre, provincial, unimaginative men lacking in courage and moral seriousness. The historian Friedrich Meinecke foresaw that they were unfit to govern effectively. The Jews among them, he claimed, were too "soft and sentimental," the others not intelligent enough. The former needed a shot of "iron" in their bloodstreams, the latter a shot of "brains."[109]

The victors in World War I were singularly shortsighted and ungenerous—as victors often are after long wars. They did little to lend the republic either stability or strength; on the contrary, they hobbled and weakened the new republican system. The imposed indemnity of 230 billion gold marks (later reduced to 132 billion) was crushing and led to hyperinflation; the surrender of 13 percent of German territory in Europe and all German colonies overseas was both painful and degrading. The victors, of course, were only emulating Germany's example: the penalties imposed on France in 1870 and on Russia in 1917 had been equally crushing.

The revolution of 1918—the word would soon seem a misnomer— fused old myths with deadly new ones. In addition to "polluting" Germanic culture, Jews were now blamed for the military defeat and considered part of a worldwide Bolshevik conspiracy to undermine Western civilization. Hitler did not have to invent these myths:

by the summer of 1919 they were already in place. Karl Kraus had them in mind in *The Last Days of Mankind* when he wrote the prophetic words "[The Germans] will have forgotten that they lost the war, forgotten that they started it, forgotten that they waged it. For this reason it will not end."[110]

10

The End

The Weimar Republic, named for the city where its constitution was adopted in 1919, began in a flurry of hope. Despite turmoil and uncertainty, it was a showpiece of intense creativity until the very end. Arts, sciences, and advanced thought flowered as never before and as nowhere else in modern Europe. In literature, music, film, theater, and design, Weimar evoked a marvelous sense of the new, the vanguard admired to this day. It was called a "republic without republicans" though this was a gross exaggeration at the time. In the first general elections for the new national assembly, the three main republican parties won 75 percent of the vote, the conservatives only 10 percent. There were many republicans, especially during the first few years, and a sizable number even at the end—and yet, after 1920, never enough. In Alfred Döblin's words, Weimar was a republic without proper "instructions for use."[1]

From the first, in fact, the new regime was mercilessly under attack, despised and derided by political extremists on both the left and the right. While in the 1919 elections the middle class voted overwhelmingly republican, after the hyperinflation of 1922 wiped out savings, it moved to the right and even the far right, which decried "Jewish capitalism" and plotted the destruction of the republic. That the rightists identified the Weimar Republic with Jews was no accident. Jews were among its most ardent supporters.

One of the mainstays of the republic during its first two years, the newly founded Deutsche Demokratische Partei (DDP), or German Democratic Party, was the brainchild of Theodor Wolff, editor of the *Berliner Tageblatt*. During the war, Wolff had been one of the few to keep a cool head, rarely using the term *national* except ironically, something in which he could now take pride. The new party was not socialist but called for agrarian reform, progressive taxes, the breakup of the estates of the landed gentry, and other far-reaching political and social reforms. It was founded in Wolff's office early in November 1918, a few days after the declaration of the republic. Albert Einstein, Walther Rathenau, the historian Hans Delbrück, the lawyer Hugo Preuss, and the sociologist Max Weber, along with fifty-seven other democratically minded academics and businessmen, publicly endorsed its platform. Under the monarchy, many of these men had been unwilling or (like Rathenau and Preuss) unable as Jews to participate in political life. In the first days of the republic, opportunists of all political shades, including tycoons of the former war industry, were eager to jump on the DDP's bandwagon. Wolff quipped that he felt like Noah: "Everybody wants to crowd into the ark and I keep having to say, 'Sorry, there's no room.'"[2] With 18 percent of the popular vote, the DDP became the third-largest party in the republican Reichstag. As minister of the interior in the new central government, Preuss drafted the republican constitution, which he hoped would serve the highest ideals of humanism.

Goethe's Weimar, the capital of *Bildung*, was a fitting setting for its adoption. Here, in February 1919, the new Reichstag convened in the pretty little court theater; the atmosphere was almost one of a Sunday matinee, cozily provincial and respectable. The deputies were seated in green silk orchestra seats and carved theater boxes painted gold and white, behind curtains that could be drawn for greater privacy. Where the great bard had once supervised the program, Preuss and his colleagues held forth on the separation of powers and the rights of men.

The cabinet (a coalition of Social Democrats, Catholic centrists, and representatives of the DDP) met backstage in the gloomy Gothic set left from a recent performance of *Lohengrin*.

The unusual location had been chosen mainly for reasons of security and of image. Berlin was still in turmoil and was not considered safe enough. The founders also wished to emphasize their link with bourgeois *Kultur* rather than Prussian military swagger. Weimar was the city not only of Goethe but of Schiller, Herder, Cranach, Liszt, Wieland, and Nietzsche. Here were the monuments, museums, schools, and archives of the greats. The "petit bourgeois character of the revolution becomes plainly visible," Harry Kessler noted in his diary. "Danton or Bismarck would seem monstrous apparitions in these dainty surroundings. . . . The representatives of all parties, with but few exceptions, belong to the lower middle class," he added. Their pants were not striped and had not been ironed quite as carefully as he would perhaps have wished. Preuss droned on endlessly, according to Kessler, his speech "tedious, colorless, spiritless," with "not a trace of the greatness appropriate to this historic moment." After an hour Kessler fell asleep and, upon waking, left. A popular cabaret had arrived in town to entertain the deputies. It "very aptly meets [their] intellectual demands," Kessler noted condescendingly.[3] Not a word on the constitution's fatal

Two Jews figured prominently in the first republican German cabinet after the revolution: Otto Landsberg (minister of justice, fifth from the left) and Hugo Preuss (minister of the interior, tenth from the left). Preuss drafted the Weimar constitution. *By permission of the Landsarchiv, Landesbildstelle, Berlin*

flaw, article 48, which enabled the president to rule by decree: in 1933, it would help Hitler legitimize his assumption of dictatorial powers in the eyes of a traditionally law-abiding people.

IN the new Germany, Jews were finally equal not only in theory but in practice. Along with millions of liberals and Social Democrats, they welcomed the republic as a hopeful fresh start. More than a century after the official emancipation, Judaism was put on the same footing as other faiths. Secularism continued to spread. On the eve of his emigration to Palestine, the budding cabala scholar Gershom Scholem confessed in his diary: "The Jewish religion is not mine." While Jews had long been prominent in the arts and the professions far beyond their numbers they had been by and large excluded from positions in government and in the upper ranks of the judiciary and public administration. Such barriers, for the most part, now fell. Politically, Jews were no longer outsiders. Twenty-four Jews were elected deputies to the Reichstag. They were also prominent in most state governments, and between 1919 and 1924, no fewer than six served as senior cabinet ministers in the central government.

German universities also finally opened up their faculties at all levels, thus enormously enriching the world of learning. More than ever before, men and women of talent and drive were able to overcome ancient barriers of class, religion, and ethnicity. Freud won the coveted Goethe Prize of the city of Frankfurt and said it was the high point of his civic life. Much of what is remembered and admired today as the golden age of Weimar culture was created by German Jews, from Einstein's theory of relativity to Schoenberg's atonal music, Freud's and Adler's psychoanalysis, Magnus Hirschfeld's research on sexuality, Ernst Cassirer's neo-Kantian and Edmund Husserl's phenomenological philosophy, Expressionist poetry, Kurt Weill's *Threepenny Opera*, and Max Reinhardt's New Theater. The Germanness of these innovators was neither an expression of self-denial nor an effort to disguise their Jewish origins but rather, according to Peter Gay, part of "a proprietarian feeling for a civilization that had produced decent cosmopolitans like Schiller and Kant, ornaments to humanism like Goethe" and that was now making a serious effort to become a pluralist democracy.[4] In a fit of bad conscience, perhaps over their jingoism during the first months of the Great War, Jewish intellectuals worked overtime for the causes of cosmopolitanism, republicanism, democracy, peace, and the multicultural society. They were patriots in the best sense of the word; love of country never blinded them to its failings.

Berlin, despite its political instability, was the epicenter of Weimar culture, a city unlike any other in Europe at the time, vibrant with sex and intellect. In the midst of great political and social disorder, Berlin was the crucible for every conceivable innovation in film, theater, poetry, painting, science, education, city planning, music, architecture, photography, radio, and journalism. "The restless age and the restless Jew," in the historian George Mosse's words, "incarnated a desperate modernity."[5] Else Lasker-Schüler established herself as the high priestess of German Expressionism. Of the five or six leading Expressionist playwrights, three—Franz Werfel, Ernst Toller, and Carl Sternheim— were Jews. Paul Cassirer's avant-garde gallery on the Viktoriastrasse, where before the war Berliners had discovered the French Impressionists, now introduced French Cubists, Italian Futurists, and Russian Constructivists. Discerning German collectors and savants eschewed the opulent grandeur of the fashionable Paris galleries in favor of Cassirer's more austere space (designed for him by the Art Nouveau Belgian architect Henri van der Velde). Writers read their works here in rooms adorned with early Picassos, Kandinskys, and Maleviches. In Berlin, the German Jewish tradition reached its apex; artists and intellectuals strove as never before to transcend nationality and religion. The flower of secular, cosmopolitan Europe sought to exorcise irrationality by trying to comprehend it rationally. After the trauma of a war that, in effect, both the victors and the vanquished had lost, Germany could not have been in more dire need of such an effort.

Einstein was perhaps Berlin's most famous "genius," a term that seems to have deeper resonance in German than in other languages, connoting something almost otherworldly. After Einstein's theory of relativity was confirmed by astronomical observation, he became a national and international celebrity. Between a visit to the former imperial palace and a performance at Reinhardt's theater, tourists would crowd into the university's Auditorium 122 to hear Einstein lecture. The

Arnold Schoenberg. From Schoenberg's atonal music to Einstein's theory of relativity, much of what is remembered today as the golden age of Weimar culture was created by Jews. *Courtesy Leo Baeck Institute, Jerusalem*

government, anxious to restore Germany's reputation as a leading scientific and cultural force, considered Einstein a national asset and was eager to please him. When one of Einstein's seminars was broken up by rioting students yelling *"Juden raus!"* the minister of culture immediately wrote to apologize and express his hope that the rumors of Einstein's planned emigration were groundless. Germany, he insisted, "was, and will forever be, proud to count you, highly honored *Herr Professor,* among the finest ornaments of our science."[6] Einstein had few illusions about the unstable republic but, as far as we know, made no plans to emigrate.

Einstein's informality was proverbial and, in a country of notoriously pompous, self-important professors, this greatly added to his popularity. He charmed all who met him. Photographers, early paparazzi, followed Einstein around, falling over one another with their cameras and lights, photographing the holes in the soles of his shoes. Einstein stuck his tongue out at them and called them *Lichtaffen* (flashbulb monkeys). Society ladies flocked to Berlin's golden-domed grand synagogue on the Oranienburgerstrasse to hear Einstein play Bach on the violin accompanied by the organ. He was also famous for his humor:

> *Looking at the Jews at leisure*
> *Tends to give me little pleasure.*
> *When to others I turn my view*
> *I feel glad I am a Jew.*

Einstein preached pacifism wherever he went. He readily agreed to accompany the Zionist leader Chaim Weizmann on a fund-raising trip to America but nevertheless annoyed him by complaining that the Zionists were overly militant and should make peace with their Arab neighbors. His simplicity and modesty were thoroughly unexpected in so renowned a personage. Harry Kessler, a man with a near-photographic memory, drew in his diary a vivid picture of Einstein explaining the relativity theory. The occasion was a dinner one night in 1922 at Einstein's home; Kessler noted the contrast between the Einsteins and their guests. "This really lovable, almost still childlike couple lent an air of naïveté" to a "typical Berlin dinner party," saving it "from being conventional and transfigur[ing] it with an almost patriarchal and fairy-tale quality." When the other guests left, Einstein and his wife held Kessler back. They sat in a corner and chatted. Kessler admitted that though he sensed the significance of Einstein's theories he did not really understand them. They were simple, Einstein replied. He couldn't see why

Albert Einstein, in the company of friends. Between visiting museums and attending Weill's *Threepenny Opera*, tourists flocked to his lectures, charmed by his humor and informality. Photograph by Erich Salomon. *Courtesy Leo Baeck Institute, Jerusalem*

people were making such a fuss. "When Copernicus dethroned the earth from its position as the focal point of creation, the excitement was understandable," he explained. But his own theory did not really change anything in "humanity's view of things." In essence, it only reemphasized the inextricable links between matter, space, and time. "I must imagine a glass ball with a light at its summit resting on a table," Kessler records Einstein as instructing him:

Flat (two-dimensional) rings or "beetles" move about the surface of the ball. So far a perfectly straightforward notion. The surface of the ball, regarded two-dimensionally, is a *limitless but finite* surface. Consequently the beetles move (two-dimensionally) over a limitless but finite surface. Now I must consider the *shadows* thrown by the beetles on the table, due to the light in the ball. The surface covered by these shadows on the table and its extension in all directions is also, like the surface of the ball, limitless but finite. That is, the number of conic shadows or conic sections caused by the theoretically extended table never exceeds the number of beetles on the ball; and, since this number is finite, so the number of shadows is necessarily finite. Here we have the concept of limitless but finite *surface*.

Now I must substitute three-dimensional concentric glass balls for the two-dimensional beetle shadows. By going through the same imaginative process as before, I shall attain the image of limitless yet finite space (a three-dimensional quality). . . . The significance of his theory . . . is derived from the *connection between matter, space, and time*, proving that none of these exists by itself, but that each is always conditioned by the other two.[7]

Frankfurt was another great center of Weimar learning. Its university, founded after the war, was the only German university where republican professors were not outnumbered by conservatives pining for the old order; its charter outlawed all racial and religious discrimination. At its famed Institute of Social Research German and European sociology flourished. The institute was generously endowed by Hermann Weil, a Jewish grain merchant who after making a fortune in Argentina had returned to his native Frankfurt. Brecht mocked Weil's generosity with an acid-tongued, typically doctrinaire epitaph: "A rich old man

(Weil, the speculator in wheat) dies, disturbed at the poverty in the world; in his will he leaves a large sum to set up an institute which will do research on the source of this poverty, which is, of course, himself."[8]

The institute's leading luminaries were Karl Mannheim, Theodor Adorno, Erich Fromm, Herbert Marcuse, Max Horkheimer, and Walter Benjamin. Gershom Scholem described the group as one of Germany's most remarkable and influential "Jewish sects." Horkheimer, the father of Critical Theory, regarded assimilation and progressive social criti- cism as the two main aspects of Jewish emancipation. Later, reflecting on his colleagues, who had been scattered far and wide by the rise of Nazism, Horkheimer mused that they had all been possessed by a superhuman but, under the circumstances, tragic faith in the per- fectibility of man.

WALTHER Rathenau, formerly a convinced monarchist, warmly wel- comed the republic. Under the old regime, he wrote, Germany had placed too much trust in the authority of "blood and office, . . . the crown, the church, professors, the army general staff, and privy council- lors."[9] He might have added that after the revolution there was too little trust in the new government—on the far left as well as the far right—by church leaders, judges, schoolteachers, university professors, bureau- crats, and militarists. The army's power had been barely dented by the war it had just lost. President Friedrich Ebert, a Social Democrat, him- self confirmed the convenient conviction that the generals had been betrayed by an occult array of treacherous forces on the home front.

Rathenau was appointed minister of reconstruction. "At night I am a Bolshevik," he told the Zionist leader Kurt Blumenfeld, "by day I seek an ethically regulated society."[10] In February 1922, against much oppo- sition and his own mother's strong misgivings, Rathenau agreed to become foreign minister. "I had to accept," he told his mother. "They couldn't find anyone else."[11] As foreign minister, he worked hard to rec- oncile Germany with its former enemies, but his policy of strict com- pliance with the terms of the unpopular Treaty of Versailles infuriated the nationalist right.

Rathenau's mother had reason to fear that he was risking his life. The Catholic politician Mathias Erzberger, who had signed the armistice agreement in November 1918, had been murdered by members of a right-wing terrorist militia. The same militia declared Rathenau Public Enemy No. 1. The police urged Rathenau to accept bodyguards. Rathenau refused—the very suggestion offended him. The Zionists were scandalized by Rathenau's readiness to put himself in harm's way; Blumenfeld urged him to resign. He and Einstein visited Rathenau one evening at his palatial home in Grunewald. The three men argued until one in the morning and parted in disagreement. A Jew should not run the foreign affairs of another people, Blumenfeld said. "You see only yourself. You don't realize that every Jew will be held accountable for your actions—and not only in Germany. You have no right to do this!" "Why not?" Rathenau responded. "I am the best man for the job. I am fulfilling my duty to the German people by offering my services. We must break down the barriers the anti-Semites have erected to isolate us."[12] Why couldn't he, Rathenau, do what Disraeli had done in England? He admitted that he would have preferred to sit in Downing Street rather than the Wilhelmstrasse. But he was not an Englishman; he was a German trying to help his country. It was his duty to serve it in this hour of need. He knew that his task would be difficult and perhaps painful. But he had to try.

Rathenau was not the only German Jew in the eye of the storm. A kindred spirit, the Hamburg banker Carl Melchior was one of two Jewish diplomats who had negotiated for less crushing economic terms in the Treaty of Versailles. Although his role in the talks had been purely technical, he was held personally responsible for the outcome. On both sides, the negotiations had been marked by cynicism and dishonesty. Melchior's demeanor was touchingly described by the economist John Maynard Keynes, a member of the British delegation, in his outspoken memoirs. According to Keynes, Melchior was the sole member of the German delegation who "upheld the dignity of defeat" although he harbored few illusions about either the victors or the vanquished, seeing only gloom in the near future:

> Melchior's emotions were towards Germany and the falsehood and humiliation which his own people had brought on themselves, rather than towards us. . . . The breach of promise, the breach of discipline,

the decay of honorable behavior, the betrayal of undertakings by one party and the insincere acceptance by the other of impossible conditions which it was not intended to carry out. . . . Germany almost as guilty to accept what she [knew] she could not fulfill as the allies to impose what they were not entitled to exact. . . . He saw no light anywhere; he expected civilization to grow dim. . . . Dark forces were passing over us.[13]

IF Jews were among the republic's strongest supporters, they were also some of its sharpest critics. They enjoyed their new rights but often saw the new republic's failings more clearly than many others. The Jewish-owned prestige papers—the *Berliner Tageblatt,* the *Frankfurter Zeitung,* and the *Vossische Zeitung*—criticized these shortcomings without ever abandoning hope that the republic would overcome them. In *Mein Kampf* Hitler reserved his most strident invective for the *Judenpresse,* especially the first two of these newpapers, which served a small but influential segment of German readers. Most Germans came increasingly to rely on the nationalist or apolitical papers of the right-wing press tycoons Hugo Stinnes and Alfred Hugenberg.

Kurt Tucholsky typified the more radical Jewish critique. "Owing to bad weather," he observed cynically, "the German revolution took place in music." Germany's most brilliant—and hated—polemicist and satirist, he was aghast at the mediocrity of its leaders and lashed out at them mercilessly. Stick the needle of reason into their bloated rhetoric, he claimed, and what remained would be a heap of bad grammar. He was even more put off by the servility and indifference of his fellow citizens, especially those of the comfortable middle class. "A fat little Berliner who tried to stop a catastrophe with his typewriter," as the writer Erich Kästner described him, he wrote under several pseudonyms for *Die Weltbühne* (The World Stage), a pacifist literary magazine edited by Carl von Ossietzky, a future Nobel Peace Prize laureate. *Die Weltbühne* was leftist but nonpartisan and non-Marxist. Of sixty-eight identifiable *Weltbühne* authors, a third, including Tucholsky, were Jews. Germany was not or not yet a republic, Tucholsky charged, it was a "negative monarchy." The monarch had simply "sneaked out," leaving the country in the lurch. Bad as the old regime had been, the republic lacked the monarchy's instinct for "self-preservation."[14] It badly neglected its most vital interests: the state bureaucracy, army, and judiciary still largely followed the prewar model and were effectively citadels of authoritarianism. The school curriculum continued to glorify war. "The glorification of one human killed in the war means three dead in the next," Tucholsky wrote prophetically.[15] He urged school reform and new teacher-training programs to raise children in the spirit of democracy. Tucholsky ridiculed the Communists for their clumsy doctrinarism: they were philistines who happened to have read Karl Marx, he said. But if he angered the Communists, he drove conservatives and Nazis downright berserk with his biting satires of every patriotic piety:

> *Anthems and flags on every spot*
> *What about Europe? Europe may rot!*[16]

Joseph Goebbels, Hitler's leading propagandist, marked him early on as a particularly dangerous Jewish *Literaturschwein*. Another Nazi, Ludwig Thoma, regretted that no one "thrashed the fellow's face with a riding whip and branded it with a Star of David."

Tucholsky's pieces were published in book form to some acclaim later in the decade. The most aggressive texts, a collection of illustrated pieces entitled *Deutschland, Deutschland über Alles,* criticized and ridiculed the military and the conservative bourgeoisie for their politics, pompousness, and fatuous self-satisfaction. The book included a photomontage of well-known German generals captioned, "Animals looking at you." George Grosz, the merciless portrayer of militarists and bourgeois fat cats, he claimed, had taught him to use his eyes. For all its rhetoric, which many found excessive, the little book is regarded today as a dramatic early warning of things to come.

Tucholsky also fought anti-Semitism. "Nothing can go wrong in this country," he said, "without some monocled face claiming it's the fault of the Jews." Conservative Jews complained that Tucholsky's unrestrained attacks on patriotic icons provoked anti-Semitism, as if there had been none before he began to write. The Zionists never forgave Tucholsky his refusal to identify as a Jewish nationalist. Gershom Scholem, who was never noted for his sense of humor, even called Tucholsky an anti-

Semite. In a hilarious series of satires on an all-too-human Berliner businessman named Wendriner—("Wendriner Cheats on His Wife," "Wendriner Goes Shopping," etc.)—Tucholsky produced the archetype of a philistine, a kind of German Archie Bunker. In Scholem's eyes they were "pitiless naked photos of the Jewish bourgeoisie." And yet Wendriner was in no way typically Jewish, whatever that may mean. Comfortable, mean, self-satisfied, and hypocritical, Wendriner incarnated the oblivious dolt of all faiths and races.*

IN the first elections after the war, the three prorepublican parties together still enjoyed a sizable majority. In subsequent elections, they saw it steadily decline. Social and political tensions mounted. Hundreds of thousands reportedly died of deprivations caused by the lost war; discharged soldiers in rags still wandered from city to city in search of work. Millions were badly disoriented—some became outright savages—by impoverishment and the demoralizing loss of social status caused by hyperinflation. Already at war's end, the mark had lost 40 percent of its prewar value of twenty-five American cents. By 1923, the dollar was worth 4.2 billion paper marks. The fixed-income middle class was annihilated. Invalids selling shoelaces and matches waited in the cold outside luxury restaurants filled with the nouveaux riches and their fur-clad and bejeweled wives. In the 1920 election, the DDP lost half its share, and antirepublican conservatives and nationalists nearly doubled their showing. Rathenau assessed the situation in words almost as bitter as Tucholsky's. There had never been a real revolution, "only a collapse of the old order," Rathenau wrote:

> The doors burst open, the wardens ran away, the captives stood in the courtyard, blinded and unable to move. Had it been a real revolution, the forces and ideas that had brought it into being would have continued to exert their influence. All the people wanted was peace and quiet, . . . which was to be expected: after all, we are a nation that loves order.[17]

---

*Much later, Scholem would direct a similar accusation against Philip Roth for his novel *Portnoy's Complaint*.

Political murders multiplied. Upon hearing that a little-known paci-fist had just been assassinated by uniformed soldiers, Harry Kessler observed that in Germany "politically unpopular" men and women were in greater danger than in the most disreputable of South American republics. Coup d'états mounted by demobilized military officers were a constant danger as well. In Berlin, in April 1920, soldiers of a marine brigade refused to be demobilized, occupied the government district, and appointed one of their own, a man named Kapp, the new German "chancellor." General Hans von Seeckt, the army chief of staff, refused to take action against the mutineers. The legitimate government, mean-while, fled Berlin. The coup collapsed only after the trade unions declared a general strike. No measures were taken against the rebels or against the army general who allowed them a free hand.

Political assassinations were mostly committed by right-wing fanat-ics. The courts tended to be forgiving toward rightist and harsh toward leftist defendants. In a pamphlet entitled *Four Years of Political Murder* (1922), Emil Julius Gimbel, a Heidelberg professor of mathematics, counted 376 political murders since the end of the war: 22 by leftist extremists (who received a total punishment of 248 years in prison), 354 by rightists (who received a total of only 90 years of prison and 730 marks in fines). Among the best-known victims of the rightists were Rosa Luxemburg, the republican cabinet ministers Hugo Haase, Kurt Eisner, and Gustav Landauer, and other Jews. Munich was especially volatile. In the murky aftermath of the Soviet Bavarian government, the newly formed German National Socialist Workers Party (NSDAP) elected a thirty-year-old war veteran named Adolf Hitler as chairman. Hitler was still drifting then. He had no regular job and appealed to his followers mainly with his rhetoric: Versailles was a crime! The Jews had been behind it! According to Golo Mann, anti-Semitism was even more ferocious during the years of hyperinflation between 1919 and 1923 than in 1933, the year Hitler finally came to power.[18]

The NSDAP's platform described Jews as vampires that had to be eliminated from Germany, if possible by legal means but ultimately through violence, deportation, and death. The party was still one of several right-wing splinter groups, active only in Bavaria, and fairly

As foreign minister, Walther Rathenau worked hard to reconcile Germany with her former enemies. Here he is on his way to the foreign ministry a few weeks before his assassination. *Courtesy Leo Baeck Institute, Jerusalem*

insignificant. The provocations of such splinter groups, however, inspired one of the last and most devastating assassinations of the early postwar years.

On June 24, 1922, at about eleven in the morning, Rathenau—still firm in his refusal to accept a bodyguard—left his villa in Berlin and drove to the foreign ministry. He had spent the previous evening with the American ambassador and then had met with a group of business-men at a downtown hotel until 4:00 A.M. At a turn of the wide Königsalle, his car was overtaken by an open vehicle. Several shots from automatic pistols were fired. Rathenau was hit in the chin and spinal cord and died before a doctor arrived.

Public agitation against Rathenau had increased since he had become foreign minister in February. The venerated General Erich Ludendorff, who was back in Germany after fleeing during the revolu-tion and was active in extreme right-wing splinter groups, had sealed Rathenau's fate by insinuating that "the Jewish prince" had sabotaged the war effort. The nationalist-conservative deputy Karl Helfferich had joined the attack on him in the Reichstag while, outside, rioters yelled in chorus:

> *Kill off Walther Rathenau*
> *The greedy goddamn Jewish sow!*

The murder, the 354th political assassination committed by right-wing extremists, shook the republic. The assassins were soon apprehended; they were young veterans, members of the clandestine right-wing terror gang Consul. Throughout his life Rathenau had idolized these blue-eyed, blond Junkers for their courage, manliness, and well-formed bodies. Under different circumstances, he might have counted his assassins among his friends. Though one of the conspirators, Erich von Salomon, later claimed the target had not been a Jew but rather a representative of the hated republic, the symbolic aspect was not limited to an attack on the republic; the assassination symbolized the crisis of assimilation.

Two weeks before the murder, Tucholsky had wondered in *Die Weltbühne* for the umpteenth time, "What does the republic really do for the republic?"[19] As a matter of fact, the republican establishment now recognized the magnitude of the crisis, but its reaction was largely rhetorical. Government posters displayed throughout the capital and major cities announced that the republic was in danger and that quick action had to be taken to save it. Nonetheless, there was widespread rejoicing over the murder. Thomas Mann's young son Golo remembered the "joyful noise we schoolboys made when we learned about [Rathenau's] assassination."[20] In *Die Weltbühne* Tucholsky claimed that "thousands of toasts are being drunk in the beer halls to celebrate the bloody deed."[21] He called on the government to fire any civil servant who conspired against the republic. The nationalist leagues, he said, must be outlawed, the school curriculum thoroughly revised. Rathenau must not have died in vain. It was up to the government to establish a genuine republic at his grave.

The government did little of the sort. No practical steps were taken to curb antirepublican forces within the judiciary, the police, or the state bureaucracy. The universities, too, continued to be infested with militant anti-Semitic student fraternities. A planned memorial service for Rathenau at the University of Berlin had to be canceled—the administration was too frightened of right-wing students. And yet millions took to the streets in mass demonstrations against the murder. In the Reichstag, Chancellor Josef Wirth looked directly at Helfferich, whose personal assaults on Rathenau had come close to calling for his assassination, and shouted, "The enemy is on the right!" Eduard Bernstein, the veteran Social Democrat, called Helfferich a murderer to his face.

Rathenau's coffin was mounted on the speaker's platform under a black canopy. The chancellor led the dead man's elderly mother to a seat in the former kaiser's box, still decorated with a crowned *W*. Although "evidently in full control of herself," she was "pale as wax, and the face behind the veil might have been carved from stone," noted Kessler, who was in the gallery. She stared only at the coffin. The high point of the ceremony, according to Kessler, was when the strains of Wagner's funeral march for Siegfried rose from an invisible orchestra. "The effect was overwhelming. Many of those around me wept. The historic significance of this death echoed from the music in the hearts of those present."[22] The funeral was the largest in German memory. Two million Berliners lined the streets in the rain as the coffin was conveyed from the Reichstag to the Weissensee Jewish cemetery. Rathenau's mother had the last word. She wrote to the mother of one of the murderers ("You poorest of women!") that if her son would confess and repent she would forgive him. "Had he known my son, the noblest of men, rather than shoot him he would have shot himself," she wrote.[23]

Five days later, an attempt on the life of Maximilian Harden, editor of *Die Zukunft*, failed, but Harden was badly injured. He had long maintained that Germany had brought its disasters on itself; only by meticulously fulfilling the hard terms of the Versailles treaty could it convince the Allies to moderate their demands. For this and for being a *Judenschwein*, two hired thugs fell on Harden in the street, beating him with iron bars, pounding his head, clearly intending to kill him. He was saved from the worst by a passerby. The would-be assassins escaped to the offices of the right-wing splinter group that had hired them, reporting that Harden was dead and demanding their fee. Some years earlier, Harden had written: "Freedom is an obsolete Jewish concept." To Kessler, who visited him in the hospital, he said: "Can I live in this country any longer?"[24]

The assailants were soon caught. One was an ex-army lieutenant, now a pimp, the other a young workman who had run away from home after a fight with his family. The man behind the crime was a conservative bookseller who was also caught and confessed. Harden attended their trial, which, with the court's acquiescence, turned into a trial of Harden for his "defeatist" and "pacifist" views. The defendants were linked to Nazi activists in Bavaria, but the court refused to admit evidence on this score; Harden walked out of the courtroom in protest. The men were released after only four years in prison. Harden closed his magazine. Once the kaiser's sharpest critic, he now told Tucholsky that life was much cheaper in the republic than under the monarchy. At least they didn't beat people to death. Now, under a Social Democratic president, they could.

The political thugs, their intellectual counterparts, the feigned objectivity of the courts that tried them, the complicity of judges, police officers, and politicians—all these would later be recognized as harbingers. At the time, few suspected that such thugs might ultimately form a government of outright criminals under the charismatic leadership of a psychopath preaching a religion of violence and death. Among those who did was the novelist Joseph Roth, later renowned for his evocative celebrations of old Austria and the lost world of Eastern European Jewry. Roth was a native of Brody in Austrian Galicia, a city with a large German-speaking Jewish population. After the war Roth became a freelance journalist for the *Frankfurter Zeitung* and the German-language *Prager Tageblatt*. In his novella *The Spider's Web* he portrayed a world in which an assortment of men like those who attacked Harden and assassinated Rathenau prepare to topple a democracy and establish a regime of terror. A gang of cunning, disgruntled war veterans roam the land in search of money and certainty in chaotic times. They fall in with rightwing conspirators and begin to kill not so much out of ideological conviction as out of simple viciousness. Some murder on their own, others on behalf of mysterious but politically powerful men behind the scenes. Hitler, Hindenburg, Ludendorff, and Hugo Stinnes are mentioned by name. One of the protagonists, a demobilized army lieutenant named Theodor Lohse, smells Jews everywhere, especially when he feels inferior.

The novella, written under the impact of Rathenau's assassination, was serialized in a Viennese newspaper between October 12 and November 6, 1923. Two days after the last installment, Hitler and Ludendorff attempted a coup d'état in Munich. Hitler still led only a small faction, one of the many splinter groups on the far right; in Munich, though, he was already a local political factor, with financial support from businessmen, landowners, and church leaders, who considered him a useful counterweight to socialism. The Richard Wagner clan worshiped Hitler. Wagner's son Siegfried considered him a splendid person with a truly German soul. Siegfried's wife, Winifred, was ready to fight for Hitler "like a lioness."[25] Hitler's popular support came from the habitués of Munich's enormous beer cellars, where, since the summer, there had been complaints about inflation and cries of "Let's march on Berlin" and "What kind of country is this anyway, where a beer costs a million marks?" On November 9, Hitler proclaimed the end of the "criminal" government in Berlin and the formation of a new regime headed by him, Ludendorff, and several local notables. He followed this verbal coup with an unsuccessful attempt to seize the seat of the municipal government in the city's historic center. Hitler, Ludendorff, and a few thousand supporters marched through downtown Munich. The police opened fire and sixteen marchers fell. History might have taken a different course had the police taken better aim. In the ensuing trial, *Bavaria v. Adolf Hitler,* the judge sympathized with the defendant, who was permitted to deliver long political speeches from the dock. The sentence (for high treason) was mild: Hitler was confined to comfortable quarters in Landsberg, a citadel renovated to provide deluxe incarceration for right-wing fanatics, where he found the time and peace to write the first volume of *Mein Kampf* and receive his followers. The "war hero" Ludendorff was acquitted. The minimum mandatory punishment for high treason was five years, the maximum a life sentence. Hitler was freed in less than a year. The same judge had shown similar leniency to Anton Arco-Valley, Kurt Eisner's assassin, whose deed, according to the court, reflected "no evil motive but rather true, deeply rooted love of the fatherland."

The judiciary was becoming one of the centers of the conservative counterrevolution. Betty Scholem felt the ground shaking under her feet. She wrote her son Gerhard, who had moved to Jerusalem with a library of some two thousand books: "Anti-Semitism has so badly infiltrated and infected people that you hear them cursing the Jews wherever you go, completely openly and with less inhibition than ever before."[26]

In 1924, the DDP lost even more votes, reducing its representation in the Reichstag to 32 deputies. The nationalists won 103, while the Nazis gained their first 24. As a factor in German politics, the DDP was finished. Even Wolff had long lost faith in it.

German Jews were caught in a vicious circle: the more they embraced the republic, the more it was discredited as a *Judenrepublik*. Popular support for it was declining anyway. The republic was identified not only with the likes of Rosa Luxemburg, Rathenau, Preuss, and other Jews but with the humiliating terms of the Versailles treaty. In short order, every unresolved problem and all the world's evils from the crucifixion of Christ to capitalism, Communism, syphilis, and the lost war were projected onto a tiny minority representing 0.9 percent of the population. The courts offered little protection against ethnic slander, dismissing remarks such as "We don't need a *Judenrepublik*" and "*Pfui Judenrepublik*" as harmless banter. The Supreme Court split hairs in a learned finding that such remarks were legitimate criticism of the "current constitution of the Reich," not an offense against the state as such. In *My Life as German and Jew*, the widely read novelist Jakob Wassermann protested with an anguish no one had expressed publicly since the emancipation:

Vain to adjure the nation of poets and thinkers in the name of its poets and thinkers. Every prejudice one thinks disposed of breeds a thousand others, as carrion breeds maggots. . . . Vain to interject words of reason into their crazy shrieking. They say: He dares to open his mouth? Gag him. Vain to act in exemplary fashion. . . . Vain to seek obscurity. They

say: The coward! He is creeping into hiding, driven by his evil conscience. . . . Vain to help them strip off the chains of slavery. They say:
No doubt he found it profitable . . . Vain to live and die for them. They
say: He is a Jew.[27]

Today Wassermann is remembered mostly for this cri de coeur
rather than for his novels; in his own time he ranked with Thomas
Mann and Hermann Hesse. Mann, in fact, tried to convince Wassermann that the enormous success of his novels was proof enough that
serious anti-Semitism did not exist. This was a little glib. Mann himself
and his wife carefully withheld from their children any information
about her Jewish origins.[28] Wassermann wrote back: "How would you
have felt if people had viewed your upper-class Lübeck background as
grounds for mistrust? In reality you experienced the opposite; you were
respected for it. To this day, however, despite all my successes, despite
all the books I've published, I still run up against the same old wall, the
same ridiculous misgivings; I continue to sense the mysterious backing
off that can cut a person to the
quick and damage his inner
being."[29]

THEN, as had happened so often
in the past, things improved,
even considerably. Successful
currency reform, Allied concessions, sustained economic
growth, the shock provoked by
Rathenau's death led to several
years of republican resurgence.
American loans enabled Germany to meet its heavy reparation payments. Between 1924
and 1928, the number of Nazi
Reichstag deputies dropped to
twelve. After Hitler's release

Jakob Wassermann. *Courtesy Leo Baeck Institute, Jerusalem*

375

from prison, he was hard put to hold together his band of loyal supporters. He quarreled with Ludendorff. The Nazis seemed destined to remain a tiny fringe party.

How little Hitler counted in the public mind is clear from Ernst Feder's extensive political diary. Feder was an engaged citizen, a true representative of the urban Jewish upper middle class, a sensitive man in a sensitive position on the editorial board of the *Berliner Tageblatt*. The editor in charge of domestic affairs, he knew just about everybody in public life and was the confidant of politicians and top civil servants. Feder dictated his diary to his wife every evening. The diary is a unique combination of political gossip and firsthand information, rumor and fact, and reflects opinions on the right and the left. Feder mentions more than a thousand names in politics, the economy, the press, and the arts, names that embodied the Weimar Republic. Significantly, Hitler's name appears for the first time only in September 1930. Before then Feder often refers to anti-Semitism but never to the Nazis. The Nazis, before 1930 on the outer fringe of the political spectrum, were not alone in their vitriol against Jews and Jewish "cultural Bolshevism," a term covering nearly everything modern or merely different: Bauhaus architecture, psychoanalysis, Expressionism, atonal music, or Bruno Walter conducting Beethoven slightly faster than Furtwängler.

Ernst Feder was an engaged Jew. His weekly column in the magazine of the Centralverein reflected the republican resurgence after 1924 and echoed a growing hope that anti-Semitism was a transitory sentiment. He was, after all, living in a civilized country. His friend Gustav Krojanker, in a book entitled *Jews in German Literature,* announced in 1924 that the aversion toward Jews, "if not yet fully overcome, is at least on its way out."[30] In 1926, Krojanker and Feder were in Hamburg when the city unveiled the first and still only public statue of Heine in Germany and the keynote speaker said: "An old wish of many Germans is being fulfilled: alive in books as well as song, much beloved, highly controversial, henceforth indisputably German, incontestably belonging to the whole world."[31] It might have been more auspicious if a major, or even minor, non-Jewish writer had given the speech. In the event, it was Alfred Kerr. Krojanker and Feder were heartened by his words.

Heine, the first prominent Jewish cosmopolite, had been realistic

enough to insist that a true cosmopolitan society was possible only in
Kuckuckshimmel (never-never land). Indeed, Heine's native Rhineland
still refused to honor him publicly. The rector and faculty of the University of Düsseldorf rejected all suggestions that the university be
named after the city's most famous son. In nearby Cologne, most people
still "lived strictly among themselves," the future literary critic Hans
Mayer claimed in his memoirs. The strictly clannish Catholic upper class
welcomed social intercourse with Jews only if they were prominent artists.
The musician Otto Klemperer and the philosopher Max Scheler, recent
converts to Catholicism, "were respected but with some discomfort."
There was something "uncanny" about them. Klemperer practiced his
new religion with demonstrative devotion but when he performed the
Missa Sacra "there were mocking whispers in the audience."[32]

In Berlin and in some of the other university cities, social intermin-
gling was more widespread and growing all the time. Yet even those who
felt integrated retained a measure of insecurity. Emil Ludwig, the biographer, visited London and sought a brief audience with the German
ambassador, who received him immediately but at first did not recognize him. "Do, please, sit down, Herr Ludwig. You are German?" Ludwig suspected a sardonic allusion to his allegedly Jewish looks. He said:
"Yes. I am the author of a Bismarck biography." The ambassador, realiz-
ing his gaffe, threw up his hands and exclaimed: "Oh Lord!" This only
made things worse. Ludwig took the remark as a dismissive comment
on Jews writing books on German patriots and quickly took his leave.[33]

Intermarriage was at an all-time high. In the late twenties, it reached
levels seen only half a century later, in the United States. Informal
liaisons must have been even more frequent. At the University of Marburg, the eighteen-year-old Hannah Arendt had a soulful affair with her
professor, Martin Heidegger, a married man with two children. There
was nothing at the time to suggest Heidegger's eventual allegiance to
Hitler and Nazism. Though their affair was brief, both were marked by
it for the remainder of their lives. Heidegger would go on to claim that
Arendt had been the muse who inspired him to write his masterpiece,
Being and Time. Almost half a century later, Arendt dedicated one of
her books to him with the words "The intimate friend to whom I was
faithful and unfaithful and always through love" but then never sent it

to him. The dedication was found among Arendt's papers after her death.

A parallel renaissance of secular Jewish culture was also in evidence, generated in part by the Zionists to encourage emigration to Palestine and in part by Martin Buber's popular books on Hasidism. But membership in the German Zionist Federation, far from growing, fell drastically; the number of "shekel payers"—contributing the minimum annual amount of one mark—dropped from thirty-three thousand in 1923 to seventeen thousand in 1929, and of those, less than a third actually voted to elect Zionist leaders and functionaries. Many were said to be only halfhearted sympathizers or philanthropists eager to resettle only East European Jews in Palestine. The liberal writer Hugo Spiegler announced the imminent downfall of Zionism.[34] Several new institutes of Jewish adult education, though, worked tirelessly to promote secular or semisecular Jewish culture. The most influential of these was Franz Rosenzweig's Freies Jüdisches Lehrhaus (Free Jewish House of Learning) in Frankfurt, which aspired to "recover" religious and cultural treasures suppressed, lost, or forgotten since the emancipation.[35] Rosenzweig was not a Zionist. He came from an assimilated family for whom Judaism had become as he put it, an "empty purse." On the eve of his own intended baptism, he dramatically reversed his decision to convert and chose instead to become more familiar with the faith he was planning to abandon. His book *The Star of Redemption* became a major text of Reform Judaism in Europe and the United States. Rosenzweig was said to have derived his new theology mainly from Goethe rather than from the sages whom he cited.[36] Hundreds, many of them non-Jews, attended the Lehrhaus's lecture series and seminars. For some, the formula "people of the book" was becoming simply an article of faith.

In the twenties, Weimar Germany was also the epicenter of the modern Hebrew revival. The poets Nachman Bialik and Saul Tchernikhovsky and the novelist Shmuel Josef Agnon, a future Nobel laureate, lived in Germany prior to moving to Palestine. Habimah, a Hebrew-language theater founded in Russia, successfully toured the major German cities. Kafka moved to Berlin and took Hebrew lessons. Walter Benjamin was pained by his inability to speak Hebrew and told Hugo von Hofmannsthal it was the "great gap in his life."[37] The department-store tycoon Salman Schocken, who had revolutionized retailing in Germany, much as Marks and Spencer had in England, established Schocken Books, which, in addition to German texts (it published Kafka's stories), produced excellent German translations of classical Hebrew and Yiddish texts. Schocken remarked that the translations were his "house gifts to Germany."[38]

The burgeoning interest in Hebrew and Jewish culture had little effect on emigration to Palestine. One notable exception was Gershom Scholem; another was Moshe Smoira, a lawyer who packed up the 134 volumes of his Weimar Goethe edition and relocated to become legal adviser to the new Zionist trade unions (and later the first president of the Israeli Supreme Court). The German Zionist Federation's 1912 resolution to make emigration the key tenet of membership (part of one's "life program") had never been taken literally, not even by its advocate, Kurt Blumenfeld; indeed, Blumenfeld bought himself a new house in Berlin shortly before the Nazis came to power. By 1933, less than two thousand German Jews had emigrated to Palestine.[39] Because of their pacifist sentiments, German Zionists proved a "difficult export article" anyway, according to Siegfried Kanowitz, an emigrant who later became a liberal Israeli parliamentarian.[40] With their fine furniture and electric refrigerators (great luxuries at the time), many German Zionists arrived in Palestine unprepared for the harshness of life there. They came, too, with an insistent engagement in human (including Palestinian) rights. In the strident atmosphere of Palestine, their technical and administrative know-how was far more welcome than their political views. The political party they founded criticized the Zionist leadership for failing to reach an agreement with the Palestinians. Berl Katznelson, a Palestinian labor leader of Russian origin, sneered that they worried more about Arab than about Jewish national interests. Soon after Scholem's arrival in Jerusalem, he and other German immigrants joined with Judah Magnes, the American-born chancellor of the new Hebrew University, in founding Brit Shalom, a union of intellectuals lobbying for a Jewish-Arab compromise. Einstein, Blumenfeld, and Buber sympathized with Brit Shalom. Einstein complained that the Zionists were not doing enough to reach agreement with the Palestinian Arabs. Peace and cooperation between Arabs and Jews was not England's problem

(Palestine was under British rule) "but our own." He favored a binational solution in Palestine and warned Chaim Weizmann against "a nationalism *à la prussienne*." Multinational Switzerland represented a "higher stage of political development than any other nation state," Einstein said.[41] Weizmann called Einstein a prima donna about to lose her voice.

THE first volume of Hitler's *Mein Kampf* was published in 1925. Few people read it. The quality press rarely reported Hitler's speeches in Munich's Krone Circus, where he fulminated against Jews, Democrats, and French *Bananenfresser* (banana guzzlers). Ridiculed as a "vegetarian Ghengis Khan" possessed of an "excremental visage," he was thought to have little if any chance of reaching high office.[42] In the kaiser's days, noted one snobbish Bavarian aesthete, servants would have refused to attend to a man like Hitler on physiognomic grounds alone. His screeching voice, commonly mocked as well, was compared to a rusty door. Arnold Zweig attended one of Hitler's speeches in 1927 and wrote his wife that Hitler was a Charlie Chaplin without the talent. Thomas Mann's son Klaus watched him in Munich's Carlton Tea Room stuffing four slices of strawberry cake into his mouth; his "half-infantile, half-predatory voracity spoiled my appetite," Klaus Mann commented.[43] George Orwell had sharper eyes. His surprising reaction to one of Hitler's carefully staged photographic portraits was that the future Führer's face was more likely to elicit sympathy; it was the hangdog visage of a man who appears to have suffered a great injustice, a manly Christ.[44]

Three years after publication, *Mein Kampf* was still considered unreadable. Theodor Wolff first leafed through it only in 1930. Arnold Zweig dropped it after the first few pages. He later regretted that *Mein Kampf* was so badly written. Had it been easier to read, he said, perhaps more people would have been alerted earlier.[45] Erich Mühsam was one of the few who warned that there was more to Hitler than was apparent from his book. He tried to listen to him more carefully and noted in his diary: "Hitler's speech is quite effective. Great honesty—except that the man's estimate of his own importance far surpasses his real capabilities."[46]

Tucholsky ignored Hitler's foaming rhetoric. He and other republican stalwarts were more frightened by the consequences of the patriotic school curriculum, the antiquated judicial system, and the reviving respect for the old military spirit.* The Versailles treaty had reduced the army to 100,000 men, but it was common knowledge that the treaty was being grossly violated; an infrastructure for a vastly larger military force was maintained clandestinely, as were training programs, some in collusion with the Soviet Union. The army had not been democratized; it was still controlled by the old officers' class, whose arrogance remained unchanged. Under the cover of obscurity, there was a dangerous enterprise brewing, Tucholsky warned. The coups and political assassinations of the early 1920s had merely been rehearsals. The danger might still be thwarted today, Tucholsky wrote; tomorrow might be too late.

The presidential election of 1925, won by former field marshal Paul von Hindenburg, reconfirmed Tucholsky in his fears of a military coup. Republicans voted for Hindenburg in the hope that his prestige among the conservatives would assure the republic a stability it could not expect from one of the Social Democratic or centrist politicians. This would indeed prove true, but only until 1929, when the political equilibrium would be shattered by the advent of the depression. Tucholsky sensed the danger inherent in Hindenburg's election. When a man "who claims to enjoy war the way he relishes taking a thermal bath at a health resort is elected president of a republic, the republic will soon cease to be one," Tucholsky correctly predicted.[47] Harry Kessler agreed:

> All the philistines are delighted about Hindenburg. He is the god of all those who long for a return to philistinism and the glorious time when it was only necessary to make money and accompany a decent digestion with a pious upward glance. Farewell progress, farewell vision of a new world which was to be humanity's conscience money for the criminal war.[48]

---

*In 1928, eight prominent intellectuals (six of them Jewish)—Alfred Döblin, Arnold Zweig, Erich Mühsam, Erwin Piscator, Erich Engel, Alfons Paquet, George Grosz, and Kurt Kersten—protested the judicial system in the land of "judges and hangmen."

Theodor Lessing, too, was uncannily prescient. In a newspaper article on the eve of the election he warned against voting for Hindenburg. The old warrior might be "a zero" and one could even say "better a zero than a Nero," he wrote. "Unfortunately, history shows that behind a zero there always hides a Nero." For his article Lessing barely escaped being lynched in the streets of Hanover, his native city. He did, though, lose his teaching position at the university. He could not have known just how accurate he was. Eight years later almost to the day, the half-senile Hindenburg, in cahoots with a handful of cynical industrialists and scheming conservative politicians, would appoint Hitler chancellor and authorize him to rule by decree under article 48 of the Weimar constitution.

On November 9, 1928, the republic's tenth anniversary, the journal *Literarische Welt* asked seven leading Weimar intellectuals, "What would you do if you were in power?" The first four respondents were Jews. The mixture of good sense, fatalism, and frivolous impracticality in their responses still seems remarkable:

> Georg Bernhard [editor of the *Vossische Zeitung*]: "If I had power, I would do something completely out of the ordinary: I would actually use it."
>
> Egon Friedell [historian]: "Resign immediately."
>
> Kurt Tucholsky: "Abolish the army; pass land reform; socialize the economy; reform the judiciary, the school system, and the universities; reform the bureaucracy and the tax system; write a new criminal code and abolish the inhuman current one. The goals I've mentioned are scoffed at today because they are the truths of tomorrow. They cannot be attained by evolution—only by revolution. And even though the terms of such revolution may have been compromised, the idea is invincible."
>
> Emil Ludwig [biographer]: "I would set up a dictatorship—that would turn everyone into a republican. It would last for just one year and during that time I would keep the borders sealed, force everyone to wear a uniform, stand at attention, hoist flags, march in processions, make babies. After one year: new elections."[49]

ARNOLD Zweig later claimed that if he had been asked to answer the questionnaire he would have proposed demilitarizing Germany immediately. Like many other German writers he had supported the war but had come back psychologically and physically damaged, a confirmed pacifist. In photographs from the early twenties, he looks burdened, frightened, almost desperate. His moral tale, *The Case of Sergeant Grischa* (1927), was one of the most incisive antiwar novels in the German language. Based on an event Zweig witnessed on the Eastern Front, it tells the story of a Russian prisoner of war who escapes from a German camp in occupied czarist Russia. He is a simple peasant who knows only that he wants to go home. A Russian woman hides him and convinces him that he will never get through the German lines. She procures false papers for him and he surrenders, pretending to be a Russian deserter. The Germans easily uncover the forgery and accuse him of being a spy. He panics and confesses the truth. The court condemns him to death anyway. Convinced of his innocence, three decent men—two old-fashioned Prussian officers and a Jewish court stenographer—intervene on his behalf but fail. A cynical major general, a caricature of Ludendorff, decides to make an example of him: to intimidate the restive population of the occupied territory, he confirms the death sentence. The failed efforts of the Prussians and the Jewish court stenographer evoke—for the last time in German fiction—the so-called German-Jewish symbiosis.

BUT for the depression of 1929, the calm and "philistine" self-satisfaction so deplored by Kessler might have continued. The depression hit Germany badly. The Allies agreed to delay the collection of war reparations but nothing could stop the steady rise of unemployment. In 1930, almost five million people were out of work; by 1932, six million. The American journalist Dorothy Thompson observed the misery everywhere and the huge army of unemployed, even as Germany boasted the world's largest airships and Europe's most advanced industries, fastest trains and luxury ocean liners, most up-to-date hospitals, and best symphony orchestras. Germany was the "best-outfitted poorhouse in today's world," she wrote in the *Saturday Evening Post*. Unemployment statistics reflected only part of the wretchedness. Postwar hyperinflation had earlier wiped out savings and pensions and reduced large parts of the lower middle class to penury. The depression hit the same people again just when it seemed that the worst was over. Other European countries, of course, were also hit by the depression. They did not, however, react to it as violently as many Germans did, by assaulting the republican system, democracy, and the Jews.

The slump gave Hitler his opportunity. He used it with consummate skill. His opponents, more numerous than his sympathizers but divided, played into his hands. In the 1930 elections, Nazi representation in the Reichstag increased nearly tenfold, to 107 deputies, making the NSDAP the second-largest party after the Social Democrats. More than six million Germans voted for it. The Communists came in third, increasing their support by 40 percent. The center parties were devastated. The republican DDP was all but liquidated.

First reactions to the Nazi upsurge were mixed. Many Jews saw it as a temporary warp in what was, after all, a civilized country. Einstein remained calm. The Nazis' strong showing, he claimed, resulted from the "momentary economic slump"—it was little more than a childhood disease of the young republic. In his diary, in which he had not yet mentioned Hitler even once, Victor Klemperer wrote: "I think I'll learn to use the typewriter." He had voted for the defunct DDP. His closest friends in Dresden, however, had voted for the Nazis, he noted. Ernst Feder's confidants in the government assured him that there was no reason to worry—Hitler, Goebbels, and their henchmen weren't dangerous.[50] They would never come to power. Otto Meissner, Hindenburg's chief of staff, assured Feder that Hindenburg was a man of extraordinary decency and personal integrity who had sworn loyalty to the republic. Even if the Nazis gained a majority, the president would never confirm Hitler as chancellor.

Hannah Arendt and Arthur Koestler saw the danger more clearly. Arendt, whom Blumenfeld had converted to Zionism, was working in the Prussian state archive, researching a book on Rahel Varnhagen, with whom she strongly identified. Her old friend Anna Weil met her in the street and was surprised to hear Arendt say excitedly that they needed to prepare for emigration. Weil disagreed. She had not experienced any anti-Semitism, she claimed, not unlike many other German Jews. Arendt, according to her biographer, looked at Weil in amazement. "You are crazy," she said and stomped off.[51] Arendt revealed her deepening sense of alienation to her teacher, the philosopher Karl Jaspers, who tried nevertheless to discourage her from emigrating. He could not understand how Arendt would want "to separate herself from Germany." It was her past, present, and future. Arendt answered, "Germany in its old splendor is *your* past but what my past is I can hardly say in a phrase."[52]

Koestler, then a reporter for the Ullstein newspaper chain and science editor of the *Vossische Zeitung,* recorded the shock among his colleagues at the sudden success of the Nazis. More than half the Ullstein editors were Jews. "Everybody was dazed. People shook hands limply with absent looks." There were among them "professional optimists and constitutional optimists. The former fooled their readers; the latter fooled themselves" that things would soon improve.[53] Koestler, secretly a member of the Communist Party, fooled only his employers by spying on them for the KGB.

The situation soon worsened. American banks called in some of the loans that were helping Germany continue paying war indemnities. Under Stalin's orders, the Communists refused to join the Social Democrats in a common anti-Nazi front; they hated the Social Democrats more than they feared the Nazis. They may even have wished for a Nazi victory. A senior Russian diplomat in Berlin assured Friedrich Stampfer, editor of the Social Democratic paper *Vorwärts,* that while a Communist victory in Germany was inevitable, it would come only after Hitler rose to power. In a crude attempt to win the anti-Semitic vote, the Communist organ *Red Banner* even announced that Jewish capital was financing the Nazis.[54] The Communist militant Ruth Fischer told the German Communist student union in July 1932: "Crush the Jew capitalists, hang them, smash them!"[55]

The year 1930 saw the beginning of the end of parliamentary democracy. Bernhard Weiss was deputy police chief of Berlin from 1927 to July 1932. A former Bavarian cavalry captain, he was tough, resolute, courageous, and, as a Jew, a target of the most ruthless personal invective of the Nazis. Short, with thick spectacles, a long nose, and large ears, he might have stepped out of an anti-Semitic cartoon. Weiss tried but was unable (perhaps because of politically inspired restrictions) to restrain the looming civil war in its early stages. Nazi and Communist militias clashed in the street and Jews were molested by Nazi hoodlums. Parliamentary democracy disintegrated under the strains of political extremism on the right and the left. Theoretically, republicans were still in the majority; many of them were Social Democrats. In practice, they were dispirited and deeply divided, prey to shortsighted, doctrinaire, or opportunistic politicians. Cabinet positions changed rapidly and were increasingly filled by conservatives, leftovers from the old regime, aristocrats, and retired military men. The Social Democrats had no choice but to go along, if only to keep the Nazis out of power. In the absence of workable parliamentary coalitions, government was possible only through presidential decrees. Hindenburg was confused and frightened; nothing in his past had prepared him for such political chaos. Isolated, he was manipulated by his staff, by his son Oskar, a major general in the army, by Meissner, who would serve Hitler in the same capacity until 1945, and by a handful of conservative politicians—mostly former soldiers, debauched noblemen, and business friends—anxious above all to break the unions and weaken the left.

The moment was one of paradox, of surging Nazism and increasing assimilation, of anti-Semitic outrages and growing prominence for Jews in every field of Weimar culture. Max Liebermann was president of the Prussian Academy of Arts. Max Reinhardt, showered with honorary doctorates from the universities of Kiel, Frankfurt, and Tübingen, was directing Hugo von Hofmannsthal's Christian morality play *Everyman* on the steps of Salzburg's cathedral. Jews mistook such prominence as an index of their successful integration. The few who suspected otherwise must have repressed their concerns.

Raymond Aron, an Alsatian Jew who later became a prominent political scientist, was a graduate student in Berlin at the time. He gave French lessons to Reinhardt, who was stoically watching his world disintegrate. Manes Sperber, one of Aron's Communist friends, continued to assure Aron that the "German working class, the best-organized in the world, would never, not for one day, suffer a Fascist dictatorship like that in Italy."[56] He promised Aron that the Communists would meet any significant increase in the Nazi vote with a general strike.

But the Nazi vote continued to grow. The general strike did not take place. As more and more intellectuals attended Hitler's rallies, true liberals felt increasingly isolated. Karl Jaspers was aghast at the prospect of an "uneducated" man like Hitler governing Germany, but Martin Heidegger reassured him: "Education is irrelevant. Just look at his wonderful hands!"[57] Ernst Feder attended a public meeting of the pacifist League for Human Rights. The novelist Lion Feuchtwanger and Kurt Rosenfeld, a Jewish socialist Reichstag deputy, spoke. "The hall was packed wall to wall. But only 1 percent of the German people were represented—the Jews."[58]

As in the first years of the republic, wild street violence erupted. Jewish storefronts were smashed. On September 12, 1931, in what was known as the Kurfürstendamm pogrom, Nazi thugs fell on Jews leaving synagogue on the eve of the Jewish New Year. The next morning, in the *Berliner Tageblatt,* Theodor Wolff warned: "This simply cannot continue. All decent people, irrespective of party, must form a common front and put these agitators to the pillory."

But it continued. During these last spasms of freedom, a remarkable series of private letters written by little-known nineteenth-century German humanists appeared in twenty-seven installments in the *Frankfurter Zeitung.* Each installment was brilliantly annotated by an anonymous anthologist, Walter Benjamin. "He had to hide his name," Theodor Adorno wrote after the war. "Fascism was already casting its shadow ahead."[59] Benjamin's selections and his annotations amounted to perhaps the greatest compliment to and saddest epitaph for German humanism ever made by a German Jew. Benjamin chose letters written between 1783 and 1883 that he had collected over the years from archives and rare books. He believed that by publishing the excerpts at that moment, he was, like an archaeologist, uncovering a lost, underground tradition, one that had first been enunciated during the Enlightenment but that had never fully taken root even though many of the best minds had spoken for it. There was nothing snobbish about his choices. The letters were written not by the proverbial *Dichter* and *Denker*—poets and philosophers—but by obscure friends, relatives, and admirers, modest, virtuous men who embodied decency, rectitude, and *Bildung:* not Kant but his brother Johann Heinrich, not Goethe but his friend Friedrich Zelter, not Nietzsche but his friend Franz Overbeck. It is perhaps no accident that all but one of the letters in this anthology were written before the foundation of Bismarck's muscle-flexing great Reich. The collection reflects a certain tension between the prosaic and the utopian that marked Benjamin's own work as well. "I won't sell my hope, not even for thousands of tons of gold," he quotes the pietist Samuel Collenbusch, a doctor, as assuring Kant. The anthology reads like the catalog of an exhibition documenting a buried civilization, conjuring up its ethos, mourning it; Benjamin's collection was a warning that "not even the dead" would be safe if the Nazis won.[60] The last installment appeared on May 31, 1932, two months before the Reichstag elections.*

THEODOR Wolff was engaged in endless battles with his publisher, who demanded that he tone down his warnings in the interest of advertising and circulation. Feder quoted him as saying that while it was barely possible to stand Hitler, his publisher completely wore him out."[61] On July 31, 1932, the eve of the election, Wolff cautioned the electorate to consider the consequences of a Nazi victory: "If National Socialism triumphs today, if the Nazis are able to dictate their will even more so than before to the reactionary forces they are allied with, then you will . . . never vote again. . . . The little liberty you have left will be shattered, and they will use the brutal methods you know so well to force you into dazed obedience and mute submission." Wolff's appeal was directed at the reader who considered himself a free citizen, a breed that was becoming rarer by the minute. But even in Berlin, where they had always lagged behind, the Nazis more than doubled their votes.

---

*In 1936, Benjamin published the anthology in Switzerland under a pseudonym so that it could be sold in Nazi Germany. It found scarcely any readers there and was pulped. Its title was *German People*. The epigraph on the cover read:

Of Honor without Fame
Of Greatness without Splendor
Of Dignity without Reward

In the copy he sent Scholem, Benjamin wrote: "This is an ark I built when the fascist flood was beginning to rise" (Scholem collection, National and University Library, Jerusalem). In a letter written when Benjamin was stateless, he explained that the book helped him remain a German. It was as important to him, he said, as a French residence permit.

With 36.9 percent of the national vote and 230 deputies they emerged as the dominant party in the Reichstag. Hindenburg vainly tried to placate Hitler with an offer to make him vice-chancellor. Hitler rejected it—only the top spot would do.

Hitler wanted full powers like Mussolini's in Italy. He knew exactly what was needed to turn a government into a "legal" dictatorship: emergency powers under article 48. Hindenburg still held back, claiming he would never appoint the uncouth "Bohemian lance corporal" chancellor. Theodor Wolff rashly called Hindenburg's refusal a truly "historic" act: Hitler's attempt to seize power "legally" had failed, he wrote. There was no way to break the constitution by using it, Wolff argued. He would soon have reason to regret his words.

Government was at a stalemate. Major banks collapsed. Daily street battles raged between Nazis and Communists. Arthur Koestler was one of the few who did not wait for the end. He had never had any faith in the Social Democrats and left abruptly for the Soviet Union. Beginning in June 1932, the *Weltbühne* ran two parallel columns, one recording "progress" during the preceding week, the other "regression." The latter column was always long, the former short or blank.

Under article 48, the constitution was intermittently suspended. Short-lived ultraconservative governments ruled by decree. One such government "deposed" the last Social Democratic bastion, the state government of Prussia. One phone call ("Chancellor's office speaking. You're fired"), backed up by a few soldiers showing up at the office of Otto Braun, the prime minister of Prussia, was enough to induce him and his ministers to relinquish their posts. One of the first things the new Prussian administration did was to dismiss Bernhard Weiss, the Jewish deputy police chief of Berlin.

The people went to the polls no fewer than five times in 1932: twice to reelect Hindenburg, twice to elect deputies for the Reichstag, once for the state legislature of Prussia. Voting was becoming a tedious, even cynical routine. Campaigns were chaotic and violent, and pernicious propaganda by both the Communists and the Nazis abounded. For Vicky Baum, a popular Jewish writer, Hindenburg's reelection was too much. She decided to leave for America. Her friends thought that she had lost her mind. Why leave now, they wondered, "when we've won the election!"

Victor Klemperer and many others convinced themselves that "the republic was saved."[62]

In September 1932, the Expressionist playwright Paul Kornfeld felt reassured enough to predict that "the Nazis are spent, they are finished. We will live to see that Hitler was just an episode."[63] During the next Reichstag elections, in November, Kornfeld and others briefly saw their fondest wishes fulfilled by a sudden drop in the Nazi vote from 36.9 to 33.5 percent. The Communists gained slightly. The Nazis' decline—and reports of an imminent split in the Nazi Party—induced the liberal *Vossische Zeitung* and *Frankfurter Zeitung* to announce that the Nazi assault on the democratic state had been "repulsed"; the republic had been "rescued." Lion Feuchtwanger, in New York to promote the English translation of his novel *Erfolg*—Success—assured American reporters: "Hitler is over!" The English poet Stephen Spender was more perceptive. From Germany, he wrote to his friend Isaiah Berlin: "It looks as if the whole system . . . will break down. . . . All people of Jewish extraction will be shot."[64]

Martin Heidegger, by now Germany's most fashionable philosopher, spoke out against what he called the growing *Verjudung*—Judaization—of the German university. Arendt had one last exchange with him about this. Her letter has not survived; Heidegger's long-winded, wooden reply has. In half-serious, half-sardonic tones, reeking with self-pity, he complained that he was being vilified and betrayed by ungrateful students and disciples. As for his anti-Semitism, he told Arendt, he was no more anti-Semitic than some of his Jewish colleagues at the university.[65]

In December, Chaim Weizmann, on a brief trip to Germany, visited Richard Willstätter in Munich. From Willstätter's he walked to dinner at the home of the head of the local Jewish community. The guests, local public figures, were all deeply depressed. Some had tears in their eyes as Weizmann left. All he could say was, "May God protect you."

ON January 30, 1933, Hindenburg gave in to his advisers and appointed Hitler chancellor of a new cabinet in which Nazi ministers were a minority of two. The cabal surrounding the old man had convinced him that responsibility would "tame" Hitler and his followers. In return,

Hitler had to give his word that the Nazis would remain a minority in any future cabinet. Former chancellor Franz von Papen crowed to the right-wing film and press tycoon Alfred Hugenberg that the conservatives had been able to "hire" Hitler to serve their cause. Papen belittled the importance of Hitler's own party program.* A few rich Jews—the Hamburg banker Carl Melchior, Oskar Wassermann of the Deutsche Bank, and Rudolf Hilferding, the former Social Democratic minister of finance—entertained similar delusions.[66] Joseph Roth slapped the face of one such banker, who offered the view that the Nazis might, at the very most, beat up a few Eastern European Jews, "but nothing can happen to us."[67]

Theodor Wolff was one of the few who warned that Hitler's appointment was merely the first stage of a coup d'état in installments. It was as though a pyromaniac, Wolff said, had been appointed fireman to extinguish the fire he himself had kindled. In an editorial the day after the appointment, Wolff predicted that "a cabinet whose members have been proclaiming for weeks and months that salvation—by which they mean their own—is at hand, in the form of a coup d'état, a breach of the constitution, the elimination of the Reichstag, the muzzling of the opposition, and in unbridled dictatorial rule . . . will do everything in its power to intimidate and silence its opponents."

For millions of Berliners nothing seemed to have changed at first. Too many chancellors and cabinets had followed one another in quick succession for this new one to assume any particular significance. Few seemed aware of the watershed they had just passed. What most surprised Raymond Aron during the first weeks of the Third Reich was the "almost invisible quality of great historical events." A newsreel screened throughout Germany featured Hitler's appointment as the sixth item, after a horse show and other sports news.[68] Manes Sperber still expected a popular uprising. Some republicans felt it was good that Hitler had been given his chance. "In a few weeks he will have burned

---

*In his memoirs, published after the war, Papen claimed that party platforms had always been irrelevant in his eyes (*Der Wahrheit eine Gasse*, Munich, 1952, p. 289).

himself out," they said, or "The army will not put up with this. They'll arrest him soon. No need to worry." Foreign diplomats in Berlin were only slightly more concerned. The Czechoslovak press attaché Camill Hoffman, a Jew, saw little significance in the new government. It was not a Nazi government, he noted, "even though it carries Hitler's name." Henry Ashby Turner, in *Hitler's Thirty Days to Power*, quotes a young Jewish copy editor on a Berlin tabloid who remembered proofing the transcript of Hitler's inaugural remarks "without the slightest feeling [or] any concern that it might affect me."[69]

THERE is little reason to delve deep into German history as far back as Luther to explain Hitler's success. His rise to power was made possible by the chaos and disintegration of government in the aftermath of the depression, but it was not inevitable. Nor was Hitler, as some Germans claimed after 1945, a mere *Betriebsunfall,* a work accident, in German history. He made his way to power through the "authoritarian gap," the flaw in the Weimar constitution that allowed excessive powers to the president, and, writes K. D. Bracher, "immediately set about destroying the constitution he had just taken an oath to defend. . . . Now the actual seizure of power began."[70] The Third Reich was, of course, also a product of the past: the failed revolution of 1848, authoritarianism, militarism, racism, the lost war of 1914–18, hyperinflation, the 1929 depression. Any one of these factors would not have been enough to bring Hitler to power. Personal and other contingencies played a role, as did misapprehensions and other errors. Hitler was undoubtedly the most gifted politician of the moment. Time and again, fortune played into his hands, so much so that he came to believe in his supernatural qualities long before masses of Germans did. When, after the drop in the Nazi vote in the November 1932 election, even some of his most loyal supporters gave him up, he was saved by Hindenburg's senility, Papen's stupidity, and the timidity and blindness of his opponents. He was not democratically elected by a free majority but appointed by a feebleminded, elderly general. But in January 1933, Hitler was not the only political possibility. Given the ineptitude and mediocrity of the Social Democratic leaders, the most obvious alternative to Hitler might have been a military regime, such as existed in several other European countries at that time. A military regime would certainly have been dictatorial, and it might have led to a war with Poland, Czechoslovakia, and perhaps France. But, as Henry Ashby Turner suggests, there would have been no Holocaust.

A few hours after Hitler's investiture, a torchlight parade of brownshirts marched for hours through the Brandenburg Gate to the nearby chancellery. The well-organized, seemingly endless parade proved the Nazis' dazzling command of the pageantry of power. From his home adjacent to the gate, the aging Impressionist painter Max Liebermann, in theory still honorary president of the Prussian Academy of Arts, was deafened by the endless pounding of boots and drums as he watched the spectral sight below his windows. He said in a thick Berlin accent: *"Ick kann ja nich so ville fressen, wie ick kotzen möchte—* "It makes me want to throw up more than I can possibly eat." Later, he told an interviewer that each time he climbed the stairs of the house in which he was born and his father had lived, "the hatred in me rises.... I no longer look out the windows. I don't want to see this new world around me."[71]

By coincidence, only a few days before Hitler's appointment Berlin's first Jewish museum had opened. It was "a real museum with a picture

The aged Max Liebermann under a portrait of his parents. His wife wanted, at the very least, to die in her beloved Berlin and committed suicide prior to deportation. *By permission of the Berlinische Galerie, Landesmuseum für Moderne Kunst, Photographie und Architektur, Berlin*

gallery, copper engravings, and handicrafts . . . very well arranged," according to the *Berliner Tageblatt*. We will never know whether its opening at that moment was an act of defiance or of naïveté. Karl Schwartz, its director, later claimed that from the first day one felt "the breath of death moving through its halls."[72]

Wealthy Jews left as usual for ski resorts. Arnold Zweig and his wife spent a fortnight at a thermal spa. An exaggerated faith in *Kultur* blocked awareness of the danger and produced a highly selective sense of reality. Wolff remained at his post. Heinrich Simon, editor in chief of the *Frankfurter Zeitung,* was certain that while the Nazis might seize power in the north, they stood no chance south of the Main River, in Württemberg and Bavaria, which would remain "free." Lion Feuchtwanger was still in America on his book tour. (He had recently finished building a three-story villa in the Grunewald section of Berlin.) With considerable difficulty, his American publisher kept him from rushing back to Germany, thus saving him from certain arrest. The Hamburg banker Max Warburg dismissed Hitler's government as a temporary intrigue. "I considered it impossible," he later confessed, "that [Hitler] could become sole leader of this most creative, able, industrious, and powerful nation."[73] Gershom Scholem's mother, Betty, assured her son in Jerusalem that the Social Democrats had more reason to fear than the Jews. She complained that 99 percent of what was printed in the foreign press was horror propaganda and lies. Scholem reprimanded her: "Our thinking about this is fundamentally different."[74]

Joseph Roth warned Stefan Zweig: "Everything leads to war. Don't delude yourself. Hell reigns." Hitler scheduled new elections to a bogus Reichstag on March 5, 1933. By terrorizing his opponents and arresting many of them, he manipulated the results to produce a better showing for his own party. Freedom of speech and assembly were curtailed by decree. A week before the election, the Reichstag went up in flames; the arsonists may well have been the Nazis themselves. Hitler took the opportunity to order mass arrests of opponents. That night, a young reporter rushed into Theodor Wolff's office to say that he had seen Wolff's name on a list of persons to be arrested. He took Wolff straight from his desk to the railway station. Wolff boarded the night train to Munich carrying only a briefcase to avoid suspicion. From Munich, one day before the elections, he sent in his last editorial, entitled "Go and Vote!"[75] In the carefully coded terms already in use to ensure that an article would actually appear, Wolff urged his readers to vote for "freedom, security, and equality under the law," but these were already gone. On election day, Wolff, eager to follow his call, returned unexpectedly to Berlin to cast his own vote. Colleagues intercepted him at the station and compelled him to board the train back to Munich.

That was the beginning. The rest followed in rapid succession: Jewish-owned shops were boycotted; Jews were expelled from the National Academy and from government positions, schools, research institutes, and universities; they were banned from practicing law and other professions and excluded from all national societies, such as the Association of Blind War Veterans (which quickly expelled its Jewish members). A few weeks in spring 1933 sufficed to reduce the University of Göttingen, a world-renowned center of advanced physics and mathematics, to the level of a provincial college. More than fifty professors were expelled, among them the Nobel laureate James Franck and the future laureate Max Born.* Protest was still possible. There was none.

In May, soon after the dissolution of all opposition parties, some fifty thousand books by Jews and other "traitors and degenerates" were burned in the large quadrangle opposite the university on Unter den Linden, between the National Library and the ornate opera house. Similar book burnings took place on the Königsplatz in Munich, on the Schlossplatz in Breslau, on the Römerberg in Frankfurt, under the Bismarck monument in Dresden, and in every other German university town. Students in boots and brown S.A. uniforms threw books into the fires and formed honor guards. In Berlin, the Nazi propaganda chief, Joseph Goebbels, led the proceedings, proclaiming "the end of the age of Jewish intellectualism." A brown-shirted herald proclaimed over loudspeakers:

---

*The mathematics and natural science faculties were the hardest hit, losing more than half their teaching personnel. In 1934, the Nazi minister of education, Bernhard Rust, visited the university. At a banquet in his honor, Rust sat next to the famous old mathematician David Hilbert. Rust asked him if the institute had suffered from the expulsion of the "Jews and their friends." Hilbert answered: "Suffered? It hasn't suffered, Herr Minister. It no longer exists."

Against overestimating base instincts to the detriment of the spirit and in the name of the noble human soul, I deliver to the flames the writings of Sigmund Freud.

Against the alien journalism spawned by the Jewish democrats, I deliver to the flames the writings of Theodor Wolff and Georg Bernhard.

Against insolence and impudence, and in the name of honor and respect for the immortal German spirit . . . may the flames devour the works of Tucholsky and Ossietzky![76]

That night, the flames consumed works by Thomas Mann, Lion Feuchtwanger, Bertolt Brecht, Erich Maria Remarque, Albert Einstein, Vicky Baum, Robert Musil, Ernst Toller, Heinrich Heine, Emil Ludwig, Stefan Zweig, and many others. Arnold Zweig, tightly squeezed in the crowd, watched his own books go up in flames. Raymond Aron, too, witnessed the event. Astonishingly, he did not mention it in a report he wrote at the time for a French magazine. In his memoirs, written many years later, he even dismissed the event as "a banality": There were "no

"The end of the age of Jewish intellectualism," proclaimed Goebbels. Tens of thousands of books are burned outside the National Library in Berlin. *By permission of the Landesarchiv, Landesbildstelle, Berlin*

enthusiastic masses, just a hundred or so Nazis in uniform, while Goebbels declaimed, 'I deliver to the flames . . .'"[77]

Arnold Zweig described a larger crowd, cheering, laughing, joking, cursing, a crowd made up of "simple people and some of the middle class. Obtuse, passive, and without the slightest idea of what was going on, they were marked by an animal-like, smug stupidity. They would have stared as happily into the flames if live humans were burning."

> "What are they burning there anyway?"
> "What do you think? Jewish books?"
> "No, it's indecent books, un-German."
> "They should take the whole pile and dump it into the Spree."
> "But that would pollute the Spree."

In the cordoned-off quadrangle next to the opera, Zweig reported, the books were stacked behind a police barrier in "an orderly pile of Prussian exactitude three meters by three." Policemen paced back and forth, "parading their importance, and street vendors made the rounds, crying, 'Cigarettes, chocolate, sausages, sausages!'" The books were brought in trucks reminiscent of the "open tumbrels that carried the condemned to the guillotine." Then it rained. The crowd called out advice on how to keep the flames going. Huge spotlights lit the vast square. All this time, Zweig wrote, "mystic, somber music in a minor key" came from unseen loudspeakers. "I was the only one among thousands who did not sing or raise his arm when the swastika flags passed by." Zweig had also only recently bought himself a fine new home with a garden in the Berlin suburb Eichkamp. The same night he made up his mind that he and his family could not remain in Germany. "We had to leave, for better or worse."[78]

THE precipitous flight of Jews and the most exposed leftists and liberals began soon after Hitler's investiture and increased after the Reichstag fire. A unique republic of letters—in many ways the flower of secular Europe—dispersed in all directions. The Nazi press rejoiced: "Something wonderful has happened. They have gone."[79] Arnold Zweig was the only prominent writer who left for Palestine, where he would soon outrage the more radical Zionists with his principled pacifism and insistence on speaking only German. Theodor Lessing, whose prophecy about the Nero hiding behind the Zero Hindenburg had come true, managed to board the night train to Prague a few hours before a planned Nazi raid on his home on the outskirts of Hanover. At the very last moment, his daughter changed his reservation and booked a berth in the sleeping car, saving him from certain arrest by armed S.A. men, who searched all the other cars. The Nazis posted a reward for his capture, dead or alive. A few months later, in Marienbad, Czechoslovakia, he was murdered at his desk. The killers succeeded in slipping back across the nearby German border.

The final issue of *Die Weltbühne* came out on March 7. Carl von Ossietzky, the editor, wrote in despair that while one might fight for a majority oppressed by a tyrannical minority, one could not beg a people to oppose what its majority wanted or condoned. He was arrested and sent to a concentration camp. Tucholsky's fate would have been worse had he not been living abroad. His name, together with Ernst Toller's and Heinrich Mann's, headed the first list of traitors stripped of their citizenship.

Alfred Kerr's books had also been among those burned outside the national library for their "insolence and conceit." He was sick at home when he learned that his passport had been revoked. Running a high fever and carrying a rucksack, he managed to cross safely into Czechoslovakia.[80] The publisher Fritz Landshof had just come back from abroad to the apartment in Berlin he shared with Ernst Toller. There was a knock on the door. An elderly lady whom he did not know stood outside. She said that the Nazis had been looking for him and his roommate. "I would urge you to leave and never return," she said. Within minutes, Landshof, with his still-packed suitcase, went into hiding; soon after he found refuge abroad. His young son remained behind with his actress mother, the mistress of a prominent Nazi in Berlin.

The fact that the exiled writers remained chained to the language of their tormentors added to their pain and trauma. They adapted to their new countries only with difficulty, while friends and colleagues who stayed behind either conformed or went into an arid so-called inner exile. (Despite the latter group's protestations after the war that they continued writing "for the drawer," they actually wrote nothing of consequence.) More than any other group, the exiled German Jewish intellectuals, as George Mosse has pointed out, "preserved Germany's better self across dictatorship, war, holocaust, and defeat."[81] They remained homesick wherever they went. Coming up the stairs of the New York subway at Columbus Circle station, Emil Ludwig happened upon a bust of Goethe. He was moved to tears. Erich Maria Remarque, the exiled author of *All Quiet on the Western Front,* was asked whether he missed Germany. "Why should I?" he answered. "I'm not Jewish."

FIFTY thousand Jews left Germany in 1933, thirty thousand in 1934, twenty thousand in 1935. The rest remained, at least for a while, unwilling or unable to leave. Some who left even returned. Although nothing went more against the spirit of the new regime, intermarriage was more prevalent in 1933 than ever before, reaching the astonishing figure of 44 percent.[82] In 1934, it fell to 15 percent and was soon outlawed. The exodus continued.

The rich had the fewest problems. Certainly, they had to abandon or sell their properties at drastically reduced prices; the Nazis further decimated their wealth by charging draconian "departure taxes." But nearly all wealthy German Jews were able to save themselves. They were easily able to settle in England, America, or Switzerland, where money was always welcome. Salman Schocken sent his children, his Chagalls, and his vast library to Jerusalem and followed them later. (His Rembrandt, Dürer, Renoir, Cézanne, Gauguin, van Gogh, and Manet remained in a Swiss bank vault.) The library comprised twenty-five thousand Hebrew and thirty thousand German volumes—the best of centuries of Hebrew and German classics—priceless medieval incunabula, and original, handwritten manuscripts of major works by Goethe, Schiller, Schopenhauer, Heine, Kraus, and Börne, along with first editions of Hofmannsthal, Mann, Werfel, and Stefan George. Erich Mendelssohn, one of the great architects of the Weimar period, was commissioned by Schocken to build a new home for his library on a leafy side street in Jerusalem. The moving of Schocken's treasures to Jerusalem seemed like an attempt to preserve the aborted German Jewish dream in the new Jewish homeland, at least temporarily. After the war, Schocken's children sold off much of the German collection. Heine's manuscripts were acquired by the French national library—as befit the work of a great Francophile, said the de Gaulle government.

The less fortunate, unable to obtain residence permits in most European countries or the United States, were forced to wander from land to land, some to as far as China. W. H. Auden portrayed their fate in "Refugee Blues":

> The consul banged the table and said,
> "If you've got no passport you're officially dead":
> But we are still alive, my dear, but we are still alive.
> . . . .
> Saw a poodle in a jacket fastened with a pin,
> Saw a door opened and a cat let in:
> But they weren't German Jews, my dear, but they weren't
> German Jews.

In England, impecunious foreigners were admitted if they were prepared to work as domestic servants. The difficulties exiles encountered in even this most liberal of European countries were evident in the case of one upper-middle-class Jewish doctor who applied for an entry permit as a tutor. The British visa officer in Paris informed him that work as a tutor did not constitute "domestic service." If that was so, the doctor replied, he would be ready to work as a butler. The vexed visa officer rejected this possibility as "absurd" since "butlering requires a lifelong experience."[83] Entry permits to Palestine, too, were tightly rationed by the British authorities. They were freely available only to "capitalists" with a minimum of a thousand (later five hundred) pounds sterling.

That so many Jews stayed in the country of their birth reflected not so much lethargy but the lingering conviction that the horrors were transitory. Baffled, incredulous, shocked, many refused to believe that the nearly two-thousand-year-old Jewish presence in Germany was coming to an end. Max Liebermann felt he was too old to leave. He wrote to the mayor of Tel Aviv that "regretfully, regretfully," he had awakened "from the beautiful dream of assimilation" to a nightmare.[84] Not long afterward, he died. Before his widow was picked up for deportation, she committed suicide "to be able to at least die here, in this city."[85] Victor Klemperer, a professor of Romance languages at the University of Dresden, felt more "shame" than "fear," shame for Germany; it hardly occurred to him to leave the country. Like many other war veterans (some of whom now bravely flaunted their medals in the hope of protecting themselves from harassment), Klemperer trusted that he was safe. "I am German forever, a German 'nationalist.' . . . The Nazis are un-German," he declared. Second thoughts came only in 1935, after his expulsion from the university. "My principles about Germany . . . are beginning to wobble like an old man's teeth." A year later, Klemperer bought a car in order to tour the beautiful Thuringian countryside with his wife. He was likely the only German Jew who invested his savings at that late date in a little villa overlooking Dresden. Three years later, he would be thrown out of the house and confined with his wife to a tiny room in a *Judenhaus* in downtown Dresden, saved from deportation to a concentration camp only because his wife was "Aryan." On May 11, 1942, he noted: "I am German, the others are un-German. I must hold on to this: The spirit is decisive, not blood. I must hold on to this: On my part Zionism would be a comedy—my baptism was *not* a comedy."[86]

Among those who stayed, suicides were rampant. Following the boycott of Jewish businesses, Robert Weltsch became a cult figure among Jews, especially Zionists, for an article in the *Jüdische Rundschau* entitled "Wear It with Pride, the Yellow Patch!" The article was credited with saving many from suicide. Weltsch later regretted it and especially its headline, which he said should have read instead: "Pack Your Bags and Run!" Suicides were also common among exiles. Among well-known writers, Kurt Tucholsky took his life in Sweden, Stefan Zweig in Brazil, Ernst Toller in New York, and Ernst Lissauer in Vienna. To the last, the author of the "Hymn of Hate against England" celebrated the "German war" of 1914–18 as a just, almost "mythic struggle." But he anguished over his fate, writing:

O people, my people!
Which people is my own?
I bear two people's load,
A basket filled with history's stones.
In German eyes a Jew, masked as a German,
In Jewish eyes a German, traitor to the cause.[87]

Ludwig Fulda, a founding member of the Prussian Academy of Arts who on his seventieth birthday in 1932 had been honored by President Hindenburg with the Goethe Medal for Art and Science, killed himself after being denied an entry permit to the United States, where his son was living. "Since I cannot join my beloved boy," he wrote, "I join my good parents in the only country that requires no hard currency, passports, or visas."[88] Walter Benjamin committed suicide on the French-Spanish border, Walter Hasenclever in a French internment camp. Each had his history and his temperament. History had failed them all bitterly.

A few days before taking his life, Tucholsky recalled in a letter to Arnold Zweig his resignation from the Berlin Jewish community in 1914. He knew now, he said, that such a withdrawal was impossible.[89] Tucholsky and others in the Weimar radical avant-garde were later accused of having encouraged anti-Semitism by being too disrespectful of national icons. Franz Werfel, who also went into exile, even castigated himself for his arrogance: "Applauded by the laughter of a few philistines, we stoked the inferno in which humanity is now roasting."[90] And yet, all that he or Tucholsky had was a voice. They used it as best they could. Had there been no Tucholsky, no Werfel, no Wolff, Hitler would have moved to seize power anyway.

Else Lasker-Schüler, a few weeks after receiving the Kleist Prize, Germany's highest poetry award, was beaten up by Nazi hoodlums in the street. Still dazed, she boarded a train for Zurich, where she was picked up in a park for vagrancy:

Homeless I rove together with the deer
Dreaming through bitter days—yes, I loved you well.[91]

Walter Benjamin was in Berlin when the Nazis took over. He was lucky enough to have a valid passport and left for Paris as soon as he could. From Paris he wrote to Scholem on March 20, 1933, that the new situation in Germany was reflected not only in "terror against individuals" but in a "general cultural decline." Paris was becoming the true capital of German literature: Brecht, Mann, Feuchtwanger, Cassirer, Döblin, Kerr, and many others, Jews and non-Jews, would be there at one point or another, some literally living out of their suitcases, others moving from one cheap hotel to another for lack of a valid residence permit.

After a brief spell in a Gestapo prison, Hannah Arendt decided to leave Germany immediately, even without proper travel documents. She spent her last evening in Berlin in Mampe's wine restaurant on the Kurfürstendamm reciting Greek poetry with Kurt Blumenfeld, her Zionist mentor. The next day she took a train to the Czech border, hoping to cross it illegally.

She, too, had her history, her loves, and her friends, and they had failed her. A circle was closing. Arendt's train out of Berlin sped south through the rolling countryside, in the opposite direction taken two centuries earlier by the boy Moses Mendelssohn, on foot, on his way to fame and fortune in Enlightenment Berlin.

NOTES

INTRODUCTION

1. M. Kayserling, *Moses Mendelssohn: Sein Leben und Wirken*, Leipzig, 1888, p. 477.
2. Report submitted to the king, quoted in H. Knobloch, *Herr Moses in Berlin*, Berlin, 1987, p. 35.
3. G. A. Craig, *The Germans*, New York, 1982, p. 34.
4. K. Zuchardt, ed., *Friedrich der Grosse. Drei politische Schriften: Regierungsformen und Pflichten der Könige*, Leipzig, n.d.
5. Karl Voss, Introduction, *Reiseführer für Literaturfreunde*, Frankfurt, 1980.
6. Kayserling, *Mendelssohn*, p. 488.
7. H. Kamen, *The Spanish Inquisition*, London, 1968, p. 13.
8. F. V. Grunfeld, *Prophets without Honor: A Background to Freud, Kafka, Einstein, and Their World*, New York, 1979, p. 1.
9. S. George, *Stern des Bundes*, Berlin, 1914, p. 35.
10. C. Schulte, ed., *Deutschtum und Judentum: Ein Disput unter Juden aus Deutschland*, Stuttgart, 1993, p. 18.
11. Ibid.
12. Quoted in M. Reich-Ranicki, *Über Ruhestörer: Juden in der deutschen Literatur*, Munich, 1973, p. 55.
13. Craig, *Germans*, p.126.
14. J.-F. Lyotard, *Le différend*, Paris, 1983, para. #93.
15. *Leo Baeck Institute Yearbook* 20 (1975): 79.

405

1. ANCIENT RENOWN

1. K. Popper, *The Open Society and Its Enemies,* London, 1950, p. 245.
2. H. Spiel, *Fanny von Arnstein, oder die Emanzipation,* Vienna, 1975.
3. R. Dietrich, ed., *Politische Testamente der Hohenzollern,* Munich, 1981, p. 167.
4. Spiel, *Fanny von Arnstein,* p. 43.
5. *Boswell on the Grand Tour: Germany and Switzerland, 1764,* London, 1954, p. 24.
6. A. A. Bruer, *Geschichte der Juden in Preussen, 1750–1820,* Frankfurt, 1991, p. 76.
7. N. Lenau, *Sämtliche Werke,* vol. 1, Leipzig, 1910, p. 408.
8. Josephus Flavius, *Antiquities of the Jews,* book 19, ch. 5.
9. H. Karasek, *Der Fedtmilch-Aufstand: Wie die Frankfurter 1612–14 ihrem Rat einheizten,* Frankfurt, 1978, p. 26.
10. Quoted in German in *Bulletin of the Leo Baeck Institute* 19 (1962): 196.
11. A. Müller, *Geschichte der Juden in Nürnberg,* Nürnberg, 1968, p. 131.
12. J. W. Goethe, *Dichtung und Wahrheit,* Frankfurt, n.d., vol. 1, book 4, p. 148.
13. H. Teweles, *Goethe und Die Juden,* Berlin, 1925, p. 90.
14. S. Stern, *The Court Jew,* Philadelphia, 1950, p. 56.
15. *Leo Baeck Institute Yearbook* 20 (1975): 69.
16. R. Glanz, *Geschichte des niederen jüdischen Volkes in Deutschland, Gaunertum, Bettelwesen und Vagrantentum,* New York, 1968, p. 134.
17. H. Heubach, ed., *Jüdisches Leben in Frankfurt, Materialen, I, 1462–1796,* Frankfurt, 1988, pp. 88–89.
18. H. Heine, *Confessio Judaica,* ed. H. Bieber, Berlin, 1925, p. 36.
19. Glanz, *Geschichte des niederen jüdischen Volkes,* p. 132.

2. THE AGE OF MENDELSSOHN

1. M. Mendelssohn, *Gesammelte Schriften,* Leipzig, 1843–44, vol. 1, p. 9.
2. Ibid., vol. 5, p. 525.
3. B. Badt-Strauss, *Moses Mendelssohn: Der Mensch und das Werk,* Berlin, 1929, p. 72.
4. Ibid., p. 22.
5. Ibid.
6. F. Nicolai, *Anekdoten von König Friedrich II,* Berlin 1788, vol. 3, p. 278.
7. A. Altmann, *Moses Mendelssohn: A Biographical Study,* Philadelphia, 1973, p. 159.
8. Mendelssohn, *Gesammelte Schriften,* vol. 5, p. 165.
9. Badt-Strauss, *Moses Mendelssohn,* p. 79.
10. Ibid., p. 87.

11. Ibid., p. 88.

12. *Goethes Werke*, Hamburg, 1958, vol. 12, p. 385.

13. J. C. Lavater, *Ausgewählte Schriften*, Zurich, 1943, vol. 1, p. 123.

14. Ibid., vol. 1, p. 217.

15. N. Boyle, *Goethe: The Poet and the Age*, Oxford, 1992, pp. 149–50.

16. Lavater, *Ausgewählte Schriften*, vol. 2, p. 231.

17. C. Schmölders, *Das Vorurteil im Leibe: Eine Einführung in die Physiognomik*, Berlin, 1995, p. 72.

18. Ibid., p. 16.

19. L. Geiger, *Goethe und die Juden*, Berlin, 1891, p. 335.

20. M. Mendelssohn, *Briefwechsel aus den letzten Jahren*, Stuttgart, 1979, p. 178.

21. Mendelssohn, *Gesammelte Schriften*, vol. 3, p. 355; vol. 8, p. 6.

22. Ibid., vol. 5, p. 605.

23. H. Heine, *Confessio Judaica*, ed. H. Bieber, Berlin, 1925, p. 110.

24. S. Maimon, *Geschichte des eigenen Lebens*, Berlin, 1935, p. 141. The translation is from *Solomon Maimon: An Autobiography*, ed. Moses Hadas, New York, 1967, pp. 72–73.

25. Maimon, *Geschichte des eigenen Lebens*, p. 17.

26. Hadas, *Solomon Maimon*, pp. 90–91.

27. H. Heine, *Über Polen, Sämtliche Schriften*, Munich, 1975–78, vol. 2, p. 71.

28. Maimon, *Geschichte des eigenen Lebens*, p. ix.

29. Ibid., p. 205.

30. C. von Dohm, *Über die bürgerliche Verbesserung der Juden*, Berlin und Stettin, 1781.

31. von Dohm, letter to Friedrich Nicolai, cited in *Zeitschrift für die Geschichte der Juden Deutschlands* 5 (1890): 75.

32. Dohm, *Über die bürgerliche Verbesserung*, pp. 34–37.

33. Dohm, *Denkwürdigkeiten meiner Zeit*, cited in A. A. Bruer, *Geschichte der Juden in Preussen, 1750–1820*, Frankfurt, 1991, p. 69; F. Oppeln-Bronikowski, ed., *Gespräche Friedrich des Grossen*, Berlin, 1919, p. 306.

34. Lavater, *Ausgewählte Schriften*, vol. 3, p. 21.

35. Quoted in M. Brenner, ed., *Deutsch-jüdische Geschichte in der Neuzeit*, Munich, 1996, vol. 2, p. 228.

36. F. Klopstock, *Oden*, Leipzig, 1798, vol. 2, p. 51.

37. G. Mosse, *German Jews beyond Judaism*, Cincinnati, 1985, p. 9.

38. F. Kafka, *The Diaries*, ed. Max Brod, New York, 1976, p. 101 (Nov. 1, 1911).

39. *Gedenkbuch für Moses Mendelssohn*, Berlin, 1829, p. 8.

40. Mendelssohn, *Gesammelte Schriften*, vol. 5, p. 566.

41. Ibid., vol. 5, p. 202.

42. H. Arendt, *Men in Dark Times*, New York, 1968, p. 18.

3. MINIATURE UTOPIAS

1. Quoted in H. Landsberg, ed., *Henriette Herz: Ihr Leben und ihre Zeit*, Weimar, 1913, pp. 6–7.
2. Quoted in A. A. Bruer, *Geschichte der Juden in Preussen, 1750–1820*, Frankfurt, 1991, p. 58.
3. K. A. Böttiger, *Literarische Zustände und Zeitgenossen (Aus dem Nachlasse)*, Leipzig, 1839, vol. 2, p. 102.
4. *Deutsches Museum*, 1 (1784): 43.
5. K. Feyerabend, *Kosmopolitische Wanderungen*, Berlin, n.d., vol. 2, p. 126.
6. F. Kobler, ed., *Juden und Judentum in deutschen Briefen aus drei Jahrhunderten*, Vienna, 1935, p. 147.
7. H. Graetz, *History of the Jews*, Philadelphia, 1895, vol. 5, p. 422.
8. H. Herz, *Erinnerungen*, Berlin, 1958, pp. 53, 121.
9. Quoted in T. M. Endelman, ed., *Jewish Apostasy in the Modern World*, New York, 1987, p. 49.
10. W. Teller, *Lehrbuch des christlichen Glaubens* and *Wörterbuch des neuen Testaments zur Erklärung der christlichen Lehre*, quoted in Bruer, *Geschichte der Juden*, pp. 219–20.
11. H. Knobloch, *Herr Moses in Berlin*, Berlin, 1987, p. 233.
12. Quoted in Bruer, *Geschichte der Juden*, p. 212.
13. Quoted in H. Arendt, "Berliner Salon," *Deutscher Almanach für das Jahr 1932*, p. 173.
14. E. Berend, ed., *Jean Paul: Sämtliche Werke*, Berlin, 1960, vol. 4, p. 41.
15. G. Mann, *Friedrich von Gentz: Geschichte eines europäischen Staatsmannes*, Zurich, 1947, p. 61.
16. Quoted in H. Arendt, *Rahel Varnhagen: The Life of a Jewess*, ed. L. Weissberg, trans. Richard Winston, Baltimore, 1997, p. 150.
17. L. Geiger, *Geschichte von Berlin, 1688–1844*, Berlin, 1895, vol. 2, p. 198.
18. Ibid., pp. 88–89.
19. *Wilhelm und Caroline von Humboldt in ihren Briefen*, Berlin, 1912, p. 236.
20. Quoted in Arendt, "Berliner Salon," p. 180.
21. Quoted in Endelman, *Jewish Apostasy*, p. 9.
22. Letter of Nov. 9, 1816, Rothschild Archive, London.
23. Quoted in H. Heine, *Confessio Judaica*, ed. H. Bieber, Berlin, 1925, p. 143.
24. Ibid., p. 83.
25. H. Heine, *Sämtliche Schriften*, Munich, 1975–85, vol. 7, part 1, p. 277.
26. B. V. Ephraim, *Über meine Verhaftung und andere Vorfälle meines Lebens*, Berlin, 1807, p. 103.
27. J. M. Raich, ed., *Dorothea von Schlegel geb. Mendelssohn und deren Söhne: Briefwechsel im Auftrag der Familie Veit*, Mainz, 1881, p. 81.

28. S. Hensel, *The Mendelssohn Family, 1729–1847*, New York, 1881, vol. 1, p. 75.

29. Ibid., p. 80.

30. *Leo Baeck Institute Yearbook* 39 (1994): 21.

31. Arendt, *Rahel Varnhagen*, p. 85.

32. K. A. Varnhagen von Ense, *Denkwürdigkeiten des eigenen Lebens*, ed. K. Feilchenfeldt, Frankfurt, 1987, vol. 3, p. 43.

33. Quoted in *Bulletin of the Leo Baeck Institute* 52 (1976): 28ff.

34. H. Brandenburg, ed., *Das Denkmal. Heinrich Heine: Denkwürdigkeiten, Briefe*, Munich, 1912, p. 18.

35. Ibid., pp. 29–30.

36. Ibid., p. 16.

37. Heine, *Sämtliche Schriften*, vol. 4, p. 572.

38. Frankfurt city archive, Uglb. D33, nos. 97, 120.

39. D. Hertz in Endelman, *Jewish Apostasy*, p. 48.

40. National and University Library, Jerusalem, Ms. collection 662a.

41. H. Spiel, *Fanny von Arnstein, oder die Emanzipation*, Frankfurt, 1962, p. 404.

42. Quoted in F. Gilbert, ed., *Bankiers, Künstler und Gelehrte*, Tübingen, 1975, p. xlvi.

43. K. W. [Grattenauer] *Über die physische und moralische Verfassung der heutigen Juden: Stimmes eines Kosmopoliten*, Leipzig, 1791, pp. 58, 122.

44. J. G. Fichte, *Sämtliche Werke*, Berlin, 1845, vol. 6, p. 149.

45. C. A. H. Burkhardt, ed., *Goethes Unterhaltungen mit dem Kanzler Friedrich von Müller*, Stuttgart, 1870, p. 57.

46. C. Brentano, *Werke*, Leipzig, 1914, vol. 3, p. 264.

47. Ibid., vol. 2, p. 959.

4. HEINE AND BÖRNE

1. H. Finke, *Briefwechsel Friedrich und Dorothea Schlegels, 1818–1820*, Munich, 1922, p. 266.

2. H. Graetz, *History of the Jews*, Philadelphia, 1895, vol. 5, p. 531.

3. The extensive correspondence between Ludwig Robert and Rahel Varnhagen appears in the *Bulletin of the Leo Baeck Institute* 52 (1976).

4. Quoted in W. Keller, *Und wurden zerstreut unter alle Völker*, Munich, 1966, p. 446.

5. Ibid., p. 449.

6. Quoted in E. Sterling, *Judenhass: Die Anfänge des politischen Antisemitismus im Deutschland (1815–1850)*, Frankfurt, 1969, p. 162.

7. Letter to Rahel Varnhagen, Apr. 18, 1815, *Bulletin of the Leo Baeck Institute* 52 (1976): 23.

8. Letter to Rahel Varnhagen, Aug. 22, 1819, *Bulletin of the Leo Baeck Institute* 52 (1976): 35.

9. *Bulletin of the Leo Baeck Institute* 52 (1976): 35.
10. R. Varnhagen, *Gesammelte Werke*, Munich, 1983, vol. 2, pp. 536–37.
11. *Bulletin of the Leo Baeck Institute* 52 (1976): 37.
12. *Leo Baeck Institute Yearbook* 9 (1964): 211.
13. *Leo Baeck Institute Yearbook* 6 (1961): 277; 38 (1993): 35.
14. Quoted in F. Kobler, *Juden und Judentum in deutschen Briefen aus drei Jahrhunderten*, Vienna, 1935, p. 259.
15. Ibid., p. 261.
16. *Goethes Gespräche, Begegnungen und Briefe*, Zurich, 1950, vol. 2, p. 191.
17. Goethe, *Gespräche*, Zurich, 1947, p. 107.
18. A. Leschnitzer, *Saul und David*, Heidelberg, 1954, p. 8.
19. *Leo Baeck Institute Yearbook* 22 (1977): 109.
20. N. N. Glatzer, ed., *Leopold and Adelheid Zunz: An Account in Letters, 1815–1885*, London, 1958, p. xvi.
21. H. G. Reissner, *Eduard Gans: Ein Leben im Vormärz*, Tübingen, 1965, p. 53.
22. Quoted in *Leo Baeck Institute Yearbook* 11 (1966): 164n.
23. Zunz papers, Ms. collection, National and University Library, Jerusalem, file 7007.
24. Ibid., p. 13.
25. Glatzer, *Leopold and Adelheid Zunz*, p. 20.
26. N. N. Glatzer, ed., *Leopold Zunz: Jude-Deutscher-Europaer*, Tübingen, 1964, p. 12.
27. Zunz papers. I am grateful to Paul Mendes-Flohr for bringing this heretofore unknown document to my attention.
28. Quoted in Glatzer, *Leopold Zunz*, p. 14.
29. Ibid., p. 17.
30. Reissner, *Eduard Gans*, p. 77.
31. Ibid., p. 56.
32. Ibid., p. 65.
33. Ibid., p. 93.
34. S. Kaznelson, ed., *Jüdisches Schicksal in deutschen Gedichten: Eine abschliessende Anthologie*, Berlin, 1959, p. 261.
35. H. Heine, *Confessio Judaica*, ed. H. Bieber, Berlin, 1925, p. 90; H. Heine, *Selected Prose*, trans. and ed. Ritchie Robertson, London, 1993, p. 179.
36. H. Heine, *Sämtliche Schriften*, Munich, 1975–85, vol. 2, p. 55.
37. *Almansor*, scene 1.
38. G. Steiger, *Aufbruch, Urburschenschaft und Wartburgfest*, Leipzig, 1867, pp. 111–12.
39. H. Heine, *Briefe*, ed. F. Hirth, Mainz, 1950–57, vol. 1, p. 92.
40. *Goethe im Gespräch*, Zurich, 1944, p. 420.
41. Heine, *Sämtliche Schriften*, vol. 2, p. 7.
42. Heine, *Briefe*, vol. 1, p. 117.

43. Heine, *Sämtliche Schriften*, vol. 2, p. 69.
44. Reissner, *Eduard Gans*, p. 95.
45. Heine to Immanuel Wohlwill, Apr. 1, 1823, in *Confessio Judaica*, p. 13.
46. Heine to Wohlwill, June 18, 1823.
47. "Zeitgedichte XI: Das Neue Israelitische Hospital zu Hamburg."
48. Heine to his brother-in-law, Moritz Embden, May 3, 1823, in *Confessio Judaica*, p. 14.
49. Heine to Moses Moser, Sept. 17, 1823, in *Confessio Judaica*, p. 14.
50. Quoted in *Heine Jahrbuch*, ed. E. Galley, Düsseldorf, 1968, p. 14.
51. M. Werner, ed., *Begegnungen mit Heine*, in H. H. Houben, *Gespräche mit Heine, 1797–1845*, Hamburg, 1973, vol. 1, p. 128.
52. Heine to Moses Moser, Dec. 14, 1825; Jan. 9, 1826, in *Confessio Judaica*, pp. 64, 68.
53. Reissner, *Eduard Gans*, p. 36.
54. Heine to Moses Moser, Dec. 14, 1825, in *Confessio Judaica*, p. 64.
55. Ibid., Apr. 23, 1826.
56. Werner, *Begegnungen mit Heine*, vol. 2, p. 180.
57. Heine, *Sämtliche Schriften*, vol. 2, p. 291.
58. M. Reich-Ranicki, *Über Ruhestörer: Juden in der deutschen Literatur*, Munich, 1973, pp. 59, 61.
59. Heine to Moses Moser, July 8, 1826, in *Confessio Judaica*, p. 70.
60. Werner, *Begegnungen mit Heine*, vol. 2, p. 394.
61. H. Brandenburg, ed., *Das Denkmal. Heinrich Heine: Denkwürdigkeiten, Briefe*, Munich, 1912, pp. 181–82.
62. Kobler, *Juden und Judentum*, pp. 255–56.
63. R. Schumann to H. von Kurrer, June 9, 1828.
64. Reich-Ranicki, *Über Ruhestörer*, p. 59.
65. M. Oppenheim, *Erinnerungen*, Frankfurt, 1923, p. 82.
66. L. Börne, *Sämtliche Schriften*, Düsseldorf, 1964, vol. 3, p. 511.
67. H. Heine, "Über Ludwig Börne," *Confessio Judaica*, p. 72.
68. Börne, *Sämtliche Schriften*, vol. 1, p. 510.
69. Ibid., vol. 1, p. 286.
70. L. Marcuse, *Revolutionär und Patriot: Das Leben Ludwig Börnes*, Leipzig, 1929, p. 211.
71. Börne, *Samtliche Schriften*, vol. 1, p. 684.
72. K. Feilchenfeldt, ed., *Rahel Varnhagen: Gesammelte Werke*, Munich, 1983, vol. 9, pp. 679–82.
73. See H. M. Enzensberger, ed., *Ludwig Börne und Heinrich Heine: Ein deutsches Zerwurfnis*, Frankfurt, 1997.
74. Heine to Anonymous, July 1, 1830.
75. Werner, *Begegnungen mit Heine*, vol. 1, p. 310.
76. Ibid., vol. 1, p. 357.
77. Ibid., vol. 1, p. 315.

78. Quoted in Steiner, *After Babel: Aspects of Language and Translation*, London, 1975, p. 240.

79. Werner, *Begegnungen mit Heine*, vol. 1, p. 273.

80. Quoted in M. Brod, *Heinrich Heine*, Berlin, 1935, p. 149.

81. Werner, *Begegnungen mit Heine*, vol. 1, p. 295.

82. F. Kafka, *Letters to Milena*, trans. Philip Boehm, New York, 1990, p. 19.

83. G. Mann, *The History of Germany since 1789*, Harmondsworth, 1985, p. 121.

84. *Jahrbuch für deutsche Literatur und Kunst*, Hanover, 1855, vol. 2, p. 230.

85. H. Heine, "Zur Geschichte von Religion und Philosophie im Deutschland," *Sämtliche Schriften*, vol. 3, p. 505.

86. Ibid. English translation in Mann, *History of Germany*, pp. 139, 142.

87. Werner, *Begegnungen mit Heine*, vol. 2, p. 555.

88. Oppenheim, *Erinnerungen*, p. 67.

89. Werner, *Begegnungen mit Heine*, vol. 2, p. 436.

90. Ibid., vol. 2, p. 362.

91. Brod, *Heinrich Heine*, p. 226.

92. Werner, *Begegnungen mit Heine*, vol. 2, p. 547.

5. SPRING OF NATIONS

1. L. Bamberger, *Erinnerungen*, Berlin, 1899, p. 18.

2. Ibid., p. 24.

3. Ibid., p. 25.

4. Ibid., p. 26.

5. H. Simon, ed., *Leopold Sonnemann: Seine Jugendgeschichte bis zur Entstehung der "Frankfurter Zeitung,"* Frankfurt, 1931, p. 53.

6. *Der Orient*, 1848, p. 121.

7. Quoted in M. Brenner et al., eds., *Deutsch-jüdische Geschichte in der Neuzeit, 1780–1871*, Munich, 1996, vol. 2, p. 297.

8. R. Payne, *Marx*, London, 1968, pp. 67ff.; P. Johnson, *Intellectuals*, New York, 1988, pp. 54, 55.

9. K. Marx, *Early Writings*, London, 1963, pp. 34–37.

10. S. Born, *Erinnerungen eines Achtundvierzigers*, Leipzig, 1898, pp. 101, 117.

11. *Der Orient*, 1848, p. 91.

12. Ibid., p. 27.

13. Ibid.

14. National and University Library, Jerusalem, Ms. collection ARC 1588/69.

15. R. Taylor, *Richard Wagner*, London, 1979, p. 85; Martin Gregor-Deilin, *Richard Wagner*, Munich, 1980, p. 266.

16. A. Bettelheim, *Berthold Auerbach: Der Mann, sein Werk, sein Nachlass*, Stuttgart, 1907, p. 212.

17. E. Fuchs, *Die Juden in der Karikatur*, Langen, 1921, p. 125.

18. *Leo Baeck Institute Yearbook* 5 (1960): 132.

19. N. N. Glatzer, ed., *Leopold Zunz and Adelheid Zunz: An Account in Letters, 1815–1885*, London, 1958, p. 132.

20. *Allgemeine Zeitung des Judentums* 12 (1848): 210.

21. R. Rürup, ed., *Jüdische Geschichte in Berlin: Essays und Studien*, Berlin, 1995, p. 65.

22. L. von Ranke, ed., *Aus dem Briefwechsel Friedrich-Wilhelms IV mit Bunsen*, Leipzig, 1873, p. 169.

23. K. L. von Prittwitz, *Berlin 1848: Das Erinnerungswerk des Generalleutenants Karl Ludwig von Prittwitz*, Berlin, 1985, p. 149.

24. Quoted in S. Baron, "The Impact of the Revolution of 1848 on Jewish Emancipation," *Jewish Social Studies*, 1949, p. 230.

25. *Berliner Strasseneckenliteratur, 1848–49*, Stuttgart, 1977, p. 87.

26. D. Kastner, *Der Rheinische Provinziallandtag und die Emanzipation der Juden im Rheinland, 1825–1845*, Cologne, 1989, p. 299.

27. M. Stürmer et al., *Wägen und Wägen: Sal. Oppenheim Jr. & Cie. Geschichte einer Bank und einer Familie*, Berlin, 1992, p. 126.

28. S. Grossmann, *Ferdinand Lassalle*, Berlin, 1919, p. 14.

29. D. Nick, *Jüdisches Wirken in Breslau*, Würzburg, 1998, p. 12.

30. N. N. Glatzer, ed., *Leopold Zunz: Jude-Deutscher-Europaer*, Tübingen, 1964, p. 258.

31. *Leo Baeck Institute Yearbook* 5 (1960): 129, 137.

32. *Der Orient*, 1848, pp. 28, 114, 165.

33. *Der Orient*, Apr. 8, 1848.

34. Quoted in Rürup, *Jüdische Geschichte in Berlin*, p. 70.

35. *Jahrbuch des Instituts für deutsche Geschichte* (Tel Aviv University) 15 (1985): 342.

36. A. Goldschmidt, ed., *Levin Goldschmidt: Ein Lebensbild in Briefen*, Berlin, 1898, p. 101.

37. Quoted in J. Toury, *Bulletin of the Leo Baeck Institute* 9 (1960): 59.

38. F. Kobler, *Juden und Judentum in deutschen Briefen aus drei Jahrhunderten*, Vienna, 1935, p. 165.

39. Quoted in L. B. Stein, *Auerbach und das Judentum*, Berlin, 1882, p. 34.

40. Auerbach papers, Deutsches Literaturarchiv, Marbach am Neckar.

41. R. Wagner, "Die Juden in der Musik," 1850.

42. Bettelheim, *Berthold Auerbach*, p. 179.

43. Auerbach to Ferdinand Freiligrath, Nov. 24, 1843, in Bettelheim, *Berthold Auerbach*, p. 161.

44. Ibid.

45. Ibid., p. 365.

46. Ibid., p. 211.

47. Ibid., p. 213.

48. Ibid.

49. Ibid., p. 436.

50. National and University Library, Jerusalem, Ms. collection ARC 4 1588/ 70.

51. B. Auerbach, *Tagebuch aus Wien*, Breslau, 1849, p. 226.

52. *Leipziger Tageblatt*, Nov. 28, 1849.

53. *Der Orient*, Dec. 8, 1849.

54. F. Lewald, *Erinnerungen aus dem Jahre 1848*, Frankfurt, n.d., p. 355.

55. Letter of Sept. 29, 1832, in E. Silberner, ed., *Johann Jacoby Briefwechsel 1816–1849*, Hanover, 1974.

56. G. Riesser, *Gesammelte Schriften*, Frankfurt, 1867–68, vol. 2, p. 671.

57. H. Laube, *Das erste deutsche Parlament*, Leipzig, 1849, vol. 3, p. 336.

58. G. Meinhardt, *Eduard von Simson*, Bonn, 1981, p. 69; J. H. Schoeps, *Deutsch-jüdische Symbiose oder die missglückte Emanzipation*, Berlin, 1996, p. 117.

59. Riesser, *Gesammelte Schriften*, vol. 2, p. 679.

60. F. J. Raddatz, ed., *Mohr an General: Marx und Engels in ihren Briefen*, Vienna, 1980, p. 28.

61. M. Werner, ed., *Begegnungen mit Heine*, in H. H. Houben, *Gespräche mit Heine, 1797–1845*, Hamburg, 1973, vol. 2, p. 110.

62. A. Herzen, *My Past and Thoughts*, New York, 1974, p. 598.

63. E. Hamburger, *Juden im öffentlichen Leben Deutschlands*, Tübingen, 1968, p. 203.

64. Quoted in W. Keller, *Und wurden zerstreut unter alle Völker*, Munich, 1966, p. 457.

65. Translation by A. Kramer, in *The Poetry and Prose of Heinrich Heine*, ed. F. Ewen, New York, 1948.

66. Werner, *Begegnungen mit Heine*, vol. 2, p. 196.

67. *Der Spiegel*, Mar. 16, 1998.

68. Bamberger, *Erinnerungen*, p. 20.

69. L. Bamberger, *Erlebnisse aus der Pfälzer Erhebung, Mai–Juni 1849*, in Bamberger, *Politische Schriften von 1845 bis 1868*, Berlin, 1985, pp. 69–71.

70. Ibid., p. 71.

6. HOPES AND ANXIETIES

1. *Leo Baeck Institute Yearbook* 12 (1967): 249.

2. L. Bamberger, *Erinnerungen*, Berlin, 1899, p. 268.

3. Ibid., pp. 257–58.

4. *Leo Baeck Institute Yearbook* 12 (1967): 250.

5. Bamberger, *Erinnerungen*, pp. 499, 500.

6. E. Feder, ed., *Die geheimen Tagebücher Ludwig Bambergers*, Frankfurt, 1933, p. 91.

7. Quoted in S. Zucker, "Ludwig Bamberger and the Rise of Anti-Semitism in Germany, 1848–1893," *Central European History* 3 (1970): 335.

8. Ibid.

9. Bamberger, *Erinnerungen*, p. 506.

10. L. von Roenne and H. Simon, *Die früheren und gegenwärtigen Verhältnisse der Juden im sämtlichen Landteilen des preussischen Staates*, Breslau, 1843.

11. Bamberger, *Erinnerungen*, p. 507.

12. Ibid., p. 508.

13. Ibid.

14. E. Hamburger, *Juden im öffentlichen Leben Deutschlands*, Tübingen, 1963, p. 186.

15. Bamberger, *Erinnerungen*, p. 508.

16. Ibid., p. 525.

17. Ibid., pp. 501, 519–20, 541.

18. Quoted in S. Zucker, *Ludwig Bamberger: German Liberal Politician and Social Critic, 1823–1899*, Pittsburgh, 1975, pp. 42, 43.

19. Zucker, "Rise of Anti-Semitism," p. 338.

20. *Im deutschen Reich: Zeitschrift des Centralvereins deutscher Staatsbürger jüdischen Glaubens*, Berlin, 1899, p. 204.

21. J. Toury, *Die politischen Orientierungen der Juden in Deutschland*, Tübingen, 1966, p. 152.

22. L. Bamberger, *Gesammelte Schriften*, Berlin, 1898, vol. 1, p. 424.

23. F. Stern, *Gold and Iron: Bismarck, Bleichröder, and the Building of the German Empire*, New York, 1979, p. 146.

24. Feder, *Die geheimen Tagebücher*, p. 87.

25. Ibid., p. 86.

26. Stern, *Gold and Iron*, p. 48.

27. Ibid., p. 146.

28. Ibid., p. 48.

29. Ibid., p. 152.

30. Hamburger, *Juden im öffentlichen Leben*, p. 135.

31. Quoted in L. B. Stern, *Berthold Auerbach und das Judentum*, Berlin, 1882, p. 33.

32. A. Bettelheim, *Berthold Auerbach: Der Mann, sein Werk, sein Nachlass*, Stuttgart, 1907, Berlin, 1899, p. 330.

33. B. Auerbach, *Briefe an Jakob Auerbach*, Frankfurt, 1884, vol. 2, p. 67.

34. K. H. Hoefele, *Geist und Gesellschaft der Bismarckzeit, 1870–1890*, Göttingen, 1967, p. 449.

35. J. Toury, *Die politischen Orientierungen*, p. 136.

36. H. von Treitschke, *Deutsche Geschichte im 19. Jahrhundert*, Leipzig, 1913–14, vol. 5, p. 139.

37. Hamburger, *Juden im offentlichen Leben*, p. 317.

38. G. Herwegh, *Morgenruf: Ausgwählte Gedichte*, Leipzig, 1969, p. 130.

39. K. Gerteis, *Leopold Sonnemann*, Frankfurt, 1970, p. 53.

40. Toury, *Die politischen Orientierungen*, p. 156.

41. L. Sonnemann, *Reichstagreden*, Frankfurt, 1901, p. 22, in Gerteis, *Leopold Sonnemann*, p. 62.

42. *Geschichte der Frankfurter Zeitung*, Frankfurt, 1911, p. 210.

43. Stern, *Gold and Iron*, p. 173.

44. Auerbach, *Briefe an Jakob Auerbach*, vol. 2, p. 56.

45. Gerteis, *Leopold Sonnemann*, p. 63.

46. Quoted in G. A. Craig, *Germany, 1866–1945*, Oxford, 1978, p. 30.

47. *Frankfurter Zeitung*, Dec. 1, 1876.

48. Heinrich E. Brockhaus, *Stunden mit Bismarck, 1871–1878*, Leipzig, 1929, p. 67.

49. E. Herz, *Before the Fury: Jews and Germans before Hitler*, New York, 1967, p. 21.

50. Comité zur Abwehr antisemitischer Angriffe in Berlin, eds., *Die Juden als Soldaten*, Berlin, 1896, p. 69.

51. T. Fontane, *Der deutsche Krieg von 1866*, Berlin, 1881, p. 143.

52. *Allgemeine Israelitische Wochenschrift*, 1870, p. 432.

53. *Allgemeine Zeitung des Judentums*, 1870, pp. 823–25, 857–61, 873–74, 893.

54. Graetz to Heinrich von Treitschke, in W. Boehlich, ed., *Der Berliner Antisemitismusstreit*, Frankfurt, 1988, p. 52.

55. F. Mauthner, *Ausgewählte Schriften*, Berlin, 1919, p. 365.

56. N. Sombart, *Nachdenken über Deutschland*, Berlin, 1987, p. 268.

57. Composite tables in *Leo Baeck Institute Yearbook* 28 (1983): 79–80 compiled from comprehensive numerical data in J. Toury, "Der Eintritt der Juden ins deutsche Bürgertum," *Das Judentum in der deutschen Umwelt, 1800–1850*, ed. H. Liebeschütz and A. Paucker, Tübingen, 1977, pp. 139–242, and in Toury, *Soziale und politische Geschichte der Juden in Deutschland, 1847–1871*, Düsseldorf, 1977.

58. M. Lazarus, *Aus meiner Jugend*, Frankfurt, 1913, p. 14.

59. H. B. Oppenheim in *Die Gegenwart* 17 (1880): 18.

60. P. Johnson, *History of the Jews*, New York, 1987, p. 345.

61. L. Heid and J. H. Schoeps, eds., *Juden in Deutschland: Ein Lesebuch*, Munich, 1994, p. 14.

62. F. Gilbert, ed., *Bankiers, Künstler und Gelehrte*, Tübingen, 1975, p. xxxvi.

63. Boehlich, *Der Berliner Antisemitismusstreit*.

64. Ibid., pp. 139, 149.

65. S. T. Taylor, *Reminiscences of Berlin during the Franco-German War of 1870–71*, London, 1885, p. 238.

66. Quoted in Heid and Schoeps, *Juden in Deutschland*, p. 14.

67. E. Bernstein, *Kindheit und Jugendjahre*, Berlin, 1926, pp. 9, 41, 65.

68. G. Seeber, ed., *Gestalten der Bismarckzeit*, Berlin, 1978, pp. 168f.

69. *Leo Baeck Institute Yearbook* 6 (1961): 114.

70. Quoted in F. Stern, *Central European History* 3 (1970): 55n.

71. *Allgemeine Zeitung des Judentums,* 1873, pp. 118–19.

72. V. Ullrich, *Die nervöse Grossmacht: Aufsteig und Untergang des deutschen Kaiserreichs, 1871–1918,* Frankfurt, 1997, p. 45.

73. W. Keller, *Und wurden zerstreut unter alle Völker,* Munich, 1966, p. 478.

74. L. Bamberger, *Bismarck,* Berlin, 1899, p. 35.

75. Boehlich, *Der Berliner Antisemitismusstreit,* p. 157.

76. Auerbach, *Briefe an Jakob Auerbach,* vol. 2, p. 81.

77. Quoted in Stern, *Gold and Iron,* p. 463n.

78. Ullrich, *Die nervöse Grossmacht,* p. 387.

79. A. Stöcker, *Reden und Aufsätze,* Berlin, 1885, p. 145.

80. P. Massing, *Vorgeschichte des politischen Antisemitismus,* in *Frankfurter Beiträge zur Soziologie,* Frankfurt, 1959, p. 40.

81. Stern, *Gold and Iron,* p. 520.

82. Ibid., p. 521.

83. M. Meyer, "Jewish Reaction to New Hostility in Germany, 1879–1881," *Leo Baeck Institute Yearbook* 11 (1966): 143.

84. Quoted in Boehlich, *Der Berliner Antisemitismusstreit,* pp. 7–14.

85. Meyer, "Jewish Reaction," p. 166.

86. Boehlich, *Der Berliner Antisemitismusstreit,* p. 140.

87. Ibid., p. 216.

88. Ibid., p. 227.

89. Auerbach, *Briefe an Jakob Auerbach,* vol. 2, pp. 441–43.

90. K. Baumbach, ed., *Eduard Lasker: Biographie und letzte öffentliche Rede,* Stuttgart, 1884, p. 32.

91. O. Hartwig, *Ludwig Bamberger: Eine biographische Skizze,* Marburg, 1900, p. 75.

92. T. Fontane, *Briefe,* Berlin, 1996, vol. 3, p. 71.

93. M. Stern, *Berthold Auerbach und das Judentum,* p. 36.

94. Toury, *Die politischen Orientierungen,* p. 177.

95. Auerbach, *Briefe an Jakob Auerbach,* vol. 2, p. 442.

7. YEARS OF PROGRESS

1. G. A. Craig, "The End of the Golden Age," *New York Review of Books,* Nov. 4, 1999, p. 13.

2. W. Benjamin, *One-Way Street and Other Writings,* trans. E. Jephcott and K. Shorter, London, 1985, p. 328.

3. P. Gay, *Freud, Jews, and Other Germans,* Oxford, 1978, p. 78.

4. Unpublished ms. cited by H. Meier-Cronemeyer in *Germania-Judaica; Kölner Bibliothek zur Geschichte des deutschen Judentums,* vol. 8, nos. 1–2, Cologne, 1969, p. 4.

5. S. Zweig, *The World of Yesterday*, London, 1945, p. 28.
6. Ibid., p. 30.
7. A. Schnitzler, *My Youth in Vienna*, trans. C. Hutter, New York, 1970, p. 63.
8. Ibid., p. 6.
9. *Zeitschrift für Demographie und Statistik der Juden*, Jan.–Feb. 1924, p. 25.
10. F. Theilhaber, *Der Untergang der deutschen Juden*, Munich, 1911.
11. Quoted in M. Richarz, *Bürger auf Widerruf: Lebenszeugnisse deutscher Juden, 1780–1945*, Munich, 1989, pp. 310–11.
12. H. Kohn, *Martin Buber: Sein Werk und seine Zeit*, Cologne, 1961, p. 25.
13. V. Klemperer, *Curriculum Vitae: Erinnerungen 1881–1918*, Berlin, 1996, vol. 1, p. 96.
14. G. Tietz, *Hermann Tietz: Geschichte einer Familie und ihrer Warenhäuser*, Stuttgart, 1965, pp. 37, 53.
15. Klemperer, *Curriculum Vitae*, vol. 1, p. 44.
16. Ibid.
17. Ibid., pp. 44–45.
18. K. Hiller, *Leben gegen die Zeit*, Hamburg, 1969, p. 33.
19. E. Ludwig, *Geschenke des Lebens*, Berlin, 1932, p. 101.
20. W. Benjamin, *Berliner Kindheit um Neunzehnhundert*, Frankfurt, 1950, p. 47.
21. M. Brod, *Streitbares Leben*, Munich, 1969, p. 222.
22. F. Kafka, *Letters to Felice*, trans. J. Stern and E. Duckworth, New York, 1973, p. 502 (Sept. 16, 1916).
23. F. Kafka, *Letter to His Father*, trans. E. Kaiser and E. Wilkins, New York, 1966, p. 77.
24. Kafka, *Letters to Felice*, p. 55 (Nov. 21, 1912).
25. F. Kafka, *The Diaries*, ed. Max Brod, New York, 1976, p. 169 (Jan. 7, 1912), p. 252 (Jan. 8, 1914).
26. W. Sombart, ed., *Judentaufen*, Munich, 1912, p. 77.
27. Klemperer, *Curriculum Vitae*, vol. 1, p. 350.
28. G. Kisch, *Judentaufen*, Berlin, 1933, p. 49.
29. Ibid., p. 17.
30. *Die Zukunft*, Mar. 6, 1897.
31. H. Kessler, *Walther Rathenau: Sein Leben und sein Werk*, Frankfurt, 1988, pp. 41–42.
32. *Die Zukunft*, Mar. 6, 1897.
33. W. Rathenau, *Zur Kritik der Zeit*, Berlin, 1912, p. 189.
34. Kessler, *Walther Rathenau*, p. 49.
35. E. Schulin, ed., *Hauptwerke und Gespräche*, vol. 2 of *Walther Rathenau: Gesamtausgabe*, Munich, 1977, p. 783.
36. B. von Bülow, *Denkwürdigkeiten*, Berlin, 1920, vol. 3, pp. 39ff.
37. A. Schnitzler, *The Road into the Open*, trans. R. Byers, San Francisco, 1992, p. 36.

38. Quoted in G. Scholem, *From Berlin to Jerusalem*, Tel Aviv, 1982, p. 70.
39. W. E. Mosse and A. Paucker, eds., *Juden im Wilhelminischen Deutschland, 1890–1914*, Tübingen, 1998, pp. 697–98.
40. *Judische Rundschau*, Oct. 11, 1918, p. 320.
41. S. Kaznelson, ed., *Jüdisches Schicksal in deutschen Gedichten: Eine abschliessende Anthologie*, Berlin, 1959.
42. S. Aschheim in S. L. Gilman and J. Zipes, eds., *Yale Companion to Jewish Writing and Thought in German Culture, 1096–1996*, New Haven, 1997, p. 302.
43. A. Paucker, "Zur Problematik einer jüdischen Abwehrstrategie in der deutschen Gesellschaft," *Juden im Wilhelminischen Deutschland*, ed. Mosse and Paucker, p. 487.
44. F. Gilbert, ed., *Bankiers, Künstler und Gelehrte*, Tübingen, 1975, p. xxxvii.
45. Willy Ritter Liebermann von Wahlendorf, *Erinnerungen eines deutschen Juden, 1863–1936*, Munich, 1988, p. 228.
46. Ibid., p. 17.
47. Ibid., p. 108.
48. Ibid., p. 27.
49. Ibid., pp. 60–61.
50. Ibid., p. 64.
51. Ibid., pp. 286, 47.
52. T. Lessing, *Einmal und nie wieder*, Gütersloh, 1967, p. 123.
53. P. Gay, Introduction to R. Gay, *The Jews of Germany: A Historical Portrait*, New Haven, 1992, p. xii.
54. E. Cahen, *Les héros de Wissembourg*, Paris, 1898, quoted in *Leo Baeck Institute Yearbook* 28 (1983): 139.
55. A. Landsberger, *Judentaufen*, Munich, 1912, p. 4.
56. J. Namier, *Lewis Namier: A Biography*, Oxford, 1971, p. 101.
57. Klemperer, *Curriculum Vitae*, vol. 1, p. 524.
58. *Leo Baeck Institute Yearbook* 3 (1958): 81.
59. E. Zechlin, *Die deutsche Politik und die Juden im Ersten Weltkrieg*, Göttingen, 1969, pp. 471ff.
60. P. Pulzer, in Mosse and Paucker, *Juden im Wilhelminischen Deutschland*, p. 199.
61. E. Reichmann, *Flucht in den Hass*, Frankfurt, 1974, p. 172.
62. A. Paucker, in Mosse and Paucker, *Juden in Wilhelminischen Deutschland*, p. 492n.
63. N. Sombart, *Die Deutschen Männer und ihre Feinde*, Munich, 1991, p. 271.
64. C. Schmölders, *Merkur: Deutsche Zeitschrift für europäisches Denken* 596 (1997): 1039.
65. P. Gay, *Freud, Jews, and Other Germans*, p. 142. The translations are by Robert P. Newton in *Your Diamond Dreams Cut Open My Arteries: Poems by Else Lasker-Schüler*, Chapel Hill, 1982, pp. 137, 251.

8. ASSIMILATION AND ITS DISCONTENTS

1. S. Volkov, "Geschichte und Gesellschaft," *Zeitschrift fur historische Sozialwissenschaft* 3 (1983): 338.

2. *Marx-Engels Werke*, Berlin, 1963, vol. 12, p. 99.

3. *Allgemeine Zeitung des Judentums*, Dec. 12, 1881, p. 862.

4. R. Wagner, *Mein Leben*, Munich, 1963, p. 747; C. Wagner, *Tagebücher*, Munich, 1982, vol. 1, p. 82.

5. C. M. M. Girardet, *Jüdische Mäzene für preussische Museen in Berlin*, Berlin, 1997, p. 31.

6. Ibid., p. 26.

7. R. Vierhaus, ed., *Tagebuch der Baronin Spitzemberg*, Göttingen, 1963, p. 348.

8. K. Schreinert, ed., *Theodor Fontane: Briefe an Friedlander*, Heidelberg, 1954, pp. 312, 309; *Briefe an F. Paulsen*, Bern, 1949, p. 6.

9. Quoted in German in P. Gay, *Freud, Jews, and Other Germans*, Oxford, 1978, p. 41. The translation is mine.

10. R. Zedlitz-Trützschler, *Zwölf Jahre am deutschen Kaiserhof*, Berlin, 1924, p. 84.

11. H. S. Chamberlain, *Briefe*, Munich, 1928, vol. 2, p. 273.

12. Quoted in H. Arendt, *The Origins of Totalitarianism*, New York, 1976, p. 185.

13. J. Reinharz and W. Schatzberg, eds., *The Jewish Response to German Culture: From the Enlightenment to the Second World War*, Hanover, 1985, p. 170.

14. C. Weizmann, *Trial and Error*, London, 1949, p. 12.

15. Ibid., p. 41.

16. W. E. Mosse, in Reinharz and Schatzberg, *Jewish Response to German Culture*, p. 171.

17. Ibid., p. 189n.

18. Ibid., p. 183.

19. M. Richarz, ed., *Jüdisches Leben in Deutschland: Selbstzeugnisse zur Sozialgeschichte*, Stuttgart, 1979, vol. 2, p. 68.

20. Reinharz and Schatzberg, *Jewish Response to German Culture*, p. 160; *Leo Baeck Institute Yearbook* 10 (1965): 10.

21. G. Mahler, *Erinnerungen und Briefe*, Amsterdam, 1940, p. 259.

22. *Die Zukunft*, Mar. 6, 1897.

23. Quoted in S. Aschheim, *Brothers and Strangers: The East European Jew in German and German Jewish Consciousness*, Madison, 1982, p. 36.

24. *Allgemeine Zeitung des Judentums*, April 19, 1881.

25. Aschheim, *Brothers and Strangers*, p. 36.

26. F. Stern, *Einstein's German World*, Princeton, 1999, p. 4.

27. *Der Kunstwart*, March 1, 1912.

28. R. Marwedel, *Theodor Lessing, 1872–1933: Eine Biographie*, Oldenburg, 1990, p. 138.

29. S. Volkov, *Jüdisches Leben und Antisemitismus im 19. und 20. Jahrhundert*, Munich, 1990, pp. 146ff.

30. Quoted in F. Stern, *Verspielte Grösse*, Munich, 1998, p. 171.

31. D. Farrer, *The Warburgs*, New York, 1975, p. 35.

32. P. Gay, *Freud, Jews, and Other Germans*, p. 130.

33. B. von Bülow, *Denkwürdigkeiten*, Berlin, 1930, vol. 1, p. 254.

34. H. and B. Ellern, eds., *Herzl, Hechler, the Grand Duke of Baden, and the German Emperor*, facsimile letters, Tel Aviv, 1961, p. 48.

35. Quoted in A. Bein, "Erinnerungen und Dokumente über Herzls Begegnung mit Wilhelm," *Zeitschrift fur die Geschichte der Juden* 11 (1960): 62.

36. T. Herzl, *The Complete Diaries of Theodor Herzl*, ed. R. Patai, trans. H. Zohn, New York, 1960, entry for Oct. 7, 1898.

37. Ibid., Oct. 9, 1898.

38. Ibid., June 3, 1895.

39. Central Zionist Archives, Jerusalem, H/4/File B.

40. T. Herzl, *The Jewish State*, trans. S. D'Avigdor, New York, 1946, p. 10.

41. T. Herzl, *Zionistische Schriften*, Berlin, 1920, p. 15.

42. Herzl, *Complete Diaries*, June 2, 1895.

43. Ibid., June 22, 1895.

44. M. I. Bodenheimer, *Wohin mit den russischen Juden?*, Hamburg, 1891, p. 3.

45. The full text is in A. Hertzberg, *The Zionist Idea*, New York, 1972, p. 188.

46. B. Cohn, *Vor den Sturm*, Berlin, 1896, pp. 9, 12, 48.

47. S. Zweig, *The World of Yesterday*, London, 1945, p. 87; Zweig memoir in Central Zionist Archives, Jerusalem, H/NX/49.

48. Quoted in W. E. Mosse and A. Paucker, eds., *Juden im Wilhelminischen Deutschland, 1890–1914*, Tübingen, 1998, p. 654.

49. A. Leschnitzer, *Saul und David*, p. 209, n. 1.

50. W. Rathenau, *Gesammtausgabe*, Munich, 1977, vol. 2, p. 787.

51. R. Kallner, *Herzl und Rathenau*, Stuttgart, 1976, pp. 292, 291.

52. Quoted in P. Mendes-Flohr, ed., *Deutsch-Jüdische Geschichte der Neuzeit, 1871–1918*, Munich, 1997, p. 354.

53. *Leo Baeck Institute Yearbook* 3 (1958): 212.

54. Mosse and Paucker, *Juden im Wilhelminischen Deutschland*, p. 666.

55. F. Oppenheimer, *Erlebtes, Erstrebtes, Erreichtes*, Düsseldorf, 1964, p. 212.

56. K. Blumenfeld, *Erlebte Judenfrage*, Stuttgart, 1962, p. 96.

57. W. T. Angress, "The *Judenwahlen* and the Jewish Question," *Leo Baeck Institute Yearbook* 28 (1983): 375.

58. R. Lichtheim, *Rückkehr*, Jerusalem, 1960, pp. 60–61.

59. Blumenfeld, *Erlebte Judenfrage*, pp. 28, 34.

60. W. von Goethe, "Suleika," *Poems of the West and East*, trans. J. Whaley, Bern, 1998, p. 281.

61. *Hannah Arendt–Karl Jaspers: Correspondence, 1926–1969*, ed. L. Kohler and H. Saner, New York, 1985, p. 198.
62. Blumenfeld, *Erlebte Judenfrage*, p. 68.
63. *Arendt–Jaspers Correspondence*, p. 244.
64. Blumenfeld, *Erlebte Judenfrage*, p. 90.
65. L. Frank, *Aufsätze, Reden und Briefe*, Berlin, 1924, p. 348; R. Schay, *Juden in der deutschen Politik*, Berlin, 1923, pp. 219ff.
66. J. Toury, *Die politischen Orientierungen der Juden in Deutschland*, Tübingen, 1966, p. 315.
67. Gay, *Freud, Jews, and Other Germans*, p. 158.
68. H. Kessler, *Künstler und Nationen*, Frankfurt, 1988, p. 279.
69. A. Einstein, *Ideas and Opinions*, trans. S. Bargmann, New York, 1964, p. 171.
70. Quoted in R. W. Clark, *Einstein: The Life and Times*, New York, 1971, p. 183.
71. Stern, *Einstein's German World*, p. 67.

9. WAR FEVER

1. H. Kessler, *Walther Rathenau: Sein Leben und sein Werk*, Berlin, 1988, p. 168.
2. S. Haffner, *Die deutsche Revolution*, Munich, 1979, p. 17.
3. K. Rietzler, *Tagebücher, Aufsatze und Dokumente*, Göttingen, 1972, entry for July 27, 1914.
4. T. Wolff, *Tagebücher 1914–1919*, Boppard, 1984, p. 66.
5. T. Mann, *Doctor Faustus*, trans. John Wood, New York, 1997, p. 318. Emphasis mine.
6. A. Hitler, *Mein Kampf*, trans. Ralph Manheim, London, 1992, p. 148.
7. E. Simon, *Unser Kriegserlebnis*, in *Gesammelte Aufsätze*, Heidelberg, 1965, p. 18.
8. C. Schmölders, *Hitlers Gesicht: Eine physiognomische Biographie*, Munich, 2000, p. 49.
9. T. Mann, *Betrachtungen eines Unpolitischen*, Frankfurt, 1956, p. 60.
10. T. Mann, *Friedrich und die grosse Koalition*, Berlin, 1916, pp. 14, 21, 126ff.
11. *Frankfurter Zeitung*, Sept. 12, 1914.
12. Quoted in F. Stern, *Einstein's German World*, Princeton, 1999, p. 212.
13. Quoted in P. Mendes-Flohr, "The *Kriegserlebnis* and Jewish Consciousness," *Jews in the Weimar Republic*, ed. W. Benz, Tübingen, 1998, p. 226.
14. N. Ferguson, *The Pity of War*, London, 1999. Colonel House is quoted on p. 153.
15. E. Zechlin, *Die Deutsche Politik und die Juden im Ersten Weltkrieg*, Göttingen, 1969, p. 88.
16. M. Sperber, *All das Vergangene*, Vienna, 1983, p. 121.
17. H. Bergmann, *Tagebücher*, Königstein, 1985, p. 59.

18. F. J. Strauss, ed., *Kriegsbriefe gefallener deutschen Juden*, Berlin, 1961, p. 22.

19. G. Kotowski et al., eds., *1914–1933: Historisches Lesebuch*, Frankfurt, 1968, p. 27.

20. P. Rieger, *Ein Vierteljahrhundert im Kampf um das Recht und die Zukunft der deutschen Juden*, Berlin, 1918, p. 61.

21. W. von Molo, *Erinnerungen und Begegnungen*, Stuttgart, 1957, p. 217.

22. A. Niekisch, *Gewagtes Leben*, Cologne, 1958, p. 283.

23. *Jüdische Rundschau*, no. 32, Aug. 7, 1914, p. 343.

24. Zechlin, *Deutsche Politik*, pp. 90, 94, n. 61.

25. *Blau-Weiss Blätter*, vol. 4, no. 4, p. 96.

26. N. Goldmann, *Der Geist des Militarismus, Der Deutsche Krieg*, ed. Ernst Jaeck, no. 52, Berlin-Stuttgart, 1915.

27. Zechlin, *Deutsche Politik*, pp. 119–20.

28. W. Ruge, *Hindenburg: Portrait eines Militaristen*, Cologne, 1981, p. 102.

29. *Leo Baeck Institute Yearbook* 30 (1985): 146.

30. W. Rathenau, *Gesammelte Schriften*, Berlin, 1925, vol. 2, p. 611, n. 35.

31. Quoted in R. Kallner, *Herzl und Rathenau*, Stuttgart, 1976, p. 363.

32. F. Fischer, *Griff nach der Weltmacht*, Düsseldorf, 1962, pp. 127, 113.

33. Quoted in G. Hecker, *Walther Rathenau und sein Verhältnis zu Militär und Krieg*, Boppard, 1963, pp. 167–68.

34. Cited in Fischer, *Griff nach der Weltmacht*, p. 355n.

35. Rathenau, *Gesammelte Schriften*, vol. 5, p. 27.

36. Kallner, *Herzl und Rathenau*, p. 363.

37. T. Buddensieg et al., eds., *Ein Mann vieler Eigenschaften: Walther Rathenau und die Kultur der Moderne*, Berlin, 1990, p. 63.

38. Stern, *Einstein's German World*, p. 64.

39. Ibid., p. 121. See also R. Willstätter's own account, *From My Life*, trans. L. S. Hornig, New York, 1958.

40. *Encounter* (London), June 1952, p. 43.

41. Quoted in W. E. Mosse, *Deutsches Judentum in Krieg und Revolution, 1916–1923*, Tübingen, 1971, p. 30.

42. W. H. Auden, "At the Grave of Henry James."

43. H. Kohn, *Martin Buber*, Cologne, 1961, p. 164.

44. N. N. Glatzer and P. Mendes-Flohr, eds., *The Letters of Martin Buber*, Syracuse, 1991, p. 162 (Oct. 16, 1914).

45. Ibid., p. 160 (Sept. 30, 1914).

46. Quoted in W. von Sternburg, *Lion Feuchtwanger; Ein deutsches Schriftstellerleben*, Berlin, 1994, p. 148.

47. C. Schulte, ed., *Deutschtum und Judentum: Ein Disput unter Juden aus Deutschland*, Stuttgart, 1993, pp. 56–59. See also S. L. Gilman and J. Zipes, eds., *Yale Companion to Jewish Writing and Thought in German Culture, 1096–1996*, New Haven, 1997, p. 348.

48. V. Klemperer, *Curriculum Vitae: Erinnerungen 1881–1918*, Berlin, 1996, vol. 2, p. 201.

49. Ibid., vol. 1, p. 315.

50. Ibid., vol. 1, p. 195.

51. Ibid., vol. 1, p. 315.

52. *Die Zukunft*, Aug. 29, Aug. 22, Sept. 5, Aug. 22, 1914.

53. *Neue Rundschau*, Sept. 14, 1914.

54. E. Ludwig, *Geschenke des Lebens*, Berlin, 1931, p. 363.

55. *Frankfurter Israelitisches Familienblatt*, no. 31, 1914, quoted in J. Toury, *Die politischen Orientierungen der Juden in Deutschland*, Tübingen, 1966.

56. A. Kerr, "Die Harfe," 24 *Gedichte*, Berlin, 1917.

57. Klemperer, *Curriculum Vitae*, vol. 2, p. 200.

58. G. Steiner, *After Babel: Aspects of Language and Translation*, London, 1975, p. 339.

59. Klemperer, *Curriculum Vitae*, vol. 1, p. 252.

60. S. Zweig, *The World of Yesterday*, London, 1945, p. 179.

61. Ibid., p. 216.

62. S. K. Brand, *Ernst Lissauer*, Stuttgart, 1923, p. 67.

63. Stern, *Einstein's German World*, p. 210.

64. J. and W. von Ungern-Sternberg, *Der Aufruf an die Kulturwelt*, Stuttgart, 1996, pp. 18, 46, 60, 64.

65. Quoted in M. A. Meyer, *German Jewish History in Modern Times*, New York, 1997, vol. 3, p. 364.

66. *London Times*, Nov. 4, 1987.

67. E. Mühsam, *Streitschriften*, Berlin, 1985, p. 53.

68. *Die Schaubühne*, vol. 11, no. 8, Feb. 15, 1915. Translation courtesy Feuchtwanger Memorial Library, Special Collection, University of Southern California.

69. G. Scholem, *Judaica*, Frankfurt, 1984, vol. 4, p. 241.

70. G. Scholem, *Dvarim bego* (Hebrew), Tel Aviv, 1976, vol. 1, pp. 12, 14, 15.

71. B. Scholem and G. Scholem, *Mutter und Sohn im Briefwechsel, 1917–1946*, Munich, 1989, p. 13.

72. A. J. P. Taylor, *The First World War*, Harmondsworth, 1980, p. 140.

73. Cited by S. Friedlander, in Mosse, *Deutsches Judentum in Krieg und Revolution*, p. 37.

74. Kessler's unpublished war diary, Apr. 14, Oct. 15, 1915, in Kessler papers, Deutsches Literaturarchiv, Marbach.

75. H. F. Young, *Maximilian Harden: Censor Germaniae*, Münster, 1971, p. 199.

76. House to W. Wilson, Mar. 21, 1915, quoted in C. Seymour, *The Intimate Papers of Colonel House*, New York, 1928, vol. 1, p. 406.

77. W. Rathenau (May 17, 1916), quoted in R. Kallner, *Heral and Rathenau*, Stuttgart, 1976, p. 366.

78. B. Guttmann, *Schattenriss einer Generation*, Stuttgart, 1950, p. 246.

79. H. Delbrück, *Vor und nach dem Weltkrieg: Politische und historische Aufsätze, 1902–1925*, Berlin, 1926, pp. 436–37.

80. Facsimile in R. Vogel, *Ein Stück von Uns: Deutsche Juden in deutschen Armeen, 1813–1976*, Mainz, 1977, p. 70.

81. Rathenau to W. Schwaner, quoted in V. Ullrich, *Die nervöse Grossmacht: Aufsteig und Untergang des deutschen Kaiserreichs, 1871–1918*, Frankfurt, 1997, p. 489.

82. Willstätter, *From My Life*, p. 235.

83. Vogel, *Ein Stück von Uns*, p. 149; *Leo Baeck Institute Yearbook* 19 (1974): 143.

84. Ullrich, *Die nervöse Grossmacht*, p. 485.

85. Simon, *Unser Kriegserlebnis*, p. 18.

86. J. Marx, *Kriegstagebuch eines Juden*, Frankfurt, 1964, p. 138.

87. *Leo Baeck Institute Yearbook* 10 (1965): 9.

88. Mosse, *Deutsches Judentum in Krieg und Revolution*, pp. 517–18.

89. Cited in Ullrich, *Die nervöse Grossmacht*, p. 567.

90. M. Harden, *Von Versailles nach Versailles*, Leipzig, 1927, p. 56.

91. Guttmann, *Schattenriss einer Generation*, p. 206.

92. C. Kessler, ed. and trans., *Berlin in Lights: The Diaries of Count Harry Kessler (1918–1937)*, New York, 1999, pp. 44–45.

93. *Berliner Tageblatt*, Nov. 10, 1918.

94. Stern, *Einstein's German World*, p. 127.

95. Cited by R. Weltsch in Mosse, *Deutsches Judentum in Krieg und Revolution*, p. 629.

96. T. Wolff, *Der Marsch durch zwei Jahrzehnte*, Amsterdam, 1936, pp. 222–23.

97. S. Friedländer, in Mosse, *Deutsches Judentum in Krieg und Revolution*, pp. 52–53, 65.

98. E. Mühsam, in *Vom Judentum*, ed. Verein jüdischer Hochschüler Bar Kochba, Leipzig, 1913, p. 254.

99. T. Dorst and H. Neubauer, eds., *Die Münchener Räterepublik*, Frankfurt, 1959.

100. Cited by P. Pulzer, in Mosse, *Deutsches Judentum in Krieg und Revolution*, p. 213.

101. Dorst and Neubauer, *Die Münchener Räterepublik*, p. 43.

102. P. Dirr, *Bayerische Dokumente zum Kriegsausbruch und zum Versailler Schuldspruch*, Munich, 1925, p. 43.

103. V. Klemperer, *Leben sammeln, nicht fragen wozu und warum: Tagebücher, 1918–1932*, Berlin, 1996, p. 29.

104. Toury, *Die politischen Orientierungen*, p. 344.

105. Haffner, *Die deutsche Revolution*, p. 184.

106. Ibid., p. 185.

107. E. Mühsam, *Gedichte, Drama, Prosa*, Berlin, 1961, p. 31.

108. E. Meyer, *Erinnerungen*, Vienna, 1949, p. 364.
109. Quoted in Mosse, *Deutsches Judentum in Krieg und Revolution*, p. 137.
110. K. Kraus, *Die letzten Tage der Menschheit*, Frankfurt, 1986.

10. THE END

1. A. Döblin, *Fluch und Sammlung des deutschen Judentums*, Freiburg, 1977, p. 11.
2. T. Wolff, *Der Marsch durch zwei Jahrzehnte*, Amsterdam, 1936, p. 204.
3. C. Kessler, ed. and trans., *Berlin in Lights: The Diaries of Count Harry Kessler (1918–1937)*, New York, 1999, p. 75 (Feb. 24, 1919).
4. P. Gay, *Freud, Jews, and Other Germans*, Oxford, 1978, p. 95.
5. G. L. Mosse, *Rassismus*, Frankfurt, 1978, p. 108.
6. *Albert Einstein in Berlin: Darstellung und Dokumente*, Berlin, 1979, p. 204.
7. Kessler, *Berlin in Lights*, pp. 155–57 (Mar. 20, 1922).
8. B. Brecht, *Journals*, ed. J. Willett, trans. H. Rorrison, London, 1993.
9. *Walther Rathenau: Ein preussischer Europäer*, Berlin, 1955, p. 329.
10. K. Blumenfeld, *Erlebte Judenfrage*, Stuttgart, 1962, p. 139.
11. E. Federn-Kohlhaas, *Walther Rathenau: Sein Leben und Wirken*, Berlin, 1927, p. 233.
12. Blumenfeld, *Erlebte Judenfrage*, pp. 132–33.
13. J. M. Keynes, *Two Memoirs*, London, 1949, pp. 50, 69.
14. K. Tucholsky, *Ausgewählte Werke*, Reinbeck bei Hamburg, 1965, vol. 2, p. 126.
15. K. Tucholsky, *Gesammelte Werke*, Reinbeck bei Hamburg, 1989, vol. 10, p. 98.
16. Translated by Harry Zohn.
17. Quoted in S. Reinhardt, ed., *Die Schriftsteller und die Weimarer Republik; Ein Lesebuch*, Berlin, 1982, p. 65.
18. Speech by Mann (1966), quoted in W. E. Mosse, ed., *Deutsches Judentum in Krieg und Revolution, 1916–1923*, Tübingen, 1971, p. 49.
19. *Die Weltbühne*, June 8, 1922.
20. G. Mann, in *Encounter*, June 1952.
21. Tucholsky, *Gesammelte Werke*, vol. 1, p. 936.
22. Kessler, *Berlin in Lights*, pp. 185–86 (June 27, 1922).
23. H. Kessler, *Walther Rathenau: Sein Leben und sein Werk*, Frankfurt, 1988, p. 37.
24. *Die Zukunft*, vol. 60, p. 77; Kessler, *Berlin in Lights*, p. 188 (July 12, 1922).
25. S. Friedländer and J. Rüsen, eds., *Richard Wagner im Dritten Reich*, Munich, 2000, p. 205.
26. B. Scholem and G. Scholem, *Mutter und Sohn im Briefwechsel, 1917–1946*, Munich, 1989, p. 32.

27. J. Wassermann, *My Life as German and Jew,* trans. S. N. Brainin, New York, 1933.

28. G. Mann, *Erinnerungen und Gedanken,* Frankfurt, 1986, p. 166.

29. S. Reinhardt, ed., *Die Schriftsteller und die Weimarer Republik: Ein Lesebuch,* Berlin, 1982, p. 82.

30. G. Krojanker, *Juden in der deutschen Literatur,* Berlin, 1924, p. 9.

31. J. A. Kruse, ed., *Heinrich Heine: Leben und Werk in Texten,* Frankfurt, 1983, p. 283.

32. H. Meyer, *Ein Deutscher auf Widerruf,* Frankfurt, 1982, pp. 56–57.

33. Kessler, *Berlin in Lights,* p. 350 (Oct. 5, 1928).

34. *Jüdische Rundschau,* June 28, 1929; *Jüdisch-liberale Zeitung,* Aug. 26, 1927.

35. M. Brenner, *The Renaissance of Jewish Culture in Weimar Germany,* New Haven, 1996, p. 70.

36. I owe this observation to Anthony David Skinner's forthcoming biography of Salman Schocken (Metropolitan Books).

37. Cited in R. Alter, *Necessary Angels,* Los Angeles, pp. 44–45.

38. Private communication from Schocken's son Gustav.

39. M. Kreutzberger, ed., *Der Zionismus im Wandel drei Jahrzehnten,* Tel Aviv, 1962, p. 15.

40. Central Zionist Archives, Jerusalem, A339/46.

41. A. Einstein, *Mein Weltbild,* Zurich, 1953.

42. F. Beck, *Tagebuch eines Verzweifelten,* Frankfurt, 1994, p. 23.

43. K. Mann, *Der Wendepunkt,* Berlin, 1974, p. 329.

44. G. Orwell, "Hitler," *New English Weekly,* Mar. 21, 1940.

45. Interview with Zweig, May 1965.

46. E. Mühsam, *Tagebücher, 1910–1924,* Munich, 1995, p. 347.

47. Tucholsky, *Gesammelte Werke,* vol. 4, p. 206.

48. Kessler, *Berlin in Lights,* p. 267 (May 15, 1925).

49. Reinhardt, *Die Schriftsteller und die Weimar Republik,* p. 165.

50. E. Feder, *Heute sprach ich mit . . . : Tagebücher eines Berliner Publizisten,* Stuttgart, 1971, p. 312.

51. E. Young-Bruehl, *Hannah Arendt: For Love of the World,* New Haven, 1982, p. 98.

52. Ibid., p. 103.

53. A. Koestler, *Arrow in the Blue,* London, 1969, pp. 295–96.

54. F. Stampfer, *Erfahrungen und Erkenntnisse,* Cologne, 1957, p. 263.

55. Quoted in K. Schneider and N. Simon, eds., *Solidarität und Deutsche Geschichte: Die Linke zwischen Antisemitismus und Israelkritik,* Berlin, 1984, p. 72.

56. M. Sperber, *All das Vergangene,* Vienna, 1983, p. 517.

57. C. Schmölders, *Hitlers Gesicht: Eine physiognomische Biographie,* Munich, 2000, p. 9.

58. Feder, *Heute sprach ich mit,* p. 293.

59. T. Adorno, Afterword to Benjamin's *Deutsche Menschen: Eine Folge von Briefen,* Frankfurt, 1984, p. 90.

60. A. Schöne, in *Juden in der deutschen Literatur,* ed. S. Moses and A. Schöne, Frankfurt, 1986, p. 350; M. Brodersen, *Spinne im eigenen Netz. Walter Benjamin: Leben und Werk,* Bühl-Moos, 1990, p. 247.

61. Feder, *Heute sprach ich mit* (entry for Sept. 9, 1930).

62. Vicky Baum, *Es war alles ganz anders: Erinnerungen,* Vienna, 1962, pp. 318–19; V. Klemperer, *Leben sammeln, nicht fragen wozu und warum: Tagebücher, 1918–1932,* 1996, p. 758.

63. K. Edschmid, ed., *Briefe der Expressionisten,* Berlin, 1964, p. 34.

64. Quoted in M. Ignatieff, *Isaiah Berlin,* New York, 1998, p. 52.

65. H. Arendt and M. Heidegger, *Briefe, 1925–1975,* Frankfurt, 1998, p. 69.

66. H. Ashby Turner Jr., *Hitler's Thirty Days to Power,* New York, 1996, p. 196.

67. D. Bronsen, *Joseph Roth: Eine Biographie,* Munich, 1974, p. 422.

68. Turner, *Hitler's Thirty Days,* p. 159.

69. Ibid., p. 159.

70. K. D. Bracher, *The Path to Dictatorship,* quoted in P. Gay, *Weimar Culture,* New York, 1970, p. 163.

71. *Pariser Tageblatt,* Mar. 15, 1935.

72. *Berliner Tageblatt,* Jan. 24, 1933; K. Schwartz, unpublished text, Robert Weltsch collection, Leo Baeck Institute, Jerusalem.

73. W. E. Mosse, ed., *Entscheidungsjahr 1932: Zur Judenfrage in der Endphase der Weimarer Republik,* Tübingen, 1965, p. 20.

74. Scholem, *Mutter und Sohn,* p. 287.

75. *Berliner Tageblatt,* Mar. 5, 1933.

76. Quoted in S. Kuscinsky, *Deutsche Schriftsteller zwischen Machtübernahme und Bücherverbrennung,* Berlin, 1978, p. 287.

77. R. Aron, *Erkenntnis und Verantwortung: Lebenserinnerungen,* trans. Kurt Sontheim, Munich, 1985, p. 54.

78. Kuscinsky, *Deutsche Schriftsteller,* p. 288.

79. Ibid., p. 206.

80. A. Kerr, *Lesebuch zum Leben und Werk,* Berlin, 1987, p. 159.

81. G. Mosse, *German Jews beyond Judaism,* Bloomington, 1985, p. 82.

82. N. Stolzfus, *Resistance of the Heart: Intermarriage and the Rosenstrasse Protest in Nazi Germany,* New York, 1996, cited in S. Aschheim, *Intimate Chronicles in Turbulent Times,* Bloomington, 2001, p. 81.

83. L. London, *Whitehall and the Jews, 1933–1948: British Immigration Policy and the Holocaust,* Cambridge, 2000, cited in *New York Review of Books,* Mar. 29, 2001.

84. F. Landsberger, ed., *Max Liebermann: Siebzig Briefe,* Berlin, 1937, p. 86.

85. H. Schütz, *Juden in der deutschen Literatur,* Munich, 1992, p. 241.

86. V. Klemperer, *I Will Bear Witness: A Diary of the Nazi Years, 1933–1941,* trans. Martin Chalmers, New York, 1998, p. 129 (July 21, 1935); *I Will Bear Witness: A Diary of the Nazi Years, 1942–1945,* trans. Martin Chalmers, New York, 2001, p. 51 (May 11, 1942).

87. *Bulletin of the Leo Baeck Institute* 5 (1960): 287, 300–301.

88. B. Gajek and W. von Ungern-Sternberg, *Ludwig Fulda: Briefwechsel 1882–1939,* Berlin, 1977, p. 249.

89. K. Tucholsky, *Ausgewählte Briefe,* Reinbeck bei Hamburg, 1962, p. 33.

90. Quoted in J. P. Stern, *Hitler: The Fuhrer and the People,* Berkeley, 1975, p. 29.

91. R. P. Newton, trans., *Your Diamond Dreams Cut Open My Arteries: Poems by Else Lasker-Schüler,* Chapel Hill, 1982, p. 285.

ACKNOWLEDGMENTS

As the endnotes show, I am indebted to many authors, but my thinking about German Jews before the rise of Nazism was primarily affected by the learned insights of three great historians far more expert than I: Peter Gay, Fritz Stern, and my friend of many years, the late George Mosse, to whose memory I dedicate this book. Responsibility for the views expressed in it is, of course, entirely my own. Paul Mendes-Flohr and Steven Aschheim read the book in manuscript and made useful suggestions. I am grateful also to the editors and authors of the numerous studies and yearbooks issued over the past fifty years by the Leo Baeck Institute of Jerusalem and New York. Apart from its many publications, this important research body has assembled a priceless collection of rare nineteenth-century texts, manuscripts, personal testimonies, and historic photos. Going through these treasures, one feels like an archaeologist sifting through the sands of a now-lost great secular civilization. I am grateful to Shlomo Mayer, director of the institute in Jerusalem, for making these treasures available to me and for authorizing the reproduction in this book of some of the graphic material owned by the Jerusalem institute.

Thanks also to Wolf Lepenies, until recently rector of the Institute for Advanced Study in Berlin, and the institute's head librarian, the resourceful Gesine Bottomley, who enabled me to consult the rich accumulation of postwar German works on my subject. Sara Bershtel, a princess among publishers, and her colleague Riva Hocherman edited the manuscript as few editors nowadays are inclined or feel free to. Their suggestions have immensely improved this book. I am grateful to Philip Boehm as well for his excellent translations.

It has become a tiresome habit of authors to thank their spouses for their generosity and forbearance. I am happy to report that, in my case, writing has never been the solitary occupation it is often said to be. My wife, Beth, shared in it and has been an endless source of ideas and encouragement, and if her patience ran out at times, these were rare indeed. *Eshet Khayil mi yimtsa.*

INDEX

ABOUT THE AUTHOR

AMOS ELON is the author of eight widely praised books, including *Founder: A Portrait of the First Rothschild and His Time* and the *New York Times* bestseller *The Israelis: Founders and Sons*. A frequent contributor to *The New York Times Magazine* and *The New York Review of Books*, he divides his time between Jerusalem and Tuscany.